AUSTIN
SAN ANTONIO & THE HILL COUNTRY

JUSTIN MARLER

Contents

DISCOVER

Austin, San Antonio & the Hill Country

W hen Austin is mentioned in casual conversation, all eyes light up. Those who have been to Austin can't help but chime in with enthusiasm, and those who have never been have heard only amazing things about this alluring city in the heart of Texas. What makes Austin so memorable and so liked? Austin is perhaps the most diverse city in Texas, and probably all of the American South. It is the land where John Wayne meets Andy Warhol. Here cowboys drive pickup trucks with abstract murals painted on the side, Christmas lights are on year-round, bizarre landmark art is everywhere, and hip youngsters and old country folk two-step together in honky-tonks.

Absolutely anyone can come here and feel right at home. The closet cowboys can safely pretend they are real cowboys without fear of looking out of place. Messy-haired hipsters can stagger down urban streets lined with clubs, diners, and music stores, while fans of folk art and Americana pillage countless boutiques and curiosity shops. The voices of passionate politicos boom throughout grand halls, while sports fans hoot 'n' holler at UT Longhorn games in jam-packed stadiums. Music fans of all genres fall in love with countless musicians and venues in a wildly eclectic scene that never shuts off its amps.

Clockwise from top left: cooling off in the Guadalupe River; Grab a pair of cowboy or cowgirl boots; Tex-Mex in San Antonio; hot rod at the Lonestar Roundup Car Show; Texas State Capitol in Austin; Continental Club in Austin.

The capital city dances to the beat of many tunes, but the fun doesn't stop at the Austin city limits. This colorful town is the porch overlooking the gorgeous Texas Hill Country. This lush region at the center of the state is lined with vast rolling hills spotted with fields of wildflowers, grazing cattle, and historic little towns founded by German pioneers who brought accordions and schnitzels to the Wild West. Folks from all over come to the region's sleepy hamlets to hunt for antiques, ride horses, explore caves, go wine-tasting, and hide out in bed-and-breakfasts.

At the southern reaches of the Hill Country is the Graceland of Texas history—San Antonio. Here pilgrims from all over venerate the legendary Alamo, stroll down the beautiful and romantic River Walk, and spend the day at massive theme parks and world-class museums.

Given half a chance, Austin, San Antonio, and the Hill Country are guaranteed to suck you in and take you for a spin, like a cow in a twister on the plains. Where else can you see Willie Nelson perform, go wine-tasting, explore underground caves, visit The Alamo, see ancient dinosaur bones, dance to German polka music, and catch a Mexican rodeo—all in one weekend? Nowhere else but deep in the heart of Texas.

Clockwise from top left: live music in Austin; Texas pride in Gruene; The Hill Country is known for juicy peaches; The Alamo.

Planning Your Trip

No matter how much time you have, it's best to know what you want out of your travel experience. **If you want an urban experience** filled with live music, tall buildings, late-night escapades, and socializing, stick to the Austin metropolitan area. **If you want to explore the great outdoors,** including many hiking and biking trails, lakes and streams, fields of wildflowers, plus maybe some wineries, you can find all this in the surrounding Hill Country. **If you want a family vacation** filled with museums and theme parks, you'll probably stick to Austin and San Antonio. Or, **if you're looking for the very best way to experience it all,** take a road trip through the entire Hill Country, from Austin to San Antonio. All this requires is an operable automobile (with air-conditioning), your favorite Willie Nelson album, a full tank of gasoline, and the will to meander.

An important thing to consider before heading to Austin, San Antonio, and the Hill Country is lodging. Because of the many festivals and events, **hotels are often booked months in advance.** The earlier you book your lodging, the better chance you have of staying in the property of your choice, or having a place to stay at all.

Getting to Austin and San Antonio is easy, as both destinations have **international airports** with flights offered by most of the larger carriers. However, getting to the Hill Country isn't as easy. Due to the lack of public transportation in the rural areas, you will need to **rent a car** for your **Hill Country** road trip.

As for getting around **Austin,** a great **metro system, pedicabs, taxicabs,** and **ride-hailing apps** make navigating pretty simple. Getting around **San Antonio** is much more complicated. There is a metro system, but everything is so spread out that you will have more fun and waste less time by renting a **car.**

San Antonio's famous River Walk

Where to Go

Austin

Although Austin is geographically south of the center of Texas, it's definitely the **heart of the state.** The Austin metropolitan area is situated at the eastern edge of the Hill Country on the I-35 corridor. The **Colorado River** winds its way through town and has been dammed off, creating a lush and beautiful lake that is the focal point of downtown. Austin is the **state capital** and the commercial heart of several industries, one of which is live music. Here in the "Live Music Capital of the World," a thriving music and nightlife scene is to be found at the base of the city's skyscrapers. The combination of rural and urban is what attracts people to Austin. The city experience offers museums for the day-tripper and a flourishing nightlife when the sun sets.

The Hill Country

The remarkably beautiful region called the Hill Country, to the west of Austin and north of San Antonio, is the **Napa Valley of Texas.** This sprawling, slow-paced region is filled with small towns—some frozen in time, others catching up. Nearly all these wide spots in the road have the signature Hill Country feature at the center of town—a beautiful, historic, ornate limestone courthouse. Between many of these towns there are **pristine parks, wineries, antiques shops,** and **roadside fruit stands.** The industry in these parts is farming, ranching, winemaking, and tourism. As you drive around the Hill Country you may notice exotic animals such as **zebras, bison,** and **antelope** grazing in fields. Many ranches in the Hill Country have become home to these rare animals.

San Antonio

The age-old city of San Antonio is just to the south of the Hill Country, southwest from Austin. If you look at a map of this vibrant, **historic city** you will notice that all roads lead to San Antonio. This river town is one of the 10 largest cities in the United States. It's also home to Texas's most visited tourist attraction—**The Alamo**—as well as the famous **River Walk,** which cuts its way through downtown, and several **Spanish missions.** The Mexican border is only 175 miles away; this proximity has given San Antonio an incredibly rich **Latino heritage.**

When to Go

Many locals say that south-central Texas has only two seasons: winter and summer. For the sake of simplicity, we'll do like the locals and lump fall and spring in with summer since they're so short. The best time to come to Austin, San Antonio, and the Hill Country is during this **long summer season,** which starts in **March** and wraps up by the end of **October.** Although June, July, and August are hellishly hot, these are the peak months for tourism. Central Texas is overflowing with people. The warm, laid-back climate and the uncanny number of **festivals** and **music events** draw thousands to the area from all over the country. Everyone is kept alive during the summer months by drinking lots of water and by air-conditioning. Anywhere you go indoors the air is a cool 74°F, and outdoors there are many swimming holes, lakes, rivers, and pools in which to keep cool.

Besides the long summer heat, the only other thing to keep in mind when planning to visit south-central Texas is **allergies.** The Hill Country is rife with **wildflowers** and trees that come to life in the spring. Sure, it's beautiful, but for the person who suffers from seasonal allergies, it can be hard to enjoy. The peak allergy times are December-January (mountain cedar), March-April (oak), and September-October (ragweed). If you plan to come during these months, be prepared to buy an antihistamine.

Although folks visit the region year-round, winter is definitely the quiet season. In Austin you can always find fun things to do; however, San Antonio and the Hill Country are pretty sleepy this time of year.

statue of Austin legendary musician Stevie Ray Vaughan by artist Ralph Helmick

Austin in a Long Weekend

Austin is a city that can easily be explored in a weekend. It's so alive and accessible that it takes little effort to be completely immersed in its life and culture.

Day 1

This is probably the only day you will wake up early. First thing on the agenda is a hearty breakfast at the **Magnolia Cafe.** To walk off all the calories you just consumed, head straight out the door of Magnolia Cafe and down the street to **Lady Bird Lake** (formerly Town Lake). Enjoy walking the overgrown trails, watch the turtles and ducks putter in the lake, and take in the stunning view of Austin's skyline. Along the trail you can pay homage to Austin music legend **Stevie Ray Vaughan** at his famous statue.

Next make your way to one of the most popular record stores in the United States, **Waterloo Records,** and check out their extensive collection of Texas music. After buying a Willie Nelson CD, walk across the street to **Whole Foods** world

headquarters and buy some granola, energy bars, or dried fruit to consume the following day on a hike.

A first day in Austin must include a visit to the **Texas State Capitol.** Walk the grounds, stand beneath the dome, and take in the gubernatorial history. If it's between 2pm and 4pm, make your way over to the **Governor's Mansion** for a tour of the historic home that some think is haunted.

Before evening descends, get a copy of the *Austin Chronicle* and look at the entertainment section. Pick a show—any show—and plan to have your socks blown off by a great night on the town. For an authentic Austin night out, catch a country band at the **Broken Spoke.** If you have the guts and gumption, try your hand at two-stepping.

Day 2

The first half of Day 2 is devoted to an education in Texas pride by visiting the **Bullock Texas State History Museum.** After you're all

Texased out, have lunch at nearby **Texas Chili Parlor,** then walk over to Austin's world-class repository for art, the **Blanton Museum of Art.** After admiring the Picassos, make your way down to the **Driskill,** Austin's famed haunted hotel. Even if you don't stay here you can marvel at the architecture and the creepy vibe, and get a confection at the **1886 Café & Bakery.**

Cross over Lady Bird Lake and keep going until you arrive at the city's most popular strip, **South Congress Avenue,** which is lined with funky shops, trendy boutiques, and restaurants. If you get hungry, order a margarita with shrimp fajitas at popular **Güero's Taco Bar.** Check out the oddity shop **Uncommon Objects** and marvel at the $3,000 cowgirl boots at **Allens Boots.** As a side note, staying at one of the trendy hotels on South Congress is highly recommended.

By this time the music scene is getting revved up. Check out music listings in the *Austin Chronicle* and catch some live music at the **Continental Club** on South Congress or any of the venues on **6th Street** or **Red River Street,** such as **Stubb's Bar-B-Q, The Mohawk,** or **The Parish.** Peruse the music listings for Austin

City Limits Live at The Moody Theater. This is a great way to see a world-class act and get close to the famous Austin City Limits stage.

Day 3

Day 3 is kicked off with a trip to the most visited presidential library in the United States, the **LBJ Library and Museum.** You're sure to be moved by the exhibit about the president's life, and may well up with tears when you walk into the JFK assassination exhibit, or feel a sense of pride at seeing the pen LBJ used in signing the Civil Rights Act. Follow up the LBJ experience with lunch at **Rudy's Country Store and BBQ** for some smoky beef brisket. If it's not over 100 degrees, make your way to **Wild Basin Wilderness Preserve,** which is close by. Walk the hills and learn about Central Texas flora and fauna through interpretive trails. At the end of the trail be sure to sit on the bench and enjoy the view of the city skyline for as long as you can. Once you've acquired peace of mind, take a walk through **Zilker Botanical Garden.** Consider how this area was the stomping grounds of dinosaurs in the **Hartman Prehistoric Garden,**

Texas State Capitol

and then get a bite to eat at nearby **Shady Grove Restaurant**. Once you've filled up on great Tex-Mex, head downtown to famous **Alamo Drafthouse Cinema**. Order a pitcher of beer and watch a random movie or attend a Michael Jackson sing-along.

Day 4

Your final day in Austin will start with a trip to **Zilker Park,** where you'll take a ride on the **Zilker Zephyr**. This mini-train takes both mini and full-size passengers throughout the park. If you're lucky your train ride will include a brief performance by "the man with the guitar in the cutoff shorts." Assuming it's a hot summer day, get off at the Barton Springs stop and jump in **Barton Springs Pool**. Plan to splash around in the constantly 68-degree water and people-watch for a couple of hours.

Before evening sets in, make your way to Lady Bird Lake and watch the **bats of Congress Avenue Bridge,** which take flight just before sundown. A great way to view them is by taking a ride on **Lone Star Riverboat**, a genuine double-decker paddle wheel riverboat. Follow this up with a visit to Austin's burgeoning **Warehouse District**. First stop off at the Irish pub **Fado's** or the popular pub **The Ginger Man** and drink a pint of beer produced by local brewhouse **Live Oak Brewing Company.** It's your last night, so if you still have ears for music, check out some more bands and musicians. Or if you prefer a calm evening, walk over to **Halcyon Coffeehouse** to roast marshmallows and make s'mores at your table.

Day 5

If you can squeeze one more day into your long weekend, a trip to **San Antonio** to visit **The Alamo** is essential. The drive is just two hours to downtown. After exploring Texas's most sacred site, walk down to The Esquire Tavern, a spot famous for pub grub and for having the longest bar in Texas. Afterwards enjoy a stroll on San Antonio's greatest feature, the **River Walk**. If you still have some time to kill before heading back to Austin, drive the **Mission Trail.**

Austin's Music Scene

Austin is the undisputed Live Music Capital of the World. With an unprecedented number of live music performances happening every night of the week throughout the year, it has earned the title. Touring national acts, local favorites, and unknowns perpetually fill Austin's venues, clubs, and bars as well as unusual places such as clothing stores, supermarkets, and even the airport.

The Quintessential Austin Music Experience

Musical styles and tastes vary greatly, making it difficult to suggest one quintessential music experience, but here's a start. The proper accommodations are crucial for the live music fan. They need to be cheap, centrally located, and near a restaurant that serves breakfast all day. Musicians and fans alike love to stay at the **Austin Motel** on South Congress Avenue because it meets all these criteria. Once you arrive in town, immediately consult the music section of the *Austin Chronicle*. All venue listings and festival and event information are found in the pages of this weekly rag.

After a night of live music followed by a visit to one of Austin's many dive bars, you'll probably wake up after noon. If you stay at the Austin Motel, saunter up the street to **Home Slice Pizza** or **Güero's Taco Bar** for great grub. If you want to continue with a music-themed visit to Austin, check out one of the most popular music stores in the country, **Waterloo Records**. If you're a vinyl collector, explore **Antone's Record Shop** or **End of an Ear**. While in town it's imperative that you pay your respects to local music legend **Stevie Ray**

Austin Motel

Dale Watson is Austin's legendary and hardest working honky-tonk musician.

Vaughan on the south-shore trail of Lady Bird Lake. On the banks of the Colorado stands a life-size bronze statue of the guitar god.

While in Austin all music lovers invariably ask themselves, "I wonder how to get tickets to a taping of *Austin City Limits*?" You have a better chance of sprouting wings than acquiring tickets to a taping of this famous PBS program. However, on off nights, the famous stage with the Austin skyline as the backdrop is utilized as a traditional venue called the **Moody Theater,** where anyone can see great national acts perform.

Venues

Austin has over a hundred places that offer live music from both regional and national acts, and nearly all of them are worth checking out. Most are in the downtown area on 6th Street, Red River Street, and South Congress Avenue. Venues generally come alive after dark, except during special benefit shows and during SXSW. Most venues have something going on every night of the week, so don't expect the good shows to be only on weekends. You're sure to catch something

interesting virtually any time doors are open at the following venues.

Antone's has been Texas's outlet for the blues for decades. In recent years it's expanded its repertoire to include pop, rock, and indie, bringing in some major national acts. **Stubb's Bar-B-Q** serves up both great barbecue brisket and superb big-name rock and indie bands in a historic limestone building; this is where the hip parties go down during SXSW. There's an intimate indoor stage for smaller acts, while the big outdoor stage features national acts such as Drake, Death Cab for Cutie, and Queens of the Stone Age.

For traditional country and two-step dancing, there's the legendary **Broken Spoke.** This real honky-tonk will blow your Stetson off when you walk through the door. The crowd is a perfect mix of country folk, young hipsters, and everyone in between, which makes it all-inviting. The premier intimate venue for all things unplugged is the **Cactus Cafe.** Big-name acoustic, singer-songwriter, country, and folk acts have graced the small corner stage for over 70 years. The space is small, upscale, and outfitted with a full bar in the back.

Antone's weekly Blue Monday jam

For those who like it loud and grungy, **Emo's** is Austin's outlet for punk, metal, and indie rock. If you don't know where to go or who to see, the best place to experience Austin's own is the **Continental Club** on South Congress Avenue or **Saxon Pub** on South Lamar Boulevard.

Lastly, if you want to see the big headliners such as Taylor Swift or Iron Maiden, the **Frank Erwin Center** or the Formula 1 racetrack **Circuit of the Americas** is where it will happen.

Festivals

Out of all the **music festivals** that happen in and around Austin there are a few you simply can't miss if you happen to be in town.

SXSW

In March, one of the biggest music festivals in the nation takes over Austin—SXSW, also known as **South by Southwest.** For one week the city is overrun by hundreds of musicians and celebrities and thousands of music fans. Restaurants, clubs, music stores, and barbecue joints are teeming with greasy-haired, tattooed, ripped-jean-wearing rock stars and rock star wannabes. The festival features literally hundreds of big names and up-and-coming artists in alternative, indie rock, and even pop. This isn't your typical music convention held in a convention center. Shows happen in all Austin venues from midday to the wee hours. You have to purchase pricy wristbands to get into venues, but it's well worth it. Oh, and good luck getting a hotel if you haven't booked it months in advance.

ACL MUSIC FESTIVAL

The biggest festival on Austin's calendar is the **Austin City Limits Music Festival.** For three days in September nearly 200,000 people fill Zilker Park and overdose on music and sun. Spun out of the famous public television show, ACL Fest features top acts, bands, performers, and musical legends in nearly all genres of music. Passes are available for all three days or for single days. Bring sunscreen and be prepared to sit in the Texas summer heat for this one.

FUN FUN FUN FEST

In the fall, Waterloo Park becomes the site of **Fun Fun Fun Fest**, which features neo-punk, indie

Craft Beer Boom

Live Oak Brewing

For almost 20 years Austin and the surrounding region has been at the forefront of the Texas craft beer boom. In the spirit of Texas do-it-yourself attitude, many creative and entrepreneurial folks developed their own beers in basements and small warehouses with antiquated systems, and these brews have quickly sprung into the mainstream. Austin-area beer producers have exploded, in large part because beer and live music are inseparable. Real Ale Brewing Co. has even created a beer and named if after its employees' favorite local metal band, The Sword.

The history of DIY beer in the state started in 1909 with Texas's oldest independent brewery, Spoetzl Brewery, best known for its diverse line of Shiner beers; since Prohibition, Shiner and Lone Star have been the preferred beers of the locals. However, it must be disclosed that Lone Star, Texas's most famous beer, was owned by Anheuser-Busch since 1895 and is now owned by Pabst Brewing Co.

It wasn't until the late 1990s that the modern boom started with breweries such as Live Oak Brewing and Real Ale Brewing Co. Today there are numerous craft breweries and brewpubs in the region. In addition, there are many festivals dedicated to hops and drinking, such as the Texas Craft Brewers Festival in Austin and Oktoberfest in Fredericksburg.

Most of the beers below can regularly be found at bars and grocery stores. The best beer bars and pubs to sample in downtown Austin include Bangers (79 Rainey St.), The Ginger Man (301 Lavaca St.), which has the largest selection on tap, and Craft Pride (61 Rainey St.).

BEST MICROBREWS

- **Live Oak Brewing** (taproom at 1615 Crozier Ln., Austin, www.liveoakbrewing.com)
  - Recommended: Big Bark (amber lager), Hefeweizen

- **Hops and Grain** (tasting room at 507 Calles St. #101, Austin, www.hopsandgrain.com)
  - Recommended: Zoe (lager), Greenhouse IPA

- **Real Ale Brewing Co.** (taproom at 231 San Saba Ct., Blanco, www.realalebrewing.com)
  - Recommended: Fireman's 4 (blonde ale), Full Moon (rye IPA)

- **Austin Beerworks** (3009 Industrial Ter., Ste. 150, Austin, www.austinbeerworks.com)
  - Recommended: Fire Eagle, Black Thunder, Heavy Machinery IPA

- **Independence Brewing Co.** (3913 Todd Ln. #607, Austin, www.independencebrewing.com)
  - Recommended: Austin Amber, Bootlegger Brown (brown ale), Convict Hill Stout (oatmeal stout)

- **Jester King Brewery** (13187 Fitzhugh Rd., Austin, www.jesterkingbrewery.com)
  - Recommended: Das Wunderkind, Atrial Rubicite

pop, electronic, metal, and random icons from punk's bygone era. Along with a messy hairdo, be sure to bring sunscreen and a penchant for FUN.

OLD SETTLERS MUSIC FESTIVAL

To kick off spring with some two-steppin', the **Old Settlers Music Festival** is held in April. For a four-day weekend banjos will be plinkin' and fiddles will be fiddlin' at the Salt Lick BBQ Pavilion in Driftwood just outside of Austin. The festival features more than two dozen of the top performers of bluegrass and Americana music on four stages.

KERRVILLE FOLK FESTIVAL

One of the biggest folk festivals in the nation, the **Kerrville Folk Festival** happens out in the Hill Country every May. This 18-day folk celebration draws the biggest names in Americana, folk, bluegrass, acoustic rock, blues, and country. Fans mill around in fields all day long listening to folk legends past and present. Most festivalgoers camp on-site.

Texas Pride

Texans have lot of reasons to be proud. Much of this pride stems from the state's history. Texas was created in a revolution against a brutal dictator and stood alone for almost 10 years as an independent nation. Eventually Texas joined the United States as a result of a treaty between two sovereign nations, not because it was a conquered territory or constituted land purchased from a European power. It's understandable that the original Texans were proud of what they created and have passed on that pride to later generations and new arrivals. Most of Texas pride finds its roots in Austin and San Antonio.

Austin

Since Austin is the capital of the Lone Star State, much of Texas pride has been generated, legislated, and spurred here. The **Texas State Capitol** alone is a testament to Texas self-adulation. After all, it's taller than the nation's capitol. Here you can gaze at the portraits of all the state's governors and peer into Texas politics. Not too far from the capitol building are the **Old State Capitol Building Ruins,** which tell ghost tales of the founding of the State of Texas. And one can't forget the **Governor's Mansion,** which is an original Abner Cook design still inhabited by presiding governors and their families.

Just a stone's throw from the state capitol is the grandest testament to Texas in all the world, the **Bullock Texas State History Museum.** Inside this enormous domed shrine are historical exhibits, dioramas, and a multimedia experience—all promoting the richness of Texas pride.

From Austin all the way out into the Hill Country is what's known as LBJ Land. Lyndon B. Johnson, the 36th president of the United States, was a proud native son of Texas. Austin is home to the **LBJ Library and Museum,** the nation's most visited presidential library. Texans are proud of LBJ, and his library/museum is a sort of mecca for them. The exhibits follow LBJ's story, from a small-town Texas upbringing to carrying the presidential torch through the civil rights movement.

The best way to actively experience it is by dancing two-step at Austin's premier honkytonk, the **Broken Spoke.** Dance to live country bands and drink Texas longneck beers (Lone Star or Shiner) in a friendly environment.

The Hill Country

Just west of Austin, in a wide spot in the road called Driftwood, is one of Texas's most famous barbecue joints, **The Salt Lick.** People drive from miles around to eat ribs, brisket, and smoked turkey in this ancient converted ranch house. Just up the road, in the town of Johnson City, is the **Lyndon B. Johnson Boyhood Home** and **LBJ State Park and Historic Site,** which is the site of LBJ's ranch and his **Texas White House.**

Texas German heritage is celebrated each October with the sounds of accordions at

The Alamo, San Antonio's famed pilgrimage sight

Oktoberfest in the Hill Country's most popular town, **Fredericksburg.** This three-day bratwurst, schnitzel, and German beer extravaganza draws big crowds to Fredericksburg. Two stages, two tents, great food, polka and waltz contests, and music with an oompah make this a great Texas Hill Country celebration.

Texas is where the art of ranching was invented and perfected. One of the state's most famous and historic ranches is **Y. O. Ranch,** with longhorn cattle drives, a classy lodge-style resort, cowboys, and zebras. Whether you stay here or just take a wildlife tour, your experience will be quintessentially Texan.

San Antonio

Out of all points of interest related to Texas pride, the one that is most revered, most iconic, and embodies the most legend is **The Alamo.** This is where the revolution went down, the independent spirit was ignited, and the pride was grafted. Ponder where and how Davy Crockett may have died, and marvel at the bravery of those men who faced certain slaughter.

Also in San Antonio is the **Institute of Texan Cultures,** which features exhibits on all the peoples that have lived in Texas and occupied prominent places in the state's history. For Texas dinosaur history there's the **Witte Museum.** Lastly, a visit to Texas wouldn't be complete without seeing the **Texas Pioneer and Ranger Museum.**

You can't talk about Texas pride without talking about Mexico and Latino heritage. The experience of Mexican food is best had at **Mi Tierra.** The old building is festively decorated with strings of lights and tinsel, and a mariachi band often strolls around the tables. Be sure to sit in the dining room, which is painted with masterfully executed murals telling the story of Mexico and Texas.

The most spectacular festival in all of Texas is **Fiesta San Antonio.** For 10 days in April San Antonio has a citywide celebration in honor of the heroes of Texas history. The festivities include carnivals, sports, fireworks, entertainment, feasts, art exhibits, and parades that float down the San Antonio River.

Lastly, Texas history can't be more enjoyable than when experienced through a simulated helicopter experience in the **Tower of the Americas** 4-D theater ride **Skies Over Texas.**

Hill Country Road Trip

A road trip in the Hill Country is an adventure into both beautiful parks with natural wonders and tiny towns that meticulously preserve remnants of Americana and the Wild West. Get ready to do some serious wine-tasting, antiques hunting, horseback riding, and hiking. Before setting out, do some planning. It may be wise to arrange for accommodations ahead of time as well as pre-arrange activities such as horseback riding.

Day 1

Start your road trip with a splash by taking a dip in **Hamilton Pool Preserve.** From Austin drive west on Highway 290, and then go north on Highway 71. If it's hot, take a dip; if it's cold, gawk for a while at the beauty. Afterward, head south on Highway 12 through Dripping Springs en route to Johnson City and eat some great Texas barbecue at **Ronnie's Ice House.** Before leaving town stop at **Whittington's Jerky,** because no road trip is complete without some additional beef to gnaw on. Swing by the old limestone jail,

which was built in 1894 and is still in use, and then proceed westward on Highway 290 toward Stonewall to **LBJ State Park and Historic Site.** This ranch was President Lyndon B. Johnson's retreat from the world. While here see the **Texas White House** and watch an old movie about the 36th president. Once you're back on Highway 290, stop off at **Becker Vineyards** to do some wine-tasting. After buying a bottle, continue westward on Highway 290, but make sure the poor sap who didn't drink is behind the wheel.

Fourteen miles down the road you'll come to the German hamlet of **Fredericksburg.** For dinner there's schnitzel, beer, and German polka music at **Auslander Biergarten.** If there's a jazz band playing at the **Hangar Hotel,** head out to the airport for a swinging time. You can also stay at this World War II-era hangar for the night.

Day 2

Walk Fredericksburg's Main Street to check out the various shops and boutiques, and pay a visit

picturesque Boerne

to the **Pioneer Museum** and funky **Gish's Old West Museum.** If you're a World War II buff, check out the **National Museum of the Pacific War,** where you can see artillery used in the war. Then head north on RR 965 to one of the Hill Country's most precious natural wonders, **Enchanted Rock State Natural Area.** Take the time to hike the face of the enormous granite-domed rock to check out the view and ponder the myths and legends that were born here. If it's not past noon, take a drive on the most scenic country road in Texas, the **Willow City Loop.**

From Fredericksburg your journey will continue south on Highway 16 to Kerrville and on to RR 1340 toward Hunt. Out here you'll be looking for **Stonehenge II,** a small version of the mysterious rock formation in Salisbury, England. After pondering this oddity, head back to Kerrville, where you'll head south on RR 173 to get to your final destination, the Cowboy Capital of the World, known as **Bandera.** Once in Bandera, have a meal at **O. S. T. Restaurant.** The food is down-home country cooking in the presence of John Wayne memorabilia. One of the area's many dude ranches, such as the **Mayan Dude Ranch,** is where you'll want to stay.

Day 3

Start the day with a big cowboy-style breakfast at the dude ranch mess hall, followed by a horseback ride. A guide will take you into the backcountry on trails that have been trodden under hoof for eons. After lunch in the mess hall and a siesta, head downtown and explore the strange Western shops that line Bandera's dirt sidewalks. Also pay a visit to the **Frontier Times Museum.**

Once you've seen Bandera, leave town by way of Highway 46, toward the historic German pioneer town of **Boerne.** This lovely spot on Cibolo Creek is a great place to hunker down for the rest of the day. The main activity here is walking Main Street, known to locals as **Hauptstrasse.** Here you'll find dozens of antiques shops, boutiques, and eateries, all in historic limestone buildings built by the German pioneers. When you get hungry, walk over to the river, turn left, and walk down to the **Dodging Duck Brew Haus.** Dinner with a beer on the outdoor patio is the only way to go. Most folks who come to Boerne stay in a bed-and-breakfast. A reservation service can help you find the right lodgings for your budget.

Day 4

The first thing you'll want to do in the morning is drive north on RR 474, where you'll explore the **Cave Without a Name.** The cave is full of intriguing rock formations, stalagmites, and stalactites. After this head back to Boerne, and then go east on Highway 46. Along the way you'll encounter **Guadalupe River State Park.** Stop off here for some incredible scenery, or even better, go tubing down the **Guadalupe River.** Afterward, make your way to New Braunfels and the charming town of **Gruene.** Explore Gruene's quaint buildings full of antiques and a few restaurants overlooking the beautiful Guadalupe River. At the base of the old town is the **Gristmill River Restaurant & Bar,** situated in the ruins of an old cotton gin.

A grand finale to your road trip should be famous **Gruene Hall.** This old structure with chicken-wire windows is Texas's oldest dance hall. Country music legends still fill this joint with great foot-stomping music.

Family Fun

Central Texas has a wide variety of activities, events, and sights that are sure to keep the kids stimulated and the adults fascinated. From theme parks and curiosity shops to museums with interactive exhibits and mysterious caves, it would take a family two weeks to soak up all the fun.

San Antonio

San Antonio is known the world over as a family town. The imaginations of both parents and children are sparked when visiting **The Alamo,** along with the other historic Spanish missions on the **Mission Trail.** A boat ride on the **River Walk** is another great experience for the whole family. The Alamo and River Walk aside, San Antonio is known by kids the world over for its internationally recognized **San Antonio Zoo and Aquarium.** All the animals kids have read about and imagined are here, ready to be viewed up close. While at the zoo, climb aboard the **Brackenridge Eagle,** a miniature train that travels a two-mile route around Brackenridge Park.

San Antonio also has two gigantic theme parks. First there's **Six Flags Fiesta Texas,** which has over 200 acres of fun for the whole family. Older thrill-seekers will enjoy the wild rides, and for the younger bunch there are less-scary kiddie rides. Six Flags also puts on campy shows that kids will clamor to see. The other mega theme park is **SeaWorld San Antonio.** The main attraction here is the killer whale Shamu, who performs in front of an audience. Be prepared to be soaked if you sit in the first rows.

San Antonio also has some popular indoor family hot spots, such as the children's museum, **The DoSeum.** This huge indoor and outdoor campus has hands-on exhibits where children can pretend, explore, imagine, and discover. There's also the popular **Witte Museum.** Inside the grand halls of the Witte the whole family will marvel at *Triceratops* and *Tyrannosaurus rex* bones, mummies, dioramas, and history and natural science exhibits. There's even a big tree house.

One of the more obscure things in town for the family is the **Texas Transportation Museum.**

Witte Museum in San Antonio

Here the kids will be enthralled by the miniature scale-model train sets meticulously built, painted, and erected with a frightening attention to detail. The scale models and their detailed environments are a must-see for the train geek and the curious.

Although your kids may not jump for joy at the idea of an evening of dancing, I guarantee if you drag them to **Leon Springs Dancehall** they will have the time of their life. Here families dance two-step to a live country band along with hundreds of other folks. This family-friendly dance hall has a massive 18,000 square feet of wooden floor that's packed Friday and Saturday nights.

Every January the San Antonio River is drained, and the **River Walk Mud Festival** begins. All weekend this mud-based festival puts smiles on faces. A king and queen of mud are elected to preside over events that include music, games, and all sorts of festivities.

After a long day of fun, enjoy a meal at **Liberty Bar.** Parents can enjoy a great lunch or dinner with upscale food, while the kids will enjoy eating in a unique two-story house. (Think Alice in Wonderland.) Another popular place to eat with kids is **Mi Tierra.** Mexican food and ambience reach a zenith here.

Austin

Family fun in Austin begins with watching the flight of the **bat colony of Congress Avenue Bridge.** This is a surefire way to get the kids excited on a summer evening. Indoor fun is to be had at the **Bullock Texas State History Museum,** where families can have a multimedia sensory overload. Also indoors is **The Thinkery,** Austin's children's museum. Here kids can come completely unglued in a safe environment. **Toy Joy** is a toy store for adults as well as kids.

Kids are crazy about dinosaurs. There are three great places where you can learn about these prehistoric animals. First there's the **Texas Memorial Museum,** which has an entire room filled with dino bones as well as pickled critters. A good way to get the kids interested in a walk through a botanical garden is by bringing them to the **Hartman Prehistoric Garden** in **Zilker**

Botanical Garden. Lastly in the dino field, there's the **Austin Nature and Science Center,** where kids can become mini paleontologists and dig for prehistoric bones.

A train ride can do a family a lot of good. You can't help but smile ear to ear while riding the **Zilker Zephyr,** a miniature train that runs through Zilker Park. If mini doesn't satisfy, there's the real deal, the **Austin Steam Train.** This old locomotive takes passengers into the Hill Country on a chugging ride to remember.

A fun place to take the whole family for lunch or dinner is Tex-Mex **Chuy's.** Kids can marvel at the junk hanging from the ceiling and color with crayons while parents can sip margaritas.

The Hill Country

The primary sights in the Hill Country for both kids and adults are the various caves and caverns. Everyone will be interested in walking through the **Natural Bridge Caverns** or the **Cave Without a Name.** For more of a theme park spin on a natural-cave experience there's **Wonder World Caverns** in San Marcos. If you prefer being high up in the trees, there's **Cypress Valley Canopy Tours.** Here the whole family can travel on cables, up in the tree-tops, for thrilling views along with adventure.

The historic German pioneer town of New Braunfels is home to Texas's largest water park, **Schlitterbahn.** A good way for a family to cool down in the summer is to ride chutes and tubes of water, and to splash in pools for a day. West from New Braunfels, in the art town of Wimberley, everyone loves to visit **Wimberley Glass Works.** Watch the world-renowned glass artists blow melted glass into beautiful shapes in a matter of minutes. In Fredericksburg, take the family to eat at the **Auslander Biergarten,** which has a Texas-meets-schnitzel menu and outdoor and semi-outdoor seating.

A fun place for the whole family to stay in the Hill Country is at the **Mayan Dude Ranch.** Families can take horseback rides in the country, eat in Wild West-style mess halls, go on hayrides, and hear ghost stories told around a campfire.

Austin

Look for ★ to find recommended
sights, activities, dining, and lodging.

Highlights

© AVALON TRAVEL

★ **Texas State Capitol:** The stately pink granite building is impressive both historically and visually (page 32).

★ **Barton Springs Pool:** The most popular way to cool down when it's over 100 degrees? Splashing, diving, and swimming in this perpetually 68-degree water (page 36).

★ **6th Street:** Catch a wide variety of live music and meet uninhibited partiers on Austin's version of Bourbon Street (page 36).

★ **The Bats of Congress Avenue Bridge:** Before dusk, pack a picnic dinner and head downtown to the bridge to watch the cloud of flying mammals swoop off into the night (page 37).

★ **LBJ Library and Museum:** No one has had more impact on recent Texas history than President Lyndon B. Johnson. Explore his life and his presidency—and even hear a mechanical LBJ tell some jokes (page 38).

★ **Blanton Museum of Art:** Check out the largest public collection of Latin American art in the country, along with works by notable artists like Pablo Picasso and Peter Paul Rubens (page 38).

★ **Bullock Texas State History Museum:** Texas's vibrant history is captured in dioramas, historical artifacts, and educational exhibits that dazzle the imagination (page 39).

★ **South Congress Avenue:** Stroll down this popular avenue lined with unique stores, boutiques, curiosity shops, and restaurants (page 42).

★ **Alamo Drafthouse Cinema:** Sip pints of beer, eat burgers, and screen independent films and long-forgotten B movies introduced by the stars and directors themselves (page 66).

★ **Lady Bird Lake:** Walk the many trails around the lake, paddle out in a kayak, or take a ride on a genuine paddle wheel riverboat (page 83).

A

t the end of the 19th century, in one of his short stories, the great American author O. Henry referred to the then small municipality of Austin as the "city of the violet crown."

In a single phrase, he captured the striking violet sunsets that often surrounded Austin in the evenings. Today this colorful evening show is the backdrop to Texas's most alluring city.

The core of Austin's life revolves around a few things: the capitol, the university, the high-tech industry, and the music. The most prominent of these is its role as the capital of Texas. If Texas were a nation, its economy would rank as the eighth largest in the world. Austin provides the stage for this powerful political and economic evolution and has hosted politicians and their ideas for well over a century. The second most important driving force of the city is the University of Texas (UT), which has always functioned as its main repository of knowledge and disseminator of progressive ideas. Consistently ranked as one of the top universities in the nation and the world, UT draws people from all walks of life to Austin, adding to the city's diverse

character. Third is the high-tech industry that was first planted here by IBM and later exploded with UT graduate Michael Dell's founding of Dell Computers. For the past few decades the tech industry has grown to such proportions that Austin has been dubbed "the Silicon Hills." Lastly is everybody's favorite, the music. Austin is proud to crank up the volume and loudly proclaim itself as the Live Music Capital of the World. With thousands of musicians, hundreds of clubs and venues, and an entire population of devout music lovers, the title is well deserved.

Austin has proven that when you combine politics, education, high technology, and music you get an extraordinary concoction. With these elements Austin has successfully forged its own unique identity and stands in stark contrast to the rest of the state. It's a city that was built with spare parts from the Wild West, pop culture, and Americana. It's urban, and it's rural; it's a big city but somehow

---

Previous: view of Austin and Lady Bird Lake; vintage amps at Austin Vintage Guitars. **Above:** the famous bell tower at the UT Campus.

Austin

© AVALON TRAVEL

ROLLINGWOOD

To One World
Theatre

UNIVERSITY
OF TEXAS

To Lady Bird Johnson
Wildflower Center and
Salt Lick

Barton Creek
Greenbelt

MANCHACA

SEE "LADY
BIRD LAKE"
MAP

Zilker Park

Town Lake
Metro Park

BROKEN
SPOKE

END OF
AN EAR

KERBEY
LANE

MATT'S EL
RANCHO

MARIA'S
TACO
EXPRESS

SEE "SOUTH
AUSTIN" MAP

BARTON SPRINGS
POOL

SOUTH AUSTIN

BULLOCK TEXAS
STATE HISTORY MUSEUM

CATHEDRAL
OF JUNK

SOUTH
CONGRESS
AVENUE

THE BATS
OF CONGRESS
AVENUE BRIDGE

DOWNTOWN

TEXAS STATE
CAPITOL

BLANTON
MUSEUM OF ART

ST EDWARDS
UNIVERSITY

6TH STREET

THUNDERBIRD
COFFEE

ALAMO
DRAFTHOUSE
CINEMA

EMO'S

ANTONE'S

HOSTELLING
INTERNATIONAL-AUSTIN

LADY
BIRD
LAKE

MR NATURAL

HOT MAMA'S
CAFE

JUAN IN A
MILLION

EAST AUSTIN

GEORGE
WASHINGTON
CARVER MUSEUM

DOG & DUCK
PUB

EL
CHILE

HOOVER'S
COOKING

THE EASTSIDE CAFE

Roy G. Guerrero
Colorado River Park

RIVERSIDE
GOLF
COURSE

LA QUINTA INN AND
SUITES AUSTIN
AIRPORT

To Airport

0   0.5 km
0   0.5 mi

retains a small-town vibe; it's rich in history, but forward-looking; it's progressive but laid-back. All the above makes this Central Texas town a thrill to visit. Exploring Austin is like being the steel ball in a Rube Goldberg invention. You simply slide down the chute and go for the ride, not fretting about what is around each twist and turn.

PLANNING YOUR TIME

If a long three- to four-day weekend is all you have to explore the town, it can help to plan your time a little. However, the best way to experience Austin is to let yourself meander. As a weekend traveler, you can plan to spend most of your time right in the downtown area because all that you could ever want is within arm's reach. Most attractions are within walking distance, such as the state capitol, 6th Street, and the museums, and everything else is accessible by an inexpensive cab ride. On foot or by cab, in a weekend you can check out some of the galleries and museums, walk around Lady Bird Lake, poke your head into some of the intriguing curiosity shops on South Congress Avenue, and eat some delicious Tex-Mex. Above all, plan on staying up late, walking down 6th Street, and catching some live music at the many varied venues downtown. Music is absolutely everywhere, and is usually good, often great.

If you plan to be in Austin for a couple weeks or longer, I would suggest a whole different approach to planning your time. Figure out where you would like to stay and settle in. Make a home base where you can leave your things and not worry too much about anything. Immediately upon checking in and unloading your luggage grab a free copy of the *Austin Chronicle* and look through the music and events pages. There's so much going on that there's bound to be something of interest for everyone. Once you've made some mental notes on events to catch, take your time exploring the town and scouring the surrounding area. Catch one of the creepy ghost tours downtown, hike in the greenbelt, relax at

Barton Springs, take a ride on Lady Bird Lake in an authentic double-decker paddle wheel riverboat, and spend half a day out at the Lady Bird Johnson Wildflower Center. After all this, if you still have a day to spare take a road trip out into the Hill Country.

ORIENTATION

Austin has several distinct areas where most of the attractions, restaurants, and accommodations are found. These areas are defined by neighborhoods and their streets—some of these streets being sights in their own right. Although Austin has several highways fanning out into the surrounding country, the two main highways that box in the city are I-35 and Highway 1. I-35 is on the east side of downtown, and is notorious for traffic accidents and congestion; Highway 1, known to locals as Mo-Pac (Missouri-Pacific Railroad), is to the west. Most of Austin's sights, best restaurants, hotels, and live music are somewhere between these two freeways.

Since there's no definitive way to explain the geographical areas that Austin comprises, it's broken up here in a way that should make it easy for the newcomer to get around.

Downtown

The first and foremost area is downtown, which encompasses the area north of Lady Bird Lake between I-35 and Lamar Boulevard. Downtown hot spots include **Congress Avenue,** which rolls down from the state capitol into town. Then there's the historic and infamous bar-studded **6th Street,** which is Austin's version of New Orleans's Bourbon Street. Sixth Street features bars, live music venues, and some tourist shops that sell junk that doesn't reflect Austin at all. For some reason tourists love 6th Street while locals are way "over it."

Just on the west side of Congress Avenue is the **2nd Street District,** which has become one of Austin's well-known dining and shopping areas. The area is noted for being the home to the *Austin City Limits* TV show, the W Hotel, and Willie Nelson in bronze.

Austin Fast Facts

- Founded in 1838

- Population: 931,830 (2016 U.S. Census Bureau data)

- Land area: 297 square miles

- Time zone: GMT/UTC-6 (Central Time)

- Fourth-largest city in Texas

- 11th-most populous city in the United States

- County: Travis

- Ethnicity: 49 percent white, 35 percent Hispanic, 8 percent African American, 8 percent other

- Sunshine: Austin averages 300 days of sun every year

- Average temperatures: 42-62°F in winter, 75-95°F in summer

- Average rainfall: 32.49 inches annually

- Major employers: City of Austin, Dell, federal government, Motorola, IBM, State of Texas, University of Texas at Austin, Apple, AMD, Applied Materials, Samsung, and 3M

- Area colleges and universities: The University of Texas at Austin, Huston-Tillotson College, St. Edward's University, Concordia University at Austin, Southwest Texas State University, Austin Community College, Southwestern University

- Median home price in 2016: $335,000

- Sales tax: 8.25 percent

Bordered by West 7th, West 8th, Guadalupe, and San Antonio Streets is the **Bremond Historic District,** a middle-class neighborhood of old Victorian homes situated under ancient oak trees. Under the glow of the Frost Building, the most distinctive structure in Austin's skyline, there's the **Warehouse District,** also known as 4th Street. In the late 1800s this was the brothel district, then it was turned into an industrial area, and in recent years has reverted to the spirit of its origins and is now lined with upscale bars and pubs.

The burgeoning **Rainey Street District** is a tiny pocket neighborhood fixed between downtown and I-35. Charming old houses have been tastefully converted into bars and eateries.

Just west of downtown is **West End,** which includes **Enfield** and the restaurants on **West Lynn Street.** Lastly, there's the **Red River District** on Red River Street. Just a few years ago this area was the quietest part of downtown, but today it's a bustling street of clubs, bars, and live music in the alternative/punk/metal/hipster vein.

South Austin

The cherished favorite for locals is South Austin. Here you have the ever-popular **South Congress Avenue,** which has some great curiosity shops, restaurants, clothing boutiques, and music clubs. A few streets west there's **South Lamar Boulevard,** where you can find some of Austin's many vintage and retro shops. South Austin is also popular for outdoor activities, with the gigantic grassy fields of **Zilker Park,** as well as trailheads to the beautiful hiking and biking area called the **Barton Creek Greenbelt.** Also in this area is Austin's premier feature, **Barton Springs.**

Central Austin

Central Austin is largely dominated by the **University of Texas** campus. The campus features some excellent museums, the LBJ presidential library, sports stadiums, and performing-arts theaters. The street that connects the UT area to downtown is **Guadalupe Street,** known to locals as **The Drag.** This used to be a main artery of action but in recent years has little pulse. Here you'll find some chain clothing stores, freak and chic shops, some cheap eats, and some bars. Also in Central Austin is the **Hyde Park** area, which is home to beautifully restored Victorians and neighborhood restaurants on **Duval Street.**

East Austin

Also referred to as the East Side, East Austin is the area in town that's experiencing growing pains. This is the "sketchy" part of town that's getting gentrified with the help of chic restaurants and city development. What Austinites consider sketchy is tame compared to similar areas in other cities. The East Side has some fine restaurants, a few boutique shops, some art spaces, and a few bars and music clubs, and is home to many of Austin's artists.

Old North Austin

Old North Austin is just starting to realize its potential. Visitors to Austin probably won't find themselves in this area without special effort. It's just north of the UT campus area, and only five miles from downtown. Although there are no sights to speak of, there are some interesting shops, boutiques, antiques stores, and "old-time" eateries. The area is popular among locals because it has a weird '70s time warp appeal. In Old North Austin there's **Old Burnet Road** (pronounced "BURN-it"), which has some of Austin's more unusual businesses and the area's best dive bars. There's also **East North loop,** which is a small bend in the road. This tiny area of shops doesn't look like much, but give it a chance and your sense of curiosity and adventure is sure to be piqued.

Sights

Austin has an eclectic and multifarious array of sights and attractions that include all of what one might expect from a large U.S. city, such as museums, grand architecture, botanical gardens, and monuments to historical figures. These are all what I would call the "typical" sights. Then there are the "atypical" sights, such as the ghostly bronze statue of Angelina Eberly firing her cannon and single-handedly saving Austin; the Cathedral of Junk; the Umlauf Sculpture Garden; the 500-year-old Treaty Oak tree, a survivor of chain saws and poisoning; and the famous bat colony of Congress Avenue Bridge. From typical to unique to downright strange, all Austin's attractions singularly and collectively stir the imagination, summon the bizarre, and foster new curiosities.

Austin's main attraction is simply nature. The parks and gardens, the lakes and streams, the hiking and biking trails, and the wildflowers and oaks are most worthy to behold, especially at twilight when Mother Nature's coronation ceremony fills the city skyline with the violet crown.

DOWNTOWN
★ Texas State Capitol

The **Texas State Capitol** (1100 Congress Ave.) is the nucleus of Austin, both historically and visually. When you see the massive statehouse on the skyline, consider that it almost never was. Over a hundred years ago a tug of war between the cities of Houston and Waterloo (Austin was initially named Waterloo) went on for years, and every so often the state government would shift between the cities. Austin eventually won the title of state capital, and this decision has since shaped the city's development.

When the capitol building was first erected back in 1888 it was believed to be the seventh-tallest building in the world. Today it supposedly stands taller than the U.S. Capitol, a detail Texans are proud to point out. The interior of the capitol exudes a hushed dignity. Each component, from the grand marble pillars down to the door hinges, is an example of the fine craftsmanship of a bygone era. Old battle flags, sculptures, and portraits of historical figures and significant events in Texas history grace the entryways, walls, and legislative chambers, leaving visitors with strong visual images of Texas's story. A large, colorful marble terrazzo covers the floor of the capitol rotunda, depicting the six sovereign flags that have flown over Texas and 12 battles significant in the history of the state. The rotunda is also home to portraits of all the Texas governors.

During the 20th century, as the state of Texas grew, so did its government, and the capitol became increasingly hard-pressed for space. Over the years quick fixes were made to accommodate the demands placed on the century-old building. Successive additions of new technologies like telephones, air conditioners, and computers, and the need for more offices, led to a maze of false walls and generations of wiring. No one was surprised when a fire broke out in 1983. The event highlighted the need for renovation and expansion. After 10 years of bureaucracy, funding woes, and architectural debate, excavation and construction finally started. In 1993, the underground expansion of the capitol was dedicated. The results of this project are truly a sight to behold. To build the 620,000-square-foot subterranean extension, nearly 700,000 tons of rock had to be removed, and a 130-foot-long, 32-foot-deep trench had to be dug through solid limestone to connect the original building to the new extension without harming the original foundation or structure.

Today, the opulent capitol and the beautiful surrounding 22-acre grounds are well worth a visit. The capitol is free and open to the public 7am-10pm weekdays, 9am-8pm weekends. Free guided tours are offered 8:30am-4:30pm Monday-Friday, 9:30am-3:30pm Saturday, and noon-3:30pm Sunday. Plan on spending about two hours at the capitol grounds to take in the history, monuments, and architecture.

CAPITOL VISITORS CENTER

If you're itching for more information on the capitol, walk over to the **Capitol Visitors Center** (112 E. 11th St., 512/305-8400, 9am-5pm Mon.-Sat., noon-5pm Sun., free), at the southeast corner of the capitol grounds. Here you'll find exhibits, a video presentation on the secret rooms and spaces in the capitol, and a salute to O. Henry.

OLD STATE CAPITOL BUILDING RUINS

Directly across from the capitol, at Congress and 11th, are the remains of Austin's first statehouse, the **Old State Capitol Building Ruins.** There's not much there but the original crumbling foundation and a cistern. It's also where University of Texas classes were held back in the late 1800s.

GOVERNOR'S MANSION

Not too far from the capitol is the **Governor's Mansion** (1010 Colorado St., 512/305-8524, 2pm-4pm Wed.-Fri., free, by reservation only). This Greek Revival-style house has been the home for every governor since it was designed and constructed back in 1856. Built with Austin-made bricks and timbers from Bastrop, this fine architectural work has survived years of politics, stuffy decor, and renovations. Today the mansion is the oldest standing public building in downtown, and is the fourth-oldest continuously occupied governor's mansion in the United States. Over the years paranormal activity has been reported, and in plain English that means some have seen "dead people." Some think it's the ghost of Sam Houston, while others think it's the ghost of a lovesick 19-year-old who shot himself in the guest room. The mansion suffered

Downtown Austin

MADAM MAM'S ▼

NEILL-COCHRAN
HOUSE MUSEUM ★

AUSTIN CITY LIMITS
(FORMER LOCATION) ★

DEAN ST   KEATON ST   (26TH) ST

25TH ST

24TH ST

23RD ST

22 1/2 ST

★ THE DRAG

STAR OF
TEXAS INN ●

AUSTIN FOLK
HOUSE B&B ●

UT TOWER

22ND ST

TEXAS MEMORIAL
MUSEUM ★

★ PERFORMING
ARTS CENTER

UNIVERSITY

OF

TEXAS

23RD ST

LBJ LIBRARY ✪
AND MUSEUM

HARRY RANSOM
HUMANITIES RESEARCH
CENTER

CAMPUS   MANOR RD

HOTEL
ELLA ●

21ST ST

AUSTIN'S INN
AT PEARL ST ●

20TH ST

MARTIN

AT&T HOTEL &
CONFERENCE CENTER ●

18TH ST

LUTHER

KING

To Aster's ↗
Ethiopian

JR   BLVD

✪ BLANTON
MUSEUM OF ART

ARTURO'S BAKERY
AND CAFE ★

17TH ST

CLAY PIT ●

16TH ST

★
✪ BULLOCK TEXAS STATE
HISTORY MUSEUM

35

81
290

To El Cilito →

AUSTIN LAND AND ▼
CATTLE CO

15TH ST

14TH ST

TEXAS CHILI ★
PARLOR

13TH ST

12TH ST

RED

RIVER

★ FRANK ERWIN
CENTER

16TH ST

★ TEXAS STATE ✪
CAPITOL

Waterloo
Park

14TH ST

Duncan
Park

11TH ST

10TH ST

9TH ST

GOVERNOR'S
MANSION ●

OLD STATE
CAPITOL
BUILDING
RUINS ★

CAPITOL
VISITORS
CENTER ★

13TH ST

LA QUINTA INN-
AUSTIN CAPITOL ●

BRICK OVEN ●

SUPER 8
MOTEL ■

12TH ST

BREMOND
HISTORIC DISTRICT

AUSTIN HISTORY
CENTER ★

8TH ST

SHERATON
AUSTIN ●

JUNIPER ST

7TH ST

HUT'S
HAMBURGERS ▼

FRANK AND ▼
ANGIE'S PIZZERIA

EXTENDED STAY AMERICA
AUSTIN-DOWNTOWN-
LADY BIRD LAKE ●

THE
CONTEMPORARY
AUSTIN ★

PARAMOUNT
THEATRE ★

OMNI AUSTIN
HOTEL
DOWNTOWN ●

FRANKLIN
BARBECUE ▼

RED RIVER
DISTRICT

10TH ST

WAHOO'S ▼
FISH
TACOS

WALTON'S FANCY
AND STAPLE ▼

THE STEPHEN F
AUSTIN HOTEL ●

VOODOO
DONUTS ▼

ALAMO
DRAFTHOUSE
CINEMA ✪

STUBB'S BBQ ▼

8TH ST

SAN MARCOS ST

FADO'S ▼

WILD ABOUT
MUSIC ●

THE
DRISKILL
HOTEL

1886 ★

MUSEUM OF THE WEIRD ★

HALCYON ▼
COFFEEHOUSE

TRULUCK'S ▼

IRON
CACTUS ▼

THE
VELVEETA
ROOM

6TH
STREET

TOY
JOY ■

LAMBERT'S ■

MEXIC-ARTE
MUSEUM ●

EDDIE V'S
EDGEWATER
GRILL ▼

ESTHER'S
FOLLIES ●

6TH ST

WRIGHT
BRO'S ▼

7TH ST

To Takoba →

2ND STREET DISTRICT

W AUSTIN ●

JO'S ●

LA
TRAVIATA ▼

O HENRY
MUSEUM ●

HILTON
AUSTIN ●

5TH ST

EAST
AUSTIN

SCOOT
INN ■

AUSTIN JAVA ▼

CESAR

CHAVEZ

WILLIE NELSON BLVD

3RD ST

35

81
290

4TH ST

3RD ST

MEDINA ST

WALLER ST

NAVASOTA ST

Auditorium
Shores

LONE STAR ●
RIVERBOAT

RADISSON HOTEL
ON LADY BIRD LAKE ●

WILLOW ST

AUSTIN
CONVENTION
CENTER

Palm
Park

MOONSHINE ●

THE LONG ★
CENTER

THE BATS OF ✪
CONGRESS
AVENUE BRIDGE

THE FOUR ●
SEASONS

IRON WORKS ▼

To G'Raj
Mahal

HOLIDAY INN ▼
AUSTIN-LADY
BIRD LAKE

2ND ST

extensive damage from a fire in 2008 but reopened to visitors in 2013. Visiting hours can vary throughout the year so be sure to check hours online or by calling ahead.

★ Barton Springs Pool

In the dead of summer, when few Austinites stray too far from the air-conditioning, there's one place that's sure to be a cool 68 degrees, and that's **Barton Springs Pool** (2101 Barton Springs Rd., 512/867-3080). This age-old artesian spring-fed pool in Zilker Park has faithfully provided Austinites with a cool place to swim, relax, and socialize for over 100 years. On any given summer day Barton Springs Pool is packed with families, flirting teenagers, sunseekers, and daredevils at the diving board showing off their tricks.

The 1,000-foot-long swimming hole is fed by several underwater springs. When the springs were dammed off to create the pool, the rock and gravel bottom was wisely left unaltered, preserving the natural ambience. If you're concerned about pollution or hygiene, you'll be glad to hear the pool has a legion of advocates (the Save Our Springs Coalition) that closely guard this precious resource. When it comes to pollution Barton Springs' pure waters have been tirelessly defended

from the constant threat of damaging development on the aquifer that feeds the pool. As for hygiene, the pool is closed when the fecal coliform count is high.

The pool is open daily (except Thursdays) 5am-10pm in the summer. Access to the pool is $3 for adults, $2 for ages 12-17, and $1 for seniors and kids 11 and under. Remember this is a cash-only operation. Swimming before 8am is free but "swim at your own risk"; lifeguards are on duty only during the fee periods. There are two ways to access the pool, with the main entrance off Barton Springs Road. For the back entrance off Barton Springs Road, turn away from Lady Bird Lake on Robert E. Lee Drive, go up the hill, and park at the gravel parking area next to the baseball field. Words of advice: Call before you go to make sure the pool is open, check the hours (which change seasonally), and don't bring food (eating on the grounds is prohibited). Hanging out at the pool can easily be a half-day leisure event, that is if you enjoy swimming, sunbathing, and people-watching.

★ 6th Street

Besides bats, Austin is probably most known for **6th Street,** which is Austin's version of New Orleans's Bourbon Street. It features

Barton Springs Pool

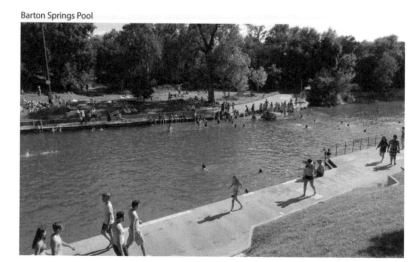

Austin Quirks

There are many subtle and strange things you may notice while exploring this town that prides itself on being weird. Here's a list in no particular order.

- **Yard Art and Lawn Statuary:** While driving around town you may notice Austin's pervasive veneration for yard art and lawn statuary. Popular yard decorations are pink flamingoes, metal kinetic art, bizarre sculptures, and yard gnomes, some of which have an uncanny resemblance to George W. Bush.

- **Freak Storms:** Austin, as well as the Hill Country, is notorious for freak mini storms that pass through the area in a matter of minutes. One second it's a nice evening at about 70°F and the next the wind will whip up and lightning will fill the skies. Then the next thing you know hail the size of golf balls is plummeting to the earth. In an hour or so the sky clears up as if nothing happened.

- **Liberal Bumper Stickers:** If you had to figure out which city you were in solely by the bumper stickers on cars you would probably guess you were in Berkeley, California. A city in Texas would be your last guess. This is one of the great conundrums of Austin. The capital of the conservative state of Texas is liberal Austin.

- *Bosom Buddies* **Theme Song:** You have to completely tap into your subconscious to catch this one. When you are about town, shopping for groceries at H.E.B., in the lobby of a motel, or even sitting in a piano bar, you will begin to notice Billy Joel's lyrics, "I don't care what you say anymore, this is my life. Go ahead with your own life, and leave me alone." This melody is a subliminal and curious soundtrack to Austin life.

bars, pubs, live music venues, and sidewalk pizza kiosks. After dusk live music comes from every crack and crevice. On Thursday, Friday, and Saturday nights around 10pm, the Austin police department closes off the street and the party begins. The scene on 6th Street is pretty rowdy, with hordes of wasted college kids and scantily clad girls. There's always a contingent of men roaming about, afflicted with an acute case of machismo, looking for a date, a fight, or both in one. The scene can get pretty sketchy later in the night—a good time to bail on this scene is around midnight, and especially before the bars close at 2am.

Besides clubs and bars there's also a slew of terrible tourist shops that feature belt buckles, Texas memorabilia with the state flag screen-printed on everything, samurai swords (don't ask why), shot glasses, and ridiculous touristy T-shirts that say things like "F*** Y'all, I'm from Texas," which doesn't represent Texas or Austin in even the slightest way.

Sure, there are some good live music spots here, but you have to put up with lots of nonsense to enjoy it. If you like spring break at Daytona Beach or New Orleans during Mardi Gras, you'll probably like 6th Street, in which case you will probably want to plan for 5 hours as you may want to catch a late dinner down here before enjoying the live music and night-life until after midnight.

★ The Bats of Congress Avenue Bridge

Austin's main attraction isn't always rock stars. **Bats** are the stars of the show every evening when they fly out from under Congress Avenue Bridge by the thousands in search of bugs. When the bridge was reconstructed in the 1980s no one had any idea this spot would become the largest urban bat colony in North America. These Mexican free-tailed bats migrate each spring from central Mexico to various roosting sites throughout the southwestern United States, their favorite being here in Austin. Out of the 1.5 million bats in this colony, most are females, who produce one offspring each June. Every night they eat somewhere between 10,000 and 30,000 pounds of insects.

You can catch the bats' dramatic exit into the night from March to early November, but the best months are July and August. Best spots for viewing the bat flight are the **Bat Observation Area** at the *Austin American-Statesman* (at the southeast corner of the Congress Avenue Bridge), at the Radisson Hotel (11 E. 1st St.), on Lady Bird Lake from a **canoe** (rent from Zilker Park Boat Rentals for $12 an hour, www.zilkerboats.com), or on an authentic **double-decker paddlewheel riverboat** (Lone Star Riverboat, 512/327-9721, $10 per person). Best time for viewing is sunset, and parking is offered at the *Austin American-Statesman* after 6pm. No public restrooms are available. For more information on the bats, such as flight times, call the Bat Hotline at 512/327-9721, ext. 3636. Be prepared to hang around the bridge for a couple of hours so you can get a good spot; in the summer, the bridge can often be packed.

The LBJ Library and Museum is the most visited presidential library in the US.

★ LBJ Library and Museum

Considered the most visited presidential library in the United States, the **LBJ Library and Museum** (2313 Red River St., on the University of Texas campus, 512/721-0200, www.lbjlibrary.org, 9am-5pm daily, $8 adults, $5 seniors and retired military, $3 college students and children 13-17) explores the life and politics of Lyndon Baines Johnson. If you know little to nothing about LBJ, the permanent exhibit that recounts his life is sure to capture your interest and foster an appreciation of the 36th president. Midway through the exhibit, expect an emotional sucker punch when the exhibit commemorates the assassination of JFK in a moving way. From here on out it explores the period in U.S. history that ushered in a new era in culture and politics—the 1960s. When you surface in the gigantic main room and look up, your breath will be taken away by a towering wall of glass, behind which are floors of red archives containing everything LBJ ever wrote, did, and darn near thought. Be

sure to listen to the mechanical LBJ tell jokes. Plan on spending at least two hours for the exhibits and in the gift shop.

★ Blanton Museum of Art

The only art museum in Austin with a permanent collection to speak of is **Blanton Museum of Art** (200 E. Martin Luther King Jr. Blvd., on the UT campus, 512/471-7324, 10am-5pm Tues.-Fri., 11am-5pm Sat., 1pm-5pm Sun., $9 adults, $7 seniors, $5 ages 13-21, free every Thurs. with extended hours on the third Thurs. of each month). Located at the edge of the university campus in downtown Austin, the Blanton is the largest university museum in the United States. Inside the 180,000-square-foot complex are both temporary and permanent exhibits, and outside is an attractive public plaza with views of the state capitol. The Blanton's permanent collection includes some 17,000 works of art, including old master paintings and contemporary American art, and is proud to be one of the largest public collections of Latin American art in the United States. Works by notable artists include those of Pablo Picasso,

Peter Paul Rubens, and Fernando Botero. Plan on spending at least two hours for the exhibits and the gift shop.

★ Bullock Texas State History Museum

Texas state pride is bigger than Texas itself. It's fitting that the museum devoted to the big spirit of Texas is gigantic, and adorned with a 35-foot-tall bronze Lone Star. In the grand polished stone halls of the Bullock Texas State History Museum (1800 N. Congress Ave., 866/369-7108, www.thestoryoftexas. com, 9am-5pm Mon.-Sat., noon-6pm Sun., $13 adults, $11 seniors, military, and college students, $9 youth 4-17), the "Story of Texas" is told. From the indigenous people who first inhabited the region to the Spanish explorers of the 1500s and the legendary battle at The Alamo, through the oil boom to the present day, Texas's history is chronicled in life-size dioramas and interactive exhibits. The facility also houses two theaters. The Texas Spirit Theater provides a multimedia, cinematic experience complete with special effects that bring Texas's story to life. The museum also boasts Austin's only IMAX theater, which operates independently of the museum. Plan on spending at least 2 hours for the exhibits and

the gift shop and 3-4 hours if you also include a visit to IMAX theater.

So who was Bob Bullock, the museum's namesake? He was a highly regarded state politician who eventually became the lieutenant governor. His vision and passion for all things Texas brought the museum into fruition. Admission prices vary. I recommend buying tickets to the museum and the Texas Spirit Theater's 20-minute movie ($5 adults, $4 students, seniors, and youths 4-17).

For those who haven't acquired Texas Pride, or just aren't in the mood for a multimedia Texas experience, "never mind the Bullocks." There are many other museums to saunter through.

Harry Ransom Humanities Research Center

There's only one place in the world where you can see a Gutenberg Bible, the world's first photograph, an original manuscript by James Joyce, and a painting by Frida Kahlo all in one place, and that's the Harry Ransom Humanities Research Center (21st and Guadalupe St., on the UT campus, 512/471-8944, www.hrc.utexas.edu, 10am-5pm Mon., Tues., Wed., and Fri., 10am-7pm Thurs., noon-5pm Sat.-Sun., free). Self-billed as "one

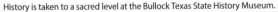

History is taken to a sacred level at the Bullock Texas State History Museum.

of the world's finest culture archives," the Harry Ransom Center is a place where scholars conduct research alongside tourists and the curious. The center houses a robust collection of over 36 million literary manuscripts, including ones by Ernest Hemingway, James Joyce, T. S. Eliot, and Tennessee Williams, and over 100,000 works of art that are rotated into view. Along with showcasing its own collections, the center also has temporary exhibits. Parking is at the Dobie Center parking garage on the corner of 21st and Whitis.

Mexic-Arte Museum

The **Mexic-Arte Museum** (419 Congress Ave., 512/480-9373, www.mexic-artemuseum.org, 10am-6pm Mon.-Thurs., 10am-5pm Fri.-Sat., noon-5pm Sun., $5 adults, $4 seniors, $1 children 12 and under) has emerged as the official Mexican and Mexican American fine-art museum of Texas. You can encounter works by contemporary Mexican, Latino, and Latin-American artists in the museum's three gallery spaces. Mexic-Arte offers a permanent collection, but the primary focus here is special exhibits and shows that both educate and get people thinking. On any given day the art here is poignant, colorful, and inspiring,

offering a glimpse into the inner life of Latino culture through the arts.

O. Henry Museum

The prolific American short-story writer O. Henry (1862-1910) made Austin his home for a brief stint. His little house, now the **O. Henry Museum** (409 E. 5th St., 512/472-1903, noon-5pm Wed.-Sun., free but donations encouraged), is a beautiful Queen Anne cottage containing some of O. Henry's personal items. Born William Sydney Porter in Greensboro, North Carolina, he came to Austin when he was 20 years old. Here he started a humorous weekly called *The Rolling Stone* (not to be confused with the pop-culture magazine of today), fell in love, married, and moved into this house, which was owned by his new wife's family. Ten years later he found himself in an Ohio prison, where his writing started taking off. Upon leaving the penitentiary he changed his name to O. Henry and moved to New York City, where his life fizzled out, with a second failed marriage and alcohol problems. The master of surprise endings eventually died of cirrhosis of the liver.

The Contemporary Austin

All things related to modern and cutting-edge

the O. Henry Museum

art are presented at **The Contemporary Austin**'s two locations. The large indoor exhibition space at the **Jones Center** (700 Congress Ave., 512/453-5312, http://thecontemporaryaustin.org, 11am-7pm Tues.-Sat., noon-5pm Sun., $5) is an indoor museum and art space dedicated to promoting and exhibiting contemporary art. Founded in 1911 to promote the works of locally celebrated artist **Elisabet Ney** (whose house is now an Austin museum), the gallery space currently has exhibitions and programs geared toward educating. The **Laguna Gloria** location (3809 W. 35th St., 512/458-8191, 10am-4pm Tues.-Sun.) is at a mansion nestled on a stunning site near the lake at Mayfield Park and Preserve. This extension of the Contemporary Austin features an outdoor sculpture park and a small indoor exhibition space. As a side note, the mansion was built by Clara Driscoll, who is dubbed "the savior of the Alamo" because she bought the historic grounds in San Antonio to prevent developers from leveling the site.

Austin History Center

Austin's rich history has been collected, archived, and made available by the **Austin History Center** (810 Guadalupe St., next to the Austin Public Library, 512/974-7480, 10am-6pm Tues.-Sat., noon-6pm Sun., free). Housed in a historic neoclassical building, the collection consists of millions of photos, maps, architectural drawings, documented customs, newspapers, and records, and is the main repository for history in the Central Texas region.

Austin Nature and Science Center

Ever wanted to pretend you're a scientist? **Austin Nature and Science Center** (301 Nature Dr., in Zilker Park just off Stratford Dr., 512/974-3888, 9am-5pm Mon.-Sat., noon-5pm Sun., $2 donation) offers many different ways to discover and explore for a day. Here you can learn about the plants, animals, and geology of Central Texas. The Discovery Lab has several mini science labs that engage and educate through hands-on exhibits. In the Dino Pit you can become a paleontologist and dig up dinosaur bones.

Museum of the Weird

If you are fascinated by the unusual and the bizarre, or you are just plain curious, this small storefront "museum" on 6th Street will fill your head with all sorts of crazy images and thoughts. **Museum of the Weird** (412 E. 6th St., Austin, 512/476-5493, 10am-midnight daily, $12 adults, $7 children under 8) is the only place in the world where you can view up close a mermaid-monkey creature, skeletons, shrunken heads, and lots more creepy stuff. If you take the tour you can also stroll up to the top floor and watch sideshow performances in a small room. A tattoo-covered performer may swallow a sword or electrocute himself. On the way up the stairs you'll have the opportunity to swallow a giant Madagascar hissing cockroach, and you can view the room where Johnny Depp stayed when he was in town filming a movie.

If all this isn't enough, for a couple extra bucks you can see the museum's most prized treasure: the giant frozen body of a prehistoric, Sasquatch-type man-creature known as the Minnesota Iceman. This specimen is frozen in a block of ice inside a specially designed coffin/freezer. Peering through the glass at this mangy face brings up all sorts of thoughts from, "is this real?" to "will he come alive if the ice is thawed?" to "this is just plain ridiculous!" Viewing hours for the Iceman are limited, so it's best to call in advance.

Emma S. Barrientos Mexican American Cultural Center

Austin is proud to have a vibrant Latino community comprising families, business owners, politicians, musicians, and artists. **Emma S. Barrientos Mexican American Cultural Center** (600 River St., 512/974-3772, www.ci.austin.tx.us/macc, 10am-6pm Mon.-Thurs., 10am-5:30pm Fri., 10am-4pm Sat.) is emerging as the official Mexican American cultural center in Austin. Here you can encounter works by contemporary Mexican, Latino, and Latin-American artists, participate in classes, and screen films from Mexico's Golden Age era of film.

Texas Memorial Museum

For the kids and parents alike there's the **Texas Memorial Museum** (2400 Trinity St., on the UT campus, 512/471-1604, www. utexas.edu/tmm, 9am-5pm Tues.-Sat., $3, $1 military, 2 and under is free), which has four floors of exhibits dedicated to the natural sciences. The big draw here is the dinosaur exhibit, which features dinosaur models, including a 40-foot-long pterosaur, fossils of saber-toothed tiger kittens, and dinosaur footprints. The 1st floor has fossils, gems, and minerals, with a paleontologist on site to answer questions; the 2nd floor displays rare specimens; the 3rd floor features wildlife exhibits with mounted birds, animals, reptiles, and amphibians; and the 4th floor has an exhibit featuring colorful and unusual insects, microscopic cave fauna, and fish. Parking is available at the UT parking garage at 2500 San Jacinto Boulevard, just north of the museum.

Treaty Oak

When you arrive at this sight you may wonder why an old tree with a plaque on it is worth seeing. Well, the venerable 500-year-old Treaty Oak is a source of legend, history, and drama, with a story of religion, truces, chain saws, poison, and endurance. It is the last survivor of the Council Oaks, a grove of trees that was once a place of religious ceremony for the area's Comanche and Tonkawa populations. According to legend, it is also the site where Stephen F. Austin signed a boundary treaty with local Native Americans in the 1800s. In the 1920s, when the Council Oaks were being cleared for urban growth, this one ancient tree was saved from a violent death by chain saw and was consecrated a historic U.S. tree by the American Forestry Association.

The Treaty Oak is remembered by most folk not for having witnessed Austin's history,

but for what happened to it in the 1980s when a lovesick lunatic poured lethal amounts of poison on the tree to get back at a lover. Don't ask why. In the ensuing months the Treaty Oak made national headlines as dendrite doctors tried to save the tree. Now about 35 percent of the tree is alive, and the Treaty Oak has become a symbol of endurance for Native Americans and Anglos alike.

If you want to see this historic tree there's no need to make a special trip. Just check it out while you're eating at Z'Tejas Southwestern Grill. The Treaty Oak is on Baylor Street between 5th and 6th Streets, just west of Lamar Boulevard.

Mount Bonnell

What is considered a hill by some is a mountain to others. Since Texas doesn't have much in the way of mountains, I suppose **Mount Bonnell** (Mount Bonnell Rd.) has earned its title. Towering 785 feet above Austin, Mount Bonnell offers a spectacular panoramic view of the city, the Colorado River, and the surrounding area. The 200-foot limestone escarpment is a strenuous climb but worth the effort. When you are on top of the mount, consider how it was once called "Antoinette's Leap" in remembrance of a settler who jumped off the cliff rather than perish during a Native American attack. Don't expect any snowcapped peaks, and don't try to find Mount Bonnell by driving toward "the mountain," as you can't see it from anywhere. It's accessed from Mo-Pac Expressway/Highway 1 by exiting at 35th Street and heading west. On your way back down the mountain, stop off at **Dry Creek Saloon** (4812 Mount Bonnell Rd., 512/453-9244) for a beer.

SOUTH AUSTIN
★ South Congress Avenue

The bat colony at Congress Avenue Bridge marks the beginning of a strip of curiosity shops, eateries, and clubs on South Congress Avenue. If 6th Street is too touristy for you, you'll love this street. Enjoy strolling around with a cup of coffee from the parking-lot kiosk

Walking up and down South Congress Avenue is a great way to let a day slip away.

Jo's Cafe. Be sure to always look up as you walk along South Congress, because many of these businesses have great signs and sculptures attached to their roofs and storefronts. For example, there's a cowboy made out of a muffler, riding a giant rabbit, and a zebra dressed up like Carmen Miranda. You can get lost for hours in the multifarious shops and boutiques, like the folk-art gallery Yard Dog, the vintage shop Uncommon Objects, the costume shop Lucy in Disguise with Diamonds, and the Western-wear shop Allens Boots. South Congress is fun during the day for window-shopping and at night for restaurants and live music. The absolute best day of the week is the first Thursday of each month when the businesses stay open late (most until 10pm). The streets are full of vendors and artists selling their wares, and bands play on the sidewalks. If you want to enjoy the shops and get a bite to eat, you can easily lose yourself for 2-4 hours exploring fajitas, bizarre taxidermy, hip clothing, luchador masks, vintage shops, and musty Elvis costumes.

Lady Bird Johnson Wildflower Center

Come spring, Austin and the surrounding Hill Country have some of the most varied and beautiful wildflowers in the state. It's no surprise there's a center devoted to these little guys. In 1982 the **Lady Bird Johnson Wildflower Center** (4801 La Crosse Ave., 512/232-0100, www.wildflower.org, 9am-5pm Tues.-Sat., noon-5pm Sun., $10 adults, $8 seniors and students, $4 children 5-17) was founded under a different name, and at a different location, by two spry advocates of native plants, former First Lady of the United States Lady Bird Johnson and a friend. In 1995 the center was moved to its current location on 279 acres southwest of Austin, and in 1998 it was renamed in honor of Lady Bird Johnson. The main grounds include 16 carefully placed and meticulously maintained gardens, all designed around the region's natural landscape, using native plants. The gardens weave through and around several stone buildings that serve as educational centers and galleries, and lead to even more gardens with wisteria-covered pergolas and flower-lined promenades. The center isn't in Austin proper, but it's well worth the drive. Since it all hinges on wildflowers and seasonal native plants, don't bother visiting in the fall or winter when everything is dead.

Zilker Park

The heart of Austin's outdoor action is **Zilker Park** (2100 Barton Springs Rd.). The park's beautiful setting is unparalleled, with 351 acres of green grass at the edge of Lady Bird Lake, groves of old oak trees, and a dramatic view of Austin's city skyline rising from the trees in the distance. Most of the city's outdoor events happen here, such as the Austin City Limits Music Festival, Austin Symphony July 4th Concert and Fireworks, Trail of Lights, Zilker Park Christmas Tree, and the Zilker Park Kite Festival, which has been held here for almost 80 years.

On the grassy knoll next to Barton Springs Pool, classical, rock, and everything in

South Austin

BARTON SPRINGS POOL

BLACK SHEEP LODGE

UMLAUF SCULPTURE GARDEN AND MUSEUM

SAXON PUB

SOUTH AUSTIN MUSEUM OF POPULAR CULTURE

ALAMO DRAFTHOUSE

GREEN PASTURES

Guerrero Park

0   0.25 Km
0   0.25 mi

HETHER ST
LAMAR
KINNEY
TREADWELL
MARGARET ST
ROBERT E LEE RD

Zilker Park
TOOMEY RD

CHUY'S
SHADY GROVE RESTAURANT
AUSTIN JAVA
FILIPNOTICS

ZACHARY SCOTT THEATRE CENTER

West Bouldin Creek
BLVD
JULIET ST
AVE
ST

VOX TABLE
UCHI
GARMENT MODERN & VINTAGE

GREEN MESQUITE
P. TERRY'S
PETER PAN MINI-GOLF

West Bouldin Creek Greenbelt

LIVE OAK ST
JOHANNA ST
MARY ST
ANNIE ST
MONROE ST
5TH ST
BOULDINE ST

BOULDIN CREEK COFFEE HOUSE
ROADHOUSE RELICS
POLVOS

East Bouldin Creek Greenbelt
BARTON SPRINGS RD
Butler Park

FREDDIE'S
GOURDOUGHS DOUGHNUTS

NEWTON
ELIZABETH ST
1ST ST
BOULDINE AVE

SEE DETAIL

S CONGRESS AVE
NICKERSON ST
BRACKENRIDGE ST

SOUTH CONGRESS AVENUE

PALMER EVENTS CENTER
LONG CENTER FOR THE PERFORMING ARTS

Auditorium Shores
Colorado River

THREADGILL'S
EGO'S
HYATT REGENCY AUSTIN
LONE STAR RIVERBOAT

FREEBIRDS WORLD BURRITO
DOMINICAN JOE
EMBASSY SUITES DOWNTOWN

THE BATS OF CONGRESS AVENUE BRIDGE

NEWNING AVE
Blunn Creek Greenbelt
Blunn Creek

THE FAIRVIEW

EMMA S. BARRIENTOS MEXICAN AMERICAN CULTURAL CENTER

AUSTIN CONVENTION CENTER

RAINEY STREET DISTRICT

MOONSHINE PATIO BAR & GRILL

© AVALON TRAVEL

TORCHY'S TACOS
WAHOO'S FISH TACO
MAGNOLIA CAFE

EVA ST
MILTON
S CONGRESS AVE
MARY ST
ANNIE ST
NICKERSON ST
BRACKENRIDGE ST

BIG TOP
FEATHERS
ALLENS BOOTS
MONKEY SEE, MONKEY DO
SOUTH CONGRESS HOTEL

YESPAÏO
LUCY IN DISGUISE
UNCOMMON OBJECTS
GUERO'S
HOPDODDY
TESORO'S
SOUTH CONGRESS CAFE
YARD DOG
STAG
HOME SLICE

ELIZABETH ST
NEWTON
GIBSON ST
JAMES ST

PERLA'S
SAN JOSE
AUSTIN MOTEL
JO'S
CONTINENTAL CLUB
AMY'S ICE CREAM
KIMBER MODERN

RIVER ST
RAINEY ST
SAN MARCOS ST

PARTS AND LABOUR
BLACKMAIL
CREATURES
HOTEL VAN ZANDT
BANGAR'S
GRAJ MAHAL
PHOENICIAN RESTO CAFE

MONROE ST
CONGRESS
SAN

81
290
35

Austin's Jack the Ripper

Early Austin history has many shades, characters, and shady characters. One of Austin's darkest chapters took place in 1885 when the young city was haunted by the shadiest character in all the town's history. Lurking in the shadows was a serial killer who is now known as the Servant Girl Annihilator. For an entire year there was a chill of horror on the streets of Austin. This Texas version of Jack the Ripper was never seen, nor caught, but his trail of blood was everywhere. He brutally murdered seven servant girls of poor origins and one man; all were hacked to death with an ax. The bodies turned up in alleys and behind homes, and one of the bodies was found on what is now West 6th Street. Headlines for that year were horrifying, and all the city's residents could do was hope and pray that either the killing spree would stop or the murderer would get caught. On Christmas Eve the last murder took place, and after that there were no more. Eventually three arrests were made and one suspect went to trial, but he was acquitted. All of the murders have remained unsolved. The uncanny twist to this tale is that three years after the Austin murders, Jack the Ripper began his infamous spree in England.

If this bit of Austin's history interests you, novelist Steven Saylor's historical fiction work *A Twist at the End* (St. Martin's Minotaur, 2001) probes into this dark tale. You can also walk in the footsteps of the Servant Girl Annihilator with **Austin Ghost Tours** (512/853-9826, www.austinghosttours.com).

---

between can be heard at the **Zilker Hillside Theater,** which also is home to the **Zilker Summer Musical** and **Shakespeare in the Park.** Down the parking lot from the theater and at the entrance to Barton Springs is the depot for the **Zilker Zephyr,** a miniature open-air train that weaves through the park—a huge hit with kids. Past the Zephyr and down the riverbank you can rent a canoe and paddle around on **Lady Bird Lake** and get a unique view of Austin. **Blues on the Green** happens on alternating summer Wednesdays at the **Rock Garden,** which is in the middle of the large grassy area that is bordered by Barton Springs Road. The park is also home to the **Austin Nature and Science Center,** where everyone can participate in interactive wildlife, nature, and science displays. Zilker Park also has an entrance to the **Greenbelt,** which has trails for hiking and biking. At any given day throughout the year, Zilker Park is a safe bet for a day in the outdoors. Parking lots are available, but it's nearly impossible to find a spot during major festivals.

Zilker Botanical Garden

The unique climate around the south shore of Lady Bird Lake has made a perfect location for the diverse gardens at **Zilker Botanical Garden** (2220 Barton Springs Rd., 512/477-8672, www.zilkergarden.org, 7am-7pm daily, $3 general admission, $2 Austin residents, $1 children 3-12 and seniors ages 62 and older). Gardens include the waterfall, ponds, and bridges of the Taniguchi Oriental Garden; the Cactus and Succulent Garden; the Rose Garden; the Butterfly Trail and Garden; and the City of Austin's Green Garden. Lastly, there's the garden that interests the whole family, the **Hartman Prehistoric Garden,** located on the site where dinosaur tracks were found in 1992. Plants in this garden represent those that existed at the time of the dinosaurs. To jump-start the imagination, small-scale bronze statues of dinosaurs that roamed here have been placed throughout the gardens. The Garden Center complex houses a little gift shop with items for kids and those with a green thumb. Parking is available.

Umlauf Sculpture Garden and Museum

The **Umlauf Sculpture Garden and Museum** (605 Robert E. Lee Rd., 512/445-5582, www.umlaufsculpture.org, 10am-4pm Tues.-Fri., noon-4pm Sat.-Sun., $5 adults, $3 seniors, 12 and under free) is truly a one-of-a-kind Austin sight. Never heard of Charles Umlauf? Well, you're not alone. The prolific and internationally recognized artist donated his home and many of his works to his own cause, and I'm glad he did. Strolling around the grounds of this museum piques the imagination and sparks curiosity. The style of Umlauf's sculpture is evocative and emotional, with subject matter ranging from alien-looking angels to pieces that tell a story about the Nazi invasion of Poland.

Cathedral of Junk

History will one day refer to our age as the age of waste, and when future archaeologists discover the **Cathedral of Junk** (4422 Lareina Dr., 512/299-7413), they may think we worshiped the gods of garbage. In the backyard of a small house in South Austin is artist Vince Hannemann's life work. Here you'll find over 60 tons of post-market-consumer junk weaved, stacked, stuffed, twisted, and screwed together, all amid overgrown vegetation. The final effect is astonishing. This temple of refuse has been featured in motion pictures such as *Spy Kids 3D*, and has been the backdrop for top-model photo shoots as well.

The artist didn't create this masterpiece to express some profound point about our consumer culture of obsolescence, or because he believes in worshiping transcendental refuse. In his own words, he did it "because it was kinda cool." Bravo! The cathedral was nearly scrapped when the city tagged it as a blatant code violation. Luckily the city and the artist figured out how to retrofit the structure to make it safer so it could be preserved. The artist opens the cathedral to the public Saturday and Sunday noon-6pm, and by appointment during the week.

South Austin Museum of Popular Culture

It should come as no surprise that there's a homespun **South Austin Museum of Popular Culture** (1516 S. Lamar Blvd., 512/440-8318, 1pm-6pm Thurs.-Sun., free)

in Austin. The best way to explain this place is by completely dismantling its name. First of all, this DIY museum is really more of a shrine than a museum—a shrine to 1960s and '70s music. And it's actually not about pop culture per se, but about the counterculture. The only thing that's correct in the title is that it is, in fact, in South Austin. Here you can marvel at the incredible world of music from the pioneering age of sex, drugs, and rock 'n' roll. The walls are filled with posters, T-shirts, and memorabilia from this era. For those who don't think poster art is fine art, the founder of this museum says, "'Fine' is a four-letter word. It's the F-word of the art world."

CENTRAL AUSTIN
Elisabet Ney Museum

The oldest museum in Texas, and one of the most interesting smaller museums in Austin, is the **Elisabet Ney Museum** (304 E. 44th St., 512/458-2255, noon-5pm Wed.-Sun., free). In the late 1900s this castlelike home was the only building in the Hyde Park area, and was the home to German-born sculptress Elisabet Ney. Now you can walk through the bright rooms and view more than 80 statues and busts of characters from Texas history as well as both known and unknown characters from Europe.

University of Texas Campus

The three things that drive this city are politics at the state capitol, live music, and the University of Texas. UT is big in both size and state importance. Founded in 1883 on 40 acres just north of downtown, the campus now occupies over 350 acres and draws some 50,000 students to the main campus alone. Many of Austin's main attractions and museums are located on campus, including the **LBJ Library and Museum, Harry Ransom Center, Texas Memorial Museum, Frank Erwin Center,** the **Battle Oaks,** the **Cactus Cafe** for live music, and the **UT Tower and observation deck.** Along with these, UT

Signs of Longhorn Pride

Local sports fans bleed orange in Austin.

There are a few things the newcomer to Austin will notice around town that may cause some confusion, or at least raise some questions. Now is as good a time as any to clarify a few points. First of all, let me explain the color orange. It's technically called **burnt orange** and is more of a rusty color. This sacred hue is seen everywhere in Austin. People even paint their houses and cars with it. It's so pervasive that it's darn near the official color of the city. However, it's actually the official team color of the University of Texas Longhorns.

Secondly, the outsider may notice the simple iconic image of **steer horns** plastered all over town. This image is just as pervasive as burnt orange, popping up on city street signs, on most cars on the roads, in advertisements, and on flags that are simultaneously flown with the Texas state flag. Again, the image of the steer—or more correctly the longhorn steer—isn't the city's official logo; it belongs to the celebrated college football team the UT Longhorns.

Finally, the most confusing thing for the outsider is the popular **hand sign** that Austinites display. This gesture, with pinky and index fingers raised, resembles the sinister hand sign of devil horns attributed to heavy metal and Satanism. But in Austin, and Texas in general, this is called the "Hook 'em Horns" and has nothing to do with old Beelzebub. In fact, in other cultures it has less evil meanings: In Buddhism it's a prayerful symbol that wards off evil, in parts of Africa it's a curse, and in sign language it means "bullsh—." In Austin this symbol is the hand sign of UT fans, devised back in the 1950s, which definitely predates heavy metal.

sports draw a phenomenal number of people to Austin and the campus.

Visitor parking is available at seven garages. Garages are located on Brazos Street (the only parking garage open 24 hours), Manor Avenue (for Bass Concert Hall and sporting events), San Jacinto Street (for Bass Concert Hall), Speedway, Trinity (for Frank Erwin Center), 27th Street (for football games), and San Antonio Street. Rates are $3 for 0.5-1 hour, $6 for 1-2 hours, $9 for 2-3 hours, $12 for 3-12 hours, and less than 30 minutes is free. For more information visit the **UT Visitor Center** (405 W. 25th St. on the 2nd floor of Walter Webb Hall, 8am-5pm Mon.-Fri., 9am-noon Sat.). Advance registration is required for tours.

Central Austin

The Drag

Every campus needs its slightly seedy commercial area where students can get textbooks and booze. The busy section of Guadalupe Street that runs along the western edge of the University of Texas campus, aptly called the Drag, is Austin's version. Although not as wild as in earlier years, the Drag is a bustling area similar to Telegraph Avenue near the University of California, Berkeley, with students mixing with street folk at late-night cafés, record stores, clothing outlets, live music venues, and bars. It may have passed its prime, and is no longer the cultural epicenter it once was, but there's still lots to see and do here.

There are several chain clothing shops clinging to any remaining threads of trendiness, great bars such as **Hole in the Wall,** tattoo shops such as **Diablo Rojo,** restaurants like **Kerby Lane** and **Madam Mam's,** and a couple of notable vintage clothing outlets. The Drag is where *Austin City Limits* and Dell computers began: The giant square, dark, ominous brown building across from Madam Mam's was home to the famous *Austin City Limits* studio where all the classic live performances were taped (before the studio moved downtown), and the Dobie Center (UT dorms) is where Dell computer corporation was cooked up. Parking on and near the Drag can be challenging, so plan on driving in circles and eventually parking a couple blocks away.

EAST AUSTIN
The Thinkery

Who needs tons of sugar to get kids amped up when there's the **Thinkery** (1830 Simond Ave., 512/469-6200, http://thinkeryaustin.org, 10am-5pm Tues.-Fri., 10am-6pm Sat.-Sun., $10, free for 0-23-month-old babies)? This is just about the most fun place in Central Texas for kids. What started out as a grassroots organization for children (without a facility) eventually became a fancy million-dollar institution, thanks to the Dell Corporation. Inside are two stories with several permanent and temporary exhibits, all very cartoon-esque, but learning oriented. Kids are bedazzled by colors, sounds, and hands-on exhibits that spin, bounce, roll, swoosh, tumble, and squeak. Caution to parents—a day here will likely end with a climactic post-fun meltdown. Along with the exhibits, the museum offers events and programs for children and families, all with the goal of inspiring the joy of learning and constructive play. Parking is available for free at the Mueller Town Center parking garage just north of the museum.

George Washington Carver Museum and Cultural Center

The **George Washington Carver Museum and Cultural Center** (1165 Angelina St., 512/974-4926, 10am-6pm Mon.-Thurs., 10am-5pm Fri.-Sat., free) is celebrated as the first black neighborhood museum in Texas. Exhibits include the country's only permanent exhibit dedicated to the history and development of Juneteenth, the Texas-born day of jubilee celebrating the end of slavery. An in-depth exhibit explores the lives of 10 African-American families who have contributed to Austin and Central Texas history.

OLD NORTH AUSTIN
Neill-Cochran House Museum

Austin's 19th-century high-society lifestyle has been petrified and is on display at the **Neill-Cochran House Museum** (2310 San Gabriel, 512/478-2335, www.nchmuseum.org, 1pm-4pm Tues.-Fri., $10 adults, $8 seniors, $5 college students and youth 12-18, children under 12 free). This old mansion built by famed Austin architect Abner Cook in Greek Revival style offers an interesting glimpse into the past. All visitors are guided through the house by NCHM staff or a trained docent (allow 45 minutes). Here you can see just how stuffy life was "back in the day," with Victorian doilies to hand wash and collars to starch. The styles of interior decoration represented here are colonial, empire, rococo revival, and Victorian. Over the years this house has functioned as a Civil War hospital and an institute for the blind.

Abner Cook: Master Builder

When exploring Austin you will undoubtedly notice the many elegant historic homes—or should I say mansions—that summon images of a more genteel era. The person behind some of these architectural masterpieces is the master builder Abner Cook (1814-1884). In 1837, the young Cook arrived in the small city of Austin, where he worked as a carpenter building coffins and furniture and later log cabins. Eventually Cook worked his way to the top and became Austin's foremost master builder and architect, and he was a pioneer of the Greek Revival style in Texas architecture.

During his career he was involved in many projects that shaped the overall aesthetic of the city, such as homes, businesses, buildings on the University of Texas campus, a state mental hospital, a state penitentiary, and the state capitol building. Many of Cook's buildings have been destroyed to make way for more modern development, but some of his elaborate and stately mansions of the late 1800s can still be seen around town. These magnificent homes are exquisite examples of his popular Greek Revival style and bear his unique trademarks, such as the X-and-stick balustrade motif on exterior rails and Greek Ionic details.

Abner Cook houses that have survived are the **Woodlawn House,** also known as Pease Mansion (6 Niles Rd.); the **Swisher-Scott House** (2408 Sweetbrush); the **West Hill House** (1703 West Ave.); the **Hotchkiss-Graham House** (2605 Salado St.); the **Donnan-Hill House** (2528 Tanglewood); the **Neill-Cochran House** (2310 San Gabriel), which is open to the public; the **Old Depot Hotel** (504 E. 5th St., now Carmelo's Italian Restaurant); and the **Governor's Mansion** (1010 Colorado St.).

Live Music and Nightlife

At night Austin lights up like a pinball machine. Downtown transitions from all business and politics to neon lights, live music, techno-thumping bars, dressed-up folks, honky-tonks, comedy clubs, fine dining, curbside pizza, and drunks young and old doing the bar crawl. All of this happening at one time and place can provide a vibrant backdrop to one's night. Under Austin's city glow you can have an evening that consists of eating at an expensive restaurant, catching a performance of a local singer-songwriter, and having a drink at a swank bar. Or you can eat a slice of pizza on a street corner and catch a metal band, do some dive bar-hopping, and wake up at 11am the following day on a stranger's kitchen floor.

There are a few areas with the greatest concentration of action. In downtown there's famous (becoming infamous) **6th Street,** which is Austin's version of New Orleans's Bourbon Street. It features bars, live music venues, tattoo parlors, and some tourist shops (traps). This is largely dominated by UT college students, tourists, and crazies looking for craziness. On Thursday, Friday, and Saturday nights around 10pm, the Austin police department closes off the street. The scene on 6th Street can get pretty rowdy, especially after midnight.

For a less sketchy scene downtown, where you'll find men who pluck their eyebrows and women who prefer tapas to an entrée, there's the **Warehouse District** on West 4th Street and the bars on West 6th Street. Historically, the Warehouse District was the brothel district, but today the scene is a bit more upscale, with classy bars, dance clubs, live music, gay bars, and pubs. These are all in converted warehouses with entrances that have steps and concrete landings that are uneven and hard to navigate after you've had a few drinks.

The area where new music can be found is the **Red River District.** Just a few years ago

Austin Live Music and Nightlife

Map legend:
- ■ LIVE MUSIC
- ▼ BAR/LOUNGE

Map labels:
- HOLE IN THE WALL
- DEAN
- KEATON ST
- (26TH ST)
- WHITIS AVE
- 25TH ST
- 24TH ST
- UNIVERSITY OF TEXAS
- SPEEDWAY
- TRINITY ST
- CAMPUS DR
- BASS CONCERT HALL
- 23RD ST
- CACTUS CAFE
- 22ND ST
- PEARL ST
- NUECES ST
- SAN ANTONIO ST
- GUADALUPE ST
- 21ST ST
- 20TH ST
- MARTIN LUTHER KING JR BLVD
- 18TH ST
- 17TH ST
- LUCKY LOUNGE
- 5TH
- LAVACA ST
- COLORADO ST
- CONGRESS ST
- HALCYON COFFEEHOUSE
- FADO
- CEDAR ST COURTYARD
- GUADALUPE ST
- 4TH
- RAIN
- OILCAN HARRY'S
- SPEAKEASY
- THE GINGER MAN
- ELEPHANT ROOM
- 16TH ST
- 15TH ST
- WEST AVE
- RIO GRANDE ST
- 14TH ST
- SCHOLZ GARTEN
- RIVER ST
- 13TH ST
- FRANK ERWIN CENTER
- 35
- 81
- 290
- RED RIVER
- 12TH ST
- 11TH ST
- NUECES ST
- SAN ANTONIO ST
- GUADALUPE ST
- LAVACA ST
- COLORADO ST
- CONGRESS ST
- BRAZOS ST
- SAN JACINTO BLVD
- TEXAS STATE CAPITOL
- Waterloo Park
- 14TH ST
- 13TH ST
- 12TH ST
- 10TH ST
- 9TH ST
- 8TH ST
- 7TH ST
- THE IRON BEAR
- THE MOHAWK
- To Donn's Depot
- LITTLE WOODROW'S
- 6TH ST
- PARAMOUNT THEATER / THE STATE THEATER
- CHEER UP CHARLIES
- STUBB'S BAR-B-Q
- MARCOS ST
- THE BELMONT
- 5TH ST
- SEE DETAIL
- ALAMO DRAFTHOUSE CINEMA
- VALHALLA
- THE SIDEWINDER
- 6TH STREET
- ELYSIUM
- THE PARISH
- BEERLAND TEXAS
- EMPIRE CONTROL ROOM
- 311 CLUB
- PLUSH
- 7TH ST
- SAN MARCOS ST
- LYDIA ST
- THE LIBRARY BAR
- ESTHER'S FOLLIES
- 8TH ST
- 2ND ST
- THE MOODY THEATER
- 4TH
- FLAMINGO CANTINA
- NECHES ST
- RED RIVER ST
- SABINE ST
- SHANGRI'LA
- 6TH ST
- To The Liberty
- AUSTIN CITY LIMITS
- 3RD ST
- 5TH ST
- CESAR CHAVEZ ST
- WILLOW ST
- (1ST ST)
- 35
- 81
- 290
- Palm Park
- 4TH ST
- 3RD ST
- 2ND ST
- WALLER ST
- MEDINA ST
- 1ST ST
- SCOOT INN
- Sattilo Park
- Butler Park
- Comal Park
- 0   0.25 mi
- 0   0.25 km

© AVALON TRAVEL

Must-See Local Musicians

The city of Austin prides itself on being the Live Music Capital of the World, and for a very good reason: It *is* the live music capital of the world. There are more venues, musicians, and music lovers here than anywhere else outside of heaven. There are over 2,000 recording acts and a total of almost 9,000 musicians in all genres of music, but I've narrowed the list down to the top artists and bands that live and perform here. If you see any of the following names in the music section of the *Austin Chronicle*, be sure to check them out.

- **And You Will Know Us by the Trail of Dead:** This punk-influenced alternative rock band got its start by playing Emo's as much as possible, but somehow they became more popular in the rest of the country before they really got recognized in Austin. Occasionally they still play in front of a sold-out crowd at Emo's and other venues around town.

- **Asleep at the Wheel:** Austinites, and all Texans for that matter, have always tapped their toes to the traditional country music pumped out by Asleep at the Wheel. This prolific Grammy Award-winning band has survived the terrors of Nashville by sticking to their cause of keeping western swing alive and kicking. If you can catch them at Gruene Hall in the Hill Country you are sure to enter western nirvana, and the only way to get there is by dancing.

- **Band of Heathens:** This group is a true Austin singer-songwriter collective. Their unique performances feature all three singer-songwriters up front. These great vocalists can do soul, blues, rock, and country, and they deliver it all with heart. Catch them any time they play at one of the many venues around town.

- **Del Castillo:** A renowned Austin Latin group fronted by Rick del Castillo and Mark del Castillo, Del Castillo is a high-energy band that blends many styles, including flamenco, rock, Latin, and world music. From their live performance you will never forget the dueling Latin guitar solos. Del Castillo has performed with many legendary acts, such as Don Henley and Willie Nelson.

- **Dixie Chicks:** Everyone has heard of the popular but controversial self-made all-girl country band the Dixie Chicks. Although they generally have to stick to stadiums, they occasionally surface around town.

- **Joe Ely:** Ely, a country, bluegrass, and rock 'n' roll artist, grew up in Lubbock. He later relocated to Austin to pursue his musical aspirations. Over his career, Ely has been in numerous bands in a variety of genres. He has performed and toured with Chuck Berry, Carl Perkins, Merle Haggard, Bruce Springsteen, and The Clash.

- **Alejandro Escovedo:** Musicians the world 'round are huge fans of Escovedo, but somehow this remarkable singer-songwriter never lands a hit song on the radio. In his case, this is a good thing. As a Hispanic coming out of the late-'70s punk rock movement, Escovedo blends what he knows into a fascinating, moving arrangement of words, melodies, and rhythms that reach all audiences. The best place to see him is at the Cactus Cafe.

- **Patti Griffin:** This spectacular singer-songwriter has been deep in the background of the music industry and hasn't fully walked onto the mainstream stage for reasons unknown. She has performed with and written songs for some of today's top folk and country acts, such as the Dixie Chicks, Lucinda Williams, and Emmylou Harris.

- **Iron & Wine:** Soft-spoken alternative folk master Sam Beam lives in the beautiful Texas Hill Country. This Sub Pop artist doesn't perform live that often, so if his name is listed in the *Chronicle* you'd best buy your tickets ASAP.

- **James McMurtry:** Blue-collar singer-songwriter James McMurtry is a staple around town.

He's perpetually performing, and people are perpetually enamored by his unique folk- and blues-based songs that talk about real down-home people in tough real-life situations.

- **Willie Nelson:** Country music legend Willie Nelson is one of the hardest-working artists in Texas. He performs all over Austin and the Hill Country. Seeing him perform here is seeing him perform in his own backyard, and his comfort on local stages really comes through. In fact, despite his age he cuts loose and takes his audience on a ride through his standards, coupled with lots of country classics, all faster and juiced up.

- **Bruce Robison:** The tradition of country ballads of love gone wrong is carried on by Bruce Robison. But don't expect a Stetson and boots on Bruce because he's more of a quiet, contemplative, urban guy who resembles John Cusack. Catch him at the Broken Spoke and other Hill Country venues.

- **Charlie Robison:** Contemporary country that I like to call tractor pop is provided by Charlie Robison. He's a strong country staple for Central Texas, and he performs all over the state and the United States. The best place to see him live is at Gruene Hall in the Hill Country.

- **Bob Schneider:** An artist who has the power and charisma to reach fans of many music genres is Bob Schneider. He's a skillful songwriter who puts on a spectacular show and somehow comes across as honest in his search for mainstream appeal. His folksy rock approach sounds like Neil Young meets Beck.

- **Charlie Sexton:** Not many Austinites have graced the cover of *Rolling Stone* in their teens, but Charlie Sexton is one of those few. This prodigy had a hit in the 1980s with "Beat's So Lonely," which was an MTV favorite, and then he seemed to vanish. For most of the '90s and into the 21st century he was a studio musician and songwriter for some top artists, such as Bob Dylan. In 2005 Charlie released a folk/alternative record to much acclaim.

- **Spoon:** Alternative rock band Spoon is Austin's music scene personified. They've been around for years and years performing and recording records that fly beneath the radar. It wasn't until 2005 that they finally broke into the mainstream, and this didn't break their original sound as mainstream success often does. They pop up around town for a low-key show from time to time.

- **The Sword:** Heavy metal and stoner rock has found its way to Austin with the rise of The Sword. These young, semi-nerdy, fully cool kids blast audiences with riff after riff—the kind that made Black Sabbath scary. If you catch them at Emo's be sure to wad up some toilet paper in your ears unless you enjoy tinnitus.

- **Jimmie Vaughan:** Grammy Award winner and brother of Stevie Ray Vaughan, Jimmie has become a blues and rockabilly legend in his own right. He plays around town all the time. The best venue to catch his performance is the Continental Club on South Congress. Tickets can be costly, but it's worth it to see a legend perform.

- **Stevie Ray Vaughan:** This American blues guitar legend passed away back in 1990, but I'm confident his ghost is cruising all around Austin's music venues. You can pay homage to one of the most influential electric blues musicians in history by visiting his life-size statue on Lady Bird Lake.

- **Dale Watson:** Country music has been carefully preserved by local legend Dale Watson. When Nashville gave the boot to country legends such as Johnny Cash and Willie Nelson and started pumping out atrocious pop sounds, Dale dug deep into the classics for inspiration. Dale is best enjoyed while sipping on a Lone Star at the Broken Spoke or the Little Longhorn Saloon.

this area was the dead tooth of downtown—now it's a bustling center for the more alternative and indie forms of live music. Some of the best live music venues in town are all within a two-block radius, which makes sampling different bands and drinks easy and fun. The scene here is mostly rockers, punks, and hipsters. Don't let the tattooed folks wearing black and sporting extreme piercings deter you, as the scene here is generally friendly and fun.

Outside of downtown there are a couple areas where you'll find action. First there's **South Congress Avenue.** It offers a few clubs, some local bars, and some restaurants featuring live music. Far away from the young angst of downtown, this area is a safe bet for a low-key and predictable night on the town.

Austin's newer scene, being pioneered by hipsters and do-it-yourselfers, is **East Austin.** This area, just on the other side of the freeway from 6th Street, is where all the artsy musician locals like to hang out. Strewn about on what has historically been considered the sketchy side of town you'll find alluring dive bars, food trucks, music venues, and unusual shacks and backyard patios to explore.

Whatever your preference is for a night on the town in Austin, before stepping out the door, grab a free copy of the *Austin Chronicle* (issued every Thursday) and check out what's happening in the events section. With the *Chronicle,* coupled with the listings here, tailor an evening that best suits you, or just wander around and let the night be a "Choose Your Own Adventure" type of experience.

LIVE MUSIC

Austin is compulsive about music. After all, it's simply and indisputably the best U.S. city for live music, and has the distinguished honor of being the Live Music Capital of the World. The town is forever inundated with touring national acts, local favorites, and unknowns crawling out of the woodwork seeking their 15 minutes of expression. Venues, clubs, and bars all across town have something going on every night of the week. Live music is so

pervasive here that you'll find it in unusual places, such as clothing stores, supermarkets (Central Market), the airport, and even the post office. I've noticed many venues offering two stages, one smaller stage inside and a bigger stage outside for larger national acts. This makes sampling music a blast.

Although venues are everywhere, the greatest concentration of music is downtown. No matter where you stand in the downtown area the sounds of live music can be heard, merging in stereophonic cacophony, and the sound is sweet. The concentration gets thick on 6th Street and Red River, where you can stand on any corner and hear blues, pop, and heavy metal all at once. Thanks to Austin's multifarious musical palate the venues and acts are diverse. There's a thriving scene here for absolutely every kind of musical taste.

It's hard to say how live music got its footing in Austin and how it has become so extraordinary over the years. But, from Willie Nelson to Janis Joplin to *Austin City Limits,* from Stevie Ray Vaughan to Alejandro Escovedo to Spoon, Austin has been greatly blessed in its calling to live music greatness. With this calling comes great responsibility, and Austinites take this seriously by religiously supporting local music. It's not uncommon for someone to catch a live act every night of the week and during the day maintain a "normal" life at the office.

Tickets for most concerts and venues can be purchased at **Waterloo Records** (600 N. Lamar Blvd., 512/474-2500) or online at venue websites. Also, tickets can be purchased online at **Front Gate Tickets** (www.frontgatetickets.com) or **Ticketmaster** (www.ticketmaster.com). Tickets purchased online are often cheaper than at the venue. For smaller venues tickets are sold only at the door or at venue websites.

Big Venues

The term "big" is relative when it comes to venues. The following listings are venues I consider to be "big" because of their size and seating capacity, and/or "big" because they feature big-name national acts. Tickets can range from $15 to $55 depending on the act or lineup and the night.

Antone's (2015 E. Riverside Dr., 512/800-4628, www.antonesnightclub.com) has been Texas's outlet for the blues for decades. They've expanded their repertoire to include pop, rock, and indie, bringing in some major national acts. This is the best place to catch Austin's own Jimmie Vaughan. The club's founder, Cliff Antone, had his highs and lows, operating the venue for 30 years until his death in 2006. Highs included receiving an award from the National Blues Foundation for his contribution to the blues, and lows included doing prison time for drugs. The record store on Guadalupe Street with the same name is owned by the venue. Scene: national acts, local legends, blues, rock, pop, and country.

Emo's (2015 E. Riverside Dr., 512/800-4628, www.emosaustin.com) is the town's premier punk, metal, stoner, and indie venue and has been for a long time. You can't use the word "alternative" to describe this scene or the music, as this term is sacrilegious, and people will smirk. Spoon and Trail of Dead got their start at Emo's, and even Johnny Cash has played here (at the original location). Parking can be tricky, so come a little early. Scene: punk, heavy metal, indie.

Frank Erwin Center (1701 Red River St., 512/471-7744, www.uterwincenter.com) is Austin's stadium for mega entertainment. The coliseum can seat up to 18,000 people, so don't expect an intimate show. The center hosts acts like George Strait, Metallica, and Lady Gaga, and has also hosted the Dalai Lama and the Ringling Bros. and Barnum & Bailey circus. This is also the home of UT sports. Scene: mega entertainment of all kinds.

The Moody Theater (310 Willie Nelson Blvd., 512/225-7999 venue, 877/435-9849 tickets, www.acl-live.com) is the new home of the famous *Austin City Limits* stage. Located in the 2nd Street district at the W Hotel, this live music venue and studio has made ACL accessible to the masses. The Moody Theater is a state-of-the-art facility with a capacity of 2,700-plus people. Scene: rock, pop, alternative, country, folk, world.

Stubb's Bar-B-Q (801 Red River St., 512/480-8341, www.stubbsaustin.com) is the place to get famous barbecue sauce and famous national acts. Housed in a historic limestone building, Stubb's is where the hip parties go down during SXSW. There's a small indoor stage and a big outdoor stage in the backyard. Scene: national acts, local acts, rock, alternative.

Small Venues

There are so many smaller venues in town that it's not practical to give them all a nod here, so I've distilled the list to the very best. Generally doors open for these venues sometime around 8pm-9pm, and there's almost always a cover charge that is somewhere between $5 and $20.

Beerland Texas (711½ Red River St., 512/479-7625, www.beerlandtexas.com) is one of the older rock venues in the Red River District. The proprietors best describe their own place by saying, "Rock & roll club seeks bands, fans, and hangers-on for all-out orgy of loud music and cheap beer." Also here are arcade games and pool. Scene: rock.

Broken Spoke (3201 S. Lamar Blvd., 512/442-6189, www.brokenspokeaustintx.com) really should be a sight as well as a venue. This remarkable local institution will blow your Stetson off when you walk through the door. Remember John Travolta in *Urban Cowboy*? Well forget it, because the Broken Spoke is the real deal. First-timers have a hard time blending in because they end up standing there with their jaws hanging. This authentic honky-tonk is an original Texas dance hall where people still come to dance to live country bands. A front-room restaurant serves up home cooking, but the real reason for being here is the humble dance floor, under a low ceiling that I swear is going to cave in in the near future. Finally there's the makeshift museum, containing dusty artifacts from country music legends and photos of the proprietor with famous folks. No one ever seems to go in there, except for newcomers and nerds. Word for the nerd: If the lady bartender asks, "What can I get ya, sugar?" she's not asking you if you want sugar. Scene: country, dancing.

Cactus Cafe (Texas Union on the UT campus, 2247 Guadalupe St., 512/475-6515) is the premier intimate venue for all things unplugged (nowadays everything's actually semi-plugged). Big-name acoustic, singer-songwriter, country, and folk acts have graced the small corner stage for over 70 years. Among them are Janis Joplin, Bob Dylan, Lyle Lovett, Bill Monroe, Ralph Stanley, Ani DiFranco, and Sean Lennon. The space is small, upscale, and outfitted with a full bar in the back. People tend to dress up a bit for shows at the Cactus. It's a safe bet that any show here is worth seeing. Scene: unplugged, singer-songwriter, folk, Americana, bluegrass, and jazz.

Cedar Street Courtyard (208 W. 4th St., 512/495-9669), in the Warehouse District, always has a groove on. The space is like none other in town: It's an open courtyard flanked by basement bars that have a party-in-the-dungeon vibe. Music on the stage is always groovy and upbeat, and dancing is unavoidable. Scene: jazz, funk, tango, groove.

Continental Club (1315 S. Congress Ave., 512/441-2444, www.continentalclub.com) is Austin's legendary retro hookup that has been around since the 1950s. With a steady lineup of regular local musicians as well as touring acts in a throwback atmosphere, the Continental is another venue where you're sure to catch something good on any given night. Patrons love showing up on their hogs or in their classic cars, looking like a million bucks. Regular acts include Dale Watson and Jon Dee Graham. Scene: country, blues, rockabilly, rock, singer-songwriter.

The best way to experience live jazz music is in the basement of the **Elephant Room** (315 Congress Ave., 512/473-2279, www.elephantroom.com). Jazz lovers come from all over to descend into this unique environment and sink back in a chair for a couple hours of toe tapping. The Elephant Room has a full bar with more than 20 drafts and wine by the glass. Scene: jazz, big band, swing, smooth.

Elysium (705 Red River St., 512/478-8385, www.elysiumonline.net) is the venue for goth and industrial music. Here the unspoken dress code is black, makeup, and chains, and the attitude is depressed and sullen. For the most part this is a dance club with a beat going on, but there's also live music. Scene: goth/industrial dance club.

Empire Control Room (606 E. 7th St., www.empireatx.com) is a punk/rocker/DIY scene that's gaining a foothold in the Red River District. Like Emo's and the Mohawk, Empire is the place to be during SXSW or Austin Free Week. Here you'll find three stages and a bar that's often so packed you can't see the bartender. There's a loud PA system, and bands push it to the limit. Toilet paper wadded up and stuffed in the ear won't save your hearing because the sound will travel straight through your skull. Be warned, the bathrooms are usually disgusting. Scene: punk, indie rock, techno, stoner rock.

Flamingo Cantina (515 E. 6th St., 512/494-9336, www.flamingocantina.com) is the premier reggae venue in town. This 18-and-up roots venue has big-name acts from all over the United States and from "the islands." Scene: reggae, hip-hop, funk.

Hole in the Wall (2538 Guadalupe St., 512/477-4747, www.holeinthewallaustin.com) is a historic little venue on the Drag that puts on all sorts of music in an average bar atmosphere. As for history, Stevie Ray Vaughan played here. The $1 beer special on Monday is crucial for the students. Scene: alternative rock, country, pop, singer-songwriter, bar bands.

If Dracula lived in a loft in Manhattan it would probably look a lot like **The Mohawk** (912 Red River St., 512/666-0877, www.mohawkaustin.com). This space has been through many incarnations over the years—from club after club, to swank bar, to full-on cocaine den. This time around the Mohawk is a micro-scene unto itself. One of Austin's bustling two-stage venues, this is the place to let

Nightlife Tips

Before embarking on a night on the town in Austin there are a few things you should take into consideration.

- Be sure to always have your ID with you. Clubs, venues, and bars have very strict ID policies, and you will get carded no matter what. If you don't have a valid ID you will definitely be barred from having a great night out in Austin.

- Drink lots of water in the summer months because you will quickly find yourself dehydrated, especially if you are seeing performances in the hot outdoors and drinking alcohol at the same time. All clubs, venues, and bars are eager to hand out water, and often you can find a self-serve water bucket somewhere.

- Have enough cash in your pocket before you start out. ATMs at bars and on the street charge a bundle for cash withdrawal. However, if you are caught in a jam, my favorite ATM is the one sticking out of an old wood fence at Stubb's Bar-B-Q on Red River Street. It charges a big fee, but it's entertaining pulling money out of a fence.

- If you are underage, be aware that bartenders, bouncers, and door dudes aren't fools. Consider the experience of one of George W. Bush's daughters, who was caught drinking at Chuy's bar.

- If you're merrily drinking at bars and clubs, don't get bent out of shape if a bartender cuts you off and won't give you another drink. According to Texas state law, bartenders are liable for those who stagger out of bars, and liable for their actions. They are very cautious about this and are looking out for the best interest of everyone.

- Don't drink and drive, and watch out for drunk drivers. It's not uncommon to see someone completely wasted struggling to find the keyhole in a car door.

your hair down and head bang, to shoe gaze, and to drink. Catch touring bands such as Bad Brains, Sleep, or No Name, or discover popular local indie acts such as The Authors or Stereo Is a Lie. Scene: punk, metal, indie, rock.

The Parish (214 E. 6th St. upstairs, www.theparishroom.com) is one of the newer live venues on the 6th Street scene. The upstairs venue caters primarily to the punk/alternative scene, and often features the type of bands that take themselves too seriously. If you are a band playing here be sure to have roadies, because you have to carry everything up a flight of stairs. Scene: indie, punk, hard rock.

The Sidewinder (715 Red River St., 512/474-1084, www.thesidewinderaustin.com) is one of the tried-and-true venues in the Red River District. Formerly called Red Eyed Fly, this place has two stages and a jukebox featuring Jane's Addiction, Son Volt, Tool, Fugazi, Johnny Cash, The Shins, and Queens of the Stone Age. Scene: punk, metal, indie rock.

Saxon Pub (1320 S. Lamar Blvd., 512/448-2552, www.thesaxonpub.com) is a venue down South Lamar that's guarded by a giant knight in shining armor. The best of Austin's local musicians are found here, both enjoying music and playing it. Besides being a great venue it's also a pub complete with darts, pool, and microbrews. Scene: folk, Americana, blues, country, bluegrass, light rock.

Touted as the oldest continuously running beer joint in Central Texas, **Scoot Inn** (1308 E. 4th St., 512/394-5486, www.scootinnaustin.com) is the East Side's quintessential dive bar music venue. Supposedly this shack was built in 1871 and was a place where weary pioneers would party. If someone from then visited now they might feel right at home. Patrons are sweaty, unshaven, and look like they rode in on mustangs. A full selection of Hill Country microbrew Real Ale is on tap, which is a treat, and staff are nice. Scene: rock and alternative.

Threadgill's (301 W. Riverside Dr., 512/472-9304, www.threadgills.com) is one of Austin's venues with the most history, as the young Steve Miller, Janis Joplin, and The Doors, among many others, have played here. In fact, Threadgill's claims to have been the first outlet in town for the '60s counterculture movement. Today, you can find all sorts of acts here as well as Austin's new residents, the Neville brothers and family, who relocated here after New Orleans was flooded by Hurricane Katrina in 2005. Scene: country, rockabilly, Americana.

311 Club (311 E. 6th St., 512/477-1630) has been the top venue for blues on 6th Street for over 20 years. This 21-and-up venue features local and national acts every night of the week in a bar atmosphere. Scene: blues, R&B, cover bands.

BARS AND CLUBS

Texas has many counties that are dry or partially dry, but Austin is definitely not in a dry county. There are thousands of bars here—some local dive bars with Merle Haggard on the jukebox, others ultra-swank clubs that feature DJs. The following are the best watering holes in town.

The high-end multilevel lounge experience has been made perfect by **The Belmont** (305 W. 6th St., 512/476-2100). This popular joint is plush and custom, outfitted with Vegas overtones and Manhattan undertones. If Dean Martin were alive, and if he were cool enough to live in Austin, he would probably be found smoking in one of the private nooks or on the outdoor patio—slightly hammered, of course. The signature drink is the Belmontini, which features locally made Tito's vodka and pineapple juice, and live music often helps to set the tone.

One of the more popular watering holes for creative people is **Cheer Up Charlie's** (900 Red River St., 512/431-2133). What started in a small building in East Austin is now housed in the former location of the defunct Club De

Ville. Inside feels a lot like being at a sophisticated party in a darkroom for developing photos. The best feature here is the patio in the backyard, chiseled out of limestone cliffs. This is one of the better spaces in the Red River District for sipping and chatting with friends. Here you have a great vegan food truck, free live music, beer and wine, DJs, and an outdoor movie screen that shows everything from kung fu to cult classics. Or better yet, *The Wizard of Oz* synched up with Pink Floyd's *The Dark Side of the Moon*.

On the quieter side of downtown toward Mo-Pac/Highway 1 is **Donn's Depot** (1600 W. 5th St., 512/478-0336). This fantastic old-time bar is housed in a former train depot and a real choo-choo. The crowd is very diverse, with old folks looking for a dance as well as spry youngsters seeking a cultural experience. Live and canned music is generally jazz, big band, bluegrass, country, and porch. Donn himself has two bands that perform here.

Amid all the live music is **Plush** (617 Red River St., 512/478-0099), Austin's premier DJ, mix, and hip-hop dance club. Toward the wee hours people can get a little too crazy and loose—think *Jersey Shore*. Yes, pumping beats, sexy dancing, and throwing up in the bathroom. It's always packed to the gills, so if you're claustrophobic you may freak out. If so, head to the secret chill spot in the back. If it's vacant you will be pleased to kick it in here, near to but at a safe distance from the craziness of the main dance floor.

It's hard to pigeonhole **Halcyon Coffeehouse** (218 W. 4th St., 512/472-9637, www.halcyonaustin.com, 7am-2am Mon.-Thurs., 7am-3am Fri., 8am-3am Sat., 8am-2am Sun.) as anything specific. This lack of definition is what makes it one of my favorite places to hang out any night of the week. Halcyon (pronounced HAL-see-yon) is a night-owl café, a classy bar, a sophisticated art gallery, and a laid-back smoke shop all rolled into one Zig-Zag. The front half is a great café space with low-lying chairs and couches, the back is the bar with loud music thumping, and on the side is a fish bowl that

Politicians, Prostitutes, and Secret Tunnels

During the last quarter of the 19th century Austin had a blossoming red-light district on the west side of Congress Avenue, in the area now referred to as the Warehouse District. Official city documents of the time called this area the First Ward, but everyone really called it Guy Town. With several brothels, slews of hard-working prostitutes, and a client base that consisted of city council members, legislators, and businessmen, Guy Town flourished under the noses of an unsuspecting genteel society. In order to conceal the identities of the "upright citizens" that were patrons of Guy Town, many brothels had tunnels that connected to secret locations. But Guy Town wasn't just for the well-to-do; it was also a place for gamblers and outlaws, and some of Austin's dubious chapters unfolded in the streets, buildings, and tunnels of Guy Town.

Only one remnant of Austin's era of prostitution can be found in town, and it's actually not in the historic area of Guy Town, but north of downtown at 1601 Guadalupe Street. This historic stone structure known as the Bertram Building (currently housing Clay Pit, the finest Indian restaurant in Austin) has a basement tunnel that historically led to a conveniently located brothel next door.

contains the tobacco shop. Everywhere in this place you will find great artwork hanging on the walls and people surfing wireless Internet and socializing. If you're craving sweets, staff will bring fire to your table so you can roast marshmallows and make s'mores.

If the downtown 6th Street scene is wearing on you, simply walk under the freeway to **The Liberty** (1618½ E. 6th St., 512/600-4791). Here you have an unfriendly jukebox joint with potent but cheap drinks. So why suggest this place? Because the unfriendly vibe and stiff drinks will toughen you up! The space out back with picnic tables is huge, and the East Side King food truck is here too. This food truck has a connection to famed local restaurant Uchi.

Another great spot on the east side of the freeway is **Shangri'La** (1016 E. 6th St., 512/524-4291). The drinks aren't fancy but they are cheap and strong. This place is fun because it's often packed, has a great jukebox, and has pool tables. Like most joints east of the freeway, this place is generally free of college folks.

Some of the bars on 6th Street are into gimmick to a degree that is stupid. Although **The Library Bar** (407 E. 6th St., 512/236-0662, www.librarybars.com) is guilty of this, it's one of the better places to hang out downtown. The library theme is cleverly integrated into the vibe, inspiring college students to visit the "library" to do homework. Under the illusion of study, the drinks are well mixed and the tone is upbeat. This place is not afraid of lighting, either. This is good because too many bars are into dark and moody environments.

Lucky Lounge (209A W. 5th St., 512/479-7700, www.theluckylounge.com) is a trendy bar with '60s decor and occasionally good live music. If you want to lounge around, have live background music, and sip apple martinis, you're in luck at Lucky's. The crowd is primarily heterosexual singles looking to schmooze and flirt in a sophisticated way.

One of the best martinis in town is at **Speakeasy** (412D Congress Ave., 512/476-8017). The entrance is in the alley, which harkens back to the Prohibition era. Suave and divine is a way of life here, with live music, a relaxed atmosphere, a brick-and-wood interior, and walls covered in vintage posters.

The bar for aspiring singers is **Ego's** (510 S. Congress Ave., 512/474-7091). Tucked away in a parking garage off South Congress, Ego's always has a wild cast of vocalists, drinkers, and people-watchers who are willing to let their guard down and be silly. The combination of karaoke and dive bar is genuine here. Karaoke starts at 10pm Sunday-Thursday, 9pm Friday-Saturday. I suggest stopping by when it's hosted by Diamond Karaoke. Ego's is also home to a competitive karaoke league, Downtown Division of the National Karaoke League, on Thursday nights.

Little Woodrow's (520 W. 6th St., 512/477-2337), on the quieter side of 6th Street, is a great place to hang out with friends for an extended stay. Sports fans will be pleased to find that there are distracting TVs everywhere, and others will enjoy the great outdoor space with picnic tables. Unlike at the dive bars and hipster hangouts in town, the beer selection is broad, so there's always something here for everyone.

Valhalla (710 Red River St.) is a cigarette loosely hanging from the bottom lip on Red River Street. It's not cool to smile too much here, or to be exuberant. The scene is a mix of denim-overall-wearing tattooed folks, cow-punks, and hipsters. Just stand around with a drink in hand and gently bang your head to the music. The wagon-wheel bar is an interesting feature that divides the bar from the live music.

Dive Bars

Have you recently been dragged through the briar patch of love? Have you lost faith in humankind because humans don't seem to be kind? Or are you just lonely and want to sit around with others who are lonely, pretending you don't want to be bothered, when you're really crying out for human contact? Austin's world-class dive bars can help you. Some of these joints have historical significance, although you would never know it from the outside—they look like they've been closed since REO Speedwagon broke up. Many of these drinking institutions are owned and operated by spry older ladies who've created their own unique cultures in their bars. For obvious reasons these places dredge up images from Nick Cave ("Jangling Jack"), Frank Sinatra ("Strangers in the Night"), and Johnny Cash ("Sunday Morning Coming Down"). Be sure to bring cold hard cash to these places because most of the following joints don't take plastic.

If your inner child likes to drink, check out the age-old **Carousel Lounge** (1110 E. 52nd St., 512/452-6790). The circus theme is taken to the limits with a big pink ceramic elephant, circus murals, and a mini carousel.

Jukebox joint **Deep Eddy Cabaret** (2315 Lake Austin Blvd., 512/472-0961) will make you feel at home. Here you can swim in your own head while listening to the eclectic tunes on the jukebox. We've all heard of Elvis (both Costello and Presley), but what kind of dive bar patron has heard of Edith Piaf (often confused with eat a pilaf)? The early-20th-century French singer gone heroin addict surprisingly adds a nice depressed touch to this dive bar experience. Pitchers of Lone Star are only $6, and snacks consist of hot nuts and pretzels.

Dry Creek Saloon (4812 Mount Bonnell Rd., 512/453-9244) is one of the oldest bars in town. This rustic shack is nestled among extravagant, million-dollar homes, but I assure you that all the patrons come from elsewhere. Only a couple kinds of beer are available, so don't expect marvelous microbrews on tap. The saloon is high up Mount Bonnell Road, but don't expect some great mountain peak 'cause this is a Texas mountain, measuring in at a whopping 780 feet above sea level. This doesn't, however, diminish the fact that there's an extraordinary view from the saloon's rooftop deck.

You don't have to be drunk at a Christmas party to see elves dancing over the bar, because it's always Christmas at **Lala's Lounge** (2207-09 Justin Ln., 512/453-2521). Years of cigarette smoke and liquor-stained carpets produce a marvelous smell. Just like the patrons, the Christmas tree is always lit, with presents under its branches—and the skeleton over the pool table is riding a giant beer bottle. There's hidden symbolism in all this, I'm sure. Frank Sinatra and Dean Martin provide the soundtrack for this joint.

The legendary mini honky-tonk **Little Longhorn Saloon** (5434 Burnet Rd.) is a place steeped in character, booze, and bird

Chicken S#!t Bingo

Don't confuse Chick S#!t Bingo with craps.

The game of bingo, which is the ultimate game of chance and boredom, has become a lively way to spend an afternoon at **Little Longhorn Saloon** (5434 Burnet Rd.). Every Sunday night this tiny honky-tonk features an amusing game of Chicken S#!t Bingo that relies entirely on the unpredictable bowels of a chicken in a cage on a pool table. Contestants throw down hard-earned cash on a number and cheer and jeer for about an hour waiting for that special moment, while Austin's favorite country act, Dale Watson and his Lone Stars, perform and provide commentary. Free chili and hot dogs are served, along with cheap Lone Star Beer. The lucky winner can walk away with up to $100. If you want to participate in this spectacle, plan on showing up early and hanging around for a while. The band starts at 4pm and tickets go on sale at 5pm. The winner is announced when the chicken takes a dump.

poop. Local mother to the bar divers, Ginny Kalmbach was the owner/operator for over 30 years when she retired and sold the windowless joint to local country legend Dale Watson. Besides being known as a place to get a drink and to hear real country music (as opposed to country pop), Little Longhorn is famous for Chicken S#!t Sunday. This is when a specially designed bingo board is placed on the pool table along with a chicken in a cage. People place bets on a number, and if the chicken poops on your number you win the pot. The soundtrack is provided by a live performance by Dale Watson and his Lone Stars.

If you thought poodles and heavy metal had no place being together, check out **The Aristocrat Lounge** (6507 Burnet Rd., 512/465-9468). You know you're there when you see a seemingly abandoned building with a giant mural of a poodle on the outside, which is a homage to its former name, The Poodle Dog Lounge. This place has a wacky scene of bearded hipster locals and grouchy bartenders. On one hand it seems like it's an old bar in its death throes, and then on Friday nights the place springs to life. This dive features several tall booths, pool tables, and games for those that enjoy activities while they are drinking. Just up the road is Top Notch Hamburgers, which was one of the shooting locations for the movie *Dazed and Confused*.

PUBS

A pub with dark nooks and crannies similar to an English pub, **Dog & Duck Pub** (2400 Webberville Rd., 512/479-0598) has 35 beers on tap, including the local Celis line, and dozens of bottled beers to choose from. The Austin Beer Club and the Homebrewing Club both meet here, which says a lot about the pub. Besides being a great place to suck down pints, Dog & Duck is a great place for the whole family. And just as in an English pub the food is greasy and is good only because it goes with beer. On St. Patrick's Day, Dog & Duck is packed. Drink specials are offered throughout the week.

The pub that most successfully replicates English-pub atmosphere is **The Draught House** (4112 Medical Pkwy., 512/452-6258, www.draughthouse.com). Dark spaces, a good selection of microbrews and commercial beers, and a mellow atmosphere make this one of the best pubs in town. It has its own Old World-style brewhouse where they cook up some excellent beers using traditional recipes. Ask for a taste before ordering one of their micros. Every day of the week they offer great deals that draw crowds. For instance, on Wednesdays if you buy a pint you keep the glass, and Saturdays there's free bratwurst, and Tuesdays all pints are $3. The pub lets people take their brews outside, which has spawned a unique lawn-chair-parking-lot social scene. After dark don't drive in with your headlights on, as this will elicit the evil eye from patrons.

Fado (214 W. 4th St., 512/457-0172) in the Warehouse District is hailed as one of the most popular Irish pubs in town. Guinness may flow in rivers here, but that doesn't make it Irish, or even a pub for that matter. The interior is faux Irish pub, featuring four different motifs: Victorian Dublin, the Gaelic Pub, the Traditional Pub, and the Irish Country Cottage Pub. You might expect to trip over a faux "Irish" sheep as you walk to the bathroom. However, this doesn't diminish Fado's popularity and the fact that it's consistently hopping and always packed after dark.

The Ginger Man (301 Lavaca St., 512/473-8801) is another one of my favorite pubs in town. Knowledgeable staff serve up bottles and pint glasses of brew produced at local breweries, as well as the ones you're most familiar with. This is the place downtown with the largest selection of beer on tap. Last I heard the number was around 82. No matter where you sit—at the booths inside or on the

The Warehouse District is full of great pubs, bars, and restaurants.

outside patio—Ginger Man is a comfortable place to hang out with family or friends, or when you're all alone.

Legacy and history make **Scholz Garten** (1607 San Jacinto, 512/474-1958) Austin's one and only *biergarten*. Established in 1866 over an old boardinghouse by a German immigrant, Scholz became a cultural center with beer as the communal glue. Scholz is still a cultural center, and the beer still flows. Along with being one of Texas's oldest continuously operated businesses, Scholz also has the distinction of being one of the top 25 best sports bars in the United States according to a *Sports Illustrated* article. True to the German *biergarten,* Scholz offers schnitzels, along with American fare. Out back is a huge space with a stage for live music and picnic tables, which makes this a grand place for big crowds of family and friends to gather.

A great place to have a beer under a covered outdoor patio perched on the side of a busy South Austin street is **Black Sheep Lodge** (2108 S. Lamar Blvd., 512/707-2744). As the name implies, this place is for the weird ones of Austin, which I suppose is most people in this town. Somehow they pull off an old lodge-style atmosphere in a tiny 1970s strip mall. This description may sound odd, but I promise, the place is a gem. Local beer on tap, good American pub-style food, $2 "white trash cans," and hefty picnic tables offer tons of character. Lastly, the place is South Austin's best place to watch the game. Honestly, it's so comfortable that it's easy to waste away your whole evening here.

GAY AND LESBIAN

You may be thinking, "Austin is in Texas. There can't be a gay scene!" Well, all you have to do is close your eyes, click your heels, and pretend you're not in Texas, and voilà—a thriving gay and lesbian scene is before your eyes. Austin's propensity for open-mindedness has allowed lots of room for a unique gay scene that is completely unrivaled—at least in Texas. Where else in the world can you see a room of cowboys in Stetsons two-step dancing with each other? Nowhere, my friends!

The North Austin neighborhood is home to a sophisticated sports bar in **'Bout Time II** (6607 N. I-35, 512/419-9192, www.bouttime2.com). Here you can play volleyball, drink draft beers, and enjoy the company of friendly, good-humored bartenders.

Want a safe and friendly place to be a big bear of a man and dance without a shirt to music spun by DJs? Make your way down to Austin's premier gay bar, **The Iron Bear** (121 W 8th St., 512/482-8993). Not everyone who comes here sports a beard or a 'stache, but it's definitely on tap. The folks here are friendly and all are welcome.

The gay men's nightclub is **Oilcan Harry's** (211 W. 4th St., 512/320-8823, www.oilcanharrys.com). This Warehouse District staple has lots of attitude Thursday-Sunday, from DJs spinning dance hits to the Malebox. The patio area is a great place to meet your mate or hang with your mates. Check out the website for drink specials and a calendar of events.

Also in the Warehouse District is the lounge bar **Rain** (217 W. 4th St., 512/494-1150). It's a classy martini joint with a disco and snooty bartenders. Some nights there's dancing and some nights live music. Happy hour is every night of the week.

Entertainment and Events

There's much more besides live music going on in Austin. After all, this is a world-class city with opera, symphony, ballet, and roller derby. Tickets for most concerts and events can be purchased at **Waterloo Records** (600 N. Lamar Blvd., 512/474-2500) or online at **Front Gate Tickets** (www.frontgatetickets. com) or **Ticketmaster** (www.ticketmaster. com). The outlet for theater, music, and dance tickets is **Now Playing Austin** (512/247-2531, www.nowplayingaustin.com). Tickets can also be purchased at the venues depending upon availability, but purchasing online is often cheaper.

THEATERS AND EVENTS CENTERS

The City of Austin's Convention Center Department operates two massive facilities that provide space for some of the area's biggest indoor events. The bigger space is the **Austin Convention Center** (500 E. Cesar Chavez St., 512/404-4000), and the smaller space is **Palmer Events Center** (900 Barton Springs Rd., 512/404-4500). Both host a wide variety of events such as conventions, consumer shows, conferences, roller derby, concerts, public dances, and trade shows. For a comprehensive calendar of events for both venues check out www.austinconvention-center.com.

Bass Concert Hall (23rd St. at 2350 Robert Dedman Dr. on the UT campus, 512/471-2787 or 800/687-6010 for ticket information) is the largest space in UT's Performing Arts Center. This venue has the best acoustics in town, and although it's big, you don't feel far from the stage even in the back seats. Here's where most of the classical and dance performances take place, including touring Broadway acts, and on occasion big stars such as Tony Bennett take the stage. The UT campus parking lots on Manor Avenue and San Jacinto Street are the most convenient places to park.

If you are driving on I-35 and wonder what the gigantic cylinder that resembles the spaceship from *Close Encounters of the Third Kind* is, it's the **Frank Erwin Center** (1701 Red River St., 512/471-7744). This megavenue hosts UT sports and big-name performers, such as Metallica, Lady Gaga, George Strait, and the Harlem Globetrotters. Parking can be downright depressing during a major event; there are a few garages in the area (San Jacinto St.), but don't count on there being a space for you.

Austin's glorious venue for the higher arts is **The Long Center** (701 W. Riverside Dr., 512/474-5665, www.thelongcenter.org). This classy facility for cross-cultural classics has events ranging from opera to modern performance arts, making the Long Center the premier venue for big and bold acts. Although the performances inside can ennoble, the grand promenades outside, which offer breathtaking views of Lady Bird Lake and the downtown skyline, are just as inspiring. Also, there's not a bad seat in the house.

On the outskirts of town is the beautiful **One World Theatre** (7701 Bee Caves Rd., 512/330-9500, www.oneworldtheatre.org). This is a favorite for world-class performers in all genres of music. Here you can see the Cowboy Junkies, the Doobie Brothers, Ricky Skaggs, George Winston, and world music and dance. The theater is housed in one of the most famous green/eco-friendly buildings in the area, designed by Marley Porter, and proves that comfort and world-class entertainment can take place without impacting the environment too much. Parking is available.

Paramount Theatre (713 Congress Ave., 512/472-5470, www.austintheatre.org), in the center of downtown near the capitol, is a beautiful historic theater that hasn't changed much since World War I. It still hosts some of the town's best shows, offering a wide variety of entertainment, such as country, folk, jazz, and classical music; comedy shows; dance; spoken word; and theater. This is also the place to see classic movies and random cult classics on the big screen. The art deco interior, ornate ceilings, and original red curtain from the early 1900s make for a great environment in which to be entertained. Downtown garage parking is available.

Wonder where John Tesh performs when in Austin? **Riverbend Centre** (4214 N. Capital of Texas Hwy., 512/327-9416, www.riverbendcentre.com) on the edge of town hosts all sorts of events, including Austin Symphony performances such as the Christmas Sing-A-Long, world music, and entertainment. The center is in a beautiful spot, and the facility is a stunning limestone-and-wood structure that makes performances here a treat.

The State Theatre (719 Congress Ave., 512/472-5143, www.austintheatre.org), next door to the Paramount, primarily offers theater. This is the home of the State Theatre Company, which provides the community with high-quality plays September-June. Wine, beer, and other beverages are sold in the lobby and are allowed in the theater, which makes for a great experience. Downtown garage parking is available.

Zachary Scott Theatre Center (1510 Toomey Rd., 512/476-0541, www.zachscott. com) is Central Texas's oldest and most popular residential theater. Here audiences are captivated by some of the best plays and musicals put on in the state. The season runs September-August, offering about eight performances by an award-winning cast. Parking is available.

Circuit of the Americas (9201 Circuit of the Americas Blvd., http://circuitoftheamericas.com) is one of Austin's megavenues. With the installation of the Formula 1 racetrack came this ginormous outdoor venue where rock bands perform and large-scale performance art takes place. In 2014 the X Games were held here.

PERFORMING ARTS

Austin may not have a world-renowned performing-arts scene, but that is bound to change in the future as the community's various companies, troupes, and organizations keep putting on world-class performances.

Austin's young opera scene is quickly gaining a footing thanks to **Austin Opera** (512/472-5992 or 800/316-7372, www.austinopera.org). This remarkable troupe is pushing the envelope with avant-garde versions of Mozart's *Don Giovanni,* more traditional expressions of Verdi's *Il Trovatore,* and modern

Paramount Theatre is one of Austin's oldest venues.

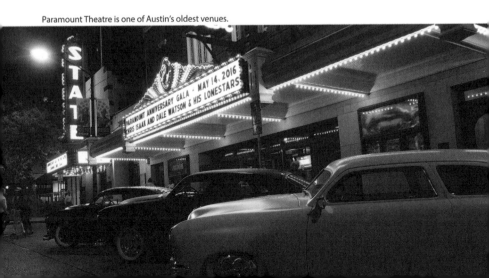

operas such as *Dead Man Walking*. All operas are held at the Long Center on Lady Bird Lake (701 W. Riverside Dr., www.thelongcenter. org). Tickets range $15-100 depending on the seat and the day of the week. Tickets can be purchased by phone or at the box office (901 Barton Springs Rd.).

Austin Symphony (512/476-6064, www. austinsymphony.org) is keeping classical music alive and well in Austin. Throughout the year the symphony has performances and series with a wide range of interests. They offer the Classical Series, which is strictly classical music performed at Bass Concert Hall on the UT campus, and the Pops Series, which is a fun and eclectic combination of arrangements in conjunction with contemporary artists at Riverbend Centre and Palmer Events Center. For the whole family there's the Family Series, which includes the Halloween Children's Concert at Paramount Theatre and a Family Concert in June at Symphony Square Amphitheatre. Finally, there are the ever-popular Holiday Concerts, including Handel's *Messiah* in December and the July 4th Concert and Fireworks at Zilker Park, which is probably the most popular symphonic event of the year. Tickets range from free to $42 depending on the event and the venue.

Proving its wide range of cultural interests, Austin also has **Ballet Austin** (501 W. 3rd St., 512/476-2163, www.balletaustin. org). The *Washington Post* proclaims Ballet Austin "one of the nation's best-kept secrets." Productions include staples such as *The Nutcracker,* but you can also catch more innovative productions as well. Most of the bigger events take place at Bass Concert Hall on the UT campus, and smaller events take place at the Paramount Theatre.

CINEMAS
★ Alamo Drafthouse Cinema

The place in town where you can get dinner, draft beers, and a movie all under one roof is **Alamo Drafthouse Cinema** (320 E. 6th St., 512/861-7020, 1120 S. Lamar Blvd., 512/861-7040, 2700 W. Anderson Ln., 512/861-7030,

Alamo Drafthouse Cinema

www.drafthouse.com). What used to be Austin's great secret is now public info, as even *Bon Appétit* has said, "The Drafthouse empire is the pinnacle of the movie/food experience." This legendary independently owned "empire" offers the usual blockbuster Hollywood movies complete with explosions and drama, as well screenings of cult classics. The Alamo's schedule also has some off-the-wall stuff, such as the Michael Jackson Sing-Along or a viewing of *Fast Times at Ridgemont High* with a special guest appearance by the pizza delivery boy. Seating begins 45 minutes before screening, which is just enough time to order food and drinks and settle in. The theater has a clever system of writing down requests to keep the food and beer coming during the film with little distraction. Plan spending at least 3 hours and be sure show up at least 40 minutes early to order food. Also, be sure to purchase tickets well in advance as seats usually sell out during busy times. Check out the website for schedule and locations.

Other Cinemas

Austin's only IMAX theater is the **IMAX Theatre** at the Bullock Texas State History Museum (1800 N. Congress Ave., 512/936-4649 or 866/369-7108, www.thestoryoftexas. com). Unlike many IMAX theaters, this one is equipped with an IMAX projector that has both 2-D and 3-D capabilities. Tickets range from $17 to $14. If you plan on visiting the Bullock Texas State History Museum, you might consider buying a package that includes tickets to both the museum and the IMAX theater.

The **Paramount Theatre** (713 Congress Ave., 512/472-5470, www.austintheatre.org) is the venue in town that screens classic and cult classic movies. In the comfort of the art deco theater you could catch a screening of *Gone with the Wind,* take in a stand-up comedy act by Penn and Teller, or see Chris Isaak perform live. Tickets are on sale at the box office in front of the theater and or online at tickets. austintheatre.org. Ticket prices vary.

COMEDY CLUBS

Austin's comedy district consists of two venues on the corner of 6th and Red River Streets. Life offers so much to laugh at, and **Esther's Follies** (525 E. 6th St., 512/320-0553, www.esthersfollies.com) mixes it up, boils it all down, and flings it in the face of the audience. Named after Esther Williams, the famed actress and water ballet pioneer whose career sank like a stone in the 1960s, this comedy troupe is composed of a wide variety of clever folks from the community. Esther's dishes out dangerously funny satire, spoofs, and monologues bedecked with costumes, clever wit, and cunning. Shows are held 8pm-midnight Thursday-Saturday. Tickets cost $20 for open seating and $25 for special reserved seating. A $2 discount is offered for students and seniors.

Next door to Esther's is Austin's stand-up and open-mic comedy club, **The Velveeta Room** (512 E. 6th St., 512/469-9116, www. thevelveetaroom.com). Local and visiting comics take the stage here and showcase

their stuff. This is definitely not for the kiddies. Admission is $10.

OTHER ENTERTAINMENT

Miniature golf enthusiasts will enjoy putting around at **Peter Pan Mini-Golf** (1207 Barton Springs Rd., 512/472-1033, call for hours). Founded in 1948, this small course on a hill overlooking the world's great fast-food chains is a great place to battle pirates, the skull bunny, and a dinosaur, all with the mighty putter. Considering the age of this institution, the course and holes are in surprisingly decent shape. Before or after golfing here, instead of eating at one of the fast-food joints go up Barton Springs Road to Green Mesquite or Shady Grove restaurants.

A friend once said to me, "If you want to take the pulse of America, put your finger on the artery of any bowling alley in the nation. Bowling alleys are a microcosm of the whole US-of-A." If that's true, then the country is in a strange state of affairs. Shoe- and ball-sharing, meals from vending machines, and carpet murals on the walls keep us all coming back to the ancient subculture of knocking down pins. Legendary bowler Ernie McCracken of *Kingpin* fame would endorse the following bowling alleys.

The Goodnight (2700 W. Anderson Ln., 512/459-5000, www.thegoodnightaustin.com, 11am-midnight Sun.-Thurs., 11am-2am Fri.-Sat.) is Austin's retro-hip place to have a plush meal with cocktails, sing some karaoke, and knock down pins. This dimly lit place is covered in upholstery and chock-full of all kinds of folks looking for an unusual evening. I find it funny that they self-promote as "vintage bowling," because this sport and culture is by definition vintage no matter where you go. The culture never moved forward into the 21st century. The Goodnight seems to bring it to the present.

If you want a bowling experience that is less hip and more gutter visit **Dart Bowl** (5700 Grover Ave., 512/452-2518, 9am-midnight daily). This 32-lane bowling alley, with big TV screens and a popular restaurant that

Austin City Limits

With the advent of PBS's popular and long-running program, *Austin City Limits*, Austin walked on to the U.S. stage and became a household name. Since the first live taping back in 1976, the program has showcased only the very best artists, musicians, and bands, and has single-handedly chronicled the greatest musicians of our time. It's futile to list all the acts that have performed in front of the famous backdrop of Austin's skyline in the studios of KLRU, but here's a sampling: Ray Charles, B. B. King, Johnny Cash, Leonard Cohen, The Flaming Lips, Beck, Coldplay, Pearl Jam, and Austin's own Willie Nelson and Stevie Ray Vaughan.

In 2011, the *Austin City Limits* stage moved to the 2nd Street District and is now located at the W Hotel on Willie Nelson Boulevard. The move was a massive shift in direction for the legendary show, but they felt that it was time to allow for growth, and to give the public more access. The new studio, called the Moody Theater (310 Willie Nelson Blvd., 512/475-9077, www.austincitylimits.org), is a state-of-the-art live music venue and studio set with a capacity of 2,700-plus people. Live tapings are free—that's right, *free!* Unfortunately, you have a better chance at going on a bike ride with the president than you have of getting tickets to a live performance at ACL. Available seats are limited, and these are taken by "insiders" and people "in the know." However, if you like playing the lottery, here's how it works: Ticket giveaways are posted about a week before a taping at acltv.com/upcoming-tapings. Here you can fill out the form to enter for the drawing. Multiple submissions will disqualify you. If you are visiting Austin, the chances of you being in town for a taping are slim, and your chances of actually winning tickets are slimmer, but it's worth a try. Two tickets per person are allowed, but a ticket doesn't guarantee admission to a taping.

Since the new location doubles as a live music venue, buying tickets to see a live show is a great way to gain access. For more information about live music visit www.acl-live.com.

serves an award-winning steak, draws a diverse crowd. Also in North Austin, up past all the dive bars, is Highland Lanes (8909 Burnet Rd., 512/458-1215, 9:30am-midnight Sun.-Thurs., 9:30am-1am Fri.-Sat.). The culture here is a bit more underbelly, and the food is terrible. Here's where you can find the best carpet mural in Texas, which covers two entire walls.

The scene where all walks of life merge for the pool, shuffleboard, darts, and foosball is **Buffalo Billiards** (201 E. 6th St., 512/479-7665, noon-2am Mon.-Sun.). This downtown entertainment joint for the 21-and-older crowd is a great place to either begin or end an evening on the town. Here you can shoot pool, eat burgers, and drink a few beers or down hard liquor. A word to pool and snooker professionals: The tables and cues are not well maintained, because this joint is for drunks and amateurs out for a good time. A word to drinkers: The drinks aren't sophisticated. However, the place is a blast once you're tipsy, and then everyone feels like a pool shark.

FESTIVALS AND EVENTS

Thanks to the great weather that Austin enjoys for most of the year, the calendar of events is chock-full of things to do. Texans love their festivals. In fact, it seems there's a festival for just about anything you can think of, from kite flying to German festivals that salute the sausage, and from jamborees that honor various fruits such as peaches and apples to festivals that venerate the wide variety of spring wildflowers. And one can't forget the many rodeos and local fairs that feature vats of chili, clouds of cotton candy, zany rides, and sunburned families with smiling, nauseated children.

In step with Austin's reputation of being diverse and eclectic one can take in pink tutus, Harley-Davidsons, and gay pride all in a single weekend, by walking the Austin Pride Parade during the day, catching Ballet in the Park in the evening, and partying at the ROT Biker

Rally the next day. Many of the festivities happen right in Austin.

For a complete guide to absolutely everything going on in Austin throughout the year, check out www.austin360.com and click on the calendar link, or go to www.austintexas.org and click on the events link.

January

The very best way to sample a wide range of Austin bands and musicians is by stumbling through all the Red River/6th Street venues during **Austin Free Week.** It is, as its name implies, a completely free week of live music. This started out as a way to cure the postholiday music industry blues and has grown into a smorgasbord for music lovers. There are no cover or door charges at venues such as the Mohawk, Sidewinders, Beerland, Empire Control Room, and the Scoot Inn during the first week of January.

February

For over two decades, every February **Carnival Brasileiro** (www.sambaparty.com) has brought Austin a party straight out of Brazil. Hailed as one of the city's weirdest and wildest celebrations, Carnival Brasileiro features only Brazilian music played on Brazilian instruments and sung in Portuguese, all for a crowd of drinking gringos. The event takes place at Palmer Events Center. Tickets can be purchased at local outlets Lucy In Disguise (1506 S. Congress Ave.) and Waterloo Records (600 N. Lamar Blvd). Tickets are $40, or $45 at the door.

March

In Texas the county fair historically was the big event of the year, when the whole town gathered to eat barbecue, be mesmerized by snake oil salesmen, and get sick on rides. The vestiges of this era can still be seen at **Star of Texas Fair and Rodeo** (512/919-3000, www.rodeoaustin.com). The fair is held at the Travis County Exposition Center (7311 Decker Ln.). The rodeo is the real deal, and the people that come out of the woodwork are the real deal too. Pressed jeans and Stetsons is what I'm talking about. Parking is available in an adjacent field.

It's an amazing sight to see thousands of kites in the sky with the Austin skyline as the backdrop. **Zilker Park Kite Festival** (www.zilkerkitefestival.com) has been going on since 1929. Not much can beat a glorious day under the sun in Zilker Park eating hot dogs, people-watching, and trying not to get your kite

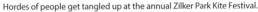
Hordes of people get tangled up at the annual Zilker Park Kite Festival.

SXSW

Imagine a major U.S. city handing over its streets, Mexican restaurants, barbecue joints, and public areas to hundreds of musicians, celebrities, rock stars, and thousands of fans for two weeks. Picture a backdrop of fireworks and dozens of film premieres. Sounds amazing, but impossible, right? Well, every spring all of this takes place in Austin during the spectacular event called **South by Southwest,** hitherto referred to as SXSW. This music and film festival has grown to mythic proportions and is now the premier event in the nation for new music and independent films.

HISTORY

SXSW started back in 1986 when the founders of the local weekly magazine *Austin Chronicle* came up with the brilliant idea of creating a music conference dedicated to independent artists. At the time, the music industry was in dire need of change, as power-ballad groups like Cinderella and Bon Jovi dominated the airwaves. The idea was quite simple: bring amazing music from outside the mainstream to one place (Austin), organize a conference with discussions about contemporary music, invite industry folk as well as fans, and have lots and lots of bands perform in venues all over town. The end result: The shape and sound of modern music has been altered forever.

Over the years SXSW has successfully brought attention to quality music that existed below the radar of the music industry. Wisely, the organizers opened the festival and conference to all genres, making the festival a cornucopia for all music lovers. Because of this, bands and musicians that have been featured at the festival over the years vary widely. A small sampling would include Jayhawks, Lucinda Williams, Mudd Puppies, Dixie Chicks, Beck, Wilco, Guided by Voices, The Fugees, Queens of the Stone Age, Trail of Dead, The Hives, The Shins, Black Eyed Peas, White Stripes, and Death Cab for Cutie. All these acts were buzz bands at the festival way back before they became household names. One of the greatest highlights in the history of SXSW was in 1994, when Johnny Cash played an acoustic set at punk rock club Emo's. A rediscovery of Cash ensued that made him a hero and icon for a new generation.

Today, SXSW is the biggest festival for new music in the world. It includes a conference with keynote speakers, private parties for indie record labels, and hundreds of shows featuring the very best new artists. SXSW has been known to have over 1,600 bands performing in 60-plus venues—and that's just the official numbers. On the periphery is a whole world of unofficial shows, parties, and showcases that take place in small juke joints, barbecue restaurants, bars, and vacant parking lots all over town.

entangled in the trees or thousands of strings connected to the sky. The day is packed with scheduled events, such as kite building for kids and a kite contest featuring stunt kite-flyers. The festival is free and is the first Sunday in March unless it's rained out. Parking gets close to impossible as the day progresses.

Every year spring comes unusually early in the Hill Country, and with it springs up a vast array of spectacular wildflowers. Every March **Wildflower Days** (www.wildflower.org) begin at Lady Bird Johnson Wildflower Center (4801 La Crosse Ave., 512/292-4100). The gardens and facility are extraordinary—a must-see for those who love the outdoors and who have allergy medication. From mid-March through the end of April the center is open 9am-5:30pm every day.

The biggest festival of the year—the mother of all mothers—is **South by Southwest** (www.sxsw.com). For one week (usually mid-March) the city of Austin is completely overrun by hundreds of musicians and celebrities and thousands of music fans. The town is plastered with the festival's acronym, **SXSW**, and the restaurants, clubs, music stores, and barbecue joints are teeming with greasy-haired, tattooed, ripped-jean-wearing rock stars and

SXSW has expanded its vision to include film. Theaters all over town premiere cutting-edge and innovative independent films, accompanied by panels and discussions on the indie film industry.

ACCESS BADGES

To attend the SXSW music or film conference you must buy an access badge. There are several different types of badges for varying levels of access for both the music and film portions of SXSW. Prices range $495-1,700. A badge gets you access to certain SXSW festival events, showcases, and the SXSW Trade Show. You also get a "Big Bag" filled with magazines, CDs, and souvenirs, as well as the program book with a directory of registrants. Buying your badge in advance is recommended, as walk-up prices are higher.

To attend both the film and music conferences it's best to buy a platinum badge. This offers access to all music, film, and interactive events. Platinum badges cost $1,295-1,695.

The easiest way to register for SXSW is online at www.sxsw.com, but registration forms can also be mailed in. Keep in mind that tickets are cheaper the earlier you buy them, and students can buy film badges at a discount. Badges are picked up at the Austin Convention Center when the festival begins.

TIPS

- There are hundreds of free shows and "unofficial" shows all over town. Some are low-key and some are major events. Before the festival begins, a schedule of free shows is circulated among those who have "connections." If you can get your hands on it, you can enjoy SXSW without buying an expensive badge. Mind you, you can't be as selective and won't get to see many of the "official" shows, but the free show circuit is a great way to experience SXSW.

- Everyone shows up the first day of the festival to pick up their badges. The wait in long lines can be brutal, so pick up your badge a day early if you can.

- For both music and film events that are getting lots of buzz, it's important to show up early and get in line. Admission is subject to venue capacity, and when big-name acts and films are being showcased, it can be very disappointing when you can't get in after paying big bucks for the "all access" badge.

- Finally, if you are itching to see somebody famous, your best bet is to eat lunch at Güero's Taco Bar or Lamberts barbecue any day during the festival.

rock star wannabes. What once was a unique underground event tailored for the ambitious DIY musician has now become a beer-sponsored, globally recognized event that includes independent film as well. If the earth opened up and swallowed Austin whole (God forbid) any day in mid-March, nearly all indie rock bands would be erased from the face of the earth, along with a few celebrities.

April

At the beginning of the month local artists, as well as artists from across the country, are peddling their wares at **Art City Austin**

(www.artallianceaustin.org, $8 adults, children under 12 free). Here you'll find sculpture, metal and woodwork, crafts, and painting in all media. This art festival is a big deal. The event takes place all weekend at Palmer Events Center, and artists set up booths so art lovers and the curious can mull about in a daze looking at all the swirling colors as they eat fair fare and live music sets an upbeat mood.

The best hot rod and classic car show in Texas is the **Lonestar Rod & Kustom Round Up** (http://hlonestarroundup.com). Every April hot rod enthusiasts, paint and piston fanatics, dolled-up pinup girls, and

greased-up guys gather at the Travis County Exposition Center (7311 Decker Ln.) for a homegrown outdoor car weekend. Be warned, there are no muscle cars here: all registered vehicles are from 1963 or earlier. Cars are slammed, chopped, loud, and some even spit fire. Live music often features Jimmy Vaughan and other rockabilly bands. The event includes booths with hot rod merchandise, food trucks, beer and margaritas, mini-bike races, and a swap meet. At the end of the weekend the trophies are passed out, as are many of the attendees. General admission is $15, kids under 12 are free, and parking is free.

Eeyore's Birthday Party (512/448-5160, www.eeyores.com) is one of the more popular and interesting citywide birthday parties held throughout the year. Founded by hippie UT students decades ago, this family festival has grown into an extravaganza of costumes, cake, and live entertainment, all in honor of the depressed donkey friend of Winnie the Pooh. He's getting up there in age so try to catch one of these before he dies. Proceeds go to nonprofit groups in town.

For the wine and food connoisseur willing to throw down some bucks there's the **Austin Food and Wine Festival** (www.austinfoodandwinefestival.com). Sponsored by the Austin Food & Wine Alliance, this three-day extravaganza showcases local and national wine and food artisans who converge in Austin to share their culinary creations. The festival takes place in venues all over town. Tickets range $55-450 depending on how much of the event you want to experience.

A favorite rite of spring for Austinites is running the **Statesman Capitol 10K** (http://cap10k.com), a 10K race on foot that begins in downtown Austin and ends on Auditorium Shores. Some run, some walk, and some just parade about in silly getups. If you have bad knees or just don't like running or walking 10 kilometers, it's worth watching the start of the race at Congress Bridge as the thousands of participants clog the arteries of downtown. The event happens the first Sunday of April and early registration costs $30-50. Every participant is actually placed and timed, so it's possible to cross the finish line in 5,142nd place.

Every April the Clyde Littlefield **Texas Relays** are held on the UT campus. This event is one of the nation's largest and most prestigious track-and-field meets. The four-day event features high school, collegiate, and professional athletes from across the nation. It is one of the earliest outdoor meets of the year, and the combination of pleasant weather and high-profile athletes draws sellout crowds.

At the end of April, down-home acoustic music enthusiasts make the **Old Settlers Music Festival** (18300 Farm to Market Road 1826, www.oldsettlersmusicfest.org) their home for a four-day weekend where the banjos will be plinkin'. Held at the Salt Lick Pavilion in Driftwood just outside of Austin, the festival features over two dozen of the top performers of bluegrass and Americana music on four stages. Camping at the festival is encouraged, but reserve your tent or RV spot in advance. Admission varies.

The **Austin Reggae Festival** (www.austinreggaefest.com), the city's premier reggae event, celebrates the legacy of peace, world unity, and great reggae music that Bob Marley introduced to the world. Held at Auditorium Shores, this Rasta mecca includes performances by reggae artists along with food vendors offering Caribbean delicacies. Bring something to sit on, sunscreen, and a Hacky Sack. A day pass costs $20, and a weekend pass is $40. A portion of the ticket sales goes to the Capital Area Food Bank.

Get in touch with your more sensitive and expressive side at the **Austin International Poetry Festival** (www.aipf.org). Held at various venues throughout town, this competition brings in over 200 poets from around the world for a four-day event dedicated to rhyme and time.

For those with a green thumb, or plant and garden lovers in general, **Zilker Garden Festival,** held at Zilker Botanical Garden (2220 Barton Springs Rd., 512/477-8672, www.zilkergarden.org) in Zilker Park, is a great way

to learn about the latest trends in gardening. Best described as a garden, plant, and craft fair, this event includes plant vendors and garden-equipment suppliers, along with purveyors of other various garden-themed goods such as jewelry, books, and games. Garden Fest is held in either April or May so check the schedule in advance. Admission is $10 adults, $4 children age 4-12, under 4 free. Parking is $5.

Wildflower Days at Lady Bird Johnson Wildflower Center continues through April.

May

If your sense of humor is on the level of Bazooka Joe gum wrappers (I used to work in a blanket factory but it folded . . .), and if you enjoy clever wit, check out the **O. Henry Pun-Off World Championships** (http://punoff.com, 512/472-1903). This duel of puns between a slew of clever word butchers is held in the backyard of the O. Henry Museum (409 E. 5th St.) with some 2,000 pun fans watching. Admission is free.

Zilker Garden Festival, held at Zilker Botanical Garden in Zilker Park, sometimes takes place in May.

Every year during the **Pecan Street Arts Festival** (www.pecanstreetfestival.com), 6th Street is shut down and the arts become king. Featuring some 300 vendors selling arts and crafts, live music stages in the streets, children's carnival games, street performers, and the smell of beef in the air, 6th Street becomes an Austin-style bazaar. This free event is held every spring on the first weekend of May and every fall on the last weekend of September, between 11am and 8pm.

June

The first weekend in June, women in pink tutus and men in tights are gracefully dancing about under the starry Texas sky. **Ballet Under the Stars** (512/246-6047, metamorphosisdance.org) is a free, open-air ballet featuring talented local dancers at the Zilker Park Hillside Theatre. For over a decade Austin Dance Ensemble has put on this nimble affair the first Friday and Saturday of June at 8:30pm.

Hailed as the biggest biker parade and street party in Texas, the **Republic of Texas Biker Rally** (www.rotrally.com) fills Austin with acres of hogs, custom choppers, leather, facial hair, and sheer brawn for an entire week. The event stretches over a four-day period at the Travis County Exposition Center (7311 Decker Ln.). Entertainment includes

6th Street and all of downtown are overrun by bikers during the Republic of Texas Biker Rally.

monster-truck rallies, white-knuckle motorcycle stunts, and live music. Headliners in the past have included Charlie Daniels, Hank Williams Jr., and George Thorogood. On Friday night the rally proceeds through downtown with a police escort and ends at Congress Avenue. Traffic is shut down for the ensuing all-night biker bash. Tickets for the Expo Center are $45; the party on Congress Avenue is free.

Starting this month, the local rock station KGSR 107.1 (www.kgsr.com) brings the blues to Zilker Park for **Blues on the Green.** Free shows are put on every other Wednesday 7:30pm-9:30pm, mid-June to mid-August. As for all events in the dead of summer, bring sunblock and lawn chairs.

July

Strike up the band and let our independence be commemorated! A grandiose way to celebrate July 4 is to attend the **Austin Symphony 4th of July Concert and Fireworks** (www.austinsymphony.org) on Auditorium Shores' outdoor stage. A free, two-hour classical music performance culminates in Tchaikovsky's famous 1812 Overture, accompanied by the firing of 75-millimeter howitzers and ending with a spectacular fireworks show over Lady Bird Lake.

August

In August it's too darned hot to do anything outside. Nevertheless, the *Austin Chronicle* cranks up the heat with the **Austin Chronicle Hot Sauce Festival.** This is an amateur and professional hot sauce competition that includes live music and great food at Waterloo Park. Warning: The combination of the 100-degree heat and hot sauce may make you feel like you're trapped in a structure fire.

During **Bat Fest** (www.roadwayevents. com), Congress Avenue Bridge turns into a fair with more than 100 booths featuring arts, crafts, and food, and more than 20 musicians and bands perform on two stages. All this is in honor of North America's largest urban bat colony, which lives under the bridge during the summer months. The bridge and Congress Avenue, Cesar Chavez Street, and Barton Springs Road near the bridge are all closed from 2am Saturday to midnight Sunday. Admission is $3 a day. A portion of the proceeds goes to Bat Conservation International.

September

Imagine the symbol of Texas—the Lone Star—on a rainbow backdrop, or a giant Texas-shaped rainbow flag proudly carried as a standard of victory by men dressed up like Cher. At the **Austin Pride Parade,** gay pride is as big as Texas. Held annually since 1991, this is an important event that is all about tolerance, acceptance, and being proud of who you are. The parade is a family event replete with floats, music, and classic cars, but it can have moments that aren't necessarily rated G.

The fall occurrence of the **Old Pecan Street Arts Festival** is held on 6th Street the last weekend of September. For more details see the complete entry in May section.

October

Spun out of the famous public television show, the **Austin City Limits Music Festival** (www.aclfestival.com) is the biggest music fest of the year. For three days the festival features top acts, bands, performers, and musical legends in nearly all genres of music. In the past the festival has featured artists such as REM, Ben Harper, and Coldplay, and the list goes on. The scene: 200,000 people, portable potties, the smell of sunscreen, parking miles away, dust in every orifice, and heat exhaustion, all in beautiful Zilker Park. Tickets can be purchased for one of the three days (Friday, Saturday, or Sunday), or you can throw down more cash for a three-day pass. In the spring an early-bird ticket special is offered, but these sell out in a matter of hours. After that tickets can be bought at a premium online. There's a long list of things that won't pass security; check the website before you bring all kinds of stuff to survive the weekend.

Founded by former librarian and First Lady Laura Bush, the **Texas Book Festival** (www.texasbookfestival.org) has become one of the biggest literary events in the Southwest. Book signings, awards ceremonies, celebrity-author book readings, and a black-tie Literary Gala including cocktails and dinner provide a great weekend that benefits the Texas Public Libraries. Tickets range $50-75, and the Literary Gala is $350 per person.

Austin has been attracting quite a bit of attention from the film industry. The event that highlights Austin and celluloid is the **Austin Film Festival** (www.austinfilmfestival.com). For eight days hundreds of film-industry folk, celebrities, and silver-screen fans converge in downtown Austin's many cinemas and hotels to view some 100 films. The festival also includes a screenwriter's conference.

Local cyclist, cancer survivor, and all-around controversial figure Lance Armstrong hosts **Ride for the Roses** (512/236-8820, www.livestrong.org) every October. This hugely popular event brings out crowds of cyclists, fans, celebrities, and spectators for a whole weekend of cycling-related events, all to raise money for cancer research.

Perhaps the most obscure event that goes on in these parts is the **Texas Gourd Society Show and Sale** (www.texasgourdsociety.org). Talk about niche: This society is made up of artists that enjoy painting and decorating gourds. The show and sale also includes a competition. Whoever has the most gourdgeous gourd wins! Believe me, some of these gourds are pretty spectacular.

When writing up events for Austin's calendar in October one can't omit **Halloween on 6th Street.** Some 60,000 dressed-up freaks and ghouls take over downtown's historic 6th Street. Overstimulated by sugar and whatever else, people party all night. The costumes are unbelievable. If you want to trick-or-treat but don't want to put time into inventing a costume, rent something from **Lucy in Disguise with Diamonds** (1506 S. Congress Ave., 512/444-2002).

November

The funnest festival in Austin is **Fun Fun Fun Fest** (www.funfunfunfest.com). Or at least it's pretty fun for all who are interested in indie rock, punk rock, hardcore, metal, and hip-hop/DJ. The festival, which started in 2006, is held in Austin's Waterloo Park close to downtown. The promoters of this show have an uncanny knack for getting bands from the bygone era of rock underground to resurface and put on amazing shows. Past lineups have included Slayer, Jane's Addiction, 7 Seconds, The Hold Steady, Descendents, High on Fire, Spoon, Explosions in the Sky, and Ice T. Even Weird Al Yankovic has done his thing, whatever that is. There are multiple stages for music and one for stand-up comedy. The event also includes BMX and skateboard half-pipes and even an amateur-wrestling ring.

A great way to sneak a peek into the lives of Austin artists is by touring artists' studios during **East Austin Studio Tour** (www.eastaustinstudiotour.com). Over a hundred artists, galleries, and studios participate in this East Austin event in mid-November each year. All media and styles are represented, from serene landscapes to bizarre abstract art. A map of the tour is available on the East Austin Studio Tour website.

December

Austin's beloved holiday tradition, the **Zilker Park Tree Lighting,** draws thousands to Zilker Park to see the park decorated in lights and watch the lighting of the 165-foot Christmas tree. The Trail of Lights, which is a mile-long display of holiday and wintertime scenes, is an Austin bucket list experience. Most locals consider spinning under the tree and eating funnel cake the only way to usher in the Christmas spirit in Austin. The tree-lighting ceremony takes place on the first Sunday of December, and the Trail of Lights is open until the New Year.

The **Armadillo Christmas Bazaar** (512/447-1605, www.armadillobazaar.com, 10am-10pm daily) is a uniquely Austin holiday market where artists and artisans from

Texas and the Southwest sell their works. This Austin original has been encouraging the public to buy from local artists since 1976. Besides all kinds of weird, wacky, original, and pop forms of art, the bazaar features great food and live music, and it all takes place at the Palmer Events Center. The bazaar operates the second half of December. Parking is available at the Palmer Events Center Garage, accessed off Riverside Drive.

Shopping

Before you defer your shopping fantasies to New York, Los Angeles, or Paris, I recommended you give Austin a full-hearted leap of shopping faith, keeping in mind one thing: Austin is the splendid crossroads of country, kitsch, and pop culture. For shopping this means obscure, secondhand vintage clothing shops, cowboy boots and Western wear, and boutiques featuring the latest in contemporary fashion. Because of all this, Austin is one of those places where the stylists of rock stars and celebrities find some of their clients' greatest fashions.

Beyond the fashion boutiques, Austin has a wide variety of other shops, such as toy stores, galleries, music stores, and curiosity shops, all displaying their wares with personalized weirdness and flair. Concept shops that I would describe as weird gift shops and oddity boutiques are springing up everywhere. They're a hip and zany version of Hallmark stores for the 21st century, peddling weird trinkets, Japanese toys, pop memorabilia, re-issued lunchboxes, and risqué cards. These do-it-yourself shops are run by creative folks who parlay their personal fetishes, hobbies, and interests into viable businesses.

Austin also has outlets of many of the big national chains, but in this book we will focus our attention on the one-of-a-kind Austin boutiques, as these are what make Austin so fabulous.

Although there are great shops all over town, there's a concentration of good stores in a few pockets of the city. The most famous shops are on **South Congress Avenue,** which is lined with funky storefronts, vintage boutiques, and trendy clothing and accessory shops. For fashionable new clothes and home decor items the shops in **2nd Street District** downtown, **6th and Lamar,** and **Guadalupe Street** are popular. For vintage and retro stuff there are the shops on **South Lamar** and **North Loop.** And for tacky touristy junk there's a smattering of shops on **6th Street.** Finally, in North Austin there's the shopping mecca of the **Arboretum,** which is a contemporary outdoor strip mall with all the big retail giants such as Gap and Pottery Barn. Hours for most of these shops are generally 10am-7pm daily. On the first Thursday of every month merchants on South Congress keep their doors open until 10pm. So get on out there and support local business at any of the following choice establishments.

CLOTHES, SHOES, AND ACCESSORIES

South Congress is home to one of the area's finest western-wear shops, **Allens Boots** (1522 S. Congress Ave., 512/447-1413, 9am-8pm Mon.-Sat., noon-6pm Sun.). Once you open that door, be prepared to be knocked down by the smell of cow skin. Inside this wood-paneled, leather-lined cowboy emporium, you'll find everything for your modern cowboy, the closet cowboy, and the wannabe, such as classy belt buckles, bolo ties, western shirts for men and women, and did I mention boots? Allens has the most extraordinary cowboy and cowgirl boot collection in the United States. With over 4,000 boots on display, they have everyday boots for the working cowboy, but they specialize in dress boots with ornate patterns, colors, and

Allens Boots on South Congress Avenue

designs, fetching up to $6,000. Even if you don't want to own a pair of cowboy boots, poke your head in here and marvel.

Finally, there's a clothing shop that sells nothing but black. Gothic meets country at fashionable **Blackmail** (1202 S. Congress Ave., 512/804-5881, 11am-7pm daily). What two words personify the style here? Johnny Cash. Here you can buy anything from a black leather jacket to a pair of black jeans to black accessories for both men and women. They even have black lotion. The only color to be found in here is in the back, where they sell vintage cowboy boots.

For fashion-conscious women and men with a fat wallet there's the local institution of fashion known as **By George** (524 N. Lamar Blvd., 512/441-8600, 10am-7pm Mon.-Sat., noon-6pm Sun.). Owned and operated by the same folks since 1977, By George has had its pulse on the state of fashion for decades. They offer the latest hip rags from contemporary big-name designers as well as some up-and-coming designers. No dusty vintage duds and

faux vintage here, just the guilty pleasures of passing fads.

Eco-wise (110 W. Elisabeth St., 512/326-4474, 9:30am-6:30pm Mon.-Fri., 10am-6pm Sat., noon-5pm Sun.) is the place to shop for all things green, and by this I don't mean the color green, I mean made with hemp. As people become increasingly environmentally conscious, shops like Eco-wise are important places to get just about anything. This place carries a small collection of clothes and accessories, as well as natural duds for kids, but don't expect much in the way of flashy design. All products are down-to-earth in the truest sense of the phrase. Here you'll also find hand creams, building supplies, toys, flooring, and other items for the home, all environmentally friendly.

Creatures (1206 S. Congress Ave., 512/707-2500, 11am-7pm daily) is a favorite for the ladies. Here you can buy cute casual dresses, flashy shoes, gifts and jewelry, all stylish for the day. I love this place because they are dedicated to supporting local and independent artists.

When shopping in Austin, get some brownie points by buying locally made goods in support of local designers from **Parts and Labour** (1117 S. Congress Ave., 512/326-1648, 10am-9pm daily). The little shop is filled with edgy designs, clever and trendy graphic T-shirts, and unusual accessories. There is no specific "look" that the proprietor is going for fashion-wise, which in turn has created a look that is totally unique. This is achieved by simply stocking the space with all locally made designs and fashions.

Finally, a boutique for the fashion-conscious male: **Service Menswear** (1400 S. Congress St., 512/447-7600, 10:30am-8pm Mon.-Sat., 11am-6pm Sun.) is a small space that is easy to overlook. In here men can buy designer, surf, and skate apparel made by Spiewak, Ben Sherman, Tyler Speed, Almost Evil, and old standbys Vans and Penguin. Service is known for its great collection of graphic T-shirts and vintage belt buckles.

Another clothing store for men in at the

South Congress area is Stag Provisions for Men (1423 S Congress Ave, 512/ 373-7824, 11am-7pm Tues.-Thurs., 10am-8pm Fri.-Mon.). This high-end outlet features trendy men's clothes by designer labels in classic and modern styles. If you're young and have a handlebar moustache and a fat wallet this place is for you.

MUSIC

Being the music-lovin' town that it is, Austin has some great music caches around town that have it all—vinyl, CDs, cassettes, and even eight-tracks, in any and every genre of music. For the vinyl fiend there are some excellent record stores.

Remember when record stores carried records? Remember that distinct smell of cardboard and plastic? It still exists at **Antone's Record Shop** (2928 Guadalupe Ave., 512/322-0660, 10am-10pm Mon.-Sat., 11am-8pm Sun.), where vinyl junkies are sure to find some old records they've been looking for. Besides having the biggest collection of vinyl in town Antone's also has a great selection of Texas music. So dig in that junk drawer and find your yellow 45 adapters.

Vinyl enthusiasts will be pleased when they visit Austin's true indie record store **End of an Ear** (4304 Clawson Rd., 512/462-6008, www.endofanear.com, 11am-9pm Mon.-Sat., noon-8pm Sun.). Although the space seems small, the collection of vinyl is full of surprises. Dig a little and you will uncover more "must-haves" than you can afford. Besides LPs and 7-inches, they also carry record players, used and new CDs of your favorite punk and metal bands, and a meager selection of country, metal, and jazz. The folks here are experts in vinyl and can help troubleshoot or answer questions.

Austin's most popular source for both new and used music is **Waterloo Records** (600A N. Lamar Blvd., 512/474-2500, 10am-11pm daily). It specializes in the most current releases in pop, country, and indie, and offers a great selection of Texas artists. Besides peddling CDs, Waterloo is the place to get tickets for local concerts, and they even put on their own live shows in-house.

BOOKSTORES

The largest bookstore in Texas is **BookPeople** (603 N. Lamar Blvd. at 6th St., 512/472-5050, 9am-11pm daily). It has everything that a major chain has, and then some. Here you'll find new books in every category, by nearly every author, as well as gifts, journals, children's books, magazines, and a café. BookPeople is also the area's top venue for author book signings, lectures, and literary information. As the name implies, it's a community bookstore and resource.

For the ladies, and the ladies who like ladies, there's **BookWoman** (5501 N. Lamar, 512/472-2785, 10am-8pm Mon.-Sat., noon-6pm Sun.). This female-oriented bookstore and community information center stocks feminist, gay and lesbian, and women's studies books, as well as T-shirts and gifts.

The area's biggest used-book resource is **Half Price Books** (5555 N. Lamar Blvd. at Koenig, 512/451-4463, www.halfpricebooks.com, 9am-10pm Mon.-Sat., 10am-9pm Sun.). Along with racks and shelves of used books you will also find new overstock coffee-table books, color folio books, and best sellers at a discount. In the back is a rare-book room for the collector in search of that first-edition *Wizard of Oz*. For other locations visit the website.

Want to bring down "the man"? Need a copy of *The Anarchist Cookbook*? **Monkeywrench Books** (110 North Loop Blvd., 512/407-6925, noon-6pm Mon.-Fri., noon-8pm Sat.-Sun.) carries literature for the counterculture and the cultural revolution. Monkey has a wide variety of zines, punk and pop-culture journals, and socialist and anarchist books.

ART GALLERIES

Every outlet for creativity abounds in Austin. Although music takes center stage, the fine arts also deserve a nod. A slew of galleries around town represent all types of artists in all mediums and styles. However, the most prevalent style is contemporary folk art best described as John Wayne meets Andy Warhol.

Wally Workman Gallery (1202 W. 6th St., 512/472-7428, 10am-5pm Tues.-Sat.) is the gallery in town where you can always find something beautiful and captivating to look at no matter what your tastes may be. Every month this small gallery in an old retrofitted Victorian house has a new exhibition that features upcoming and innovative artists.

Local artist Todd Sanders has created a little world for himself at **Roadhouse Relics** (1720 S. 1st St., 512/442-6366). A while back he bought the corner storefront location, plunked a trailer in the back, and hunkered down. Now he flings paint and neon where he wants without worrying about a thing. He opens his world to the public by appointment or by chance. If you drop by and he's not there, peek into the backyard at the giant chicken, the huge "Austin" neon sign, and all the other bizarre things Todd has collected. His stuff is best described as vintage neon and decor.

Austin's only outlet for master artists of Europe is the **Russell Collection** (1137 W. 6th St., 512/478-4440, www.russell-collection. com, 10am-6pm Tues.-Sat.). This gallery is perfect for the art collector who wants to own a Chagall, Renoir, Manet, Pissarro, or Picasso but has a budget of around $1,000-5,000. You may shudder at this and ask how this is possible. The collection consists, for the most part, of signed lithographs and works on paper that were cranked out either during the artist's lifetime or were produced in recent years from the original plates. How about the original oils? Well, look closely at the name and you will see these are painted by relatives of the masters, not the masters themselves.

Yard Dog (1510 S. Congress Ave., 512/912-1613, www.yarddog.com, 11am-5pm Mon.-Fri., 11am-6pm Sat., noon-5pm Sun.) is an art gallery that represents artists from around the country who create abstract folk art with a bite. The artwork in here is always amusing, quirky, and both colorful and off-color. Paintings, sculpture, and a unique array of things in between seem to take a tongue-in-cheek approach to Americana without becoming irreverent.

WEIRD GIFTS AND ODDITIES

Every travel destination has its particular souvenirs that folks bring back to their friends and families. For Austin it's all about music doodads, country-western stuff, or pretty much anything that's weird or unusual. The best touristy shop in the downtown area with all things music related is **Wild About Music** (615 Congress Ave. 512/708-1700, www.wild-aboutmusic.com, 10am-9pm daily). This is the place to get your touristy music-related knickknacks such as snow globes, key chains, T-shirts, hats, buttons, and random oddities. You can also find tons of junk related to Willie Nelson and Stevie Ray Vaughan.

Electric Ladyland, aka **Lucy in Disguise with Diamonds** (1506 S. Congress Ave., 512/444-2002, 11am-7pm Mon.-Sat., noon-6pm Sun.), is the biggest costume and prop outlet around. Here you can rent or buy costumes for anything, and this is not hyperbole. There's a wall of costume jewelry that can make any woman—or man for that matter—into Cleopatra, Carmen Miranda, or the Jolly Green Giant. Inside the showroom there's an amazing collection of theme-park-quality getups, such as Tweety Bird, which includes a big, fuzzy, unwieldy mask. There's also an entire room of scary rubber masks and prosthetics that range from a Freddy Krueger mask to a triple "breast"-plate.

Monkeys are known for "aping" what others do, but **Monkey See, Monkey Do** (1712 S. Congress Ave., 512/443-4999, 11am-8pm daily) isn't copying anyone. This boutique filled with new junk, such as Japanese toys, silly kitsch, retro clocks, pop-culture books, and the largest refrigerator-magnet collection in Texas, fits in perfectly on South Congress Avenue.

The shop with the most color is **Tesoros** (1500 S. Congress Ave., 512/447-7500, 11am-6pm daily), Austin's Latin American import extravaganza. Here tourists can be bedazzled

Funky Signage

Driving around Austin one can't help but take notice of the numerous funky, creepy, bizarre, and clever signs that many Austin businesses are adorned with. When it comes to zoning laws for signage Austin is pretty laissez-faire, which has opened the door for some creative approaches to attract the passerby. These businesses and their signs have become landmarks for locals and tourists, and collectively give Austin an amusing and fascinating image.

For example, what would normally be a very mundane light-bulb shop is completely transformed when topped with a three-dimensional bust of a giant, creepy, grinning man with a light bulb suspended over his head. Like a moth drawn to a light bulb one can't help but stroll into **The Light Bulb Shop** (6318 Burnet Rd.), even if there's no need for a light bulb. Just down the road is another peculiar sign worth noting. In front of **Atomic Tattoo** (5533 Burnet Rd.) is a pole topped with a skull, wearing a cap (not to be confused with a skullcap), mounted on an octopus. Eye-catching? Yes! But whether this makes one crave a tattoo or not is another story.

Other signage worth mentioning would be the grotesque massive red bulging arm in full flex protruding from **Hyde Park Gym** (4125 Guadalupe St.). Or there's the much more soothing retro/hippie sign of **Groovy Lube** (3511 Guadalupe St.) or the lesser-known, daffy-looking boxer standing proud and tall above **Richard Lord's Boxing Gym** (5400 N. Lamar). One can't leave

by an enormous space filled with treasures, religious and superstitious items, and folk art, all imported from south of the border. This emporium of colorful kitsch is a great place to get unique gift ideas. The endless litany of items includes handmade jewelry, unusual trinkets, colorful wall hangings and tapestries, carved figures and figurines, Mexican wrestling masks, pottery, toys made from soda cans, ex-votos/*milagros,* religious paintings and art, woodblock prints, and much, much more.

South Congress's Latin import connection is the **Turquoise Door** (1208 S. Congress Ave., 512/804-0618, 10am-7pm Mon.-Sat., 10am-6pm Sun.). This small retail space is chock-full of Latin American folk art, including hand-woven ceremonial Peruvian wall hangings, larger-than-life Oaxacan Día de los Muertos (Day of the Dead) figures, folk dolls, Mexican punched-tin art, religious items, wooden masks, and colorful and exotic jewelry. Chances are you aren't going in this place looking for something specific, but you'll like what you find.

Oat Willie's (617 W. 29th St., 512/482-0630, 10am-midnight Mon.-Fri., closed Sat.-Sun.) is the oldest continuously operating smoke shop in town. Oat's straddles the fine line between selling tobacco and being a head shop. I tip my hat to all who smoke tobacco in a bong.

FOR KIDS

Austin is an all-around fun place with a persistent lightheartedness and an unspoken maxim: "Don't take things too seriously." That said, everything in town for children isn't exclusively for children. Frank Sinatra's famous song explains what I'm trying to say with this lyric: "For it's hard, you will find, to be narrow of mind, if you're young at heart." This is especially true if you are in **Toy Joy** (403 W. 2nd St., 512/320-0090, 10am-9pm Mon.-Fri., 10am-10pm Sat., 10am-8pm Sun.). Rated one of the top 10 toy stores in the nation by *Child* magazine, Toy Joy is lined floor to ceiling and beyond with toys, gags, flying things, shooting things, noisemakers, squishy things, giant things, and tiny things, all in primary colors. One very important word of advice to grown-ups: Before you enter, leave your adult persona at the door. Open late at night, this is a great place to visit in the "wee" hours. Inside Toy Joy you'll find things that cheer up every girl and boy, such as: Things that go swish, things out the string of shops on South Congress Avenue. The sign and sculpture above **Uncommon Objects** (1512 S. Congress Ave.) begs the question, "What the heck were they thinking?" A cowboy made out of a muffler, riding a giant rabbit? Wow!

Among all of Austin's landmark signs there are two vying for the position of sign diva. One is a little waitress girl with a big Fender guitar that used to be on top of **Fran's Hamburgers** (her whereabouts are unknown since Fran's closed); the other is the mother of all mothers, the colossal woman's bust with open arms beckoning all the world to enter **Maria's Taco Express** (2529 S. Lamar Blvd.). This sign features the actual likeness of the proprietress. Once you see Maria's open arms from the road it is highly suggested you pull over and let her embrace you with her delicious tacos.

The Light Bulb Shop

that go squish, flying birds, and swimming fish. Things that tumble, things that roll, and music by Raffi, not Dave Grohl.

If the commercial plastic side of the toy industry has you turned off, consider visiting Austin's miniature haven of homemade wooden toys, **Rootin' Ridge Toymakers** (1206 W. 38th St., Ste. 1105, 512/453-2604, 10am-5pm Mon.-Sat.). This little shop, founded by husband-and-wife team Georgean and Paul in 1976, has all kinds of toys and games that seem like they were made for the set of *Little House on the Prairie*. The fun part of visiting this little shop is you can watch the toys being made on the spot.

Another great locally owned toy store is **Terra Toys** (2438 W. Anderson Ln., 512/445-4489, 9am-8pm Mon.-Sat., noon-6pm Sun.). If you're a kid, it's as good as a candy store, and if you're a depressed and jaded adult, Terra Toys will cut a smile into your face. This collection of toys steers clear of the consumer garbage that has captivated kids for so long, such as action figures and Barbie. Instead, you can find educational toys, handmade toys, learning games, wooden toys, musical instruments for tots, and a small selection of expensive clothes.

RETRO, VINTAGE, AND ANTIQUES

Austin's love affair with kitsch is best experienced by strolling through the many shops and boutiques that specialize in wacky and rare retro furnishings, vintage clothing, and country and folk antiques. In any number of these shops you can throw down some hard-earned dollars for a musty old Western shirt that looks like something worn by a member of the Carter family on the stage of the Grand Ole Opry, an amoeba-shaped chair that looks like it came from Frank Sinatra's Las Vegas home, a hand-carved shrine to the Virgen de Guadalupe, or an antique stuffed rabbit perched on a lacquered piece of burl. And by "stuffed" I mean taxidermy—you can tell by the creepy smell.

For the most part these shops are clustered together on a few of the main drags in town, which makes it easy to just step out on a street and follow your curiosity where it leads you. South of town there are some fantastic shops on South Lamar and South Congress, and just north of downtown there are a couple of shops on Guadalupe Street. Farther north there are some shops on Old Burnet Road and North Loop. Generally these places are close to great coffee shops and excellent places to break for lunch. For a complete list of vintage outlets in Austin check out www.vintagearoundtown-guide.com.

South Austin

First of all, I highly suggest kicking off your shopping on South Congress by fixing your caffeine maintenance at Jo's Cafe. Only then will you be able to focus properly for the transactions of the day.

For upscale trinkets, **Off the Wall** (1704 S. Congress Ave., 512/445-4701, 10am-6:30pm Mon.-Sat., noon-6pm Sun.) has lots of oddities you can buy at collectors' prices. The proprietors have made a living out of treasure hunting. With 25 years of experience they've developed an excellent sense for what attracts the antiques moths to the virtual flame. Here you'll find furniture along with an intriguing array of collectibles ranging from swords to early versions of Mickey Mouse in porcelain, from weird inventions from bygone times to expensive antique ashtrays.

The best curiosity shop in town is **Uncommon Objects** (1512 S. Congress Ave., 512/442-4000, 11am-7pm Fri.-Wed., 11am-9pm Thurs.). Here 18 purveyors of random items, knickknacks, oddities, trinkets, and collectibles peddle their weird stuff. Everything in this dark, 4,000-square-foot space is a conversation piece, such as vintage priest vestments, Victorian and cowboy clothes, human bones, bronze busts of whomever, and taxidermic animal corpses. Take your time browsing because there's stuff in every corner and junk hanging from the ceiling. You won't want to miss a thing.

Feathers (1700-B S Congress Ave., 512/912-9779, 11am-7pm daily) has flawlessly merged vintage and modern fashion, without being too dusty or too slick. This small retail shop specializes in '70s to '90s' fashions and home knickknacks as well as jewelry.

One of the long-time staples in Austin's vintage/retro scene is **Amelia's Retro-Vogue & Relics** (2213 S. 1st St., 512/442-4446, noon-7pm Tues.-Sat., noon-5pm Sun.).

This is a favorite place for designers and stylists to the celebrities, musicians, and drag entertainers to get ideas. Inside you'll find dramatic glamour outfits from the 1950s show-business era, children's vintage clothes, and a massive hat collection. You know you have arrived at Amelia's when you see a giant wire globe in the front yard of an old house.

For vintage and retro shopping for men and women, there's **Flashback** (1805 S. 1st St., 512/445-6906, 11am-7pm Thurs.-Sat., noon-5pm Sun.). Here you'll find an excellent collection of early-20th-century women's evening wear, men's shirts, and thrift-store art. The amount of vintage duds in here is phenomenal. The most interesting vest in the world is in here—a snake vest outfitted with pockets made from cobra heads (no joke).

The owners of **Garment Modern+Vintage** (701-F S. Lamar Blvd., 512/462-4667, 11am-7pm Mon.-Sat., noon-6pm Sun.) go to great length to find vintage clothing of quality, rarity, and desirability. Find the perfect clothes to look vintage rock-n-roll or to exhibit some flare from the past. They also stock new and vintage wearable accessories and jewelry.

North Austin

If you're out and about in Old North Austin and want to hunt for nothing in particular, make your way to the burgeoning North Loop DIY business district. This small bend in the road of a residential area is well worth your time. Here you'll find **Revival Vintage** (100 E. North Loop Blvd. #A, 512/524-2029, 11am-7pm daily), one of Austin's newest vintage stockpiles, featuring a small but well-curated collection of clothes, furniture, and stuff from the 1970s TV show *All in the Family*.

Just across the street is **Room Service Vintage** (107 E. North Loop Blvd., 512/451-1057, 11am-7pm daily). Upon entering through the double doors one can't help but be overwhelmed by the lights, colors, and shapes in here. With over 3,500 square feet of "modern" amoeba-shaped furniture, 1950s light fixtures, costume clothes and jewelry, vinyl records, vintage *Playboy* magazines, and paint-by-numbers artwork, everyone is bound to find something that tickles their fancy.

Wrap up your North Loop retro shopping day at **Blue Velvet** (217 W. North Loop Blvd., 512/452-2583, 11am-8pm Mon.-Sat., noon-8pm Sun.). Blue Velvet, six-time winner of the *Austin Chronicle*'s Reader's Poll for Best Vintage Store, is a one-stop shop for all your trendy clothing wants. In addition to the large collection of both new and vintage duds, this retro shop also sells costumes and unique handmade items from local DIY crafters.

Close to the North Loop area is **New Bohemia** (4631 Airport Blvd #116, 512/326-1238, 11am-8pm daily). This thrift store is cool enough for teenagers and retro enough for the parents. The upbeat environment seems to draw customers in and keep them coming back. In here you will find old clothes one notch above Goodwill, art that appears to be inspired by the great Bob Ross (the public television guy with the afro), some furniture, and of course that classic junk-store smell that is similar to granny's living room. Hats off to whoever made the catchy sign out front.

One man's junk is another man's treasure, especially at **Out of the Past** (5341 Burnet Rd., 512/371-3550, 10am-6pm Mon.-Sat., noon-5pm Sun.). This place wins the award for most stuff crammed into a small room. Browsing here is like digging through your uncle's garage and uncovering movie, music, and sports posters; collectible toys such as Star Wars, Barbie, and Hot Wheels; miniature furniture made from clothespins; and religious kitsch. They have the whole kit and caboodle—whatever that means.

Uptown Modern (5111 Burnet Rd., 512/452-1200, 11am-6pm Mon.-Sat., noon-5pm Sun.) is Austin's emporium of mid-century modern furniture, art, and accessories. The showroom is so impressive you will wish the time machine that Austin Powers used was real so as to go back in time. Be warned that most of the items in here are pretty pricy.

Top Drawer Thrift (4902 Burnet Rd., 512/454-5161, 10am-6pm Mon.-Sat.) is a secondhand store with a fashion sensibility. Paint-by-numbers art from the 1960s, old clothes and graphic tees, old appliances, and shelves of weird stuff are sitting around begging to find a home.

Recreation

Being in the most beautiful and diverse natural setting in Texas, Austin has become a favorite for lovers of the outdoors. Numerous lakes, rivers, hills, caves, trails, and parks have wisely been preserved for people to use and enjoy. There's kayaking, biking, backpacking, boating, scuba diving, spelunking, rock climbing, camping, rafting, skiing, golf, disc golf, tennis, volleyball, and numerous swimming holes—all for the taking.

★ LADY BIRD LAKE

The greatest attraction Austin has to offer is the stretch of the Colorado River called Lady Bird Lake, formerly known as Town Lake. This wide, slow-moving river winding through the heart of downtown Austin is banked with lush vegetation, ancient trees, and wildlife, such as turtles, swans, and ducks. What makes Lady Bird Lake so remarkable? By taking just a few steps you can go from bustling urban downtown to an alternative world that's peaceful, beautiful, and natural.

Lady Bird Lake's hike-and-bike trails are some of the best urban trails in the country, with several loops over and around the lake that are in three 10-mile increments. Each loop's bridge provides a different view of Austin, the lake, and surrounding hills. Although the trails are fit for bikes as well as pedestrians, and during peak hours bikers find it pretty hard to navigate all the joggers

Austin Recreation

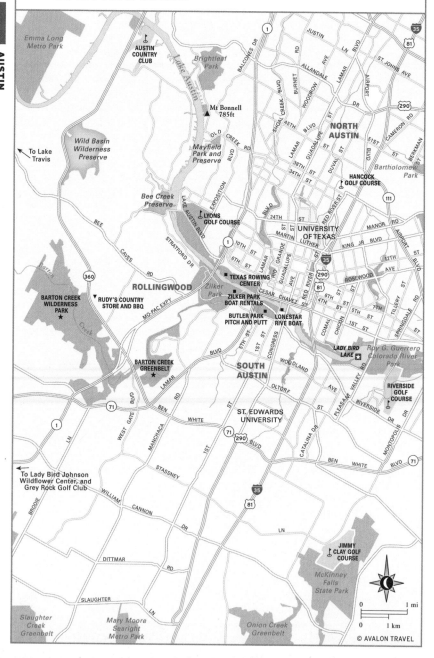

© AVALON TRAVEL

and speed-walkers, everyone seems to sweat in harmony. The trails are all lakeside and have lots of shade, benches, water fountains, and Stevie Ray Vaughan. That's right! On the south shore of the lake is a life-size bronze statue of the Austin legend proudly standing as a sentinel with guitar in hand. Free water stations are set up at various locations along the trail. The trail is considered very safe, so no need to worry about crazy people doing crazy things. However, watch out for poison oak. The trail is laced with this evil plant, and if you are not paying attention, or decide to pet the cute dog running up to you, you may end up with some serious itching. During the peak months nice people will put little flags on branches to help identify the stuff.

Other activities that take place on Lady Bird Lake include crewing, canoeing, kayaking, and stand-up paddleboarding, which are great ways to get up close to giant white swans and turtles. You might even catch a glimpse of the elusive gar. This is a long, prehistoric-looking fish with spots and a crocodile-like nose. From the water the city skyline looks pretty impressive—even breathtaking. For many locals, spending time on the lake in some sort of vessel is the best way to spend a Saturday. For visitors, planning your time

here all depends on whether you want to take a leisurely walk for an hour or want to spend half of the day on the lake in a canoe or on a stand-up paddleboard.

Canoes can be rented through **Zilker Park Boat Rentals** (512/478-3852, www.zilkerboats.com, 10am-dark Mon.-Fri., 9am-dark Sat.-Sun. in summer and early fall, 10am-dark Sat.-Sun. in winter as weather permits, $15 an hour or $45 per day) at Zilker Park near Barton Springs Pool. They have 17-foot Alumacraft, Grumman and Michicraft canoes, and both Frenzy (one-person) and Malibu Two (two-person) ocean kayaks. Paddles and life jackets are provided.

If you prefer standing while traversing the lake, stand-up paddleboards can be rented from **Texas Rowing Center** (512/651-5710, www.texasrowingcenter.com, open daily during daylight hours). This boat rental go-to is located on the north side of Lady Bird Lake on the trail near Mo-Pac on Stephen F. Austin Drive across from Austin High School. The weird-looking recreational sport of standing on a surfboard has become very popular. Texas Rowing Center also has rentals for other water sports, such as canoes and kayaks. Rates for paddleboards are $15 per hour and $35 per day. Rates for kayaks are $10 per hour

Canoeing on Lady Bird Lake is one of the best ways to spend a Saturday morning.

Lady Bird Lake

and $25 per day and canoes are $20 per hour and $45 per day.

The most glorious way to experience the lake under the city skyline is by tour on a double-decker paddle wheel riverboat. **Lone Star Riverboat** (512/327-1388, www.lonestarriverboat.com, $10) operates this Mark Twain-style adventure March-October on weekends at 3pm.

Lady Bird Lake's trails can be accessed at any of the downtown bridges and from several of the hotels on the river. The most convenient parking lot is at Auditorium Shores, on the south side of the lake at the foot of the 1st Street Bridge. However, a better place to park is in Zilker Park, on Stratford Drive under the Mo-Pac overpass. Peak recreation hours are before and after the workday, during the weekend, and on holidays. Swimming in Lady Bird Lake isn't allowed due to dangerous whirlpools.

LAKE TRAVIS

Just northwest of Austin along the Colorado River is the Highland Lakes area. Five winding lakes draw hordes of people from spring to fall: Lake Austin, Inks Lake, Lake LBJ, Lake Marble Falls, and Lake Travis. These lakes are wide spots in the Colorado River that became wider when six dams were built back in the 1930s and '40s. The primary function of these dams was to give water a place to go during flash floods. The lakes that have formed are all about recreation under the sun, the most popular lake being Lake Travis.

Lake Travis is the second largest of the lakes and has an average surface area of nearly 19,000 acres to play on. People come from all over Texas to lie in the sun on and around Lake Travis and participate in every form of water recreation imaginable. There's swimming, boating, fishing, sailing, scuba diving, parasailing, and all kinds of water sports, as well as the only nude beach in the state.

The best way to gain access to Lake Travis is through Travis County Parks locations. The most popular and largest facility is at **Mansfield Dam Park** (4370 Mansfield Dam Park Rd., 8am-dark daily, $10 for the day, $20 for primitive camping). It has four boat-launching ramps, swimming areas, barbecue grills, picnic tables, and restrooms. The other popular access to the lake is at **Pace Bend Park** (2011 N. Pace Bend Rd., Spicewood, 512/264-1482, sunrise-9pm daily, $10 for the day, $15 for primitive camping). With nine miles of Lake Travis shoreline and beautiful vistas only 45 minutes from downtown Austin, this park provides an easy way to experience the lake. You can camp, swim, hike, and launch boats. To get to Pace Bend from Austin take Highway 71 west 11 miles to RR 2322 (Pace Bend Park Rd.). Turn right on RR 2322 and travel 4.6 miles to the park entrance.

If man-made water recreation is more your style there's **Shore Club Volente Beach** (16107 FM 2769, 512/258-5110, www.volentebeach.com, 10am-8pm daily Apr.-Oct., $16 for those shorter than 42 inches, $21 for those 42 inches and taller). This is the closest water park to Austin, and it has everything from waterslides to tropical-style swimming pools. To get to Volente Beach go north on Highway 183 then west on Anderson Mill Road, which turns into FM 2769. The park is seven miles up FM 2769.

HIKING AND BIKING
Barton Creek Greenbelt

If you want to disappear into nature but don't want to spend any time getting there, the **Barton Creek Greenbelt** (512/974-1250,

5am-10pm, free) has it all. Second in popularity only to Lady Bird Lake, this well-preserved stretch of wilderness along Barton Creek has mountain biking, hiking trails, swimming holes, and rock climbing. The Greenbelt is about 7.9 miles long and consists of 809 acres. The terrain is mostly rough with sheer cliff walls, lush vegetation, and a creek that is at its peak in the spring. Once you descend into the Greenbelt you feel far away from civilization, provided you don't look up and see the occasional home on the cliff. The trails are rocky and semi-primitive and cut through scenic wildflowers, trees, limestone cliffs, caves, meadows, swimming holes, and waterfalls. The trail varies from narrow ledges to wide walkways. Wildlife is abundant, which can make the park sound and look like the Amazon.

The trail starts above Barton Springs Pool at Zilker Park and extends westward past Loop 360 to Lost Creek. There are several trailheads throughout the park, mostly in adjoining neighborhoods. The three easiest places to access the Greenbelt are **Spyglass Trail Access** on Spyglass Drive just off Mo-Pac; **Loop 360 Trail Access** at Loop 360

Lake Travis

Cedar Park

Lago Vista

183

1431

ROUND ROCK AVE

SHORE CLUB
VOLENTE BEACH

Volente

Lake Travis

620

183

HIPPIE HOLLOW

Pace Bend Park

BEE CREEK

2322

Briarcliff

Mansfield Dam Park

BULL CREEK

LOST PARROT CABINS

MANSFIELD DAM

RD

71

LAKEWAY RESPORT AND SPA

ROBIN'S NEST

360

AUSTIN

Lakeway

QUINLAN PARK RD

Colorado River

RIVERBEND CENTER

Lake Austin

620

0   2 mi
0   2 km

© AVALON TRAVEL

THE BACKYARD

71

3238

LAKE AUSTIN SPA RESORT

Bee Cave

ONE WORLD THEATRE

West Lake Hills

1

just south from Mo-Pac; and **Gus Fruh Trail Access** at 2642 Barton Hills Drive (wheelchair-accessible). Dogs are permitted on leash only. Mountain bikers must yield to hikers and stay on designated trails. In spring, creek crossings may require wading through water. When enjoying the Barton Creek Greenbelt, remember to pack your trash. Call for up-to-date trail conditions.

Mayfield Park and Preserve

One of the more off-the-beaten-path outdoor areas is **Mayfield Park and Preserve** (3505 W. 35th St., 10am-10pm daily, free). This often-forgotten park, on a small stretch of Lady Bird Lake, is perfect for a casual evening stroll for families and couples. The winding network of paths twists through old groves of oak trees, across several footbridges, over small creeks, and through a lakeside grove of moss-draped oaks. Being next to the historic building of Laguna Gloria art museum just

adds to the romance. The park has a paved parking lot, restroom facilities, and drinking fountains. The best way to get to Mayfield is by heading west from the 35th Street exit off Mo-Pac.

Wild Basin Wilderness Preserve

The perfect antidote to a busy schedule is **Wild Basin Wilderness Preserve** (805 N. Capital of Texas Hwy., 512/327-7622, www.wildbasin.org, trail hours sunrise-sunset, office hours 9am-4pm Tues.-Sun., $3). Smaller in scope than the Barton Creek Greenbelt and less crowded than Lady Bird Lake, Wild Basin is a favorite secret Austinite retreat. The 2.5 miles of hiking trails on 227 acres are well maintained and generally quiet. The trails take you through a valley, over streams, and to a panoramic view. The trail also includes informative trail markers that give insight into the native plants and animals that live in the

Naked in Texas

There's only one place in Texas where you can "be as proud as you can be, of your anatomy" in public, and that's at **Hippie Hollow** on Lake Travis. This little Garden of Eden on the lake is the only clothing-optional public park in the state. The park is in a secluded spot that offers spectacular views of Lake Travis, a paved walking trail, and a hiking trail that hugs the cliffs. Although the shoreline itself is pretty steep and rocky, Hippie Hollow is good for sunbathing, swimming, and fishing. Whether you're a first-timer curious about strutting in the nude, or a dedicated nudist, only the serious are welcome here—it's not a place to gawk or giggle at people. Speaking of gawking, one time a boat passing by Hippie Hollow capsized because everyone rushed to one side of the boat to get a better view.

The park is 20 minutes from I-35. From Mo-Pac or I-35, take RM 2222 west to Highway 620. Turn left on Highway 620 and go 1.3 miles. Turn right at the first traffic light onto Comanche Trail. Travel two miles to the park entrance on the left. A paved parking area, drinking water, and restrooms are available.

region. Interpretive trail brochures are available at the trailhead. Dogs and bikes aren't allowed. The entrance to Wild Basin is right off of Loop 360, which makes it an easy getaway.

HORSEBACK RIDING

At the very top of the short list of things a traveler to Texas should do at all costs is a trip on horseback through the countryside. Fortunately, there is an easy way to include horseback riding in your visit to Austin without dedicating an entire day venturing way out into the Hill Country. On the southern edge of Austin is **Texas Trail Rides** (9606 Farm to Market 1826, 512/697-9722, www.texastrailrides.com). Setting aside just two hours, wannabe cowboys and cowgirls can get acquainted with a horse, saddle up, and enjoy an awe-inspiring trail ride, all before lunch.

Their signature Ranch Trail Ride is a guided tour through a nature preserve that includes a water crossing, scampering up bluffs, spectacular views, and fields of wildflowers, and there's even one point on the trail where the Austin city skyline is visible in the distance. The Ranch Trail Ride takes about two hours and costs $125 per rider.

ROCK CLIMBING

Out of the four basic types of rock climbing—sport climbing, traditional climbing (aka Trad), gym climbing, and bouldering—sport climbing is, by far, the most popular and best represented in the Austin area. The **Barton Creek Greenbelt** has a decent number of routes that have their own names, like Seismic Wall, Gus Fruh Wall, and New Wall. They are all very short (30-40 feet max), but really, you can't beat it considering that you don't have to leave the city limits. This sort of "urban cragging" (climber speak for climbing in urban areas) has really put Austin on the map for being a place where you can climb right after work and still make happy hour somewhere.

The Austin Rock Gym (8300 N. Lamar Blvd., Ste. B-102, and 4401 Freidrich Ln., Ste. 300, 512/416-9299, www.austinrockgym.com, noon-10pm Mon.-Fri., 10am-10pm Sat., 10am-7pm Sun.) is the only gym that is exclusively dedicated to climbing.

There are a couple of great online resources, such as www.bloodyflapper.com. Here you'll find lots of good information, a bulletin board for hooking up with other climbers, and great descriptions of all the rock-climbing spots in the Austin area. Another website that has some good info is www.texasclimbers.com, which has a set of rough topographical maps and area descriptions that can be really handy. **Whole Earth Provision Company** (1014 N. Lamar Blvd., 512/476-1414, 10am-8pm Mon.-Fri., 10am-8pm Sat., 11am-6pm Sun.) offers an extensive line of climbing equipment and shoes. There aren't a whole lot of places where you can rent used gear in town, since climbers' lives depend on the condition of their gear.

SPELUNKING

If you enjoy being in dark places in the belly of the earth, Austin has some good caves to explore. There are two known caves in town. First, there's **Airman's Cave** in the Barton Creek Greenbelt. This is the longest known cave in the county. Here you'll see the Keyhole, which is a tight space that can freak out even the most advanced spelunkers, and the Aggie Art Gallery, which is a room full of clay art that has been preserved in this underground environment.

The other cave in town is at **Goat Cave Preserve** (3900 Deer Run) in southwest Austin. For more information on caving in Texas check out www.utgrotto.org.

GOLF

Austin is a golf town—after all, it has been home to Harvey Penick, the legendary golf pro and teacher, as well as Ben Crenshaw, Tom Kite, and Hilary Lunke, a U.S. Women's Open champion. There are world-class courses in the area, both public and private. The following are the best golf courses in Austin.

Hancock Golf Course (811 E. 41st St., on 38th St., 512/453-0276, dawn-dusk daily, $14 for 9 holes) was built in 1899 and is the oldest course in Texas. The 9-hole, par 35 course is in the heart of Austin in the Hyde Park area. No reservations are required. Another course that's been around for a long time is **Lions Golf Course** (2910 Enfield Dr., 512/477-6963, sunrise-sunset daily, $16-29). This 6,001-yard, 18-hole, par 71 course requires reservations.

Grey Rock Golf Club (7401 Hwy 45, 512/288-4297, greyrockgolfandtennis.com, hours vary by season, call ahead) is one of the best public courses in Texas. A picturesque Hill Country setting, covered biergarten, and a casual yet elegant clubhouse make this a safe bet for visiting golfers. The Salt Lick barbecue restaurant is nearby, and a stop here after golf would finish your day perfectly.

In South Austin there's the tiny but popular **Butler Park Pitch and Putt** (201 Lee Barton Dr., 512/477-4430, $9-11). This 9-hole, par 27

Sporting Goods Stores

- Sports & Outdoor Recreation: **REI** (601 N. Lamar Blvd., 512/482-3357; 9901 N. Capital of Texas Hwy., Ste 200, 512/343-5550)

- Hiking & Outdoor Recreation: **Whole Earth Provision Company** (2410 San Antonio St., 512/478-1577)

- Running & Jogging: **Luke's Locker** (115 Sandra Muraida Way, 512/482-8676)

- Canoe & Kayak Gear: **Austin Canoe and Kayak** (9705 Burnet Rd., Ste. 102, 512/719-4386)

---

course is perfect for getting in a quick golfing fix. You only need three clubs carried in hand and a couple of golf balls in your pocket. The best golf gear shop is **The Golf Club** (1315 W Ben White Blvd., 512/916-4653).

DISC GOLF

When driving past Pease Park on North Lamar Boulevard, you may notice small gatherings of young folks throwing Frisbees into chain hoops with complete concentration, solemnity, and earnestness. This is the fairly young outdoor recreational sport called disc golf, also known as Frisbee golf. Austin has several courses that are very popular to folks who play this niche sport. On the surface this sport seems a bit funny, but people take this very seriously. The most centrally located course is at **Pease Park** (Lamar Blvd. at 24th St.). Other courses in town are at **Bartholomew Park** (51st St. near I-35 in East Austin) and **Mary Moore Searight Park** (Slaughter Ln. in South Austin). For more information, check out www.hookshot.com.

SPECTATOR SPORTS

Austin may not have a major-league franchise, but that doesn't stop this sport-loving town from hosting some of the biggest sporting events in the state. Most of the athletic world in Austin circles around the UT football and baseball teams; both are among the top programs in the nation. UT's sports program also includes tennis, golf, swimming, volleyball, track and field, and women's softball. Besides university games, Austin is also home to the popular minor-league baseball team Round Rock Express, a hockey team called the Ice Bats, and the outlandish return of women's roller derby, which is becoming a wildly popular cult spectator sport.

Football

From the small rural towns where absolutely every citizen can be found in the stands on Friday night to the pro-football mania of the Cowboys, football is Texas's version of the Roman gladiators. Austin happens to be home of UT Longhorns Football (www.texassports.com), one of the most popular college football teams in the United States. This excellent program commands higher ticket prices than pro football teams, and the networks have hopped on this bandwagon and paid handsome amounts to broadcast Longhorn games. Football season is September-November, and home games take place at Darrell K Royal-Texas Memorial Stadium (1701 Red River St.). Tickets are very hard to get, and the ones available are sold as season passes, but it's possible to land tickets for one event for $55-75. Tickets can be purchased at the UT Athletics Ticket Office (2100 San Jacinto Blvd., on the UT campus), by phone at 512/471-3333 or 800/982-2386, and online at www.texasboxoffice.com.

Baseball

Baseball may not be as big as football, but it still has an important place in Austin. The UT Longhorns Baseball team produces some great ballplayers, some of whom go on to the majors. The Longhorns have won six national championships. UT Longhorns baseball season is February-June, and games take place at Disch-Falk Field (corner of MLK and I-35). Tickets are $8-12 and can be purchased at the UT Athletics Ticket Office (2100 San Jacinto Blvd., on the UT campus), by phone

at 512/471-3333 or 800/982-2386, or online at www.texasboxoffice.com.

The other baseball team worthy of mention is the Round Rock Express (www.roundrockexpress.com). This AAA affiliate of the Texas Rangers was founded by Nolan Ryan and computer kingpin Michael Dell. The Express is gaining popularity to such an extent that they often break minor-league attendance records. The team plays about 70 home games April-September at the Dell Diamond (3400 E. Palm Valley Rd.) in Round Rock.

Basketball

The hoops scene in town is dominated by UT Longhorns Basketball, with both men's and women's teams. Both men's and women's basketball games take place at the Frank Erwin Center (1701 Red River St., 512/471-7744). Tickets run $6-15 and can be purchased at the UT Athletics Ticket Office (2100 San Jacinto Blvd., on the UT campus), by phone at 512/471-3333 or 800/982-2386, or online at www.texasboxoffice.com.

Roller Derby

One of Austin's hottest and most distinctive forms of entertainment is the roller derby. Put on by Texas Rollergirls (www.texasrollergirls.com), this skater-owned and -operated league comprises four very competitive teams: Hotrod Honeys, Honky Tonk Heartbreakers, Hell Marys, and the Hustlers. The roller derbies take place every spring and summer at Austin Convention Center (500 E. Cesar Chavez St.) and skating rinks throughout Texas. Typically there are two bouts per night, and every bout starts at 6pm, but you should plan on showing up an hour early. The Convention Center has two parking garages, on 2nd and 5th Streets. Street parking downtown is also available. General admission is $15 and kids are charged $5.

Roller Derby Revival

The most outrageous form of entertainment of the golden 1970s, roller derby, is back! The skates are laced up, the short shorts are donned, the roller rink is aflame, and the catfights have begun. But instead of disco, punk and heavy metal are the soundtrack to this over-the-top spectacle. Austin's unique and dazzling form of underground entertainment is put on by a legion of feisty women from all walks of life. A few years back these ladies started skating for fun and found that people loved the idea of roller derby and would pay to see them beat each other up in the rink. Seeing a grassroots opportunity to resurrect a spectacle sport that died with disco, they organized and started taking it seriously. A flurry of attention ensued, such as a cover story in *Rolling Stone* and an A&E TV show.

Today there are two Austin-based, skater-owned and -operated leagues: **Texas Lonestar Rollergirls** and **Texas Rollergirls.** A sampling of team names includes: Hotrod Honeys, Cherry Bombs, Honky Tonk Heartbreakers, Hell Marys, Holy Rollers, and the Texecutioners. With all manner of theatrics, these ladies get dressed up in crazy getups composed of fishnet stockings, plaid skirts, and war paint, and take on various personalities, such as Lucille Brawl, Rice Rocket, Kitty Kitty Bang Bang, Cherry Chainsaw, and Dinah-Mite, to name a few.

So what exactly is roller derby? Don't expect this to be a WWE-style choreographed event. This is real women going in circles at high speeds on skates, knocking each other down to win. In brief, here's how it works. There are three positions: the pivot sets the pace for the pack and is the last line of defense; blockers try to stop the jammer and knock around the opposing team's blockers; and the jammer sprints through the pack, scoring points by passing members of the opposing team. The pack starts with a pivot from each team in front, three blockers from each team in the middle, and a jammer from each team in the back. When the whistle blows, the pack takes off, and on a second whistle, the jammers start fighting their way through the pack in an attempt to be named lead jammer. The jammers lap the pack, and when they reenter the pack they receive one point for each member of the opposing team that they pass. A jam lasts a maximum of two minutes, but the lead jammer has the right to call off the jam at her discretion.

If you're feeling brave the best seating is rinkside. There are no rails, and very few seats, so plant yourself down on the rink just outside the ring of flashing lights. At rinkside you can get up close to the action, so much so that you can smell the BO as it mixes with the smell of popcorn. Always be on guard and keep your eyes on the women on skates. They often crash, wipe out, or barrel off into the crowd. Spacing out even for one moment can cost you your fingers.

The roller derbies take place every spring and summer at **Palmer Event Center** (900 Barton Springs Rd.) and **Austin Convention Center** (500 E. Cesar Chavez St). Ticket prices are usually $15 a seat and doors usually open at 6pm. A band always performs at halftime. For times and dates and more information check out www.txrollergirls.com and www.txrd.com.

TOURS
Walking Tours

Austin is best imbibed by strolling around on foot. Most points of interest are within walking distance of one another, and the town is easily traversed thanks to good city planning and pedestrian-friendly motorists. Free guided walking tours are put on by **Austin Convention and Visitors Bureau** (512/454-1545 or 866/462-8784, www.austintexas.org). They offer tours of Congress Avenue, 6th Street, the state capitol grounds, and Bremond

Block. Tours are offered March-November at the capitol's south steps and take about an hour. Call for tour schedules and information.

Austin has enough ghosts in its closet that **Austin Ghost Tours** (512/853-9826, www.austinghosttours.com, $20) came along to give these ghouls their due recognition. Tour organizers have pieced together the past and organized several fascinating tours that include the Haunted 6th Street Tour, Servant Girl Annihilator Tour, and Graveyard Tour, to name a few. Tour guides walk the curious through the streets of Austin and unfold the darker side of town. Tours are about 90 minutes and take place outside for the most part, and all are wheelchair-accessible except for the Haunted Pub Crawl Tour. Tickets generally cost $20. Reservations are required for all tours; call in advance.

Sightseeing Cruises

The best view of Austin is from Lady Bird Lake, and the best way to be on the lake is by floating in an authentic double-decker paddle wheel riverboat. **Lone Star Riverboat** (512/327-1388, www.lonestarriverboat.com) offers narrated sightseeing cruises March-October on Saturday and Sunday at 3pm. Boarding begins at 2:15pm and costs $10 for adults, $8 for seniors over 60, and $7 for children under 12. Lone Star also offers Friday night tours at 10:30pm (boarding time 9:45) for $10. You can BYOB for this cruise. Along with the riverboat, Lone Star also has a pontoon boat that offers a sunset cruise for a buck less. This is the best seat in town for watching the bats fly out of Congress Avenue Bridge. Departure time for the evening pontoon boat cruise is 30 minutes before sunset and the cruise costs $10.

Also offering aquatic tours on Lady Bird Lake is **Capital Cruises** (512/480-9264, www.capitalcruises.com). Public sightseeing cruises depart Saturday and Sunday at 1pm, and bat-watching cruises depart before sunset. Rates are $10 for adults, $8 for seniors, and $5 for kids 3-12. Also available is a dinner cruise with cocktails and entertainment. Rates range $26-100 depending on options. The local phone book has a 20 percent discount coupon. Both Capital Cruises and Lone Star Riverboat offer cruises March-October, and docks for both are on the south side of Lady Bird Lake between the 1st Street Bridge and Congress Avenue Bridge near the Hyatt Regency.

Land Tours

AO Tours (512/659-9478, www.aotoursaustin.com) offers great comprehensive 90-minute tours of town in a brightly colored minibus.

Tours include more than 30 points of interest and are narrated by a father-son team of Texas history buffs who know their stuff. Tickets are $25 for adults and $17 for children 12 and under, and can be purchased online. Departure locations are 615 Congress Ave. (Wild About Music) or 602 E. 4th Street (Austin Visitors Center). Be sure to arrive 20 minutes early.

Perhaps the most touristy thing to do in Austin is to take the amphibious tour of town with **Austin Duck Adventures** (209 E. 6th St., 512/477-5274, www.austinducks.com). Board a domesticated British Alvis Stalwart (amphibious military vehicle from the 1960s) and traverse both land and water, exploring Austin's main sights, such as the state capitol, Congress Avenue, and 6th Street, before splashing into Lake Austin.

For a nostalgic chug into the past the **Austin Steam Train** (401 E. Whitestone Blvd., Ste. A-103, Cedar Park, 512/477-8468, www.austinsteamtrain.org) is a great way to see the beautiful countryside north of town. The Austin Steam Train Association operates two classic steam trains on a leg of the original Southern Pacific railroad between Austin and the town of Llano. The boarding location is in Cedar Park, which is 20 minutes northwest of Austin. In addition to regular hours (9am-4pm Mon.-Fri.), the ticket office is also open 90 minutes before each train departure. Although walk-up tickets can be purchased at the boarding locations, advance reservations are recommended. Fares range $38-53, depending on the route and the train. Call or go online for schedules and fares.

A horse-drawn carriage is the most romantic way to see downtown, provided you don't feel guilty for making the horses sweat. Companies vying for your business include: **Austin Carriage Service** (512/243-0044, www.austincarriage.com), **Angeli Carriages** (512/659-0591, www.acarriage.com), and **Die Gelbe Rose Carriage** (512/477-8824). The carriages are drawn by Belgian and Percheron horses and charge $100 per hour and $50 for half-hour tours. Carriages can always be seen around downtown, especially in the evenings. You can schedule a ride or just pick one up out front of the Driskill Hotel on 6th Street, or you can call and have one dispatched to a restaurant, nightclub, or wherever you are. Drivers can include narrative on the tours, but they are pleased to shut up if couples want a more romantic ride.

A new and unusual way of touring the town is on a Segway Personal Transporter (PT). **Gliding Revolution** (512/495-9250, www. glidingrevolution.com, $66 for a downtown tour) offers these two-wheel tours complete with Segway training and a standing jaunt through the downtown sights with a tour guide. If a tour of building facades and Lady Bird Lake is too mundane for you, consider going on the Ghost Tour for $59.

Adventure Tours

A brilliant idea has come to fruition with **Cypress Valley Canopy Tours** (1223 Paleface Ranch Rd., Spicewood, 512/264-8880, www.cypressvalleycanopytours.com). Out in the Hill Country in Spicewood, just 30 miles west of Austin, this outfit offers an adventure on wires high up in the trees. The tours include three sky bridges and six zip lines that land on tall platforms amid the trees. Guides prepare the adventurous by running them through a detailed orientation explaining the gear and the tour. Tours cost $75 per person. Reservations are necessary. Special rates are available for families, but children under 10 are not permitted. During the summer the facility is open every day except Monday, and in the fall and spring it's open only on weekends.

Food

In Austin, eating out is a pleasure and a pastime. There's an endless amount of breakfast tacos, barbecue brisket, microbrews, organic veggies, and confections waiting to be devoured, and it's "all good." Austin is chock-full of hundreds of eateries, many of which have their own unique story and funky spin on ambience and food, keeping in step with the town's flavor for weirdness. On occasion the gimmick of the restaurant is better than the food. Although you might think that a Texas town such as this would be all about meat and potatoes, Austin takes care of the herbivores too. In 2013 Paul McCartney himself awarded Austin for being the most accommodating city in the country for vegan diets. The former Beatle said, "The influx of forward-thinking musicians and techies, the thriving University, and the food trucks all over the city run by young veg-friendly hipsters have made Austin the absolute cutting-edge place for green eating."

One word of caution is offered: Your money goes a long way in Austin's eateries, making it easy to eat out until you either burn out on restaurants, burn a hole in your wallet, or simply explode. With the exception of fine dining, your average meal will cost somewhere between $10 and $15. Hours of most establishments are typical: Breakfast joints open around 6am, lunch is generally served 10:30am-4pm, and dinner happens 5pm-10pm, with some eateries staying open as late as midnight. So come hungry—all the eateries mentioned here are sure to satisfy.

AMERICAN AND DINERS

Austin is inundated with burger joints and diners that offer up hearty plates of American standards. Texas has proven that anything can be chicken fried and that acid reflux is a virtue. Due to Austin's love of health, there are some eateries that offer healthier versions of these standard plates. But let the salt pour, the oil flow, and the butter fry, 'cause it's all about

Food Truck Scene

Austin has fallen head over wheels for the new food truck craze. Carts, trucks, silver bullets, and even wagons are strategically set up all around town, making a variety of foods readily available. Besides amazing taco trucks, you can also find trucks that serve up Indian food, duck, *pho*, crepes, and even cupcakes. There are even a couple of farm-to-market trucks that specialize in fresh and organic foods. New carts are popping up everywhere, almost daily it seems. Although trucks can be found on sidewalks and street corners all over downtown, there are miniature food trailer parks on South Congress, South Lamar, South 1st, and on Red River just south of downtown. The best way to sample food truck cuisine is by attending Austin's festival dedicated to these mobile food vendors, **Gypsy Picnic Trailer Food Festival,** which takes place in the fall. It should be noted that most of these trailers don't serve alcohol, and some are BYOB establishments. Also, it's a good idea to show up with cash, not plastic. The best resource for food truck info, hours, maps, and reviews can be found online at www.austinfoodcarts.com. Here is a list of some local favorites.

- **East Side King** (1618½ E. 6th St. behind Liberty Bar and The Grackle, 512/407-8116) has unusual Asian fusion plates, such as fried beets, brussels sprout salad, and pork belly buns.

- **Four Brothers ATX** (2201 S. 1st St., 512/550-5650) serves arepas and other Venezuelan favorites in a parking lot with outdoor picnic tables.

- **Hey Cupcake** (1720 Barton Springs Rd. and 1511 S. Congress Ave., 512/476-2253) has—you guessed it—cupcakes!

- **Holy Cacao** (1311 S. 1st St., 512/851-2253) serves cake balls and other sweet stuff.

- **Kebabalicious** (1720 Barton Springs Rd. and W. 3rd St. at Congress Ave., 468-1065) has chicken, beef, and lamb kebabs and other Middle Eastern foods.

- **La Barbecue** (1906 E. Cesar Chavez St., 512/605-9696) is the best food truck for brisket, ribs, and barbecue sandwiches.

- **Not Your Mama's Food Truck** (2209 E. Cesar Chavez) features fancy fried comfort food.

- **Luke's Inside Out** (1109 S. Lamar Blvd., 512/589-8883) features globally influenced griddled sandwiches, like brisket banh mi and Szechuan chicken.

- **Torchy's Trailer Park** (1311 S. 1st St., 512/366-0537) is the best taco truck in town.

good old-fashioned sodium and cholesterol at some of these greasy spoons.

For the fickle person who has a hard time deciding what to eat, **Austin Java** (1206 Parkway at 12th and Lamar, 512/476-1829, 301 W. 2nd St., 512/481-9400, and 1608 Barton Springs Rd., 512/482-9450, www.austinjava. com, 7am-11pm Mon.-Fri., 8am-11pm Sat. and Sun., $10) has an eclectic menu that has something for everyone for either breakfast, lunch, or dinner. If after looking at the soups and salads you still can't decide what you want, you can piece together a lunch combo that suits your taste buds. Thai sesame salad,

smoked-gouda bacon burger, and Cajun-blackened crawfish pasta are among the favorites. Then there's the wide variety of organic coffees of various blends, flavors, and colors.

In Old North Austin everybody loves **Billy's** (2105 Hancock Dr. at Burnet Rd., 512/407-9305, 11am-midnight Mon.-Fri., 11am-1am Sat., noon-midnight Sun., $12). Here sports fans, neighborhood locals, and families can eat burgers, drink the best beers on tap, and see Billy sweeping the floor. Happy hour is 2pm-7pm Monday-Friday. There's also a huge deck outside, beer specials, a jukebox, and a pool table, and the game on TV.

For the cheapest meal in town there's **Dirty Martin's** (2808 Guadalupe St., 512/477-3173, 11am-11pm daily, $8). Dirty's is one of the older continuously owned and operated eateries in Austin. This doesn't necessarily mean that as with wine, the food at Dirty's is better with age. But the onion rings and fries are homemade, the hamburger meat is fresh, and the shakes and malts are terrific.

★ **Hoover's Cooking** (2002 Manor Rd., 512/479-5006, 11am-10pm Mon.-Fri., 8am-10pm Sat.-Sun., $12) is a classic place to eat barbecue on Sunday after church in East Austin. Hoover describes his cooking influence as "Home cooking—nicely seasoned vegetables, smoked foods, pan-fried dishes, and spicy foods with a nod toward Tex-Mex and Cajun." Hoover's has the best meatloaf in Austin and the Jamaican jerk chicken is sent from Jah. This is a popular brunch and breakfast spot so a wait may be necessary, but it's well worth it.

After going through many decades of transformations (from drive-in to Mexican to lounge), **Hut's Hamburgers** (807 W. 6th St., 512/472-0693, 11am-10pm daily, $12) finally settled on the American staple—hamburgers. There's a reason Hut's is always packed at mealtime. The menu is "outside the bun" with items such as the Ritchie Valens Burger: guacamole, grated cheese, chopped tomatoes, onions, and jalapeños. Their vintage/retro decor of seminude photos, pop memorabilia, sports heroes, and music posters only adds to this distinctive flavor.

Another burger joint that begs mention is **Hopdoddy Burger Bar** (1400 S. Congress Ave., 512/243-7505, 11am-11pm daily, $15) on South Congress Avenue. The focus of the menu is the perfection of pairing beer and burgers. The plates are sophisticated and creative, and the beer selection is high caliber. You must be forewarned though: The lines are super long to even get in the door, the wait is absurdly long, and the process to get the food is not conventional. Patience is required for all the above, but it's worth the hassle. Favorite burgers are The Greek, Buffalo Bill, and The Diablo (hot and spicy), and the truffle fries are amazing.

Magnolia Cafe (2304 Lake Austin Blvd., 512/478-8645, and 1920 S. Congress Ave., 512/445-0000, http://themagnoliacafe.com, 24 hours daily, $10) is a good bet for a good dish any time of the day or night. Great breakfasts, hamburgers, sandwiches, soups, and salads, as well as some Tex-Mex dishes, can be ordered any time, as this is Austin's best 24-hour grub facilitator.

The best milk shake in town happens to be in an inconspicuous establishment—the pharmacy. Decades ago **Nau's Enfield Drug** (1115 W. Lynn St., 512/476-1221, 7:30am-8pm Mon.-Fri., 8am-7pm Sat., $8) was the place to get a burger, a shake, and your prescriptions, and nothing has changed in the past half a century.

The hamburger is one of the world's most profound culinary creations. It is inexpensive yet rich with flavor, it is globally accepted yet markedly strange in how it is made, how it is eaten, and what it tastes like. I have no fear in going out on a limb by saying that Austin is home to the world's greatest hamburger. It is cooked up at a burger joints scattered around town called **P. Terry's** (404 S. Lamar Blvd., 512/473-2217, 3303 N. Lamar Blvd., 512/371-9975, 11am-11pm daily, $8). The owner opened his first burger stand near Barton Springs after reading the book *Fast Food Nation*. The burger is simple and old-fashioned, and made of 100 percent all-natural Black Angus beef and all-natural ingredients. The focus here is simplicity, quality, and taste, so don't expect a flashy menu. The architecture for each P. Terry's location is unique, retro, and pretty cool.

The crossroads of Louisiana and Texas is on North Lamar at **Shoal Creek Saloon** (909 N. Lamar Blvd., 512/474-0805, 11am-midnight daily, $12). This sports bar was transformed when chef Bud George moved in from Louisiana, bringing with him authentic Cajun cuisine. Gumbos, fried catfish, crawfish étouffée, oysters, and hush puppies flow like the bayou. Wait—does the bayou flow? Daily specials are a great value, and happy hour is 11am-7pm Monday-Friday.

At **South Congress Cafe** (1600 S. Congress Ave., 512/447-3905, 10am-4pm and 5pm-10pm daily, $13) the approach to things is minimalist. They don't believe in dramatic decor, fancy signs and logos, or anything of a commercial nature. They simply offer quality food and service in a modern, sophisticated atmosphere. Items on the menu vary from crab cakes to pan-seared tuna salad, which sounds expensive, but don't be deceived by the fancy-sounding menu—it's affordable.

Star Seeds Cafe (3101 N. I-35, 512/478-7107, 24 hours daily, $7) is one of those places in town that completely personifies Austin. This 24-hour joint has no pretense, just past tense, as it seems to be frozen in time. Here you can eat greasy, nothing-fresh diner food, such as sandwiches, burgers, nachos, and breakfast. Effortlessly funky and offbeat, Stars is a great place to eat after waking up at noon, without showering or brushing your teeth.

If you've just finished a tour of the Texas State Capitol and you're fixin' to eat, stroll down the street to the ★ **Texas Chili Parlor** (1409 Lavaca St., 512/472-2828, 11am-2am daily, $10). This sports bar is where Texas politicians, UT students, and UT sports fans converge to enjoy a beer and some food. Obviously it is known for the chili, which comes in three variations of spiciness: X for mild, XX for medium, and XXX for habanero hell. They may even make you sign a release form when you order the XXX. Note for non-Texans: There are no beans in Texas chili, just meat and sauce.

One restaurant that is a historic landmark in its own right is **Threadgill's Home Cooking** (301 W. Riverside Dr., 512/472-9304, 11am-10pm Mon.-Thurs., 11am-10:30pm Fri.-Sat., 10am-9:30pm Sun., $12). Founded in 1933 by bootlegger Kenneth Threadgill after obtaining the county's first alcohol license, this down-home kitchen became a local favorite for hootenannies and old-time cookin'. In the 1960s, Threadgill's was one of Austin's

cultural epicenters for live music. Hippies and rednecks alike would converge here to watch the cultural revolution go down. It's said that Janis Joplin even developed her unique singing style here. As for the down-home cooking, it's just like granny makes it—lots of butter and oil, meat and potatoes, sodium and white bread. Threadgill's is especially famous for its meatloaf, chicken-fried chicken, and chicken-fried steak.

Upper Crust Bakery and Cafe (4508 Burnet Rd., 512/467-0102, 6:30am-6:30pm Mon.-Fri., 7am-5pm Sat., 7am-1pm Sun., $7) serves gorgeous baked goods and sandwiches. You don't have to take my word for it; the *Austin American-Statesman* ranked the avocado sandwich one of the top 10 sandwiches in Austin. This is easily the best place in town for any kind of sandwich.

BARBECUE, STEAK, AND SAUSAGE

Eating meat in Austin can be a profoundly gluttonous experience. At many barbecue joints you order brisket by the pound, choose from a selection of sides such as coleslaw, beans, and potato salad, and eat it all off butcher paper. This approach to eating can pose a hazard to those whose eyes are bigger than their stomachs. Texans love their beef, and you will too at the following restaurants.

Austin Land and Cattle Co. (1205 N. Lamar Blvd., 512/472-1813, 5:30pm-10pm Sun.-Thurs., 5:30pm-11pm Fri.-Sat., $30) is Austin's most popular steak house. Although the menu offers enough choices for everyone (except the vegetarian), people come here for beef. It can be served up in many different ways, but the best is the 22-ounce bone-in rib eye or sirloin cooked medium rare. The white stucco walls and exposed-beam ceiling make for a comfortable environment. The staff knows the menu and can guide you through your beef-eating experience. As for the sides, they tend to be a notch above your average steak house, such as baby spinach leaves sautéed in olive oil and carrots julienne. The portions are so big you might as well ask for a to-go bag when you order.

★ **Banger's Sausage House & Beer Garden** (79 Rainey St., 512/386-1656, 4pm-11pm Mon.-Wed., 11am-2am Thurs.-Sat., 11am-2am Sun., $13) is a must-eat Austin establishment. Here are a few things that make a perfect Austin dining experience: exotic game sausages and a wall of beer on tap, all consumed under trees on picnic tables. This is the only place where you can sample unusual sausages such as wild boar, duck, bacon and fig, and the flavorful "currywurst." Jalapeño mac-and-cheese is a pleasant surprise too. Every weekend a random event takes place, like yodeling, baton twirling, or pig roasting. And here's a tip for the late-night partiers: If you're out on the town and it's 11pm and you decide you're hungry, this place is profoundly satisfying.

If you have a car to get there, the **County Line BBQ Restaurant** (5204 FM 2222, 512/346-3664, 11:30am-2pm and 5pm-9pm daily, $14) is a terrific spot on Bull Creek near Lake Austin that feels rural but is close to town. The waterfront patio looks out onto limestone cliffs and dense tree cover. After chowing down on great barbecue everyone will have a blast feeding the ducks and turtles that come right up to the dock. The food is a little pricy but very tasty.

In South Austin there's **Green Mesquite** (1400 Barton Springs Rd., 512/479-0485, 11am-10pm Sun.-Thurs., 11am-11pm Fri.-Sat., $10). Standard, inexpensive barbecue, burgers, and some Cajun food are what's on offer at this staple Austin lunch and dinner joint. It's near Zilker Park and has a friendly staff, a relaxed atmosphere, and live music on Friday, Saturday, and Sunday nights. This is a good place for families with children.

Fancy and barbecue usually are a contradiction in terms. However, ★ **Lamberts** (401 W. 2nd St., 512/494-1500, lunch 11am-2:30pm Mon.-Fri., dinner 5:30pm-10pm Sun.-Wed. and 5:30pm-10:30pm Thurs.-Sat., brunch Sat.-Sun. 11am-2pm, $12) has concocted a combination that works. A location in the

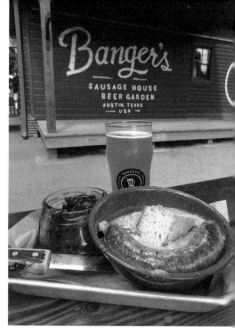

Banger's creative sausage plates have to be paired with a locally made beer.

up-and-coming 2nd Street shopping district makes Lamberts an easy springboard for a night on the town. Besides barbecue, chefs Louis Lambert and Larry McGuire have put together some classic dishes in true Austin form—casual but classy—such as steak and seafood with family-style sides accompanied by locally made microbrews.

Downtown Austin has been in dire need of a kick-ass barbecue joint. **Franklin Barbecue** (900 E. 11th St., 512/653-1187, 11am-1pm Tues.-Sun., $10) has risen out of the food truck/trailer trend to deliver the best cracked-peppercorn brisket and ribs in central Austin. The founder started as a Texas kid helping out with his dad's barbecue joint, then did the trailer thing, and now has a wildly successful restaurant going. The brisket slices are thick and the pork ribs are salty with the right amount of large cracked pepper chunks. The ribs are so tender you don't have to roll up your sleeves and get messy to eat 'em. Just pull the meat off with your plastic fork. The vibe in here is unpretentious but with the right amount of retro to be comfortable, the music is old country classics playing loud, and local Live Oak beers are on draft. There's only one drawback: Franklin is only open until it sells out of food. Most days this happens by 1pm.

There's also **Iron Works** (100 Red River St., 512/478-4855, 11am-9pm Mon.-Sat., $9), a local favorite for barbecue. Set in a historic iron shop, this is the one meat joint where you can counterbalance all the beef with all-you-can-eat salad.

Nearly every barbecue spot in the state has a shingle out front that claims, "Best BBQ in Texas." But **Rudy's Country Store and BBQ** (2451 Capital of Texas Hwy., 512/329-5554, and 11570 Research Blvd., 512/418-9898, 7am-9:30pm daily, $10) gladly proclaims "The Worst Bar-B-Q in Texas." Don't be fooled by this slogan and the fact that Rudy's is a chain, albeit a small Texas franchise. The barbecue is fabulous and the beans are musical. No dishes required—just fingers, a fork, and the need for beef. After fully glutted, wash your hands and face in the industrial-size kitchen sink in the dining room.

The area's best barbecue is provided by ★ **The Salt Lick** (18300 FM 1826, Driftwood, 512/858-4959, 11am-10pm daily, $15). It's so far out of town that it's in another town, but that shouldn't stop you from enjoying an Austin tradition. Eating here is one of the great experiences Central Texas has to offer. Here's why: It's located in an old limestone ranch house, the recipe is ancient, the barbecue pit is the dining room, you bring your own alcohol, and the barbecue is brutally good. The menu also offers sausage, turkey, ribs, the usual sides, white bread, and those pickles that every barbecue restaurant seems to have. Warning: There is no air-conditioning. For some this adds to the appeal, but for those who fear perspiration it can ruin their day. Otherwise, sit in front of the fan, relax, and eat beef. Salt Lick accepts only cash, so be sure to bring greenbacks if you plan to drive all the way out there.

In the downtown area there's **Stubb's Bar-B-Q** (801 Red River St., 512/480-8341, 11am-10pm Tues.-Wed., 11am-11pm Thurs.-Sat., 11am-9pm Sun., $12). Yes, this is the establishment behind the famed Stubb's barbecue sauce. Christopher Stubblefield founded the first Stubb's restaurant in Lubbock, Texas, where he combined good live music and barbecue. Perfect combo! Artists such as Johnny Cash, John Lee Hooker, and Muddy Waters would "play for their supper." Stubblefield eventually moved to Austin, bringing with him his concept of live music and barbecue. Today Stubb's Bar-B-Q is one of Austin's premier live music venues and still serves up great barbecue.

BREAKFAST & BRUNCH

A true Austin breakfast experience can be had at historic **Threadgill's Home Cooking** (301 W. Riverside Dr., 512/472-9304, 11am-10pm Mon.-Thurs., 11am-10:30pm Fri.-Sat., 10am-9:30pm Sun., $12). The breakfast menu is as down-home as you can get, featuring lots of butter and oil, meat and potatoes, and pancakes and eggs in an all-American atmosphere. Breakfast on Sunday is highly recommended, as there is a live gospel band in the back serving up classic hymns.

The **Omelettry** (4631 Airport Blvd #131A, 512/453-5062, 7am-5pm daily, $8) is one of Austin's best-kept secrets. Slackers, students, old-timers, and young families have chosen it as the best place to start a weekend morning. It's a no-frills restaurant that specializes in tasty omelets and pancakes that prove that crepes are just too flat. Don't expect flashy decor or bells and whistles, just great breakfast food.

One of the top picks of a former U.S. president is ★ **Moonshine Patio Bar and Grill** (303 Red River St., 512/236-9599, 11am-10pm Mon.-Thurs., 11am-11pm Fri.-Sat., 10am-10pm Sun., $14). Popular for making typical American fare classy and a little pricy, Moonshine is always a hub of important folks. Although this is a great spot for dinner, Austin's best Sunday brunch can be found here. The buffet tables are chock-full of every breakfast food imaginable, all cooked to please those with a refined appetite. There's southwestern-style eggs, sausage links, waffles, buckets of fruit, smoked salmon, goodies from the bakery, and jugs of sauces and syrups. It's pricy, but darn worth it.

Local favorite mini diner is the notch in the wall that is **Counter Café** (626 N. Lamar Blvd., 512/708-8800, 7:30am-4pm daily, $12). The name says it all: It's literally one long, very narrow counter with café/diner food. Seating is limited, which makes for a cozy and/or claustrophobic dining experience. Food here is fancier than your average greasy spoon. Although all-day breakfast is always good, they are nationally known for their cheeseburger. Be warned that street parking can be challenging.

The local favorite for Mexican breakfast, brunch, and lunch is **Juan in a Million** (2300 E. Cesar Chavez St., 512/472-3872, 7am-3pm daily, $8). The experience at this hole-in-the-wall (said with deep affection) begins with a greeting at the door from Juan himself. You then take a seat and order, but before you do, understand that everything here is huge and heaping. If you're thinking this place is familiar, it landed on the map when Adam Richman of *Man v. Food* was unable to eat eight of the breakfast tacos. Remember, I said they were heaping.

MEXICAN

Austin is only 250 miles from the border, giving the town a great advantage over most places for serving up excellent Mexican as well as creative variations on south-of-the-border foods. These variations need some clarification. First, there's good old-fashioned Mexican food, which is rice, beans, tacos, enchiladas, chopped beef, chicken, and salsa. Second, there's Texas's version of Mexican, called Tex-Mex. All you do is add catfish to the enchiladas, corn to the rice, and smoke to the salsa. Finally, there's a new hybrid that has emerged, which I call gringo-Mex. This is an upscale Mexican and Tex-Mex combination where you "encrust" the enchiladas, "sear" the meats, add citrus to the sauces, and

charge more. Think Pancho Villa but replace the bandolier with a silk scarf.

East Austin's best place for upscale Mexican is ★ **El Chile** (1809 Manor Rd., 512/457-9900, 11am-10pm Mon.-Sat., 11am-9pm Sun., $12). The food is very sophisticated gringo-Mex. Everything on the menu is well crafted, from the smoky salsa that's so tasty I wish they had it on IV drip, to their signature spicy, orange-infused margaritas (the best in town); El Chile is worthy of high accolades. Although it's upscale, the atmosphere is casual. Happy hour is 4pm-7pm. Parking is kitty-corner from the restaurant.

For more casual and affordable Mexican, El Chile opened up a small taco shop, **El Cilito** (2219 Manor Rd., 512/382-3797, $6), just down the street. It offers street versions of El Chile's award-winning food. This place is great for takeout or relaxing in the outdoor covered patio. No indoor seating means no air-conditioning. Braised pork and carne asada tacos are top menu picks.

While on South Congress, after a day of shopping for retro clothes and antiques, stop off at the best Mexican/Tex-Mex restaurant in Austin: ★ **Güero's Taco Bar** (1412 S. Congress Ave., 512/447-7688, 11am-11pm Mon.-Fri., 8am-11pm Sat.-Sun., $15). In 1994 the old Central Feed & Seed building was transformed into this fabulous taqueria. The aged brick walls are adorned with giant photos from the Mexican Revolution. The dining is casual, the handmade corn tortillas are excellent, and the margaritas are a local favorite. The portions are hearty, and the food, such as the shrimp fajitas, is truly mind-blowing. Let's not forget the self-serve salsa bar, which is a crucial part of the experience. Former president Bill Clinton loved this restaurant—hence his favorite dish is called the El Presidente. It should be noted that Güero's also successfully wears two hats: one is for Mexican food (a sombrero), and the other is for an excellent live music venue (a cowboy hat). Next door they have a great casual outdoor stage and bar with free live music.

mouthwatering combinations such as the Jamaican jerk chicken taco. Their most popular plates are the green chili pork tacos and the Trailer Park, which is fried chicken with pico de gallo. They are also famous for amazing breakfast tacos heaped with cheese and bits of bacon, and *migas* (Mexican-style scrambled eggs) tacos. For SXSW folks Torchy's is the morning hangover cure.

Everybody's favorite breakfast taco comes from **Maria's Taco Express** (2529 S. Lamar Blvd., 512/444-0261, 7am-3pm Mon., 7am-3pm Tues.-Fri., 8am-3pm Sat., 9am-4pm Sun., $8). Now run by Maria's son, this taco shack has become legendary for its cheap Mexican fare, fast service, and friendly neighborhood clientele. During SXSW Maria's is overtaken by musicians and fans who come here to start off their day. Although Maria's is the best place to go in the morning with a hangover, it also serves up great Mexican dishes for lunch and dinner.

The beautiful hacienda setting makes **Matt's El Rancho** (2613 S. Lamar Blvd., 512/462-9333, 11am-10pm Sun.-Mon. and Wed.-Thurs., 11am-11pm Fri.-Sat., $13) a safe bet for Mexican for the family. It's one of the older Mexican restaurants, as it's been in business since 1952. The food gets passionately mixed reviews, yet the restaurant has been an Austin tradition for decades. Try the Bob Armstrong dip, steak *tampiqueña*, and a margarita.

A great way to enjoy 6th Street and Mexican food in the early evening hours is by rooftop dining at **Iron Cactus** (606 Trinity St., 512/472-9240, 11am-11pm Mon.-Sat., 10am-10:30pm Sun., $15). Out on the second-level balcony the view of the hustle and bustle of Austin's famous street is unmatched. This popular upscale Mexican grill doubles as a tequila bar with a mind-numbing array of specialty drinks and creative Mexican dishes. Eat pulled pork and shrimp enchiladas and enjoy spicy tequila, in an ambience of sirens from the street below, under the glow of the city's neon skyline. Yes, better Mexican food can be found elsewhere in town, but the experience and location are unmatched.

Güero's Taco Bar

The closest you can come to having Mexican food on a beach is at **Takoba** (1411 E. 7th St., 512/628-4466, 11am-10pm Mon.-Fri., 10am-10 Sat.-Sun., $11) in East Austin. Yes, there is a beach in the side yard—or should I say large sandbox. The food is fresh authentic Mexican with homemade chips, creative drinks (white sangria), and some of the best fish tacos around. The ambience is a little polished and gringo, but makes for a pleasant environment for a friendly lunch or dinner.

South Austin's **Polvos** (2004 S. 1st St., 512/441-5446, 7am-11pm daily, $10) is famous for build-your-own enchiladas, its salsa bar, and margarita pitchers. The atmosphere is loud, and the patio is big, which can be fun for some and overwhelming for others. Parking and wait times can be tricky, so plan ahead.

★ **Torchy's Tacos** (2801 Guadalupe St., 512/494-8226, and 1311 S. 1st St., 512/366-0537, 1822 S. Congress Ave., 512/916-9025, $7) started out as a food truck on South 1st Street. They have the predictable tacos and burritos, along with a more creative menu that features

TEX-MEX AND SOUTHWESTERN

Near the capitol is popular lunch spot **Arturo's Bakery and Cafe** (314 W. 17th St., 512/469-0380, 7am-2:30pm Mon.-Fri., 10am-12pm Sat., 10am-3pm Sun., $8). Don't let *bakery* or *café* in the name fool you, as this place is much more than either. The fare is reliable southwestern/Tex-Mex and some American items. This basement restaurant looks like a New York loft, with modern art hanging on brick walls and a hip clientele. With low-key but hip decor and a diverse yet affordable menu, Arturo's has become a favorite downtown breakfast and lunch spot.

For Tex-Mex with a thrift-store Elvis flair, **Chuy's** (1728 Barton Springs Rd., 512/474-4452, 11am-10pm Sun.-Thurs., 11am-11pm Fri.-Sat., $12) will make your hips shake. The first thing one sees when entering Chuy's is a grandiose shrine to Elvis built into the entrance. From this point on it's all an experience. Yes, this establishment is heavy with gimmick, with its ceiling covered in hubcaps and fish and its retro/Salvation Army decor, but the food is great and the service is fast. They're famous for their handmade tortillas, fajitas, margaritas, overstuffed enchiladas, and Mexi-Cobb salad. Order their charro beans instead of refried.

Trying to place some food establishments in a particular category can be tricky. **Freebirds World Burrito** (515 S. Congress Ave., 512/462-3512, and 1000 E. 41st St., 512/451-5514, 11am-10:30pm Sun.-Thurs., 11am-10pm Fri.-Sat., $7) is free of categorization. It's not Mexican, it's not Tex-Mex, it's not American, and it's definitely not Eritrean, but it is good, filling, and cheap. This place was built with spare parts from a Harley-Davidson, your local Mexican joint, Whole Foods, and of course, the remaining members of Lynyrd Skynyrd. If you don't like what you eat, it's your fault, because you build your own burritos, tacos, and wraps here.

★ **Shady Grove Restaurant** (1624 Barton Springs Rd., 512/474-9991, 11am-10pm

Tex-Mex at Chuy's is an essential Austin experience.

Sun.-Thurs., 11am-11pm Fri.-Sat., $14) is one of the best places in town to dine al fresco. A stylized 1950s theme mixes with reliably good Tex-Mex, American, and health-nut fare. This place can get extremely crowded, so go when you have time to wait for a table. Have a beverage, enjoy the outdoors, and watch the beautiful people. Through the summer months Shady Grove is a great spot to see top-notch local musicians perform for the "Unplugged at the Grove" concert series presented by local radio station KGSR.

With a friendly environment that is light on the gimmick and heavy on taste, **Z'Tejas Southwestern Grill** (1110 W. 6th St., 512/478-5355, 11am-10pm Mon.-Thurs., 11am-11pm Fri., 10am-11pm Sat., 10am-10pm Sun., $12) is the eatery extraordinaire of Austin. A culinary zenith can be reached by sitting outside under the trellises on a sunny afternoon while eating their famous blackened-catfish enchiladas, stuffed pork tenderloin, crab-stuffed chicken, diablo chicken pasta, or virtually anything on the menu. After a big meal at Z'Tejas, walk down the street to the Treaty Oak and ponder the venerable tree's history.

ITALIAN

The genuine Italian food experience must have big tables, Italian songs tableside, oversized bowls of noodles, olives, cheerful waiters in white, wine, and lots of family. One might think this would be hard to find in Texas, but it's possible at the following Italian eateries.

One of the best places to eat in the Hyde Park area is **Asti** (408C E. 43rd St., 512/451-1218, 11am-10pm Mon.-Thurs., 11am-10:30pm Fri., 5pm-10:30pm Sat., $12). This popular lunch and dinner spot looks like it was decorated by a graphic designer, not an Italian grandmother. Here you'll find classy versions of the Italian favorites, such as salmon and goat cheese pizza and penne with grilled chicken and spinach, along with a great wine list and the best fried calamari this side of the Colorado River. The best part about Asti? This upscale menu has great prices.

The best upmarket pizza in town is at the **Brick Oven** (1209 Red River St., 512/477-7006, and 10710 Research Blvd., 512/345-6181, 11am-9pm Mon.-Sat., 5pm-9pm Sun., $18). The core of this casual family restaurant is the 100-year-old brick oven and the smoky thin-crust pizzas it produces. The crust is infused with "special ingredients" that the proprietors will not reveal. This lends to an amazing, soft, flavorful crust that is unparalleled in Austin. The menu also offers lasagna, chicken formaggi, ravioli, pasta primavera, and calzones. Being close to the capitol, 6th Street, and the UT campus makes Brick Oven an easy, safe pick for lunch or dinner.

A great place to bring the family is **Frank and Angie's Pizzeria** (598 West Ave., 512/472-3534, 11am-9:30pm Mon.-Thurs., 11am-10pm Fri., noon-10pm Sat., 5pm-9:30pm Sun., $12). This downtown establishment has bizarre murals, Frank Sinatra memorabilia, and a patio overlooking Shoal Creek. Two-for-one specials are offered on Monday and Tuesday. The themed menu includes gourmet pizzas, pasta, calzones, and salads, all prepared well and at great prices.

If you're on South Congress Avenue and "the moon hits your eye like a big pizza pie," make your way to ★ **Home Slice Pizza** (1415 S. Congress Ave., 512/444-7437, 11am-11pm Sun.-Thurs., 11am-3am Fri.-Sat., $8). This innovative pizzeria has mastered the art of interior decorating for the trendy crowd. Luckily, it's also mastered the world's most popular Italian dish. What makes this place so fabulous is that it's a great place to hang out with friends: They have Italian wines, a couple of beers on tap, and an upbeat environment. While waiting for the pie to cook kids can play with pizza dough. Just ask your server.

The downtown Italian food scene is dominated by **La Traviata** (314 Congress Ave., 512/479-8131, 11:30am-2pm and 5pm-10pm Mon.-Fri., 5:30pm-10:30pm Sat., $15). During the day La Traviata is a popular business lunch spot, and at night it becomes a place for romance. Wine connoisseurs will be pleased to find there's an extensive wine list here, and fans of exquisite Italian dishes will be thrilled by the creative but traditional menu. It's a bit pricy, but worth it. Note for non-opera people—it's named after one of the best Italian operas of all time.

A popular family-style Italian restaurant north of the UT campus area is **Mandola's Italian Market** (4700 W. Guadalupe St. #12, 512/419-9700, $12). Decked with fake Italian signs, plastic slabs of meat, and beadboard walls, Mandola's has authentic Italian food served amid bustling ambience. The lasagna is a personal favorite. Other menu items include gnocchi with meat sauce and chicken parmesan. After a super-unhealthy meal one can mosey over to the gelato bar or buy some imported Italian food—the market at the front of the store isn't just for looks.

Rounders Pizzeria (1203 W. 6th St., 512/477-0404, 11:30am-10pm Sun.-Thurs., 11am-11:30pm Fri.-Sat., $12) has received an award for best pizza many times since its inception in 2002. This Las Vegas-themed pizzeria serves a special pie with unique presentation and a smile. The crust is crunchy, which soft-crust pizza fans won't admire. Besides pizza, Rounder's serves up classic arcade games such as Galaga and Ms. Pac-Man.

OTHER INTERNATIONAL FOOD

★ **Clay Pit** (1601 Guadalupe St., 512/322-5131, 11am-2pm and 5pm-10pm Mon.-Thurs., 11am-2pm and 5pm-11pm Fri., noon-3pm and 5pm-11pm Sat., $12) is one of America's best Indian food restaurants, according to *Bon Appétit* magazine, and I am in full agreement! This five-star restaurant serves contemporary Indian cuisine in a sophisticated atmosphere. The orgy of flavors includes several curries, naan, and tandoori dishes. Although this is a great spot for dinner, the affordable lunch buffet brings in hordes of folks looking for a bargain for top-notch Indian. Clay Pit is affordable yet upscale, which makes it a perfect place for any type of occasion.

Imagine sitting at a table near a lake, drinking mango margaritas and eating pupu, all in the presence of the Polynesian tiki gods. **Hula Hut** (3825 Lake Austin Blvd., 512/476-4852, 11am-10pm Sun.-Thurs., 11am-11pm Fri.-Sat., $10), situated on the banks of Lake Austin, is a world unto itself. The atmosphere is festive, especially on weekends when the weather is nice. The cuisine is a "unique mix of Mexican and Polynesian, otherwise known as Mexonesian." Getting into specifics, this means dishes such as Thai barbecue fajitas and mango poblano chili quesadillas. Sitting outside is an absolute must.

Madam Mam's (2514 Guadalupe St., 512/472-8306, and 4514 W. Gate Blvd., 512/899-8525, 11am-10pm daily, $10) brings the noodle to Austin in an affordable and reliable way. Although the core of this place is Thai cuisine, with dishes such as pad thai, you can also order curry dishes with tangy lime and Chinese mushrooms. The versatility of the menu and the good prices make Madam Mam's a great place to come with friends before a night on the town.

If you suddenly find yourself completely bored with food and flavor, and if nothing seems to tickle your palate anymore, I recommend going on a food adventure to Phoenician Resto Café (84 N. Interstate 35 Frontage Rd, 512/712-5904, 11am-10pm Mon.-Thurs., 11am-11pm Sat., 11am-9pm Sun., $10). This place is all about spice exploration, savory meats, soups, and sandwiches that will render anyone speechless. This Mediterranean café offers a healthy menu with variations of hummus, chicken, lamb, and veggies, all surprisingly inexpensive.

Locals with diverse palates love to eat under the freeway at **Aster's Ethiopian** (2804 N. I-35, 512/469-5966, 11am-9pm daily, $9). The tender beef and greens mixed with lentils is super filling. With a wide variety of vegetarian and meat dishes, this is a great low-key place to bring a few friends and sample a variety of tasty and healthy dishes. The lunch buffet is all-you-can-eat, so be careful.

★ **Thai Kitchen** (3009 Guadalupe St., 512/474-2575, 11am-midnight Mon.-Thurs., 11am-1am Fri., noon-2am Sat., noon-midnight Sun., $12) simply has to be mentioned when expounding on Austin's Asian cuisine options. A popular place for both people and pigeons, Thai Kitchen has consistently been rated the best Thai restaurant by the *Austin Chronicle*. The food is surprisingly expensive for a dive Thai joint, but it's worth it. The Thai tea (often mispronounced as tai chi or chai tea) summons contentment and pleasure.

The healthiest and tastiest meal on a shoestring is at **Zen** (3423 Guadalupe St., 512/300-2633, and 1303 S. Congress Ave., 512/444-8081, 11am-9:30pm Mon.-Sat., 11:30am-9pm Sun., $8). Their motto is "Japanese Food Fast." It may be fast, but it's healthier than fast food. What can beat four-piece California rolls for $3 or a bowl of spicy chicken with noodles for $5? And what beats sushi prepared by gringos? The restaurants are clean, the decor is modern, and the concept is brilliant.

For a unique indoor/outdoor Indian food dining experience try **G'Raj Mahal** (73

Whole Foods

Well before eating healthy and organic was trendy, Austin was a center for everything all-natural. People are always surprised to hear that this Texas town was the place where organic supermarket giant Whole Foods got its start back in 1980. At the time there were fewer than half a dozen natural-food supermarkets in the United States. These stores were pricy and relegated to the hippie fringes of our society. Thanks to the popularity of eating organic, the profile of healthy foods has become accessible to all. Whole Foods may still be pricy, but food tastes so much better when it hasn't been genetically modified, manipulated, and bleached to death.

The Whole Foods corporate headquarters is above the **flagship store** (525 N. Lamar Blvd.) at the corner of Lamar and 6th Street, west of downtown Austin. Folks from out of town are consistently bedazzled, enamored, and overwhelmed by the sheer quantity and quality of the products here. If you're in the neighborhood it's suggested you poke your head in and look around. Or better yet, stay and have lunch.

Rainey St., 512/480-2255, 5pm-10pm Mon., 11am-midnight Tues.-Thurs., 11am-1am Sat.-Sun., $15), tucked away in the Rainey Street District just south of 6th Street. Here you can dine in tents with stylish pillows and aromas that transport you far from Texas. Traditional fresh Indian plates are flying out of the tandoor oven.

HEALTHY AND VEGETARIAN

Being the Berkeley of Texas, Austin has some great fare for the health nut, vegetarian, and vegan. Many of these establishments have been around for a long time and are tried and true. Remember, Paul McCartney himself awarded Austin for being the most accommodating city in the country for vegan diets—and for good reason!

In East Austin there's **The Eastside Cafe** (2113 Manor Rd., 512/476-5858, 11:15am-9:30pm Mon.-Thurs., 11:15am-10pm Fri.-Sat., 10am-9:30pm Sun., $10), which has its own vegetable garden on-site, meaning extraordinarily fresh produce graces the plates. Patrons have the choice of eating in the soothing garden room or the classy antique interior of a converted bungalow. Delicious menu options include baked brie with chutney, sesame catfish, and salmon dumplings with coconut curry sauce. On weekends, an extremely popular brunch is offered 10am-3pm

with scrumptious choices like apple almond waffles and smoked salmon Benedict. It's wise to make a reservation, especially on the weekends.

South Austin's morning-all-day, breakfast-all-day hangout is ★ **Bouldin Creek Coffee House** (1900 S. 1st St., 512/416-1601, 7am-midnight Mon.-Fri., 9am-midnight Sat.-Sun. $9). The previous location was basically a shack chock-full of Austin's weirdest. Now Bouldin has officially entered the mainstream, and to me this is a good thing. The food is fantastic, and the vibe is electric with artists, students, and shoe gazers getting jacked on coffee. Along with scrambled tofu or eggs, the menu includes some creative plates that are uniquely hippie Tex-Mex. Examples: tofu chorizo tacos, hummus, gluten-free offerings, and the Slacker's Banquet. Most of the menu is or can be made vegan.

A great choice for healthy food for everyone is **Kerbey Lane** (3704 Kerbey Ln., 512/451-1436; near UT campus at 2606 Guadalupe St., 512/477-5717; and in south Austin at 2700 S. Lamar Blvd., 512/445-4451, 24 hours daily, $8). Here you can have vegetarian fare and your friends can have meat if they prefer. Expect locally grown, organic, pesticide-free vegetables and free-range beef and pork, prepared with precision. Kerbey Lane is known for its excellent queso, salads, and unusual entrées. All this is available 24 hours a day.

Mother's Cafe and Garden (4215 Duval St., 512/451-3994, 11:15am-10pm Mon.-Fri., 10am-10pm Sat.-Sun., $9) is the oldest and probably the best. All dishes are prepared with the highest-quality ingredients and without any meat products. Many items on the menu can be prepared vegan as well. The food is so good here that the skeptic of vegetarian fare is sure to forget that the food is vegetarian. The owners take great pride in the eclectic menu choices, which range from enchiladas to stir-fry to quiche.

For pauper vegetarians and nonvegetarians broadening their horizons, **Veggie Heaven** (1611 W. 5th St. #135, 512/457-1013, 11am-9pm Mon.-Fri., noon-9pm Sat.-Sun., $6) offers up a fresh, Asian-based vegetarian menu that's quite overwhelming. Most dishes have tex-tured vegetable protein or tofu, and they're so well put together even carnivores can walk away satisfied. This sunken little restaurant is popular, and usually so packed the windows are completely steamed up. Oh wait—maybe that's just grime. Service is curt and to the point, but it's hard to complain because it's so cheap.

If you are vegetarian or vegan, and you're on the verge of backsliding, quickly make haste to **Mr. Natural** (1901 E. Cesar Chavez St., 512/477-5228, 8am-8pm Mon.-Sat., $6). This humble restaurant in East Austin is nondescript, but don't pass it over. Vegetarian and vegan Mexican has been perfected by Mr. Natural. Each intelligently designed plate is filled to the brim with all-natural ingredients and flavors. Besides great vegan meals, Mr. Natural also has a vegan bakery, with sweets such as tofu cheesecake and tres leches cake (a brilliant contradiction!). Mr. Natural is sure to seduce any questioning vegan back to the healthy side.

FINE DINING

Of the five senses we humans are equipped with, the one that is the most finicky to please is the sense of taste. Luckily, fine dining in Austin satisfies, with open kitchens, chef hats, long wine lists, Texas-style hospitality, and brilliant tastes whose origins you can't quite pin down.

True to Austin's laissez-faire approach to everything, most fine-dining establishments have no dress expectations. In fact most high-end restaurants don't even want to be classified as "fine dining"; they just want you to be comfortable and enjoy the ride. Plan on bringing plenty of money because the ride can be pricy.

Austin's most enduring high-end restau-rant is the ★ **Driskill Bar and Grill** (604 Brazos St., 512/391-7162, 5:30pm-10pm Tues.-Sat., $40), located inside the Driskill Hotel. The Driskill has been winning awards for years. The interior is dark and Victorian with a rich Texas flair. Popular among the city's elite, such as musicians, politicians, actors, and local celebrities, the Driskill has mastered fine dining. Chef David Bull has developed a three-course menu that includes duck, seared foie gras, baked Alaska halibut, and tender-loin. Here you can find nothing but the very best in service and taste. The Driskill is a per-fect place to start a romantic evening, followed by a horse-drawn carriage ride.

The tradition of Southern hospitality and fine dining has been well maintained for de-cades at **Green Pastures** (811 W. Live Oak St., 512/444-1888, 11am-2pm and 6pm-10pm daily, $30). South Austin's best-kept secret, this large estate features ancient oaks and an old Victorian house. In the 1950s the house was converted into a restaurant for Austin's elite. Eating here is like being a guest in a grand Southern home. Sip wine and savor small portions of artistically presented French-inspired gourmet cuisine, while look-ing around at all the antiques, pictures, and manicured lawns with peacocks. Reservations are highly recommended, as the place quickly fills up.

When you see the giant fork in the sky you know you have arrived at **Hyde Park Bar and Grill** (4206 Duval St., 512/458-3168, 11am-midnight daily, $18). The interior is swank, the staff is professional, and all meat products are organic. The cows may not be drinking fine wine and getting massages, but they are range fed and hormone-free. Hyde Park is famous for its batter-dipped fries, chicken-fried steak, and peach pudding. The restaurant and bar are open until midnight every day.

Being at the center of the state of Texas you may think good, fresh seafood just isn't a possibility in Austin. **Eddie V's Edgewater Grill** (301 E. 5th St., 512/472-1860, 4pm-11pm Mon.-Thurs., 4pm-midnight Fri.-Sat., 4pm-10pm Sun., $40) proves all logic wrong. Every day fresh fish is flown in from Boston, because Eddie V's motto is "we won't serve it unless it's fresh." When the menu is five pounds and leather bound, you know it's fine dining. This steak and seafood menu includes Chilean sea bass steamed Hong Kong-style, snapper and crab, seared Pacific ahi tuna steak, broiled Georges Bank sea scallops, roasted rack of Colorado lamb, and filet mignon. The menu is à la carte, which adds up pretty quickly, but once you have a nice glass of wine in front of you, you won't even think about it.

If you want to instantly feel like you've come to the right place, go to **Jeffrey's** (1204 W. Lynn Ave., 512/477-5584, 6pm-10pm Mon.-Thurs., 5:30pm-10:30pm Fri.-Sat., 6pm-9:30pm Sun., $40). A creative and gregarious chef is behind the menu, and this comes through in each dish. New American and southwest flavors, coupled with wine and total confidence, make this menu superb. For starters there are crispy oysters on yucca-root chips and ginger beef dumplings. Entrées include duck and shrimp with a rice pecan cake, beef tenderloin with rosemary potatoes, and Alaskan halibut with linguine, trumpet royale mushrooms, and orange champagne cream. Is your mouth watering yet? It should be!

A mainstay for upscale Mexican food is **Fonda San Miguel** (2330 W. North Loop Blvd., 512/459-4121, 5:30pm-9:30pm Mon.-Sat., 11am-2pm Sun., $30). The environment is quite impressive, with its extravagant hacienda interior complete with original Mexican paintings, tall ceilings, lush foliage, and large tin lanterns. Everything on the menu is excellent, but my favorite is the *carne asada a la tampiqueña*. The beef is the best-tasting meat in town. All of the above is why Fonda San Miguel has been one of Austin's premier restaurants since 1975. Be sure to make a reservation for Fonda San Miguel, as the seats fill up quickly.

If you enjoy a bustling dining experience with a big wine and cocktail list and small entrées, ★ **Vox Table** (1100 S. Lamar Blvd. #2140, 512/375-4869, 5pm-10pm Mon.-Thurs., 5pm-11pm Fri.-Sat., brunch 11am-2pm Sat.-Sun., $18) is waiting for you—if there is an open table. Although in the spirit of tapas, this place serves up small creative dishes in a modern but not snooty environment. Dishes like pork cracklins and octopus and noodles come glazed and garnished with crisp, crunch, and savor. Along with tasty food, Vox Table has a great wine and beer list, an inventive selection of house cocktails, and a bar that is always active and inviting. If this is your main meal, be sure to order enough for everyone so you don't walk away hungry at the end of the night. Also, a word of warning for the person new to tapas: Since the food is light and spread out over the course of the evening, the wine tends to kick in at plate 3 of 8, so spread it out. Reservations are recommended on weekends.

Also in the Warehouse District is **Truluck's** (400 Colorado St., 512/482-9000, 5pm-10pm Mon.-Thurs., 5pm-11pm Fri.-Sat., 5pm-9pm Sun., $40). The classy atmosphere includes waiters in chef coats and art deco decor. With a wide variety of wines, perfectly prepared seafood dishes, and big-band music piped in, Truluck's will convert seafood haters to lovers. The first time I'd ever eaten lobster was here, and it was a profound experience.

Perhaps the most popular dining venue in the city is **Vespaio** (1610 S. Congress Ave., 512/441-6100, 5pm-10pm daily, $18). This darling of all the critics, and glamorous favorite of the people, is housed in a small space on popular South Congress. The kitchen is run by celebrated chef Alan Lazarus, who engineers brilliant Italian food by mixing innovation with tradition. The wine list is excellent, the food is perfectly designed and prepared, the atmosphere is lively—and did I mention the food is perfect? Italian flavor reaches a climax with dishes like veal ravioli, gnocchi with duck, cioppino (Livorno-style seafood stew), and spaghetti alla carbonara with handmade noodles. *Vespaio* is Italian for beehive, and the restaurant lives up to its name by always buzzing with action. There aren't many tables in this small space, and they're guaranteed to be full every night of the week, so the wait may be long, but it's worth every second.

According to *Texas Monthly* magazine, ★ **Uchi** (801 S. Lamar Blvd., 512/916-4808, 5pm-10pm Sun.-Thurs., 5pm-11pm Fri.-Sat., $30) was one of the top five best new restaurants in Texas the moment it opened. It's considered Japanese, but don't expect the usual Japanese fare. It's actually Asian fusion with a dramatic, original flair. I consider Uchi the best white-knuckle eating experience I've ever had. If you have a fat wallet and razor-thin nerves, order anything from the menu and explore the mind of highly decorated chef Tyson Cole. Every item on the menu is extremely flavorful, wildly unique, and highly recommended. Warning to the squeamish—you may end up going away hungry. Praise for the brave—you will walk away an enriched person. The one item on the menu that deserves mention is the sawagani. This is a plate of several miniature freshwater crabs cooked whole to perfection and eaten like popcorn. You'll be surprised how easy the shell crunches and pincers go down the hatch.

The founders of Lamberts go fishing with the owners of the fancy South Congress seafood joint **Perla's** (1400 S. Congress Ave., 512/291-7300, 11:30am-3pm and 5:50pm-10pm daily, $20). This is Austin's best place for raw or fried oysters. Sampling the different oyster sauces with wine out on the front deck is the height of decadence. Notable menu items include lobster stock grits, calamari, and escolar. The decor gives you the impression you're eating with the rich in the Hamptons. Perla's is a great choice for seafood far from the sea, for either brunch, lunch, or dinner.

DESSERTS AND CONFECTIONS

There are just a few boutique dessert and confection shops in town, and ★ **Amy's Ice Creams** (1012 W. 6th St., 512/480-0673; 5624 Burnet Rd., 512/538-2697; and 3500 Guadalupe St., 512/458-6895, www.amysicecreams.com, 11:30am-midnight daily, $4) is the queen of them all. Amy's uses natural ingredients and a local dairy, and offers 16 flavors daily. One of the tricks to this parlor's popularity is that they manually smash and blend your favorite candy bars into your choice of ice cream using a dramatic process that happens before your eyes. There are nine locations in Austin.

One of the grand additions to the South Congress strip is **Big Top Candy Shop** (1706 S. Congress Ave., 512/462-2220, 11am-7pm Mon.-Fri., 10am-8pm Sat., 11am-7pm Sun., $2-25). These folks have created a bizarre and wonderful atmosphere that can only be described as a 19th-century circus of candy that has an honest-to-God soda fountain. Everyone under 60 who never had the chance to experience this "back in the day," should rush here. Besides hand-jerked sodas, there are bins of hard candy, rivers of malts, and mountains of chocolate.

For classy and refined fineries there's **Dolce Vita** (4222 Duval St., 512/323-2686, 8am-midnight daily, $10). If you have dinner at any of the restaurants in the Hyde Park area, such as Hyde Park Grill or Asti, a stop here is essential. Dolce Vita offers espresso along with a selection of ever-changing gelato, ice creams, pastries, and chocolate desserts. It also has an exceptional assortment of scotches and liqueurs that can't be found anywhere else in town.

Austin's original socializing parlor is the ★ **1886 Cafe and Bakery** (116 6th St. at the Driskill Hotel, 512/391-7066, 7am-midnight daily, $8). With a checkered floor, stained glass, dark woodwork, pillars, and arches, the interior looks like it hasn't changed much since 1886. Although this historic café offers breakfast, lunch, and dinner, the reason for coming here is the pastries and desserts. With a great location in the center of downtown in the Driskill Hotel, this is a great place to go if you get a craving for coffee and something sweet.

Imagine eating a small tower of chocolate mousse in a flower shop without flowers with Sandra Bullock. Sounds like heaven, right? It's actually **Walton's Fancy & Staple** (609 W. 6th St., 512/542-3380, 7am-8pm Mon.-Fri., 8am-8pm Sat., 9am-5pm Sun., $6). Although Walton's is actually a deli, I recommend this place for the sweet stuff. Baked goods are absurdly decadent, and sodas are in bottles, which means they are sweeter. Everything is sweet about this place, including the fact that it was founded by Ms. Bullock.

For bizarre treats on 6th Street you can't pass up **Voodoo Doughnut** (212 E. 6th St., 512/215-8586, open 24 hours, $8). This is a great place to have a random experience after midnight. The décor of this place is weird, and the doughnuts are even weirder. There's the Pot Hole (their take on the chocolate bar), a maple bacon bar, and even a dark chocolate doughnut of a voodoo doll.

COFFEE SHOPS

In this day and age, when nearly everyone has a daily caffeine maintenance, cafés are everywhere. Some frequent cafés to sip coffee with friends, some to surf wireless Internet, some to read the paper or a book, but all just want a place to go. Humans, like fish, are social creatures, and humans drink lots of water, only many humans like their water to be filtered through the "bean." Here are some of the top places to hang out and drink coffee.

Wright Bros. Brew and Brew (500 San Marcos St. #105, 512/493-0963, 8am-midnight daily, $5) is a perfect place to hang out, read the *Austin Chronicle*, and drink a cup of coffee after waking up at noon. This coffee shop features a menu of AeroPress, drip and espresso, featuring beans from local roaster Flat Track.

★ **Halcyon Coffeehouse** (218 W. 4th St., 512/472-9637, www.halcyonaustin.com, 7am-2am daily, $5) is a night-owl café, a bar, an art gallery, and a smoke shop in one, and a great place to hang out. People come here to surf wireless Internet, to socialize, and to meet people. If you happen to have a random

Make your own s'mores at Halcyon Coffeehouse.

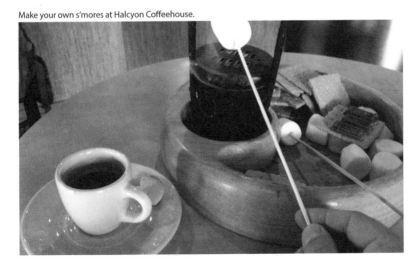

craving for s'mores, staff will bring fire to your table, as well as chocolate and marshmallows, so you can satisfy that craving. Seriously!

Jo's Cafe (1300 S. Congress Ave., 512/444-3800, 7am-9pm Sun.-Fri., 7am-10pm Sat., $2-5) is the boy who can do no wrong on South Congress. This outdoor café is strategically positioned in the best area of the bustling street, near all the great curiosity shops and boutiques. Jo's is a shack, albeit a stylish shack, that offers only outdoor seating in a parking lot. Jo's has a conventional coffee shop in the 2nd St. District (242 W. 2nd St., 512/469-9003). They're proud to serve up hot coffee, a few food items, and cold beer to a stream of people all day.

The café with the absolute best location is **Mozart's Coffee** (3825 Lake Austin Blvd., 512/477-2900, 7am-midnight Mon.-Thurs., 7am-1am Fri., 8am-1am Sat., 8am-midnight Sun., $6). Set on a quiet part of Lady Bird Lake, with outdoor seating, an in-house bakery, classical music playing, and coffee being roasted in the background, Mozart's is simply marvelous. Baked desserts are $6 and sweet pastries are $3. Wireless Internet is available. The only drawback is that parking can require patience.

Pacha (4618 Burnet Rd., 512/420-8758, 7am-9pm Mon.-Fri., 8am-9pm Sat.-Sun., $5), north of downtown, is one of those charming little homespun cafés that everyone prays will survive. Everything in here, from the tables to the hand-forged doorknobs, was made by family and friends of the two owners. Besides great coffee, Pacha sells imported Bolivian handmade arts and crafts from two cooperatives. Buying any of these crafts helps families in rural Peru and Bolivia.

Doesn't matter if it's morning or nighttime, one of my favorite places to hang out is **Spider House Cafe** (2908 Fruth St., 512/480-9562, www.spiderhousecafe.com, 11am-2am daily, $5). This mostly open-air café features coffee, breakfast, beer, and free Wi-Fi, all in one of Central Austin's best patio settings. The food is not so great, but the coffee and beer are excellent when enjoyed on the outdoor patio. Junk is stuffed in every corner of this place, Christmas lights are on year-round, and sometimes there is live music on the tiny stage.

Accommodations

A fly on the wall in any of Austin's motels, hotels, and bed-and-breakfasts would probably report seeing all kinds of folks coming and going throughout the year, such as families, politicians, sports fans, celebrities and movie industry folk, business professionals attending conferences, and leisure travelers. It's risky putting words in a fly's mouth, but I would venture to say the type of traveler a fly would report seeing the most is musicians. Being the Live Music Capital of the World, Austin generates an unprecedented amount of band traffic. That said, Austin has a place to stay for everyone. Here you can find a room in a quiet Victorian with doilies, down pillows, and blueberry muffins, or a room in a plush four-star luxury hotel with a rooftop pool, whirlpool bathtubs, and impeccable room service.

So what's the best area to lay your head? Downtown is the most desirable area because this is where everything is happening. All the chain hotels know this and their prices reflect it. Rates vary depending on the season and whether there's an event taking over the town. But those desiring comfort and a deal shouldn't lose heart. The upswing of this is that bed-and-breakfasts are plentiful and affordable, and many are within close range of downtown.

The main thing to keep in mind when planning your trip to Austin is to book your reservations way in advance. When there's an event in town it can be difficult, and sometimes nearly impossible, to find a place to stay at the last minute. To be sure you have a good chance of getting a reservation where you prefer to stay, book your lodgings at least 2-3 months in advance if possible. Also, all hotels and rooms are much more expensive when the town is overrun by people when there is a major festival or event going on, which is practically every month.

UNDER $100

The most affordable bed in town is at **HI Austin Hostel** (2200 S. Lakeshore Blvd., 512/444-2294 or 800/725-2331, $22-65). Set on the banks of Lady Bird Lake near downtown, this spacious hotel is comfortable and clean. Of course, it has dormitory-style accommodations. Rates are $22 per night for HI members, $25 per night for nonmembers. Private rooms are available for a $75 a night. Bed linens and parking are included in the rate, and towels rent for a buck. Bicycle, canoe, and kayak rentals are available, as is Internet access. Front desk hours are 8am-10pm. Dormitories are open 2pm-11am. No curfew.

There's something about staying in a dingy motel in Austin that's very appealing, and even romantic, especially for the Sid-and-Nancy-type couples. Let's start off with the good ol' American roadside mainstay **Super 8 Motel** (1201 I-35 at 12th St., 512/472-8331, www.super8.com, $65-139). I put this entry in here simply because it's cheap and close to downtown. With rates like these, don't expect anything except a bed, clock radio, coffeemaker (with bad coffee), TV, bathroom, and a Gideon Bible.

$100-150

A little more money can go a long way. While in Austin, $100-150 is what you will spend if you want to stay in accommodations that don't feel budget, but still offer value for your buck. If you want the motel atmosphere minus some of the dubious activities we all know go down in motels, there's the **Austin Motel** (1220 S. Congress Ave., 512/441-1157, www.austinmotel.com, $105-150). This family-owned Austin institution has a unique and quirky style, and is in a great location on South Congress Avenue. The motel's motto is "So close yet so far out." The Austin Motel is a favorite place to crash for musicians because it's safe, cheap, and sorta-kinda clean, but has all the charm and charisma of a total dive.

Situated in one of Austin's older neighborhoods north of downtown is **Adam's House** (4300 Avenue G, 512/453-7696, www.theadamshouse.com, $149-199). This beautiful, historic home was tastefully converted into a bed-and-breakfast that offers five charming rooms decorated with antiques. Located in the historic area of Hyde Park, just north of downtown, it's not too far from the Elisabet Ney Museum and the excellent restaurants of Duval Street. Adam's House is an excellent place to stay for romance. During the weekdays a light breakfast of granola, cereals, homemade muffins, and juices is offered, and on the weekends a full breakfast is served in the dining room. Pets and children under 12 are not welcome. Texas residents get the "state traveler discount."

The bed-and-breakfast closest to the action downtown is the **Brava House** (1108 Blanco St., 512/478-5034, www.bravahouse.com, $149-195). This old Victorian decked with art deco flair is classy, clean, and understated. Brava House offers appealing prearranged packages for an additional fee. For example, there's the "Enchanted Evening," where champagne, chocolate-covered strawberries, and candles are waiting for you in your room; "Romance in the Air," where an entire romantic evening is arranged that includes dinner for two at a local restaurant followed by a carriage ride through downtown; or the "Spa Getaway."

Also north of downtown is **Austin Folk House B&B** (506 W. 22nd St., 512/472-6700, www.austinfolkhouse.com, $130-280). This cheerful bed-and-breakfast offers clean rooms and great hospitality. Breakfasts are a few notches above most bed-and-breakfasts, as they offer *migas* (Mexican-style scrambled eggs), ginger pancakes, crepes, and a few fruit-based dishes such as banana enchiladas.

The **Star of Texas Inn** (611 W. 22nd St., 512/472-6700, www.staroftexasinn.com, $130-250) is run by the same people who operate the Austin Folk House B&B, and here you will have the same great hospitality, clean bedrooms, and of course the breakfast, all with a down-home touch.

Extended Stay America Austin-Downtown-Lady Bird Lake (600 Guadalupe St. on 6th St., 512/457-9994, www.extendedstayamerica.com) is a cheap choice for centrally located lodgings downtown. What this place lacks in charm it makes up for in privacy and location. Each unit has a full kitchen, wireless Internet, and cable TV, and laundry is available on the premises. Weekly rates are $85-149 per day, and daily rates start at $175.

A cheap hotel downtown is **Holiday Inn Austin-Lady Bird Lake** (20 N. Interregional at I-35, 512/472-8211, www.holidayinn.com). Located on Lady Bird Lake, this archetypal hotel has it all: outdoor pool, a restaurant, Internet access, on-site fitness center, and views of the city, all for around $150 a night. A kayak rental shop is close by, making kayaking on the lake an easy day excursion. The one drawback with this hotel is it's hovering over I-35. If you stay here ask for a room away from the freeway.

Also in this no-frills hotel genre is **La Quinta Inn-Austin Capitol** (300 E. 11th St., 512/476-1166, www.laquinta.com, $109-149). Here you get just the usual inexpensive hotel amenities you would expect from a budget hotel. It's a cheap place to stay, and centrally located, as it's next to the capitol. But don't be surprised if the paint is moldy in the bathroom. Also, you may see the flashing lights of Austin PD in the parking lot at night, as it can get slightly shady after dark. Nonsmoking rooms are available upon request.

One of Austin's best deals for chain hotel lodgings downtown is at **Embassy Suites Downtown** (300 S. Congress Ave., 512/469-9000 or 800/362-2779, www.embassysuites.com, $139-219). Located at the crossroads of South Congress and Barton Springs Road, this hotel is within walking distance of many of Austin's prime attractions. All the suites here have a separate room for entertaining with a bedroom in the back, and a complimentary cooked-to-order breakfast is included.

Austin has always been at the forefront of environmental awareness. **Habitat Suites** (500 East Highland Mall Blvd., 512/467-6000 or 800/535-4663, www.habitatsuites.com, $100-187) is a natural outcome of this local ecofriendly movement. Here you can enjoy all the pleasures of a four-star hotel and feel good about not contributing to the world's environmental problems. The hotel provides nontoxic, phosphate-free, natural shampoos and soaps for guests, and uses natural cleansers. The solar-power system used here is the largest of its kind used at a U.S. hotel. The facility is a nonsmoking, pet-free environment, and a member of Green Hotels Association (www.greenhotels.com). The one drawback is that it's up in Old North Austin, which is about five miles north of downtown.

For inexpensive accommodations near Austin-Bergstrom International Airport there's **La Quinta Inn & Suites-Austin Airport** (7625 E. Ben White Blvd., 512/386-6800, www.laquinta.com). If you have a flight leaving early in the morning, stay here and catch a free shuttle to the airport. This La Quinta is all about convenience, not four-star comfort. Rates can be as low as $109 even in the high season.

On the shores of beautiful Lake Travis is **Lakeway Resort and Spa** (101 Lakeway Dr., Lakeway, 512/261-6600 or 800/525-3929, www.lakewayresortandspa.com, $140-199), a premier resort designed to make guests do absolutely nothing except bask in leisurely delights. The resort is in the small town of Lakeway, which is about 20 miles from Austin. You have access to top-notch private golf courses, spas, and tennis courts, and can even charter a sailboat for a day on the lake. Getaway packages for golf, families, and romance cost more but offer more.

Note that during droughts the lake levels can get pretty low, which affects the views at the resort.

$150-250

Perhaps the most popular locally owned hotel in town is ★ **Hotel San Jose** (1316 S. Congress Ave., 512/444-7322, www.sanjosehotel.com, $145-300). This place is so hip it's almost an entire pelvis. Hotel San Jose is highly rated due to its chic vibe with minimalist decor that I would describe as postmodern Japanese rustique. Some would say Hotel San Jose is all pretense, while others would say it's all romance. You decide. The snooty staff can be unpleasant, but the wisteria-covered arbors and quiet atmosphere are pleasant. The hotel offers a great deal that is often overlooked: If you aren't opposed to sharing a bathroom you can get a posh room for only $145.

A top-notch B&B in the South Congress Avenue area is **The Fairview** (1304 Newning Ave., 512/402-6214, fairviewaustin.com, $199-300). The Fairview is a calm place for the leisure traveler. Sitting on the porch or patio and reading a book or having a gluten-free breakfast outside is the way to go. The plantation-style house has many modern updates inside. Décor is clean and modern but still Texan. Each room has modern king-size beds with organic mattresses, Wi-Fi and HDTV.

In the downtown area there are several luxury chain hotels. They may lack historic charm but they have boilerplate luxury-hotel service and amenities. They're big, they're fancy, and totally predictable, which is what some travelers prefer. At the crossroads of downtown and South Austin is the **Hyatt Regency Austin** (208 Barton Springs Rd., 512/477-1234, www.hyatt.com, $180-350), one of the city's four-star hotels. Perched on the banks of Lady Bird Lake, the Hyatt is in close range of the Palmer Auditorium, Austin Convention Center, and the great shops and restaurants of South Congress Avenue as well as 6th Street. A good choice for the health-conscious traveler, the Hyatt has a fitness center and a pool and is close to the trails around

Lady Bird Lake. The rooms on the north side have views of bats flying out from under Congress Avenue Bridge in summer months. The open atrium inside and artificial creek running through the restaurant make this a classy place to meet and do business.

Another luxury hotel is **Hilton Austin** (500 E. 4th St., 512/482-8000, www.hilton.com, $150-240). Hilton's downtown location, with a terrace pool on the roof of the 8th floor, a fitness center, an in-house steak and seafood restaurant, and extravagant decor, will make you forget all the complications of life. Views are spectacular, service is high caliber, and comfort is unavoidable. Promotional rates can sometimes be as little as $100.

The hotel with the best central location is the **Sheraton Austin** (701 E. 11th St., 512/478-1111, www.sheraton.com, $200-299). Although it's not at the heart of downtown, the Sheraton Austin provides easy access to everything, such as the capitol, 6th Street, the Red River District, the business district, many attractions, and the University of Texas main campus. Because of this, the Sheraton is a great place to hunker down for a few days. The views are great and the restaurant isn't bad either.

Omni Austin Hotel Downtown (700 San Jacinto Blvd. at 8th St., 512/476-3700 or 888/444-6664, www.omnihotels.com, $200-300) is a four-diamond hotel in the heart of downtown. A favorite of celebrities, rock stars, and rich folks, the Omni is 20 floors of elegance topped with a rooftop pool and hot tub. Guests are spoiled rotten by the in-house fitness center, on-site massage, sauna, cocktail lounge, and restaurant.

The **InterContinental Stephen F. Austin Hotel** (710 Congress Ave., 512/457-8800, www.austin.intercontinental.com, $209-299) embodies the best of old and new in Austin luxury lodgings. The historic hotel is smack-dab in the middle of all the downtown action but retains a calm, upscale vibe, standing serenely above it all. Everything is within a stone's throw—the capitol, music clubs, great restaurants, and museums. The hotel was built in 1924, and although it has gone through major renovations, it still retains the historical class of a bygone era. Besides offering guests elegant rooms with amenities that pamper, the hotel has a balcony bar that is very popular, especially with legislators. There's also a health club featuring a lap pool, a Mediterranean-themed café called Julienne, and a restaurant called Roaring Fork, which serves first-class southwestern cuisine.

Radisson Hotel on Lady Bird Lake (111 E. Cesar Chavez St., 800/395-7046, www.radisson.com, $198-300) is one of the better downtown accommodations in this price range. This centrally located hotel offers great views of the city and quality service. If you stay here you simply must take the time to walk around Lady Bird Lake, which is just out the back door. Breakfast and rooms with stunning views will cost you a tad more; rooms on the south side have views of Austin's famous bats in summer months. Booking online can get you better rates. The TGI Friday's restaurant in the hotel is one of the best spots in town to watch the bats fly from their roosts on summer evenings.

If you are less interested in Austin downtown nightlife and want to be near the UT campus or Austin's museums, consider a stay at **AT&T Hotel & Conference Center at the University of Texas** (1900 University Ave., 512/404-1900, $219-300). The hotel is modern, with all expected amenities. The best thing about this place is the location. Situated in the heart of Austin, it is within walking distance (a city block or two) of the Bullock Texas State History Museum, Blanton Museum of Art, the UT campus, and the Drag at Guadalupe Street. The Texas State Capitol is pretty close by as well. Just remember this is a run-of-the-mill hotel. Nothing weird here, which is what some folks need when traveling.

On the West End is ★ **Austin's Inn at Pearl Street** (809 W. Martin Luther King Blvd. at Pearl St., 800/494-2261, www.innpearl.com, weekday rates from $165, weekend rates from $355). With wicker chairs, kitsch in every nook and cranny, floral patterns on the walls, and a calm, spiritual feel, this establishment personifies the bed-and-breakfast. There are 12 rooms, each with a different theme, such as safari, Oxford, Venetian, and even tree house. Does Shirley MacLaine live here? No—but it sure does seem like she's the decorator. There's a two-night minimum on weekends.

For a rustic and romantic experience outside of town there's **Lost Parrot Cabins** (15116 Storm Dr., 512/266-8916, www.austincabinrentals.com, $225-285), which is situated on eight acres near Mansfield Dam, about 1.5 miles from Lake Travis. This wildly colorful little Mexican-style villa is a perfect place to get away from it all. All cabins are private, complete with hammock and rocker, and to make it even easier you can park next to your cabin. Pets are welcome with an additional fee.

The best weekend-getaway bed-and-breakfast at Lake Travis is **Robin's Nest** (1007 Stewart Cove, 512/266-3413, www.robinsnestlaketravis.com, $149-250). Beautiful views of the lake, comfortable lodgings, and proximity to water sports, fishing, and swimming holes make this nest an easy choice for an excursion away from town. Lodgings include three homes and nine guest rooms.

OVER $250

Romantic fine dining, horse-drawn carriages, and old Western Gothic architecture collide right in the heart of downtown at ★ **The Driskill Hotel** (604 Brazos St., 512/474-5911 or 800/252-9367, www.driskillhotel.com, $290-390). The Driskill has been Austin's premier luxury hotel since 1886. They've mastered Texas charm, opulence, and drama by providing guests with lavish rooms decked with gigantic curtains, fancy tile bathrooms, and ornate beds. The hotel also has an award-winning restaurant, a piano bar, and a fitness studio. With a great downtown location right on 6th Street, there's access to bars, live music, museums, touristy shops, and the capitol. Out front you can catch a horse-drawn carriage for

The Driskill Hotel

a romantic tour through downtown. Rates vary depending on room and season, but an average rate can start at around $300 a night and go as high as $1,000.

Finally, someone brought the dusty old bed-and-breakfast model into the 21st century. Say good-bye to Bob Newhart and say hello to Mork and Mindy! Sleek, modern, whitewashed, and downright soothing, the **Kimber Modern** (1220 S. Congress Ave., 512/441-1157, www.kimbermodern.com, $285-450) is a choice high-end place to stay off South Congress. You can shop, eat, catch some music, and return to your futuristic digs and soak in a tub. The lady who runs the place is friendly, the breakfast is fresh and healthy, and the common lounge is an excellent space to read and sip coffee.

Austin's classiest four-star hotel is **The Four Seasons** (98 San Jacinto Blvd., 512/478-4500, www.fourseasons.com/austin, $300-900). This is a luxury hotel for the crème de la crème, the beau monde, the privileged class, and for celebrities—as well as the average Jack or Jill who wants to spend some hard-earned cash on a fancy bed. Okay, the Four Seasons is more than a bed, it's a swank hotel set on a quiet piece of Lady Bird Lake, affording a tranquil space, rooms with unforgettable views of the skyline, private balconies, oversized cotton bath towels, down pillows, terrycloth bathrobes, and bend-over-backwards hospitality. The Queen of England stayed here when she visited Austin. If it's good enough for the queen. . . .

One of the top 10 best spa resorts in the world is right here just outside Austin. According to *Travel + Leisure* magazine, **Lake Austin Spa Resort** (1705 S. Quinlan Park Rd., 512/372-7300 or 800/847-5637, www.lakeaustin.com) is world class. Located only 25 minutes from downtown Austin on a quiet spot on the shores of Lake Travis, this resort is an extraordinary place to immerse yourself in yourself. In their own words, this is "an exquisite escape into natural beauty and personal discovery." Thanks to soothing minimalist architecture, classy modern Asian flair, beautifully manicured gardens, and exquisite hospitality, you can't help but completely forget about the outside world. Although they offer vacation packages, they also offer day packages. So what goes down here? Water aerobics, water yoga, swimming in indoor and outdoor pools, tai chi classes on the shores of the lake, kayaking, cooking classes, boat cruises, and relaxing in hammocks. Vacation packages can be 3-7 days, and rates vary depending on what you want to experience, ranging $1,400-2,300. Guests are free to participate as much or as little as desired.

Austin's fancy place to stay downtown is the ★ **W Austin** (200 Lavaca St., 512/542-3600, www.starwoodhotels.com). Besides being the hotel in the middle of Austin's newer downtown 2nd Street District, where shopping and restaurants are plentiful, the LEED-certified W Austin shares a roof with the new *Austin City Limits* studio, where live performance taping happens. Guests can expect the ultimate in service with the hotel's signature

Whatever/Whenever service, pampering guests with "whatever you want, whenever you want it." Rates range $300-400 depending on room size and amenities. If you are a rock star or want to be treated like one, you can enjoy one of the Marvelous Suites for $1,000 per night.

New to Austin is the trendy **Hotel Van Zandt** (605 Davis St., 512/542-5300, $300-450). Yes, this place is a little pricy, but for the upper-class traveler there's a lot you can get for the money. The decor is beautiful and the location can't be beat: It is situated in the Rainey Street District, which has great bars, restaurants, food trucks, and fabulous nightlife. The hotel has a stunning pool area with city views and free daily happy hour of wine and margaritas in the lobby is also something that has to be mentioned. Also, free bicycle rentals are available.

If you want stylish lodgings near the action on South Congress Avenue, **South Congress Hotel** (1603 S. Congress Ave., 512/920-6405, $250-400) is highly recommended. The overall tone of this place is alluring, with its midcentury modern design and classy but friendly atmosphere. There are few things better than walking out of a retro hotel and down South Congress to the funky shops or to catch a show at the Continental Club. Because of its location, you can do all the above with a buzz and simply walk back to your room. The hotel features an outdoor pool, a bar in the lobby, a café, and a full-service bar and grill.

Hotel Ella (1900 Rio Grande St., 512/495-1800, www.hotelella.com, $250-350) has historical charm and modern class. Just northwest of downtown in a quiet neighborhood near the UT campus, this converted mansion, which was built in the late 19th century, has spacious contemporary rooms, an interior courtyard with a pool, private cabanas, a fine-dining restaurant, fitness center, and a lounge. Some rooms have an added touch of romance with balconies overlooking the hotel grounds and courtyard access. All you could need for a pleasant, romantic, relaxing evening is right here.

The world got you drained? A weekend getaway to a wellness spa is a great way to recharge your inner battery. **Travaasa** (13500 FM 2769, 877/261-7792, www.travaasa.com/austin, $250-475), just 20 miles northwest of Austin, offers peaceful accommodations along with a busy schedule of workshops and conferences for guests. This is the only place in the area where you can enjoy spa treatments, mechanical-bull-riding workouts, cooking classes, horseback riding, and learning to dance the Texas two-step. The breathtaking 205-acre campus has hiking trails, pools, green architecture, and a spectacular view of Lake Travis. Guests are welcome to just shack up here or get involved. A discount is offered for those who combine spa and/or workshops with accommodations.

Information and Services

TOURIST INFORMATION

The **Austin Convention and Visitors Bureau** (800/926-2282, www.austintexas.org) is a great resource for travel and tourism information before you land in Austin. The easy-to-navigate website offers lots of concise information, and the person at the other end of their toll-free number can offer advice and information on anything Austin-related as well. For a brick-and-mortar information center, there's the **Austin Visitor Center** (602 E. 4th St., 512/478-0098, 9am-5pm daily) The knowledgeable staff can help you find the right accommodation on short notice, supply maps of the town, and help with anything else necessary for survival in Austin.

You can call **Austin's 311** information line (512/974-5000) to get answers to most questions about Austin, transportation, and even lost and found.

EMERGENCY INFORMATION

In the event of an emergency involving injury or danger dial **911.** Other nonemergency numbers are as follows: **Austin Police Department** (311 or 512/974-5000); **Brackenridge Hospital** (601 E. 15th St., 512/324-7000), downtown; **St. David's Hospital** (919 E. 32nd St., 512/476-7111), north of downtown; **Seton Medical Center** (1201 W. 38th St., 512/324-1000), near the UT campus; **Dell Children's Medical Center of Central Texas** (4900 Mueller Blvd., 512/324-0000); and **People's Community Clinic** (2909 N. IH 35, 512/478-4939 or 512/478-8924), for uninsured patients who pay on a sliding scale.

If you're on vacation and have a shoe emergency there's **Austin Shoe Hospital** (720 Congress Ave., 512/477-5078). In addition to the downtown location there are several others in the Austin area where they can fix your sole.

PUBLICATIONS

The local newspaper, the *Austin American-Statesman,* is an average medium-size-city newspaper—nothing to write home about. The *Statesman* covers all the basics, including local, national, and international news; sports; business; classifieds; and entertainment. Every Thursday the paper has an entertainment section called "Xlent." The *Statesman* can be found anywhere in town.

The city's alternative weekly rag, the *Austin Chronicle,* on the other hand, is excellent. What it lacks in design and layout it makes up for in colorful, opinionated content. Look to the *Chronicle* for information on music, events, films, the arts, food, kids' activities, and local politics. The *Chronicle* comes out every Thursday and is free for the

taking at almost every restaurant, café, and shopping center in town.

Many U.S. cities take a stab at having a classy, sophisticated, hip magazine, and most totally fail. But *Austin Monthly* is a high-caliber city magazine that works. In here you'll find articles that cover everything current, including culture, politics, entertainment, and tasteful celebrity cover stories.

The full-color, glossy magazine *Texas Monthly* is the best state magazine in the country. It can be purchased at most supermarkets and corner stores and is a great resource for state news, politics, and celebrity gossip. It offers a great listings section in the back with restaurant reviews.

INTERNET AND WI-FI

Internet access is so readily available in Austin that it's literally in the air. If you have a laptop with a wireless card you will be pleased to know that Austin has more free Wi-Fi hot spots than anywhere else on the planet. Walk into almost any café in town and chances are you can surf for free on your own computer. Businesses in the downtown area sure to have wireless Internet are: **Halcyon Coffeehouse** (218 W. 4th St., 512/472-9637), **Jo's Cafe** (1300 S. Congress Ave. and 242 W. 2nd St., 512/444-3800), **Mozart's Coffee Roasters** (3852 Lake Austin Blvd., 512/477-2900), **Wright Bros.** (500 San Marcos St., 512/493-0963), **Dominican Joe** (515 S. Congress Ave., 512/448-3919), **Thunderbird Coffee** (2200 Manor Rd., 512/472-9900), **Austin Java** (1608 Barton Springs Rd., 512/482-9450, and 1206 Parkway, 512/476-1829), **La Tazza Fresca** (519 W. 37th St., 512/453-0403), and **Spider House** (2908 Fruth St., 512/480-9562). Most hotels have Internet service as well.

For those without a laptop there are many outlets to get connected. All Austin public libraries offer free Internet access provided you have a valid ID such as a driver's license and one other form of ID. For locations call 512/974-7400. For everyone else there's a **FedEx Office** (327 Congress Ave. #100, 512/472-4448) downtown and elsewhere around Austin. Rates are $0.20 or $0.40 per minute depending on the computer.

MUSICIANS' RESOURCES

Since thousands of bands and musicians make their way through Austin on tour every year, it seems fitting to offer some tips on where to get your guitar set up, where to rent gear, and where to sneak in a rehearsal. The largest selection of equipment and gear rental is offered by **Rock N Roll Rentals** (1420 Oltorf St., 512/447-5305, www.rocknrollrentals.com). Here you'll find guitars, basses, amps, drums, and keyboards. When festivals are happening gear can be hard to find, so reserve equipment in advance.

If you are on tour and want to work on new material or brush up on your chops, **Music Lab** (1306 Oltorf St. and 500 E. St. Elmo Rd., 512/326-3816, www.musiclab. net) offers affordable rehearsal rooms by the hour. Prices range $12-15 per hour and rooms include PA and mic stands. Any gear beyond this can be rented for reasonable hourly rates.

Several shops in town offer guitar and amp repair but most are generally booked out a few days. The best shops in town for guitar repair are **Austin Vintage Guitars** (6555 Burnet Rd., 512/428-9100), **Strait Music** (2428 W. Ben White Blvd., 512/476-6927), and **South Austin Music** (1402 S. Lamar Blvd., 512/448-4992). The best shops in town for amp repair are **Austin Vintage Guitars** (6555 Burnet Rd., 512/428-9100) and **Audiotech Austin** (2213-B S. 1st St., 512/673-7141).

With many vintage guitar boutiques and new music shops in Austin, buying new and used gear can be a blast. Amazing selections of vintage guitars and basses can be found at **Austin Vintage Guitars** (6555 Burnet Rd., 512/428-9100) and **South Austin Music** (1402 S. Lamar Blvd., 512/448-4992). The place to buy drums and accessories is **Tommy's Drum Shop** (1100 S. 8th St., 512/444-3786). Lastly, the music store that offers just about everything is

Strait Music (2428 W. Ben White Blvd., 512/476-6927).

LAUNDRY

For coin-operated laundry machines in central Austin there's **Laundry Works** (606 W 29th St., 512/482-9274). In South Austin there's **Quick Wash Laundry** (6800 West Gate Blvd #129, 512/609-8858), and near UT campus there's **Convenience Coin Laundry** (909 W 24th St.). For environmentally friendly dry cleaning there's **EcoClean** (4012 N. Lamar Blvd., 512/236-8645).

POST OFFICE

The centrally located post offices are as follows: **Downtown** (823 Congress Ave. Ste. 150, 512/473-8334); **Capitol Station** (111 E. 17th St., 512/477-7082) downtown near the capitol; **Central Park Station** (3507 N. Lamar Blvd., 512/420-0310) in Central Austin; and **University** (2201 Guadalupe, West Mail Building, 512/232-5488) on the UT campus. For information on other locations call 800/275-8777. UPS Stores are all over town. For locations call 800/742-5877 or visit www. ups.com.

MONEY

It takes money to get money. ATM kiosks are everywhere, but beware: The ATMs you find on the street, such as on 6th Street, Red River, and Congress Avenue, all charge extraordinarily high fees. It's always best to get money from your own banking institution, but if your bank isn't to be found, at least use a national bank. You may still incur a fee, but it will be much less than at kiosk ATMs.

My favorite ATM in town, and possibly in the world, is the one planted in the rickety old wooden fence on Red River Street at Stubb's Bar-B-Q. I would never get money from it—it's just an interesting sight to behold. Also, Austin doesn't seem to have a problem with pickpocketing, so you don't need to be looking over your shoulder like you do in other cities.

Transportation

GETTING THERE

Air

The main airport that services the Austin metropolitan area is **Austin-Bergstrom International Airport** (300 Presidential Blvd., 512/530-2242), eight miles southeast of downtown. This converted air force base offers international connections that can get you to anywhere in the world. Major passenger airlines include America West (800/235-9292), American Airlines (800/433-7300), Delta (800/221-1212), Frontier Airlines (800/432-1359), Southwest (800/435-9792), and United (800/241-6522).

The airport terminal has several restaurants (including the famous barbecue of the Salt Lick), coffee shops, and, of course, the usual airport gift shops filled with irritating flying toys, paperbacks, coffee mugs, tourist T-shirts, and key chains. There's one shop that is worth making an attempt to check out if you aren't running to catch a plane, and that's the **Austin City Limits** store. And, true to Austin's love of live music, the airport often has live music. Because of this Austin's airport has landed on *USA Today*'s list of "10 great places to hang out during a layover."

The one big drawback to Austin-Bergstrom International Airport is that passengers often have a connecting flight, and this can eat up most of a travel day. There are only 52 destinations with nonstop service to and from Austin, and nearly all are domestic cities that are "lesser traveled." However, what ABIA is lacking in connections is made up for by convenient parking, which is close to the terminal and easily accessed, with no wait and no hassle. Airport parking is free for the first 30 minutes, $3 each additional hour, and $7 per day. The day rate for the close-in covered parking garage is $23 per day. Travelers heading to Austin-Bergstrom can call the airport for parking availability and other airport information 24 hours a day.

There are several ways to get from the airport to town. The most economical way is **SuperShuttle** (512/258-3826 or 800/258-3826), which costs about $18 to take one person to the downtown area. Taking a cab to downtown costs about $22-25.

An alternative way to get to the city is by using a ride-hailing company/app. Uber and Lyft left Austin in 2016. However, **Ride Austin** (rideaustin.com) and **Fasten** (fasten.com) are recommended. Ride Austin is a nonprofit raising money for local Austin charities, so you get a ride and do some good. The fare from the airport to downtown is around $17.

To drive from the airport to downtown, exit the airport and take Highway 71 west. Follow Highway 71 until you get to Interstate 35 and go north. The drive takes 20 minutes.

Car

If you are driving from Dallas to Austin, take Interstate 35 south, which goes through the heart of downtown Austin. The drive takes about 3-4 hours.

If you are driving from Houston to Austin, take Highway 290 west. Once you arrive in Austin, take Interstate 35 south to downtown. The drive takes about 2.5-3 hours.

If you are driving from San Antonio to Austin, take Interstate 35 north, which will take you right to the heart of downtown Austin. The drive takes about 2.5-3 hours.

Bus and Train

If you have a fear of flying, a low budget, or a fascination with the underbelly of America, there's always ground transportation to get you to and from Austin. The two bus lines available are **Greyhound** (800/231-2222, www.greyhound.com), which services just about anywhere in the contiguous United States, and **Kerrville Bus Company** (800/474-3352), which serves many of the smaller Texas towns, including many in the Hill Country.

Using Greyhound bus service to get to Austin from Dallas, Houston, or San Antonio is very affordable and travel times are surprisingly efficient. This is also a great way to see the countryside and meet some interesting folks. Buses to Austin from Dallas, San Antonio, and Houston are available every 2-3 hours. The bus ride from Dallas takes about 3-3.5 hours and the standard fare is around $20-25. The ride from San Antonio takes about 1.5 hours and the standard fare is $11-16. The ride from Houston takes about three hours and the standard fare is $16-22.

The **bus station** (916 E. Koenig Lane, 512/458-4463) is inconveniently located far north of downtown. Capital Metro bus 15 (Red River) or 7 (Duval) going south can get you from the bus station in North Austin to downtown; the buses run approximately every 30 minutes and the fare is about $1.

Traveling by train via **Amtrak** (250 N. Lamar Blvd., 800/872-7245, www.amtrak. com) is also a great and nostalgic way to make your way to and from Austin. However, travel times can be much longer than via bus. Trains to Austin from Dallas are available daily and leave around noon. The travel time is about 6.5 hours and the standard fare is $35. Trains to Austin from San Antonio are available daily and leave at about 7am. The travel time is about 2.5 hours and the standard fare is $17. Trains to Austin from Houston are available twice a day, one in the morning at 7am and one in the evening at 7pm. The travel time is about 2-5 hours, depending on scheduled stops along the way, and the standard fare is $51.

The Amtrak **train station** (250 N. Lamar Blvd., 512/476-5684) is conveniently located right in the heart of downtown, near Lady Bird Lake.

GETTING AROUND

It's fairly easy to get around Austin, which makes for less time traveling and more time enjoying the city. Most everything is conveniently accessible either by foot, bus, cab, or bike. However, if you plan on hiking some of the trails in and around Austin, visiting the Lady Bird Johnson Wildflower Center, or exploring the Hill Country, you'll want to rent a car.

Car

Getting around Austin by car is not necessary, but a car can provide the most freedom and is the best way to make the most of your time. There are only a few major freeways in the metropolitan area, and only a few major streets connect everything to downtown, which makes it easy to find your way around. One minor drawback to using a car is downtown parking, which can require patience and a good eye. Fee parking garages are available to eliminate parking woes.

All the usual rental car companies are represented on the ground floor at Austin-Bergstrom International Airport as well as around town. Car rental agencies include **Advantage Rent-A-Car** (800/777-5500), **Alamo Rent-A-Car** (800/462-5266), **Avis Car Rental** (800/331-1212), **Budget** (800/527-0700), **Dollar Rent-A-Car** (800/800-3665), **Enterprise** (800/261-7331), **Hertz Rent-A-Car** (800/654-3131), **National Car Rental** (800/222-9058), and **Thrifty** (800/847-4389).

If you prefer not having a rental car as a ball and chain, a practical and effective way to get around in by using a ride-hailing company/app. Uber and Lyft left Austin in 2016. However, **Ride Austin** (rideaustin.com) and **Fasten** (fasten.com) are operating.

Garage parking rates, hours, and allowed length of stay vary by location. Outside of special events, rates are typically a minimum of $5. The best parking for the 2nd Street Shopping District and for ACL Moody Theater is the **City Hall Garage** (200 Lavaca St., open 24 hours, $4 per hour). The best parking for live music in the Red River District is **Lot 119** (500 E. 8th St., open 24 hours, $6 per hour). The best garage for the 6th Street District is **Car Parked** (615 San Jacinto Blvd., open 24 hours, $14 per day). The best garage for visiting the capitol building and grounds is the **Capitol Visitors Parking Garage** (1201 San

Jacinto Blvd., open 24 hours, first 2 hours free, $1 each additional 30 minutes, $8 per day).

Bus

Austin's public transportation system, **Capital Metro** (512/474-1200, www.capmetro.org), is intuitive, easy to get the hang of, and inexpensive. Buses operate 24 hours for most main lines. Most individual rides are $1 (exact change only), but you can get the most for your money if you buy a $9 seven-day pass that offers unlimited rides for a week. Passes are available at any H.E.B. grocery store and at the **Capital Metro Transit Store** (323 Congress Ave.).

Capital Metro's very informative website is a great place to get schedule and route information. This information can also be found at most supermarkets in town and at the Capital Metro Transit Store.

A map of the bus lines can be downloaded at www.capmetro.org. A printed map can be picked up at the **Austin Visitor Center** (602 E. 4th St., 512/478-0098).

Taxi

Taxi service is available 24 hours a day, seven days a week. Smoking and nonsmoking cabs are available thanks to city regulations. Hailing a cab downtown can take some time, so I recommend calling one of the following cab companies to get faster service: **Yellow Cab** (512/452-9999), **Austin Cab** (512/478-2222), and **Lone Star Cab** (512/836-4900). Fares are $4.50 for the first mile and $2.40 for each additional mile.

Bicycle

Austin is a bicycle-friendly town, but it hasn't always been that way. Before Lance Armstrong became a celebrity athlete, cyclists were considered an inconvenience out on the motorways. Now Austin has miles of designated bicycle lanes and very respectful motorists. The City of Austin's Bicycle and Pedestrian Program (www.ci.austin.tx.us/bicycle) has a helpful map of suggested routes. It's also good to note that all Capital Metro buses are equipped with bike racks. However, if you plan to use a bicycle to get around, be forewarned that Austin has a dreadful problem with bike thievery.

Cycling around downtown Austin can be a great way to see the sights and get from South Congress to the metro area. Austin has introduced a cool bike-sharing service called **Austin B-cycle** (512/954-1665, austin.bcycle.com). With a network of 24/7 on-demand bicycle stations throughout downtown, Austin B-cycle provides an easy, fast way to navigate the city core. To access the network of bikes you need to purchase a weekly pass online or purchase a day pass at any of the stations. Day and week pass holders swipe the credit card they used to purchase the pass at the station kiosk to check out a bike. When you are done riding, return your bike to any station in the system and plug it into any empty dock in the station. Annual memberships are $80, weekly passes $25, and day passes $8. Your access pass or membership gives you unlimited checkouts up to 30 minutes at no charge for the access period. Bike-share locations can be found all over downtown and on South Congress. Check the website for more details or download the handy app for iPhone or Android.

Other bike rental services are available. The premier place to rent a bicycle for the day is **Bicycle Sport Shop** (517 S. Lamar Blvd., 512/477-3472, 10am-7pm Mon.-Fri., 9am-6pm Sat., 11am-5pm Sun.). They rent just about anything, including mountain bikes, road bikes, tandems, kids' bikes, and trailers. Prices range $28-35 for four hours and $18-50 for 24-hour rentals. Rates vary depending on the type and make of bike.

For quick and easy transportation around downtown, **Heart of Texas Pedicab** (512/930-8791), **Capital Pedicab** (512/448-2227, www.capitalpedicab.com), and **Metrocycle** (512/825-1276) can sweat it out for you. Service is available primarily around 6th Street, Congress Avenue, and the Warehouse District. Pedicab rates vary; a trip from one part of downtown to another can be $10-20, not including tip.

The Hill Country

The central region of Texas, known as the Hill Country, is perhaps the most lush, beautiful, and culturally interesting area in the state.

It's characterized by rolling hills, oak trees, dance halls, wildflowers, wineries, abandoned cars in fields, honky-tonks, dude ranches, state parks, and frontier towns scattered throughout the hills. Every square mile and every corner of the Hill Country is spilling over with history and legend. From clashes between the native Apache and Spanish settlers, to the founding of towns by German settlers, to old ranches as large as 50 square miles, the history here is rich and compelling. Over the years the Hill Country has been home to many wildly interesting characters, such as outlaws, pioneers, presidents, rodeo cowboys, and musicians.

Today the Hill Country is a place where people come to get away and have a unique Texas experience. In the Hill Country you can be a cowboy for a weekend at one of Bandera's many dude ranches; hike to the top of an enormous pink granite rock at Enchanted Rock State Natural Area; see an original Rembrandt hanging on a wall in a bank in Uvalde; go horseback riding in the Hill Country State Natural Area; catch a live performance at Gruene Hall, Texas's oldest dance hall; tube down the Guadalupe River in New Braunfels; and encounter the German heritage of Central Texas by visiting Fredericksburg. Although it's expected that visitors will romanticize the Hill Country as being a living Wild West, it's still 21st-century America. Some areas in the Hill Country look like scenes from the movie *Deliverance*, while some are reminiscent of Napa Valley. This combination is what makes this region so interesting.

PLANNING YOUR TIME

Because all the points of interest in the Hill Country are spread out, it's wise to plan your time before setting out on your journey. There are two ways people experience this region; the most common is by choosing a town and settling in for the weekend. This approach is great for a weekend getaway because it is low stress, low travel, and totally relaxing. The other approach, which is less common but becoming more and more popular,

Previous: Hamilton Pool; inside Gruene Hall, one of Texas's oldest dance halls. **Above:** Texas flag.

Highlights

★ **Hamilton Pool Preserve:** The grotto-like pool is a great swimming hole is the most beautiful spot in all of Hill Country—and a gorgeous place to hike (page 125).

★ **The Salt Lick:** This famed barbecue mecca offers a Civil War-era brisket recipe, unmatched hospitality, and a remote setting that is worth the drive (page 130).

★ **Becker Vineyards:** Sip a glass of wine on the porch at sunset and be sure to walk away with at least one bottle of Texas's best wine (page 134).

★ **Fredericksburg:** With bed-and-breakfasts, quaint shops, schnitzel, and polka music this Texas version of Bavaria bewitches and bedazzles visitors (page 134).

★ **Enchanted Rock State Natural Area:** Legend and mystery surround this giant pink granite dome, which affords spectacular panoramic views (page 141).

★ **Natural Bridge Caverns and Wildlife Ranch:** The Hill Country is beautiful on the outside and dark and mysterious on the inside—in the many caves at Natural Bridge Caverns (page 146).

★ **Stonehenge II:** In a field in the middle of nowhere is a smaller version of the mysterious monument in Salisbury, England. This version wasn't created by aliens or druids, but by a local attorney with a crazy idea (page 150).

★ **Lost Maples State Natural Area:** This remote state park explodes with color in the fall (page 154).

★ **Tubing the Guadalupe River:** In the summer you'll find thousands of folks sunning, relaxing, and drinking as they bob down the river (page 156).

is road-tripping through the Hill Country. It can take up to seven days to fully explore the whole region as outlined in this chapter. However, a three- to four-day weekend can be sufficient for a road trip that includes major attractions.

All towns in the Hill Country are a one- to two-hour drive from Austin and/or San Antonio. The distance between towns is generally under 50 miles, with some as close as 30 miles, which is great because drive time doesn't eat up too much of the day. Out of the dozens of towns in the Hill Country, there are only a few that will lure you in for a night or two: Fredericksburg, Bandera, Kerrville, Boerne, Gruene, New Braunfels, and Wimberley. For these towns plan on setting aside a full day for exploring, eating, and just meandering. All the little towns in between are good for some barbecue, roadside peaches, antiques, and maybe an hour or two of poking around.

ORIENTATION

Although there is no agreed-upon boundary that circumscribes the Hill Country, it can generally be defined as the incredibly vast area smack-dab in the center of the state of Texas. The area of the Hill Country with towns and attractions that merit mention as travel destinations is best broken into the following regions: the **Central Hill Country,** which includes some of the more touristy spots; the **Western Hill Country,** which stretches as far as Vanderpool; and the **Eastern Rim,** also known as the Austin-San Antonio corridor, which travels along I-35 south of Austin en route to San Antonio.

Central Hill Country

The gateway to the Hill Country is the small town of Dripping Springs on Highway 290 west of Austin. This little backgammon-loving, slow-moving wide spot in the road is known to locals simply as Drippin'. Dripping Springs once was a country-bumpkin ranch town, but it's quickly being swallowed by Austin. People are buying acreage, building mansions, and driving SUVs to and from the "big city." Once you pass through Dripping Springs into the Hill Country, all its grandeur rolls out like a red carpet before your very eyes.

HAMILTON POOL ROAD

Just north of Dripping Springs, about 30 miles west of Austin, there's FM 3238, better known as Hamilton Pool Road. Out on this rural country thoroughfare are three main attractions that are drawing increasing numbers of outdoors lovers, and there are caves, waterfalls, rivers, swimming holes, and trails all within a few miles of each other. This off-the-beaten-path region of outdoor activities has been discovered and developed only in recent years. As this area's popularity grows I hope and pray it doesn't get overrun.

From Dripping Springs go north on Highway 12 and turn left on FM 3238 (Hamilton Pool Rd.). From Austin take Highway 290 west, then go north on Highway 71. When you come to FM 3238 (Hamilton Pool Rd.), turn left. Everything is about 10 miles up the road near the Pedernales River.

★ Hamilton Pool Preserve

This preserve may be over 230 acres, but the main attraction is a swimming hole. Whether you want to take a dip or not, **Hamilton Pool** (Hamilton Pool Rd., FM 3238, Dripping Springs, 512/264-2740, 9am-5:30pm daily, $10 per vehicle, cash only) is a sight worth seeing. It's considered the most beautiful natural swimming hole in Texas because a majestic 45-foot waterfall spills into a deep, grotto-like pool that was formed when the dome of an underground river collapsed hundreds of years ago. In the hot summer months the

The Hill Country

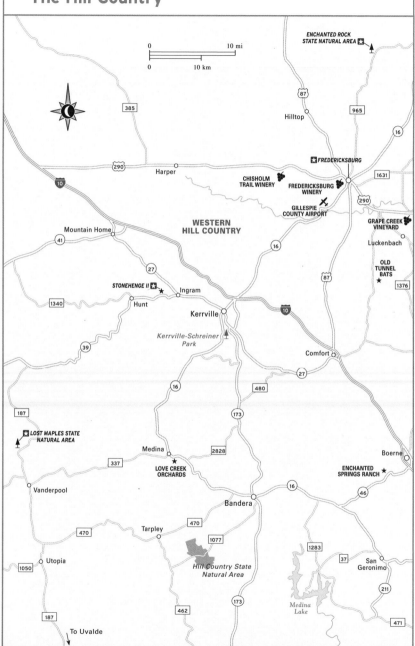

0   10 mi

0   10 km

ENCHANTED ROCK STATE NATURAL AREA

87

965

385

Hilltop

16

290   Harper

FREDERICKSBURG

1631

CHISHOLM TRAIL WINERY

FREDERICKSBURG WINERY

290

10

GILLESPIE COUNTY AIRPORT

GRAPE CREEK VINEYARD

Luckenbach

WESTERN HILL COUNTRY

Mountain Home

41

16

OLD TUNNEL BATS

1376

27

87

STONEHENGE II   Ingram

1340   Hunt

Kerrville

10

39

Kerrville-Schreiner Park

Comfort

16   480

27

187

173

LOST MAPLES STATE NATURAL AREA

Medina   2828

Boerne

337

LOVE CREEK ORCHARDS

ENCHANTED SPRINGS RANCH

Vanderpool

16

46

Bandera

470   Tarpley   470

1077

1283

37

San Geronimo

Utopia

1050

Hill Country State Natural Area

211

462   173

Medina Lake

471

187

To Uvalde

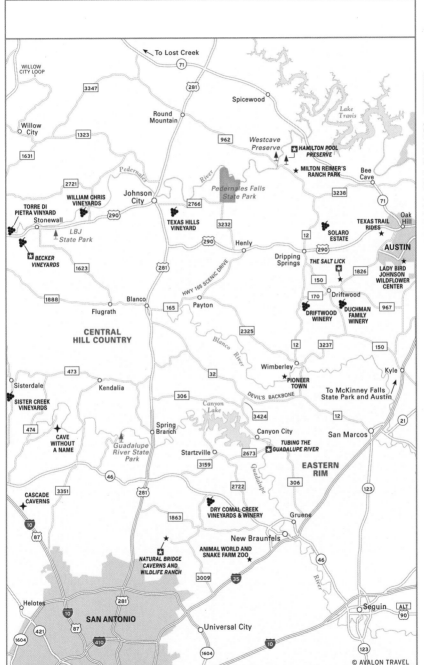

© AVALON TRAVEL

Hill Country Festivals and Events

Thanks to the great weather that the Hill Country enjoys for most of the year, the calendar of events is chock-full of things to do.

APRIL

Folks in Wimberley love butterflies so much they have a day dedicated to these little larvae that turn beautiful. On a weekend in April the **Emily Ann Theatre Butterfly Day** (1101 FM 2325, 512/847-6969, www.emilyann.org) becomes the focus of town. There's live music, plays and skits, and fun for kids and the whole family.

Wimberley offers a peek into the studios of some of its artists during **Arts Fest** (Wimberley Visitors Center, 512/847-2201, www.wimberleyartsfest.com). Near the Blanco River, Wimberley's Waters Point Retreat is filled with booths and arts spaces visited by over 3,000 art lovers. Artists represent a number of media, including oil painting, watercolor, mixed media, and sculpture. Most artists are locally, nationally, and even internationally renowned.

MAY

The biggest and longest-running festival in the Hill Country is the **Kerrville Folk Festival** (830/257-3600, www.kerrville-music.com). Starting the Thursday before Memorial Day, this 18-day folk implosion draws the biggest names in Americana, folk, bluegrass, acoustic rock, blues, and country. Live music, arts and crafts, fun for the kids, camping, and food and beverages are all within arm's reach. The festival takes place at Quiet Valley Ranch, nine miles south of Kerrville on Highway 16. Tickets vary by day but generally run $30 in advance and $40 at the gate. Tickets for all 18 days can be $400-600.

JUNE

For a peach of a time, the town of Stonewall has its annual **Peach JAMboree and Rodeo** (830/644-2735, www.stonewalltexas.com). At the height of peach season, locals get together for live music and dancing in honor of the fuzzy fruit.

SEPTEMBER

Celebrate Bandera (www.celebratebandera.com) is where to be on Labor Day weekend in the Hill Country. Every year the town of Bandera becomes a giant celebration that includes a real cattle drive, an intertribal Native American powwow, bull-riding competitions, concerts, parades, rodeos, and a Bloody Mary street party. Some events charge a fee and some are free. Check out the website for specific information.

At the Quiet Valley Ranch is the **Kerrville Fall Music Festival** (830/257-3600 or 800/435-8429, www.kerrville-music.com). Songwriters and entertainers from all around the United States make their way to Kerrville for this three-day festival, which includes camping. The ranch is nine miles south of Guadalupe River on Highway 16 between Medina and Kerrville. Tickets are $25 in advance and $30 at the gate.

Fredericksburg hosts the **Renewable Energy Roundup & Green Living Fair** (830/997-2350, www.theroundup.org). This green-building fair features exhibits, demonstrations, and workshops all espousing the new products and technologies related to the field of renewable energy

preserve is usually filled to capacity. The parking lot can fit about 75. Because the park is so small and ecologically sensitive, reservations are required to enjoy Hamilton Pool during peak travel months. The park is often full, so making reservations online well in advance is recommended. You can do so at parks.travis-countytx.gov/reservations.

Thanks to a diligent parks and recreation department, the pool is carefully protected, and green building. It's hard to determine whether this environmental awareness spills out from Austin's liberal hippie-ness, or whether it comes from Texas's long history of DIY independence from everything. Nevertheless, this event is essential for the green do-it-yourselfer. The roundup is held downtown at Market Square; tickets cost $10 each for Friday and Sunday and $12 for Saturday.

OCTOBER

Festivals abound in the historic German settlement town of Fredericksburg, but the one that gets everyone's lederhosen in a bunch is Oktoberfest (830/997-4810, www.oktoberfestinfbg.com). Held every year during the first weekend in October, this three-day bratwurst, schnitzel, and German beer extravaganza draws big crowds. Two stages, two tents, great food, polka and waltz contests, smiles, and music with an oompah make this a great weekend getaway for the family. Oktoberfest takes place at Marktplatz in the center of downtown. Hours are 6pm-midnight Friday, 10am-midnight Saturday, 10am-6pm Sunday. Tickets are sold at the entrance and cost $8 for single-day passes, $14 for two-day passes, and $18 for three-day passes. Children 7-12 are $1, and ages 6 and under are free.

At the end of the month there's the Fredericksburg Food and Wine Fest (830/997-8515, www.fbgfoodandwinefest.com), a celebration of Texas food and wine that includes live music, specialty booths, and lots of clinking of glasses. The festival is held at Marktplatz in downtown Fredericksburg. Admission is $25.

At Love Creek Orchards is one of Texas's largest and most popular pumpkin patches, The Great Hill Country Pumpkin Patch (14024 State Hwy. 16 North, Medina, 10am-4pm, admission $6). With a scheduled full of family-fun events, this is worth the drive.

NOVEMBER

For over 50 years Bandera has hosted the annual Hunters BBQ and Outdoor Expo (3862 TX-16, Bandera, 830/796-3280, www.banderahuntersbbq.com). Everyone gets all gussied up in camo and heads out to Antler Oaks Lodge for barbecue and beer and hunter-gatherer fellowship. The expo includes interactive exhibits, demonstrations of the latest hunting equipment, wildlife exhibits, and a live auction.

The best fest in New Braunfels is Wurstfest (800/221-4369, www.wurstfest.com, 4pm-11:30pm opening day, 11am-midnight Saturdays, 11am-9:30pm Sundays, 5pm-11:30pm Thursdays and Fridays). This 10-day salute to sausage features accordion music, dancing, and, of course, bratwurst. It takes place at Landa Park; admission is $10 for adults, while children 12 and under are free.

The Saturday after Thanksgiving the historic downtown of Comfort is taken over by Christmas in Comfort (830/995-3131, 10am-9pm, free). Over 150 vendors sell arts, crafts, and homemade foods, all to the soundtrack of live music. A trolley brings shoppers to the various businesses around the downtown area.

DECEMBER

The month of December means the Lights Spectacular in Johnson City. The Blanco Country Courthouse at the center of Johnson City's downtown is bedecked with 100,000 Christmas lights that remain lit the entire month. It's a remarkable show of BTUs and candlepower worth checking out. Local homes and businesses also get into the spirit.

and visitors are asked to be respectful of the environment. Swimming is allowed only when the water quality meets safe standards, so it's best to call for swimming information before trekking out to the preserve. The preserve also offers limited day use for picnicking, hiking, swimming, and nature study. Pets are not allowed, even on leashes. Drinking water and concessions are not available at the preserve, but there are toilets. Hamilton Pool Preserve is about 30 miles west of Austin.

Westcave Preserve

Just down the road from Hamilton Pool Preserve is **Westcave Preserve** (24814 Hamilton Pool Rd., 830/825-3442, westcave. org), another natural spot that demonstrates the dramatic topography and geographical history of the Hill Country. At this well-preserved, often-overlooked park, there's a cave, spectacular waterfalls, and an award-winning environmental learning center. The trail in the park can only be accessed with a guide. Canyon trail tours are offered Saturday and Sunday at 10am, noon, 2pm, and 4pm and cost $5 for adults, $2 for children under 12, and $15 for families. No pets are allowed on the grounds, even in cars. Toilets are available but there is no drinking water.

Milton Reimer's Ranch Park

Milton Reimer's Ranch Park (23610 Hamilton Pool Rd., 512/264-1923, 7am-sunset, $10 per vehicle) has exploded onto the scene as a popular spot for outdoor recreation in the Hill Country. Reimer's was originally a privately owned ranch where people could pay a few bucks to do some fishing, camping,

and rock climbing. Mountain bike trails have increased the list of activities. The ranch is on the banks of the beautiful Pedernales River, which makes for a great place to cool off on hot days. Getting to the ranch can be tricky. On Hamilton Pool Road there's a sign that says Milton Reimer's Fishing Ranch. Turn here and follow the rugged dirt road until you come to a gate. Go through the gate and stop at the house, where someone will come out to take your money. Then park and play.

★ THE SALT LICK

Animals on the ranch congregate around what's called a salt lick, which is a big block of sodium sitting in a field. Humans in Central Texas have a place to congregate too, and it's called **The Salt Lick** (18300 FM 1826, Driftwood, 512/858-4959, www.saltlickbbq. com). If barbecue was a religion, its devout followers would make this age-old landmark their hallowed pilgrimage site. This mecca for the golden calf of brisket is nearly 45 minutes outside of Austin in a wide spot in the road called Driftwood. The Salt Lick's award-winning barbecue is truly legendary, as its recipes have supposedly been handed down since the Civil War. With time-tested and time-honored beef brisket, sausage, smoked

Legendary barbecue is cooked up at The Salt Lick.

pork tenderloin, moist smoked turkey, potato salad, and beans on the menu, it's hard to find something even remotely close to this Texas tradition elsewhere. Besides having the best barbecue in the Austin vicinity, the Salt Lick is also known for its remarkably beautiful location. Situated on an old ranch in rolling hills of oak trees, the restaurant is housed in old buildings made of stone quarried from the ranch. The setting is almost European in feel.

One important thing to know before driving all the way out to the Salt Lick is that you need to bring cash—they don't take credit or debit cards. However, there are some ATM machines that charge a hefty fee. Also, if you like beer with your beef, you must bring your own beverages, as the Salt Lick doesn't sell alcohol (they do have nonalcoholic drinks available). It may seem weird to some to show up with your own beer, but that's the way it's done here. Lastly, if you arrive at suppertime, be prepared to wait at the outdoor picnic tables for up to an hour to get seated. This is the time that your BYOB comes in handy.

From Austin take MoPac (Hwy. 1) south. MoPac will turn into Highway 45 and deadends at FM 1826. Turn left on FM 1826 and the Salt Lick is about seven miles down the road on the right. If for whatever inexcusable reason you can't make it out to the Salt Lick during your visit, you can have a mini Salt Lick experience at Austin-Bergstrom International Airport. However, nothing is as good as driving out to the original barbecue mecca in the Texas Hill Country.

PEDERNALES FALLS STATE PARK

Along a dramatic and twisting part of the Pedernales River is **Pedernales Falls State Park** (2585 Park Rd 6026, 830/868-7304 or 800/792-1112, 8am-10pm daily, $6 per person). This rugged 5,000-acre park, featuring cypress-lined riverfront, waterfalls, and nature trails, is located just east of Johnson City and was acquired from private owners in 1970. The main attraction here is the falls, viewed from a scenic overlook at the north end of the

park. Crashing down over a distance of about 3,000 feet onto limestone, the falls are most dramatic after a heavy downpour. Besides the waterfall, the park also offers hiking, mountain biking, fishing, bird-watching, horseback riding, and picnicking, and there are some wide spots in the river that are great swimming holes.

The park is between Dripping Springs and Johnson City. From Austin take Highway 290 past Dripping Springs and go north on RR 3232. From Johnson City take RR 2766 east until you come to the entrance. Leisure camping with restrooms, showers, water, and electrical hookups is available as well as primitive camping, and both are on a first-come, first-served basis when the park isn't full. Reservations are suggested.

JOHNSON CITY

The Podunk town of Johnson City (pop. 1,700) is far from being a city. Things haven't changed a whole lot in the past 50 years in these parts. A testament to this resistance to change is that the old limestone jail built back in 1894 is still in use. The town center, where the jail is located, is a relic from the past. It's laid out in the typical town square fashion with the historic limestone county courthouse at the center surrounded by old businesses, most of which are windswept and vacant.

So what's the reason for mentioning this little town? Johnson City was the boyhood home of President Lyndon B. Johnson (LBJ), which is a big deal to small-town Texas. Although Johnson City was originally named after an ancestor of his, LBJ has become its patron saint. Everything around these parts revolves around him and his memory in one way or another.

Sights and Activities

The main attraction in Johnson City is the **Lyndon B. Johnson Boyhood Home** (100 E. Ladybird Ln., 830/868-7128, 9am-noon and 1pm-4:30pm daily, free) in the heart of downtown just two blocks south of Highway 290. LBJ lived in this old house from age

The Story of LBJ

Most people agree that in the 20th century, the 1960s were the tipping point in American history for social and political change. The one man at the center of this was Lyndon Baines Johnson, a native son of the Hill Country. His story is one that both exemplifies and defines the character of this heartland of Texas. Johnson was born in 1908 in the small town of Stonewall, between Johnson City and Fredericksburg. When he was five years old his family moved to Johnson City, where he graduated from high school. He received a college education in San Marcos at Southwest Texas State Teachers College, where he supported himself by working as a janitor.

Lyndon Baines Johnson

A few years later Johnson ended up in Washington DC, where he landed a job as the secretary to a U.S. congressman. Here he learned the trade of politics and acquired a taste for public office. In 1934, while visiting his hometown of Johnson City, he met Claudia Alta Taylor, better known as Lady Bird; shortly thereafter they got married in San Antonio. The following year his political career took off when President Franklin D. Roosevelt appointed LBJ as the Texas director of the National Youth Administration (NYA). In 1937 LBJ was elected to Congress, and he would ultimately serve five more terms in the House of Representatives. After the bombing of Pearl Harbor in 1941, Johnson became the first member of Congress to volunteer for active duty in the armed forces, and he received the Silver Star from General Douglas MacArthur for heroic efforts during an aerial combat mission over New Guinea. After World War II, LBJ was elected to the U.S. Senate.

In 1960, John F. Kennedy was elected president, with LBJ as his running mate; the accomplishment LBJ is most noted for during his stint as vice president is jump-starting the space program's goals of getting a man on the moon. On November 22, 1963, President Kennedy was assassinated in Dallas. Beneath a shroud of turmoil, tragedy, and mourning, high up on Air Force One, Johnson was sworn in to the office of the presidency. LBJ's career in politics culminated in the highest office, in the lowest of circumstances. In 1964, he was elected president in his own right. His presidency has been characterized as one of the most complex. He achieved many great things, such as furthering the U.S. space program, signing the Civil Rights Act of 1964, signing the Voting Rights Act, creating the Great Society program, and ushering in landmark legislation such as Medicare. It's also important to note that he was the first president to host a barbecue on the White House lawn. The more complex side to his term in office relates to his ushering in the Vietnam War, along with the cultural upheaval that ensued. In 1969, LBJ's presidency ended. He chose not to run for another term, and instead he retired to his ranch outside Johnson City. He died only three years later.

LBJ is characterized by his love of his Texas roots. The Hill Country, or as he called it, "a special corner of God's real estate," was where he hung his hat and left his heart. Today you can hear a virtual LBJ tell stories and jokes at the LBJ Library and Museum in Austin. You can also visit his ranch in the Hill Country and his boyhood home in Johnson City.

5 to 26, when he married. Today the house is furnished with items from LBJ's childhood, such as photos and quilts made by relatives. Unfortunately, it's hard to get inside the house due to funding and staff cuts. Nevertheless, the history buff may find the home interesting.

Between Johnson City and Fredericksburg is the land of LBJ known as **LBJ State Park and Historic Site** (199 Park Road 52, off Hwy. 290 near Stonewall, 830/644-2252, 8am-5pm daily, free). This beautiful sprawling ranch belonged to LBJ and his wife, Lady Bird, and was their special retreat from the world. Highlights of the park include the old house where LBJ was born, the house the president had built called the **Texas White House**, his presidential plane and cars, and the cemetery where he is buried. There are also old metal trailers where Secret Service used to reside. LBJ referred to his Hill Country ranch as a "special corner of God's real estate," and this hasn't changed. The visitors center has lots of great information about the life of LBJ and his ranch. You can also watch a 25-minute movie presentation that shows LBJ driving around the ranch explaining the history and telling stories about the area. Guided bus tours of the ranch are available.

During the winter holidays the beautiful old county courthouse downtown is draped with thousands of Christmas lights. People all around the Hill Country come to gaze at the dramatic display of holiday cheer that's called **Lights Spectacular.** The lights are on sunset to sunrise from the end of November to January.

The most popular local business in town is **Whittington's Jerky** (604 Hwy. 281/Hwy. 290, 877/868-5500). Founded in 1963, this country jerky maker has a little store on the highway where you can find all sorts of Texas-style canned goods, country knickknacks, gifts, and of course, the jerky. It comes in several flavors, including original beef jerky, garlic beef jerky, teriyaki jerky, and turkey jerky, all smoke-dried the traditional way. The result is sticks of meat that are dry and tough to chew—perfect for gnawing during a road trip in the Hill Country.

If you find yourself in town at lunchtime, stop by **Ronnie's Ice House** (211 Hwy. 281, 830/868-7553). Some of the area's best barbecue can be had in this humble and unassuming roadside eatery. The meats are flavorful and fall off the bone, and desserts such as banana pudding and buttermilk pie will make you feel like a

the home where LBJ grew up in Johnson City

fatted calf before you crawl out the door. Road-trippers, beware! Designate a driver, someone who won't fill up on smoked meats and sugar—driving after this meal is a challenge because the urge to sleep is mighty.

★ BECKER VINEYARDS

It should come as no surprise that one of the most beautiful settings in the Hill Country is at a winery. Visiting **Becker Vineyards** (464 Becker Farms Rd., 830/644-2681, www.beckervineyards.com, 10am-5pm Mon.-Thurs., 10am-6pm Fri.-Sat., noon-6pm Sun.) is like being transported to Napa Valley in Northern California. Honestly, you would never know you were in the heart of Texas. At Becker Vineyards the hills are golden and the fields are rife with grapes on the vine. The wine-tasting room and attached wine production area are housed in buildings made of limestone, with expansive porches affording spectacular views. Wine-tasting fees are $12 for six samples. A quintessential Hill Country moment is had sitting on this porch with a glass of wine at sunset. The winery is four miles west of Stonewall, off Highway 290 on Jenschke Lane.

★ FREDERICKSBURG

The most popular getaway destination in Central Texas is Fredericksburg (pop. 10,800). This big town, one of the largest in the Hill Country, is spilling over with German charm, Wild West allure, and Texas hospitality. Main Street, which runs straight through town, is lined with historic limestone buildings with wrought-iron balconies, vintage storefronts, and German *biergartens,* all in a Wild West setting. In a few words, Fredericksburg is Roy Rogers in Bavaria. This German frontierism isn't just made up for tourism—it's the real deal. In the mid-1800s after annexation, Europeans, most of whom were German, were the first white folks to settle this frontier region. These pioneers brought with them all their traditions, including schnitzel, oompah music, and beer. The vestiges of this German

Luckenbach, Texas

Between Johnson City and Fredericksburg, just a few miles south of Highway 290, is the sleepy town of Luckenbach. Not much is happening here, but this dusty old town deserves some sort of a nod. After all, it was the subject matter for a hit song by Waylon Jennings and Willie Nelson called "Luckenbach, Texas." Ironically, the chaps who wrote the song were a couple of songwriters from Nashville who had never been to the remote, out-of-the-way, three-building town. In fact, Waylon had never been there either. So how did it merit mention in a country song? Maybe the songwriters threw a dart at a map of Texas?

heritage haven't eroded over time—on the contrary, they have become what defines Fredericksburg.

Today the town is a small grid of streets lined with old trees, creating neighborhoods of historic houses and bungalows. These neighborhoods are small-town America at its height, and remind one of the sentimental paintings of Thomas Kinkade. Main Street is lined with shops and boutiques that peddle all sorts of stuff for the middle class, such as home furnishings and decor, Western wear, country kitsch, and frontier-themed souvenirs. There are also a few interesting museums and historic sights to meander through, antiques stores in which to find treasures, and wine-tasting shops, as well as hundreds of bed-and-breakfasts to pamper you during your stay. Just north is Enchanted Rock State Natural Area, which adds to the town's draw.

Because there is a lot to see and do here, and I recommend spending the weekend in Fredericksburg. Two nights in a B&B, wine-tasting, window shopping, hiking, and reminiscing about the pioneer days and WWII can all be enjoyed at a relaxed pace. However, if you only have one night and a day, skip the calorie burning/hiking. The **Fredericksburg Convention and Visitors Bureau** (302 E. Austin St., 830/997-6523,

Fredericksburg

Texas Hill Country Wine Trail

For thousands of years grapes have grown on the banks of rivers and streams all over Texas. The climate is so conducive to the vine that there are more grape species here than anywhere else on the planet. Of the 36 species of vines in the world, 15 are native to Texas. For some strange reason, when the Spanish arrived in the 1500s, they never took advantage of these local varieties. They made the first wine on American soil in El Paso with a variety brought over from Europe. It wasn't until the 1800s that the grape potential of Texas was recognized. It all began when German immigrants in the Hill Country started fermenting the local grapes, as well as producing wine from grapes brought from the Old World.

By the late 1800s wine research and production in Texas was fully underway. At the same time in Europe the phylloxera epidemic was wreaking havoc on French grape crops, threatening the future of French wine production. A grape researcher by the name of Thomas V. Munson of Denison, Texas, discovered that American species were resistant to the insect and brought vines from Texas to France, essentially saving the French wine industry. Ironically, 40 years later the U.S. Congress was successful in killing the Texas wine industry when it enacted Prohibition.

The Texas Department of Agriculture lists 21 wine varieties grown in Texas. Cabernet sauvignon and chardonnay have the highest number of plantings in the state, followed by merlot, syrah, and muscat canelli. Texas is also home to zinfandel, tempranillo, sangiovese, and viognier plantings.

The Texas Hill Country has rediscovered its viticulture roots. Wineries have been cropping up all throughout the state, 27 of which happen to be west of Austin in the beautiful Hill Country. These wineries have joined forces to create what is called the **Texas Hill Country Wineries Trail** (866/621-9463, www.texaswinetrail.com). Here are a few of the best wineries in this region.

- **Becker Vineyards** (464 Becker Farms Rd., Stonewall, 830/644-2681, www.beckervineyards. com) Location: four miles west of Stonewall, off Highway 290 on Jenschke Lane

- **Chisholm Trail Winery** (2367 Usener Rd., Fredericksburg, 830/990-2675, www.chisholm-trailwinery.com) Location: 9 miles west of Fredericksburg on Highway 290 west, then 2.4 miles south on Usener Road

www.fredericksburg-texas.com, 8:30am-5pm Mon.-Fri., 9am-5pm Sat., noon-4pm Sun.) is your local source for information.

Sights and Activities

One of the first U.S. Army outposts in Texas was **Fort Martin Scott** (1606 E. Main St., 10am-5pm Tues.-Sun., free), at the eastern end of Fredericksburg. There's not much here except for a few buildings in a field, but it does offer an interesting look at what a frontier Texas fort looked like before the Civil War. Only one original building remains; the rest are re-creations. The fort was active 1848-1853; once it closed as a military outpost it was used by Texas Rangers and homesteaders and was the site of the county fair for a few years. The fort grounds are open to the public.

The most off-the-beaten-path attraction in town—which happens to be my favorite—is

Gish's Old West Museum (502 Milam St., 830/997-2794, by appointment only, free). Joe Gish, collector of Wild West memorabilia and artifacts, has opened his collection to the public. The museum is in an old cabin on his private property. The place is covered from floor to ceiling in sheriff's badges, old rifles, saddles, cowboy hats, chaps, and spurs. Gish also has memorabilia from the silent-movie cowboys, as well as a fascinating collection of old photos of weathered faces from the frontier days.

World War II buffs from all over come to Fredericksburg to visit the **National Museum of the Pacific War** (340 E. Main St., 830/997-8600, www.pacificwarmuseum. org, 9am-5pm daily, $14 general admission, $10 seniors and military, $6 students, under 6 free). The museum, dedicated exclusively to telling the story of the Pacific Theater battles

- **Driftwood Vineyards** (4001 Elder Hill Rd./CR 170, Driftwood, 512/692-6229, www.driftwoodvineyards.com) Location: six miles south of Highway 290 on RR 12 between Dripping Springs and Wimberley

- **Duchman Family Winery** (13308 FM 150 W., Driftwood, 512/858-1470, www.duchmanwinery.com) Location: two miles south of Driftwood on FM 150

- **Dry Comal Creek Vineyards & Winery** (1741 Herbelin Rd., New Braunfels, 830/885-4121, www.drycomalcreek.com) Location: six miles west of New Braunfels off Highway 46 West

- **Fredericksburg Winery** (247 W. Main St., Fredericksburg, 830/990-8747, www.fbgwinery.com) Location: downtown Fredericksburg

- **Grape Creek Vineyard** (97 Vineyard Ln., Stonewall, 830/644-2710, www.grapecreek.com) Location: nine miles east of Fredericksburg on Highway 290, three miles west of Stonewall

- **Sister Creek Vineyards** (1142 Sisterdale Rd., Sisterdale, 830/324-6704, www.sistercreekvineyards.com) Location: 12 miles north of Boerne on FM 1376

- **Solaro Estate** (13111 Silver Creek Rd., Dripping Springs, 832/660-8642, www.solaroestate.com) Location: north of Dripping Springs off Highway 12

- **Texas Hills Vineyard** (878 RR 2766, Johnson City, 830/868-2321, www.texashillsvineyard.com) Location: one mile east of Johnson City on RR 2766

- **Torre di Pietra Vineyards** (10915 East US Hwy 290, Fredericksburg, 830/644-2829, www.torredipietra.com) Location: Highway 290 between Stonewall and Fredericksburg

- **William Chris Vineyards** (10352 Hwy. 290, Hye, 830/998-7654, www.williamchriswines.com) Location: off FM 1320 between Johnson City and Fredericksburg

of World War II, has over 1,000 artifacts from the Pacific War, including Allied and Japanese aircraft, tanks, and guns. The nine-acre complex also includes a shrine to WWII heroes in the **Admiral Nimitz Museum,** which is housed in the historic Nimitz Hotel. The grounds also contain the **George Bush Gallery;** the **Japanese Garden of Peace;** the **Pacific Combat Zone,** complete with artillery and a PT boat; **Veterans Walk of Honor;** the **Plaza of the Presidents;** and the **Center for Pacific War Studies.**

The **Pioneer Museum** (325 W. Main St., 830/990-8441, 10am-5pm Mon.-Sat., 10am-5pm Sun., $5), is a must-see when in Fredericksburg. This well-put-together complex of historic buildings furnished with artifacts offers a rare glimpse into the day-to-day life of the pioneers of the Hill Country. The focal point of the complex is the historic home and store of the Kammlah family. All the other buildings were brought in for preservation. The museum and complex are run by a few elderly women in period clothes. They and their outfits add to the museum's charm by being stuffy and old-fashioned.

Shopping

Although Fredericksburg has museums and historic sights, most people come here to stroll up and down Main Street and to meander through the many shops and boutiques. People who don't like shopping, don't panic! Don't think you'll be dragged through this street all day with nothing to do, because many of the shops have such a thick Wild West theme that your attention will surely be caught. And if you don't want to do the shopping thing at all, go hang out at a *biergarten.*

The best place to get an edible souvenir is

Scenic Drive: Willow City Loop

All roads in the Hill Country are beautiful and scenic, but a few are truly unbelievable. Willow City Loop is one of these. This 13-mile celestial drive takes the road-tripper through heavenly landscapes of wildflowers, wildlife, and terrain that seems too beautiful to be real. The road travels along a ridge for many miles, then drops down into what's called the Devil's Kitchen. This valley has a large crater in the ground that was formed by a meteor. Although it's a rural country road, in the spring Willow City Loop can have a surprising number of bicycles, motorcycles, and cars, so don't think this is some unsung Shangri-La.

To get to Willow City Loop from Fredericksburg, go north on Highway 16 for about 12 miles, then turn east on FM 1323. About three miles up the road at the small town of Willow City, look for the sign that marks the beginning of the Willow City Loop.

Rustlin' Rob's (121 E. Main St., 830/990-4750, 10am-5:30pm Mon.-Fri., 10am-6pm Sat.). This little old-style general store is chock-full of homemade canned and dried goods sourced from the region.

The most interesting clothing store for both men and women is **Parts Unknown** (146 E. Main St., 830/997-2055, 10am-6pm Mon.-Thurs., 10am-7pm Fri.-Sat., noon-6pm Sun.). Here you'll find fashions fit for upscale Texans, such as country western, rockabilly, and Patsy Cline-style cowgirl boots, men's bowling shirts, and sequins for the ladies and the men.

The local art gallery that represents many Fredericksburg artists is **Fredericksburg Art Gallery** (314 E. Main St., 830/990-2707, 10am-5:30pm Mon.-Sat.). Original paintings and works of art are sold for reasonable prices. Although these artists probably won't become world renowned, the pieces here definitely capture the spirit of the Hill Country.

Amish Market (410 W. Main St., 830/990-2977, 10am-5pm Sun.-Fri.) is an interesting place to pop your head in. This is the local outlet for handmade items from folks in the Amish and Mennonite communities. Things you'll find for sale here are Amish furniture, chests, curios, and arts and crafts. Everything here is made with care and craftsmanship.

If you didn't take the time to visit any of the local wineries, you can taste products from them all at **Texas Vineyards and Beyond** (329½ E. Main St., 830/990-9199, 11am-7pm Mon.-Tues. and Thurs.-Fri., 11am-8pm Sat., noon-6pm Sun., closed Wed.).

Food

Fredericksburg is, for the most part, an affluent community, and because of this the dining scene is of a high quality. City zoning and planning ensure there isn't a slew of fast-food restaurants on Main Street. With the German influence, many of the eateries have a Texas-meets-schnitzel menu, which makes eating here fun and unique. The place that personifies this combination is ★ **Auslander Biergarten** (323 E. Main St., 830/997-7714, 11am-9pm daily except Wed., $13). Although this eatery leans heavily toward the tourist crowd, locals also claim Auslander for themselves. The menu offers the best of the "wursts," such as knackwurst, pepperwurst, and the popular bratwurst. You can also get local favorite chicken-fried steak and other chicken and fish dishes. Outdoor and semi-outdoor seating is nice on a spring evening. Although the restaurant closes after the dinner crowd leaves, the bar is open until midnight.

For gourmet German cuisine with beer or cocktails on an outdoor patio there's **Otto's German Bistro** (316 E. Austin St., 830/307-3336, 4pm-11pm daily, $15). The duck schnitzel or Wurst Platte are most popular dishes. Demi-glace and sauerkraut undress your American taste glands and then clothe them in lederhosen. The atmosphere here is cozy and inviting.

The place on Main Street for authentic German cuisine and atmosphere is **Der Lindenbaum** (312 E. Main St., 830/997-9126, 11am-10pm daily, $13). Owned and operated by a feisty German woman who is a globally trained chef, Der Lindenbaum produces high-quality soups, salads, schnitzels, and upscale meat dishes. No reservations needed; seating is on a first-come, first-served basis.

Considered by many to be the best brewpub in Texas, **Fredericksburg Brewing Company** (245 E. Main St., 830/997-1646, http://yourbrewery.com, 11:30am-9pm Mon.-Thurs., 11:30am-10pm Fri.-Sat., 11:30am-7pm Sun., $15) proudly serves fine microbrews and German and American foods. The founder researched breweries in Europe and eventually decided to pattern this establishment after the Bavarian *gasthhausbrauerei*, which means bed and brew. The end result? Fredericksburg Brewing Company has beer vats in the restaurant and guest rooms upstairs.

Many fine-dining establishments come and go in Fredericksburg, but one that endures is **Navajo Grill** (803 E. Main St., 830/990-8289, 5:30pm-9pm daily, $15). This local favorite is a safe bet for a fine-dining experience free of the German theme. The seasonal menu includes steak, pork chops, and crab cakes. It's casual-elegant, so you may want to primp or dapper up.

The **Old German Bakery & Restaurant** (225 W. Main St., 830/997-9084, 7am-3pm daily, $12) is the place to get baked goods and casual German fare for breakfast or lunch. Housed in a historic building, this little local favorite serves up amazing German pancakes, potato pancakes, waffles, and omelets for breakfast. Lunch favorites include any of the schnitzels topped with eggs, mushrooms, or bell peppers with a side of German pan fries. If you want carbs for later, don't leave without some German bread.

Java Ranch (114 E. Main St., 830/990-4517, 7am-5pm Mon.-Wed., 7am-6pm Wed.-Sat., 8am-5pm Sun., $8) is the local

disseminator of Starbucks coffee. Besides having great coffee, this is the cheapest breakfast in town. Whether you're thirsty or not you have to poke your head in the door and check out the massive mural. Local folks, including the resident donkey, modeled for this excellent work of art.

If you don't want to make a big deal about lunch and just want a burger, there's **Wheeler's Restaurant** (204 E. Main St., 830/990-8180, 11am-3pm daily, $11). Here you can get familiar and affordable American or German food. Consider Texas chili with onion rings or chicken-fried steak.

Accommodations

There are hundreds of bed-and-breakfasts, ranches, and guest cottages in and around Fredericksburg. A few clever people have created companies that help connect travelers to accommodations with an easy one-stop-shop approach. These reservation services have been so successful that it's hard to find lodgings without going through them. The thing that's good about these services is you can easily find just the right accommodation for your liking because the research is all done for you. The drawback is that the personal touch that bed-and-breakfasts are famous for can be lost in the process.

If you like the one-stop-shop approach try **Gastehaus Schmidt** (231 W. Main St., 830/997-5612 or 866/427-8374, www.fbglodging.com), **First Class Bed and Breakfast Reservation Service** (830/997-0443, www.fredericksburg-lodging.com), **Main Street B&B Service** (830/997-0153 or 888/559-8555, www.travelmainstreet.com), or **Absolute Charm** (866/244-7897, www.absolutecharm.com). All these reservation services have access to hundreds of accommodations ranging from old farmhouses to historic limestone buildings and old Victorian homes. Perusing these websites is a great way to find the bed-and-breakfast that is right for you, as they have photos, maps, reviews, and amenity information. Reservation-service accommodations generally start at $129 a night and can go as high as $300. Whether you plan to use a reservation service or find a bed-and-breakfast to your liking on your own, it's important to book far in advance.

One of the cheapest rooms in town is at the **Frederick Motel** (1308 E. Main St., 830/997-6050 or 800/996-6050, $99-109). The proprietors like to call themselves an "unconventional B&B" because they offer quality hospitality and a continental breakfast in the mornings. For a motel, the rooms are clean and well maintained; however, they are small and just off Highway 290. Smoking and nonsmoking rooms are available.

A few blocks behind Main Street, in a quiet neighborhood, is ★ **Magnolia House** (101 E. Hackberry, 830/997-0306 or 800/880-4374, www.magnolia-house.com, $135-235). This bed-and-breakfast is housed in a historic landmark that's a perfect example of a Craftsman bungalow. The decor of the common rooms and the suites is country Victorian, and the breakfasts include American staples such as bacon, eggs, waffles, and coffee, all served on crystal. The backyard has a pleasant seating area under the trees and a small pond. There are five guest rooms in all, with the proprietors living in a cottage in the back.

One of Fredericksburg's earliest pioneer homes is now a place to stay. The **Loeffler-Weber Haus** (508 W. Main St., 866/427-8374, www.fbglodging.com, $100-120) may be shockingly rustic and pastoral, but it can be alluring. This Ma and Pa Kettle-style log cabin has been altered just enough to be comfortable for today's traveler. The kerosene lamps are mostly for looks but can be fired up if you want an 1800s experience.

Another place that specializes in rustic lodgings is **Barons Creekside** (316 Goehmann Ln., 830/990-4048, www.baronscreekside.com, $198-269). Just minutes from downtown Fredericksburg, this pastoral location features rolling hills with an assortment of little one-room cabins and an old Victorian house. The cabins are built out of logs from an old tobacco-drying barn from Kentucky and windows and doors from a 250-year-old house

from Switzerland. The accommodations are a perfect combination of rustic and luxury for both couples and families: Think log walls and a whirlpool tub, where you can listen to the sounds of crickets while drinking a bottle of exceptional wine. Also, a trail leads down to a creek and a natural pool, and the cantilevered lookout can't be left out.

The romantic place to stay in Fredericksburg is **Austin Street Retreat** (408 W. Austin St., 866/427-8374, www.austinstreetretreat.com, $185-215). This exotic and spectacular setting was originally a 19th-century family home made of Texas limestone. The home was meticulously converted into a lovely guesthouse with five private rooms, all under old pecan trees. Once you step off the street you feel like you're in a small village in Europe. Amenities can include fine linens, custom-designed bedding, whirlpool tubs, and private terraces. If you are traveling with a dog, you pet is welcome in some cabins for an additional $25.

For a classic B&B experience just south of Main Street, there's **Das Garten Haus Bed and Breakfast** (604 S. Washington, 830/990-8408, http://dasgartenhaus.com, $150-265). This old Craftsman style bungalow features three suites replete with doilies, pictures of flowers, and Wi-Fi, all under old pecan trees. Rooms are clean and well maintained, and have a great balance of charm and simplicity. The upstairs suite can house up to four guests.

One of the best privately owned and operated bed-and-breakfasts in downtown is **Keidel Inn** (403 E. Main St., 866/244-7897, www.absolutecharm.com, $129-299). This charming villa-style home has rooms with great views, creature comforts such as big fluffy beds, and an outdoor area with a brick patio and a fountain. The historic home wasn't renovated to be a bed-and-breakfast, so most rooms share a bathroom with other guests. The best part about this inn is its location. Das Keidel is on Main Street, a block away from everything that's great about Fredericksburg.

Picture the last scene in Casablanca—the

airstrip, the old plane, and the romance of it all. The ★ **Hangar Hotel** (155 Airport Rd., 830/997-9990, www.hangarhotel.com, weekdays $119, weekends $149-189) at the Gillespie County Airport brings this scene to life in a unique way. Although this hotel looks like it's in an old World War II airplane hangar, it's actually completely new, with modern amenities worthy of a four-star hotel. All 50 rooms have a king-size bed, classy brass New York Library-style lamps, honeycomb-tile bathrooms, Egyptian cotton sheets, and army blankets, all in a South Pacific WWII motif. There's also a diner and a bar on the premises. All this, and you don't have to be a pilot, or even arrive by plane—you can drive up in a car. Rooms are quiet, which is surprising for being on an airstrip. For the quintessential Hangar Hotel experience, pilot John Barnett (210/844-4463) offers plane rides for $100 for 30 minutes. Gillespie County Airport is two miles south of Main Street off Highway 16.

For predictable, chain-style amenities, there's **La Quinta** (1465 E. Main St. on Hwy. 290, 830/990-2899, $115-179) and **Fredericksburg Inn and Suites** (201 S. Washington St., 830/997-0202 or 800/446-0202, www.fredericksburg-inn.com, $99-179).

Getting There and Around

Most travelers arrive in Fredericksburg by car. However, there is a **Greyhound** station (2204 Hwy. 16 S., 800/231-2222), which can be an affordable way to get here from Austin and San Antonio. If you don't have a car you should know there is no bus system for this small town. However, taxi service is available through **Big Country Cabs** (830/307-0467) and **Bluebonnet Taxi & Shuttle** (830/998-2886). Since the area is small, cab fares probably won't exceed $10.

★ ENCHANTED ROCK STATE NATURAL AREA

Just north of Fredericksburg is an amazing park called **Enchanted Rock State Natural Area** (16710 RM 965, 830/685-3636, 8am-10pm daily, $7, children 12 and under free). Once you drive around the bend and get your first glimpse of the massive outcropping of pink granite, I guarantee you will be amazed. A popular weekend expedition for locals is to walk up the face of the enormous dome to the top, which offers incredible panoramic views of the Hill Country. The rock is the size of a city block, and looks more like it should be set in Australia, or Utah—anywhere but Texas.

the Hangar Hotel

Legend has it that the area was considered "enchanted" by the Tonkawa, who believed a ghost lived in the rock. The Tonkawa heard weird creaking and groaning at the site, which they attributed to spirits. Today's geologists say these sounds come from the rock contracting and expanding due to temperature changes. Another story is that a conquistador captured by the Tonkawa escaped by getting lost in the rock area. This gave rise to an Indian legend of a pale man who was swallowed by the rock and reborn as one of their own.

Activities at the park include hiking, camping, picnicking, bird-watching, and rock climbing. Climbers love this spot because it's great for traditional climbing as well as crack climbing. The parking lot fills up early on weekends, and the park often reaches capacity and can be closed because of this. One can spend a couple hours here hiking and taking in the beauty.

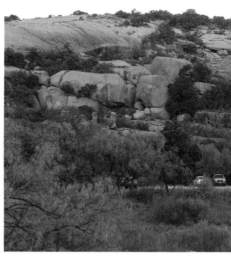

Enchanted Rock State Natural Area

COMFORT

Like most Hill Country towns, Comfort (pop. 2,300) was founded in the 1850s by German immigrants who left New Braunfels to settle more remote parts of the Hill Country. The name came about just as you might imagine—the location was a comfortable place to settle. The German word for comfort is *Gemütlichkeit*. They found this to be a little bewildering to non-Germans so they settled on the English translation. This group of settlers was different from other German pioneers in that they opposed slavery, and they weren't particularly religious. It took them over 40 years to build their first church, unlike other Hill Country towns that erected lots of churches quickly.

Comfort hasn't changed much over the years. It's a small town with almost no tourism infrastructure and no attractions—just a collection of historic buildings and a few shops, one of which is the oldest general store in Texas. In a sense the town *is* the attraction. For more information contact the **Comfort Chamber of Commerce and Visitors Center** (630 Hwy. 27, 830/995-3131, www.comfortchamber.com).

Sights and Activities

Comfort's downtown **business district** is considered to be the most intact original business district in Texas. Taking a stroll around town and shopping for antiques is what visitors do here. All the old buildings are appealing to the eye and pique the imagination. Some have historical information inscribed in a cornerstone, or have a name and date in relief somewhere on the exterior. Current business owners often know the history of the buildings they occupy, while other buildings speak for themselves, such as the old post office.

The only municipal monument to Union soldiers south of the Mason-Dixon line is in Comfort. The **Truer der Union Monument,** a simple obelisk erected in 1866, honors a group of German men slain by Confederate soldiers. The daring freethinkers refused to sign a Confederate oath of allegiance and fled

Attack at Enchanted Rock

The granite dome of Enchanted Rock was witness to some of the earliest Wild West showdowns in Texas. In 1841, Texas Ranger captain Jack Hays was exploring the region with a company of Rangers. They were looking for members of the Comanche tribe who had recently raided San Antonio. Hays decided to climb Enchanted Rock to get a better view of the surrounding countryside. He became separated from his men and while high up on the mountain was attacked by a large band of Comanche. In ordinary circumstances, this would have been a fatal error on the part of Captain Hays. On this day, however, he was armed with a brand-new weapon invented by Samuel Colt: a pair of five-shot Patterson Colt revolvers. These pistols were the most modern and innovative handguns yet created.

The tactics of the Comanche were simple. They would rush a lone defender, causing that person to fire his single-shot weapon. Following this, the individual was at the mercy of the Indians. The Comanche charged Jack Hays, he fired his single-shot rifle, and they came at him with a vengeance. However, he used his Patterson Colts to great effect, and the stunned attackers fled in terror. They had never faced multi-shot weapons before. Ever after Hays was known as "Devil Jack." Having proven themselves in battle, Samuel Colt's revolvers became increasingly popular, and Colt subsequently became one of the most successful gun manufacturers in the country.

to Mexico to escape. On their way south, they were discovered by Confederate soldiers. Most were executed, while a few escaped and later returned to tell the tale. But all were "true to the Union."

Food

The sleepy town of Comfort may not be known for world-class dining, but the following spots will satisfy hunger and an appetite for charm. **Double D Family Restaurant** (1004 Front St., 830/995-2001, 8am-8pm Sun.-Wed., 8am-9pm Thurs.-Sat., $10) is popular for family-style dining. Here you can get sandwiches, hamburgers, and *migas* for breakfast.

A diverse menu that includes German and Cajun dishes is found at **Guenther's Creekside Grill** (220 Hwy. 473 at 6th St., 830/995-5370, 11am-2pm Tues.-Sat., 5pm-9pm, $10). The exterior may seem a little shabby, but this is probably a trick to keep nonlocals off the trail of great comfort food.

Next to Hotel Faust is **814 A Texas Bistro** (713 High St., 830/995-4990, 6pm-9pm Thurs.-Sat., brunch 11:30am-2pm Sat.-Sun., $15). This upscale yet rustic place is housed in the historic post office building. Plates include lamb, Alaskan halibut, quail, and

mussels, making 814 the most exotic restaurant in the region.

Accommodations

An easy way to find bed-and-breakfast accommodations in Comfort is by going through **Meyer Bed and Breakfast** (845 High St., 888/995-6100, www.meyerbedandbreakfast.com, $120-200). Meyer has several suites in unique historic buildings on beautiful Cypress Creek.

The historic building known as the Ingenhuett-Faust Hotel is home to an excellent bed-and-breakfast, **Hotel Faust** (717 High St., 830/995-3030, www.hotelfaust.com, $80-125). Buildings in the complex include log cabins, Victorian cottages, and old farm buildings, as well as some antiques shops.

Getting There and Around

All travelers arrive in Comfort by the comfort of their own car or by hitchhiking. If you don't have a car you should know there is no bus system for this small town. Also, there are no taxi services.

OLD TUNNEL BATS

Between Fredericksburg and Comfort, inside an abandoned railroad tunnel called Old

Tunnel, is a massive colony of Mexican free-tailed bats. Some say the bat count is over 3 million. The site has been preserved since train stopped using this rail line in 1942. Now the place is called **Old Tunnel State Park** (10619 Old San Antonio Rd., Fredericksburg, 866/978-2287, 6am-5pm daily, free). Every evening in the summer months the bat colony flutters off in search of bugs to eat. A few viewing areas have been designated by the park service, and on peak days someone will step out and give a presentation on the phenomenon. Another spot to view the bats is **Alamo Springs Café** (107 Alamo Rd., Fredericksburg, 830/990-8004, 11am-9pm daily, $8). Bat viewing is nightly May-October, but the Old Tunnel is open year-round from sunrise to sunset. The state park is eight miles east of Comfort off FM 473 on Old San Antonio Road/Old No. 9 Road.

BOERNE

The bucolic little town of Boerne (pop. 13,000), just 30 miles north of San Antonio, is one of the Hill Country's bastions of German heritage. Boerne (correctly pronounced BUR-nee) was originally a village called Tusculum, which was overrun in the mid-1800s by German pioneers who settled here, built a town, and named it after a German writer named Ludwig Börne. Today the attractive downtown features many old limestone buildings built in the 1800s, narrow streets, bridges, and old towering trees. On Main Street, which is also known by its German name of Hauptstrasse, there are many little shops, boutiques, art galleries, and antiques stores that draw tourists year-round.

Although Hauptstrasse is a delight to take in, the town's most beautiful feature is Cibolo Creek, which flows right through the heart of Boerne. This creek—known to locals as "the river"—is home to ducks, geese, and other wildlife, making the setting almost too charming. For more information stop by the **Boerne Convention and Visitors Bureau** (1407 S. Main St., 888/842-8080, visitboerne. org, 8am-5pm Mon.-Fri., 10am-2pm Sat.).

Sights and Activities

No one comes to Boerne for major attractions, grand museums, and big entertainment. People come here to stay in a bed-and-breakfast, walk through the shops, and visit the most beautiful attraction in Central Texas—nature.

History and majesty are to be found in the caves at **Cascade Caverns** (226 Cascade Caverns Rd., 830/755-8080, www.cascadecaverns.com, 9am-5pm daily, $17.95 adults, $11.95 children 11 and under). These living caves have lots of stories to tell visitors. For example, the first cave was the secret hideout for a German recluse running from the law at the turn of the 20th century. Going back further in time, this same cave was a place for Native American ceremonies. Finally, going back to prehistoric times, the remains of a mastodon were found in the cave; its bones are still there. The cave tour lasts about an hour and ends at a 100-foot inner-cave waterfall. Cascade Caverns is south of Boerne just off Highway 10.

Another cave in the area is the **Cave Without a Name** (325 Kreutzberg Rd., 830/537-4212, www.cavewithoutaname.com, 9am-6pm daily in summer, 10am-5pm daily in winter, $20 adults, $18 military and seniors, $10 children 6-12, children under 6 free). This spectacular underworld was discovered in the 1930s. Before it was opened to the public a contest was held to name the cave. Legend has it that a little boy said the cave is too beautiful to name. Thus the cave got its name, or didn't, depending on how you want to look at it. Inside these immense vaulted rooms are intriguing rock formations, stalagmites, stalactites, and delicate soda straws. The cave is northeast of Boerne on Kreutzberg Road, just off RR 474.

The most intriguing thing in Boerne is the **Boerne Village Band**. Established in 1860, this outfit is the oldest continuously active German band in the country, and the second oldest in the world. This is one of the best obscure, historic traditions in the country. You can see the band perform for what's called

Abendkonzerte every other Tuesday night in June and July at the Boerne Main Plaza. If you're in town, you have to see this. But don't expect 150-year-old folks on the tuba—the members have changed over the years.

Shopping

Boerne is a main-street town lined with wine-tasting rooms, trendy boutiques, antiques shops, and art galleries, all housed in historic buildings made of limestone or wood. Walking up and down these sidewalks is an excellent way to not spend your time wisely, which is what this experience is all about. Most shops are open between 10am and 6pm daily. A shop that all must visit is **Carousel Antiques and Pickles** (101 S. Main St., 830/249-9306, 10am-5pm Mon.-Sat., noon-4pm Sun.). The great and unique combination of pickles and antiques is surprisingly brilliant. Other shops worth checking out are **Flashback Funtiques** (248 S. Main St., 830/331-2200, 10am-5pm daily), the Texana crafts-and-stuff store called **Calamity Jane's Trading Co.** (404 S. Main St., 830/249-0081, 10am-5pm Tues.-Sat., noon-5pm Sun.), and **The Green Bull Jewelry Store** (325 S. Main St., 830/249-7393, 10am-5pm Tues.-Sat.).

Food

The local favorite spot to take visitors is **Po Po Restaurant** (829 FM 289, 830/537-4194, 7am-9pm Sun.-Thurs., 7am-10pm Fri.-Sat., $12). The world's largest plate collection in a restaurant covers the walls. American standards are served on the plates.

A popular lunch spot at the center of Boerne, near antiques shops and boutiques, is **Cypress Grille** (170 S. Main St., 830/248-1353, 11am-2pm and 5pm-9pm Tues.-Sun., $12). The new American menu includes sandwiches, homemade soup of the day, and an assortment of salads. People come here to meet up, socialize, get a late start to a day downtown, and to eat home cooking.

Across from Cibolo Creek is the ★ **Dodging Duck Brewhaus** (402 River Rd., 830/248-3825, 11am-9pm Sun.-Thurs., 11am-10pm Fri.-Sat., $11). Standard American fare, such as burgers, beef tenderloin, and salmon, is on offer. Dodging Duck also brews its own beers, which are quite good. Outdoor seating makes this a great place to relax any time of day.

The local favorite breakfast joint is **Bear Moon Bakery** (401 S. Main St., 830/816-2327, 6am-5pm Tues.-Sat., 8am-4pm Sun., $10). Besides cooking up eggs, pancakes, and waffles, Bear Moon has the best baked goods in town.

Boerne fine dining happens at **The Creek Restaurant** (119 Staffel, 830/816-2005, 11am-3pm Tues.-Sun., 5pm-9pm Tues.-Sat., $12 lunch, $28 dinner). The restaurant is housed in an old bungalow on the banks of Cibolo Creek. They've also added a water mill, pond, and outdoor decks, all smothered with southern charm that resembles Georgia more than Texas. The food is upscale but affordable, with a menu that has items such as mushroom fondue, crab cakes, and schnitzel.

Accommodations

The most celebrated historic place to stay in the area is ★ **Ye Kendall Inn** (128 W. Blanco, 800/249-9954, www.yekendallinn.com, $119-249). In 1859 this grand limestone building rented rooms out to stagecoach travelers seeking upscale comfort in the rustic Hill Country. Today the tradition is carried on in the property's 30 rooms filled with antiques and decor that harks back to the pioneer days. There's a bar and a restaurant on the premises.

A charming and centrally located place to stay is **The William** (170 S. Main St., 830/249-2138, www.thewilliamboerne.com, $200-300). Housed in one of Boerne's older landmark buildings in the heart of historic downtown, this newly renovated hotel is romantic and luxurious. If you came to Boerne for the window shopping and wine-tasting, this is the best place to stay—it's all right outside the front door.

The best way to find a bed-and-breakfast in Boerne is by going through **Boerne Reservations** (132 S. Main St., 866/336-3809, www.boernereservations.com, 9am-10pm daily). This reservation service books rooms and cottages in and around town, and can easily match a lodging with a guest. The website has accommodation information, photos, rates, and amenities all in one place, which makes it easy to find the lodging that best suits your needs. The service is at no extra charge to guests.

For chain hotel accommodations, there's **Best Western Texas Country Inn** (35150 Hwy. 10 W., 830/249-9791, $72-127).

GUADALUPE RIVER STATE PARK

A magical place for outdoor recreation of all kinds is **Guadalupe River State Park** (3350 Park Road 31, near Spring Branch, 830/438-2656, 8am-10pm daily, $7 pp). This 2,000-acre park has miles of river frontage in a spectacular setting, not too far from civilization (San Antonio). The thing that makes this place so magical is the Guadalupe River, which is lined with bald cypress trees and filled with wildlife. Visitors to the park enjoy a wide variety of outdoor activities, including canoeing, swimming, fishing, tubing, hiking, and camping. The park has a five mile trail for horseback riding and mountain biking. Admission

includes a two-hour guided tour through Honey Creek State Natural Area, where visitors learn about local plant life, geology, and wildlife. The tour is usually given Saturday at 9am; call to confirm. The park is off Park Road 31 just off Highway 46, eight miles from Highway 281.

★ NATURAL BRIDGE CAVERNS AND WILDLIFE RANCH

If you've ever wanted to explore the belly of the earth in a safe and easy way, **Natural Bridge Caverns** (26495 Natural Bridge Caverns Rd., 210/651-6101, www.naturalbridgecaverns. com, 9am-7pm in summer, closes at 4pm the rest of the year, $21.95 adults, $13.99 children 3-11) has the experience all figured out. The three tours offered vary depending on your interest and level of claustrophobia. The most popular is the Discovery Tour, which is a 75-minute excursion that takes you underground for a half-mile exploration of massive caverns. The second is the Jaremy Room Tour, which is a short-and-sweet trip to a 120-foot-deep chamber—perfect for the whole family. Finally, there's the Adventure Tour, where the brave are outfitted with caving gear and lowered into the entry room by rope. They then

Guadalupe River State Park

proceed on a mile-long journey. All the caves are awe inspiring, from the stalagmites to the stalactites to the constant temperature of 70°F.

Next door to Natural Bridge Caverns is **Natural Bridge Wildlife Ranch** (26515 Natural Bridge Caverns Rd., 830/438-7400, www.wildliferanchtexas.com, 9am-5pm daily, $22 adults 12 and up, $13.50 children 3-11, $20 seniors). Kids love to take the drive through this Texas-style African safari and see giraffes, rhinos, zebras, and many other exotic animals. For the driving tour factor in about 1.5 hours and add an additional 2 hours if you want to enjoy the petting zoo and include lunch in the restaurant.

Western Hill Country

Although all of the Hill Country shares the age-old brand of the Wild West, the western Hill Country is particularly wild and western. The farther west you travel, the more rural the scenery gets, and the more down-home the folks get. When exploring this region, expect to see things out of the ordinary, such as a replica of Stonehenge, folk music jamborees, and dude ranches with real cowboys.

KERRVILLE

All the hard work and the dreams of the western pioneers are fulfilled in the small main-street town of Kerrville (pop. 22,000), on the banks of the Guadalupe River. Although Kerrville wasn't founded by French settler Captain Charles Schreiner, he has become the iconic figure that everyone remembers. In the 1850s, after serving as a Texas Ranger since he was 15, Charles ended up in Kerrville and quickly became a successful businessman. At the peak of his career he found himself in banking, ranching, and promoting the value of mohair (the product of angora goats), and his empire stretched over 600,000 acres. Through his wealth many of the town's historic buildings were erected, and eventually Kerrville established itself as a viable mark on the map of Texas.

Today Kerrville is considered by many to be the capital of the Hill Country. The town is a must-visit hamlet that promotes leisure, great music, and lots of outdoor activities. The revitalized downtown retains old-world charm but offers modern comfort and style.

It's easy to get sucked in to the boutiques, galleries, shops, and cafés, which makes Kerrville a tourist trap in the truest sense of the word. But getting trapped here is exactly what you want. The town is sleepy and quiet until one of the many festivals held here injects hustle and bustle into the streets.

Kerrville is situated on the banks of the Guadalupe River, at the quiet edge of the Hill Country just 104 miles from Austin and 65 miles from San Antonio. Because of the town's location, it's considered one of the healthiest places to live in the United States, boasting clean air, an unpolluted environment, and a great climate. Kerrville is just off Interstate 10, south on Highway 16. From Austin you would travel west on Highway 290 and at Fredericksburg take Highway 16 South. Once there, the **Kerrville Convention and Visitors Bureau** (2108 Sidney Baker St., 830/792-3535 or 800/221-7958, www.kerrvilletexascvb.com, 8:30am-5pm Mon.-Fri., 9am-3pm Sat., 10am-3pm Sun.) is a great place to start, as it offers copious amounts of information about the town and surrounding area, including easy-to-use maps, a great brochure on historic buildings of Kerrville, and a guide (with checklist) to local birds.

Sights and Activities

In the center of historic downtown Kerrville is the **Schreiner Mansion Museum** (226 Earl Garrett St., 830/895-5222, by appointment only, free). Hailed as a pioneer of the region, Captain Charles Schreiner was a Frenchman who left his castle (literally), relocated to San Antonio, and eventually settled in the Texas Hill Country. This mansion—which was his castle, so to speak—is a museum piece itself, offering a glimpse into the life of the wealthier early settlers. Marvel at the elegance of the fiesta gowns worn by the ladies of Hill Country high society, the bronze fountain imported from France, the primitive Texas art, Civil War memorabilia, and molds used to make bullets by hand. People with money were able to pull off a highbrow way of life even though they were in a rugged frontier, thanks to laborers who performed the more arduous chores. The piano in the formal parlor was brought to Kerrville by covered wagon in the late 1800s.

The talent of local artists is showcased at **Kerr Arts and Culture Center** (228 Earl Garrett St., 830/895-2911, 10am-4pm Tues.-Sat., 1pm-4pm Sun., free). Housed in the historic post office building, the slick gallery space displays high-quality works including pottery, paintings, quilting, woodwork, and jewelry.

The headquarters of famed jeweler **James Avery** (145 Avery Rd. N., on the north side of Hwy. 10 off Harper Rd., 830/895-1122, 10am-8pm Mon.-Sat., noon-6pm Sun., free) is in Kerrville. Whether you're a jewelry buff or not, Mr. Avery's designs are sure to impress. Started in a two-car garage in 1954, this little homespun shop has grown into a national mail-order business. Designs include everything from bracelets to earrings to crosses, all bearing the unique style of the artist. Here you can visit his shop and purchase jewelry, but the most interesting thing is the visitors center, where guests can watch artisans at work.

This riverside town's best natural feature lies just to the south at **Kerrville-Schreiner Park** (2385 Bandera Hwy., 830/257-5392). The Guadalupe River winds its way through the upper edge of the park, creating a lush and rugged landscape of rolling hills and live oaks. Camping, fishing, hiking, swimming, canoeing, picnicking, tubing, and wildlife-watching are why people come here. The hiking is easy,

Scenic Drive: Route 16

The windy stretch of road between Kerrville and Medina is especially fantastic. At the start you may think, "what's the big deal?" But keep driving, because at a certain point you will feel like you drove straight out of small-town Texas and right into a Dr. Seuss book. This magical country road takes you through hill and dale, and through miniature gorges that are absolutely gorgeous. The hills are unusually bumpy and pointy, and the road is squirrelly to the point of nausea.

as most of the trails don't have much of an incline and are clearly marked. Wildlife you are bound to encounter include white-tailed deer, wild turkeys, rabbits, armadillos, and rare birds. Ornithologists should note that the Texas Hill Country is one of a few places to see rare birds such as the golden-cheeked warbler and the black-capped vireo. There are 58 designated tent sites with access to restrooms, 62 RV sites, and 23 mini-cabins available for rent. The entrance fee is adults $4, children $1, seniors $2, not to exceed $10 per vehicle. Camping is $10 a night, water and electric sites are $23, and full-hookup sites are $26. Reservations are recommended. The park is off Highway 173.

The **Museum of Western Art** (1550 Bandera Hwy./Hwy. 173, 830/896-2553, www.museumofwesternart.com, 10am-4pm Tues.-Sat., $7 adults, children under 8 free) is a one-of-a-kind gallery that features contemporary art about cowboys and created by cowboys. Dramatic sculptures and paintings romanticize cowboys on the range in a way that captures the imagination and fosters a desire to eat rattlesnakes and drink coffee boiled over an open fire, without filters. The artistry and craftsmanship in all pieces on exhibit is spectacular and truly world class. For the kids there's the permanent exhibit featuring things used in the everyday life of a cowboy. The building is constructed of heavy timbers and limestone, and the grounds are dotted with life-size bronze statues, making this a long-lasting monument to the Wild West and the artistic tradition that captures it. The museum is on the southern side of the Guadalupe River.

Cultural and natural history merge at **Riverside Nature Center** (150 Francisco Lemos St., 830/257-4837, www.riversidenaturecenter.org, 10am-6pm Mon.-Sat., free). This former farm is now a sanctuary for wildlife and native plants. Inside the main building are feature exhibits, educational programs, a gift shop, and a natural sciences library. Outside, on the grounds of the center, there's an arboretum of Texas trees, a wildflower meadow, butterfly gardens, and millions of insects. The gardens and trails are open daily from dawn to dusk.

Food

Every Hill Country town has great barbecue. In Kerrville it's served up at **Bill's Bar-B-Que** (1909 Junction Hwy., 830/895-5733, 11am-7pm Tues.-Sat., $10). Bill's is *the* local favorite for all meats barbecued to perfection. True to Texas form, your dining experience is among a flock of mounted deer heads on the walls.

The local favorite for food downtown is the reliable **Rails—A Café at the Depot** (615 E. Schreiner St., 830/257-3877, 11am-9pm Mon.-Sat., $15) Expect burgers, wraps, salads, and some creative and mouthwatering dishes such as shrimp tostadas, beef masala, and tilapia tacos. The homey environment makes the experience fun.

Hill Country Café (806 Main St., 830/257-6665, 6am-2pm Mon.-Fri., 6am-11am Sat., $9) is a local institution that serves American standards for breakfast and lunch only. Being smack-dab in downtown, it's popular and often packed.

Accommodations

For an inexpensive bed with no fanfare there are a couple options: **Flagstaff Inn Motel** (906 Junction Hwy., 830/792-4449, $40-70)

and **America's Best Value Inn** (1804 Sydney Baker St., 830/896-8200, $45-70).

One of the Hill Country's most famous and historic ranches is ★ **Y. O. Ranch** (1736 Y. O. Ranch Rd., west of Kerrville, 830/640-3222 or 800/967-2624, www.yoranch.net). Picture longhorn cattle drives, a classy lodge-style resort, cowboys, and zebras, and you've envisioned Y. O. Ranch. This exotic game and hunting ranch spans 50 square miles, which is equivalent to 40,000 acres. Zebras, antelope, giraffes, and good ol' fashioned longhorns are among the 56 species of exotic and native animals that roam these parts. Established back in 1880 by Captain Charles Schreiner (of Kerrville fame), the ranch now offers exotic wildlife tours, horseback riding, rustic accommodations, and cowboy suppers featuring—you guessed it—meat and potatoes. Reservations are necessary. Guided hunts cost $250 a day for up to three people. Accommodations are around $150 per night, per person, and include three meals. Tours for wildlife viewing are $33 for adults, but if you are staying on the ranch tours cost only $18.

The classiest place to stay in the Kerrville area is **Inn of the Hills Resort** (1001 Junction Hwy., 830/895-5000, www.innofthehills.com, $90-250). Amenities include room service, an Olympic-size pool and a kiddie pool, tennis courts, and a fitness club. There's also an upscale restaurant that offers breakfast, lunch buffets, and dinner daily.

For a classic Texas cabin experience, **Trails End Guest Home** (180 Gay Dr. N., 830/995-2812, $129-194) offers rustic cabins in a quiet spot 15 miles outside Kerrville that makes for a great getaway. A big country-style breakfast is brought to your door each morning. For hot summer nights there's a pool, and some rooms have hot tubs. Farm animals linger on the property, adding to the ambience.

Getting There and Around

Most travelers arrive in Kerrville by car. However, there is a **Greyhound** station (206 Schreiner St., 800/285-2425), which can be an affordable way to get here from Austin and San Antonio. If you don't have a car you should know there is no bus system for this small town. However, there is taxi service available through **Kerr Kab & Deliveries** (830/928-5222). Since the area is small, cab fares probably won't exceed $10.

WEST OF KERRVILLE
★ Stonehenge II

The area's most peculiar attraction is **Stonehenge II.** Situated on a flat spot in a field a few miles west of Kerrville, before the small town of Hunt, is a 60 percent scale version of Stonehenge, the iconic rock structure near Salisbury, England. Unknowing folks traveling down this small Hill Country road who happen to see this amazing monument to God-knows-what are completely baffled, and unsure of what they're seeing. Just as mysterious as the original, this smaller version begs the question: "What were they thinking?" Was it created by aliens trying to contact their motherland? No! How about druids? Nope! Stonehenge II was conceived and constructed by two locals, Al Shepperd and Doug Hill. Material: concrete. Reason: none needed. The site is located on Highway 39 before the town of Hunt. Stonehenge II is on private property, but visitors are welcome during daylight hours. I recommend bringing a packed lunch and hanging out for about an hour.

LOVE CREEK ORCHARDS

If you plan on leaving the Kerrville area on Highway 16 going south you will probably want to stop off at **Love Creek Orchards Cider Mill and Country Store** (14024 State Hwy. 16, south of Medina, 830/589-2588, http://lovecreekorchards.com, 9am-5pm daily). This is a place where the apple is worshipped and glorified in its many forms. Although the orchards are lovely, the real reason why everybody comes here is the country store. To find it, follow the distinct smell of baking apples, which wafts down the highway. Once the unsuspecting visitor walks onto the grounds they are transported into a Norman Rockwell painting where America seems to be

Marvel at a weird replica of Stonehenge that is out in the far reaches of the Hill Country.

perfect and free of sin, at least until the apple is served up. Here you'll find apple pies, apple cider, applesauce, apple turnovers, apple muffins, apple rings, apple butter, and apple jellies and jams. In all, the folks at Love Creek produce more than 33 different products from apples. Yes, the temptation is great, but you can't blame Eve—this place is owned and operated by the Adams family.

BANDERA

The authentic, honest-to-goodness western town of Bandera (pop. 1,000) considers itself the Cowboy Capital of the World. When you show up you may wonder if this is true, because it can come across as a bleak little town at first. Sure, it's not a set from a spaghetti western, and it doesn't have a sexy hunk galloping down Main Street looking for the sheriff. But if you scratch the surface just a little, you will see there's much to discover and experience here that is truly western.

According to legend, many bloody battles between Apache and Comanche and

Back in the Saddle Again

Bandera is a popular place for saddling up and heading out into the country. Many of the dude ranches in and around Bandera offer horseback-riding packages with accommodations or day-trip horseback riding at an hourly rate. Experienced riders can head out on trails alone, and the inexperienced can ride with a guide. Most ranches don't have addresses, as they are out in the country, so it's good to look them up on the Internet or call to get directions before heading out. Children under six usually can't ride, and reservations are required.

For a guided stroll through the countryside for a few hours, there's **Bar M Ranch** (RR 1077 W., 2.5 miles southwest of Bandera, 830/796-9096, www.bar-mranch.com, $35 per person per hour). Trails will take riders over brook and dale, through pastures, and in the shadows of cliffs. Wildlife abounds, so bring a camera. Rates vary by trail. Trails are generally 2-3 hours; those three hours and longer require experienced riders.

Another ranch that offers hourly horseback riding is **Rancho Cortez** (RR 1077, 830/796-9339, www.ranchocortez.com, $35 per hour). Hourly rates are higher for rides in Hill Country State Natural Area.

For a ride on the trails of the beautiful Hill Country State Natural Area, call **Desert Hearts Cowgirls Club** (830/796-7001, http://desertheartscowgirlclub.yolasite.com, $65 for the first two hours, $30 for each additional hour), founded by Jeanne Beauxbeannes (pronounced "BOH-bee-nee"). She's been riding the park longer than any of the rangers. Her idea of hiking in this park is simply hiking your leg over a saddle. Jeanne offers interpretive guided trail rides that last a minimum of two hours. Half-day and all-day rides are offered only in fall and spring.

the Spanish conquistadors took place in Bandera Pass (now 12 miles north on Hwy. 173). Supposedly a red flag (*bandera* is Spanish for flag) marked the boundary between Spanish and Native American territory. In 1852 the town was officially founded, and Bandera became a staging area for western cattle drives, a Mormon colony, and the largest Polish settlement in the United States.

Today Bandera is still an emblem of the American frontier. It's home to world-champion rodeo cowboys, craftspeople who produce fine furniture and leather products, and old-style Texas dance halls. So what draws people here? The living spirit of the old West, camping under the stars, rodeos, kayaking and canoeing, catfish and bass fishing, honkytonks and country music, horseback riding, and Texas-style R&R.

Bandera's population hovers around 1,000. The downtown is small and the centerpiece is the Old Bandera County Courthouse, which is now the library. Its distinct Renaissance Revival architecture evokes the Spanish era, while the rest of the town harkens to the old West, demonstrating the richness of Bandera's history.

For more information about Bandera there's the **Bandera County Convention and Visitors Bureau** (126 Hwy. 16 S., 830/796-3045 or 800/364-3833, www.banderacowboycapital.com, 9am-5pm Mon.-Fri., 10am-3pm Sat.). The helpful staff can assist in finding just the right lodgings for you as well as offer information about anything, from rodeo schedules to a historical walking tour of downtown.

Sights and Activities

The best small-town museum in Texas happens to be in Bandera: the **Frontier Times Museum** (510 13th St., 830/796-3864, www.frontiertimesmuseum.org, 10am-4:30pm Mon.-Sat., $5 adults, $3 seniors, $2 children 6-17, under 6 free). This homespun museum is more like an antiques store where you can't buy anything—you can only look. Here you can imbibe the luster of the old days and breath in the scent of old wood and dusty artifacts from the Wild West's cowboy lore and Bandera's history.

The 5,400 acres that make up the **Hill Country State Natural Area** (830/796-4413) were originally the site of the Merrick Ranch. Located 10 miles west of Bandera on FM 1077, this park has virtually nothing to offer in the way of amenities—just good ol' nature. Camping is permitted in a 20-acre designated area, but don't expect restrooms and showers here, as primitive camping is what this park is all about. Make sure you bring water, food, and toilet paper, bury all waste matter, and take all your trash with you when you leave. This largely undeveloped, nearly pristine park offers a rugged place for hiking, walk-in camping, backpacking, mountain biking, and horseback riding among canyons, springs, and rocky hills. More than 20 caves and 10 springs add to the majesty of the park.

Six miles southeast of town on Highway 16 is **Polly's Chapel,** built in 1882 by José Policarpo Rodriguez. He came from Mexico to Texas and became famous as a scout for the U.S. Army and a mercenary. He later joined the Methodist church and became a licensed preacher and built this tiny chapel. José, known by locals as Polly, is buried in the graveyard. The chapel is often open to the public.

Living up to the prestigious title of Cowboy Capital, Bandera hosts a wide array of **rodeos** from spring to fall. Every Tuesday and Friday night from Memorial Day weekend in May through Labor Day weekend in September, the **Twin Elm Guest Ranch** (810 FM 470, 830/796-3628, www.twinelmranch.com) hosts open rodeos. Professional rodeos are put on by the **Bandera Pro Rodeo Association** (www.banderaprorodeo.org) every year on Memorial Day weekend.

One unusual activity that is highly recommended is venerating a jukebox in town. Yes, there are jukeboxes with George Jones and George Strait everywhere in the United States. However, this machine in the **Bandera County Kronkosky Library** (505 Main St., 830/796-4213) is special. This dusty little town has been home to many musicians over the years. Some locals organized and created the **Bandera Music History Project** to honor these folks. Their efforts resulted in a little shrine with a jukebox.

Music and Dancing

Bandera is known for keeping honky-tonk alive with live country music, line dancing, and sawdust floors. Live dances are held Wednesday-Sunday nights throughout the year at the various honky-tonks and dance halls in and around town. Bandera is also known for jam sessions that grow into full-on hootenannies. Expect to see accordions, Stetsons, guitars, and beer bellies at the following bars: **Arkey Blue's Silver Dollar** (308 Main St., 830/796-8826), **Chikin Coop** (402 Main St., 830/796-4496), and the **11th Street Cowboy Bar** (307 11th St., 830/796-4849).

Food

In Bandera, eating out is cheap and amusing. Sometimes the cuisine can be a bit too cowboy, though. By this I mean too greasy, meaty, and salty. You can expect to spend under $10 for a meal and a drink.

For barbecue, there's **Busbee's Bar-B-Que** (319 Main St., 830/796-3153, 10:30am-8pm Sun.-Mon. and Wed.-Thurs., 10:30am-9pm Fri.-Sat., $7). They unabashedly declare themselves the cowboy's choice for barbecue, and if this is true, how can one go wrong eating here? Beef is served up by the pound with the usual sides.

The landmark eatery in town is **O. S. T. Restaurant** (305 Main St., 830/796-3836, 6am-9pm Mon.-Sat., 7am-9pm Sun., $8), also known as Old Spanish Trail. Down-home cooking here includes chicken-fried steak, roast, meatloaf, and other American fare. One room in the restaurant is entirely devoted to the memory of Marion Morrison. Who's this, you might ask? The Duke—better known as John Wayne.

Accommodations

Although Bandera has a couple of typical motels, the popular way to lodge is in a dude ranch or a guest ranch. For most people, staying in a dude ranch is a once-in-a-lifetime opportunity. Most ranches offer rustic accommodations and a wide range of activities, such as campfire storytelling, marshmallow roasting, horseback riding, swimming, and nature walks. Rates for dude and guest ranches are more than those of your average motel/hotel but often include up to three meals a day.

For predictably clean and affordable accommodations within walking distance to shops and restaurants there's **Bandera Lodge** (700 St., Hwy. 16 S., 830/796-3093, $63-90). Nothing fancy here, just a TV, a bed, Internet access, and a bathroom.

A comfortable ranch that offers hotel-style amenities is the **Flying L Guest Ranch** (800/292-5134, www.flyingl.com, $180-300). On over 700 acres, this ranch offers 41 cottages and suites, many with fireplaces. Here you can spend the day horseback riding along the San Julian Creek, swimming, fishing, and playing sports. The Flying L also has an 18-hole championship golf course and packages for golfers that make for a resort getaway with a ranch feel. All cottages and suites require a two-night minimum stay.

Fun for the whole family is to be had at **Mayan Dude Ranch** (Pecan St., 830/460-3036, www.mayanranch.com, $130-150 for adults, $70-95 for children under 18). This ranch has been hosting people for decades, providing couples and families with rustic rooms and cottages, horseback riding, hayrides, tubing, fishing, hiking, golf, and tennis. The facility is huge, and it takes a lot of concentration to be bored here. Included in the price are three cowboy-style meals and a horseback ride.

Across from the Medina River are the cozy cottages of **River Front Motel** (1103 Maple St., 830/460-3690, $74-125). These semi-rustic, clean rooms are furnished by local craftspeople and offer convenience, location, and quiet.

For rustic ranch lodgings, the **Twin Elm Guest Ranch** (Hwy. 470, 830/796-3628, www.twinelmranch.com, $105-115 adults, $80 teens, $65 children under 12) can draw the inner cowpoke right out of you. Twin Elm has 21 units, all clean and with air-conditioning; some have bunk beds and porches. Rates vary for high and low seasons. Rates include three big cowboy-style meals a day, access to the rodeos held every Tuesday and Friday night during the summer, marshmallow roasting, swimming, and relaxing in hammocks. For a few more bucks, guided horseback riding is offered.

A dude ranch retreat isn't complete without spending some time with horses.

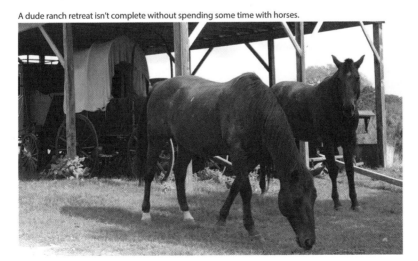

VANDERPOOL

The small town of Vanderpool (pop. 91) is primarily a center for sheep, goat, and cattle ranching. Back in 1885, when a post office was established out here for settlers and ranchers, they decided to give this place a name. Not much has changed since then—the main feature here is still the post office. So what's out here? This quiet area at the western edge of Bandera County is exceptionally beautiful, with some of the most scenic rural roads in the Hill Country. The town, if it can even be called a town, is situated on the lazy Sabinal River near a state park that is a popular getaway for city folk.

The only sight out here is the **Lone Star Motorcycle Museum** (Hwy. 187 N., four miles north of Vanderpool, 830/966-6103, www.lonestarmotorcyclemuseum.com, 10am-5pm Fri.-Sun., $5). This labor of love was pieced together by a motorcycle connoisseur who had extra money to spend on a hobby. The collection spans the entire history and evolution of the motorcycle, from the first motorized bicycles to the hogs of our time. The recent resurgence of the chopper and custom motorcycle has brought more traffic than usual to this small museum. The scenic roads leading up to the museum make this a great destination for a weekend motorcycle ride.

★ LOST MAPLES STATE NATURAL AREA

The main reason for going as far west as Vanderpool is **Lost Maples State Natural Area** (37221 FM 187, 830/966-3413, 8am-10pm daily, $5 Dec.-Sept., $6 Oct.-Nov.). The beautiful bigtooth maples are the big attraction here, and they aren't "lost" or even hard to find. In the fall these delicate but enormous trees explode with color. Fall foliage is most dramatic in November, and that's when the crowds come. Hikers are encouraged to stay on trails, as the trees can be damaged by soil compaction. Bigtooth maples require very specific conditions and have shallow roots, making them rare and vulnerable.

Lost Maples State Natural Area

The park is home to three State Champion Big Trees: an escarpment chokecherry, a Texas ash, and a bigtooth maple, nominated by the American Forestry Association. Park facilities include campsites with water and electricity, picnic areas, and restrooms with showers. Primitive camp areas are also available, but you have to hike in about 11 miles to get to them. The park is four miles north of Vanderpool on FM 187. Plan on walking the park for about an hour. If you bring a packed lunch, make it two hours.

UVALDE

At the far reaches of the western Hill Country is the slow-paced town of Uvalde (pop. 16,000). This Wild West frontier town was first settled by the Spanish back in 1674 as part of a missionary effort to convert the Apache population. The Spanish bailed on this effort after repeated attacks by local Lipan-Apache; they returned in 1709 under the military leadership of Spanish governor Juan del Ugalde (Uvalde), who defeated the Apache. According to legend, Uvalde Canyon is the spot of this decisive battle.

Although there are traces of the Spanish era, Uvalde is most remembered as a Wild West town, and as the stomping grounds of the notorious gunslinger, outlaw, and sheriff J. King Fisher. Although Fisher died in a gunfight in the Vaudeville Theater in San Antonio, he's buried here in Pioneer Cemetery. The other historical character who called Uvalde home was John "Cactus Jack" Garner, vice president under Franklin D. Roosevelt, whose home is now a museum.

Uvalde is the most remote town covered in this guidebook. Although it's out in the middle of nowhere, Uvalde is the most noteworthy town at the farthest southwestern rim of the Hill Country, and it can make for an interesting day trip from both San Antonio and Austin. From San Antonio, go west 80 miles on Highway 90. From Austin, it's probably best to go through Bandera and take Highway 173 south to Highway 90, then go west. The **Uvalde Convention and Visitors Bureau** (300 E. Main St., 830/278-4115 or 800/588-2533, www.visituvalde.com, 9am-5pm Mon.-Fri.) is the best place to get information.

Sights and Activities

Housed in a World War II-era hangar at the Uvalde municipal airport is the **Aviation Museum of Texas** (201 Sul Ross Blvd., hangar number 1 at Garner Field, 830/278-2552). See WWII aircraft and memorabilia, such as a disassembled Martin B-26, a Stearman, PT-17, Liason-4, 1946 Ercoupe, and a Fairchild. Due to a lack of volunteers museum hours are limited (9am-4pm Tues. and Fri., 1pm-4pm Sat., or by request); a donation of $2 will get you in.

If you make it all the way out to Uvalde have to check out **Briscoe Art and Antique Collection** (200 E. Nopal St., in the First State Bank, 830/278-6231, www.fsbuvalde.com, 9am-3pm Mon.-Fri., free). People are always surprised to find that out in this remote Texas town, inside a bank, there's an extensive, multimillion-dollar art collection that includes original masterpieces by Rembrandt and Gainsborough, and works by American Western artists Salinas and Warren. The collection was developed by rancher, oilman, banker, and former Texas governor Dolph Briscoe and his wife, and can be seen by simply strolling into the bank and looking around. For a guided tour, call in advance.

Built in 1891, the **Janey Slaughter-Briscoe Grand Opera House** (100 W. North St., 830/278-4184, 9am-3pm Mon.-Fri., free) was once the center for cultural activity in southwestern Texas. The opera house is now an active performing-arts center. Whether there's something happening here or not, it's worth poking your head into this historic building. The stage and most of the interior have the original turn-of-the-20th-century decor.

The **Briscoe-Garner Museum** (333 North Park, 830/278-5018, 9am-4pm Tues.-Sat., free) is in the home of John "Cactus Jack" Garner, vice president under Franklin D. Roosevelt. On display are items associated with Mr. Garner's life, including items from his political career as well as area history. A floor of the house is dedicated to Dolph Briscoe.

Food

At the Amber Sky Motel is the **Amber Sky Coffee Shop** (2001 E. Main St., 830/278-3923, 6am-3pm Mon.-Sat., $7), where locals have been getting their coffee and conversation for years. Here you can get a delicious home-cooked meal, a pie and a paper, and slow start to the day.

Long-time Uvalde tradition is offered at **Evett's Barbecue** (301 E. Main St., 830/278-6204, 10:30am-6pm Tues.-Sat., 10:30am-4pm Sat., $7). Choose smoked-to-perfection barbecue and sides, or a sandwich, all dirt cheap.

For a plate of country cooking there's **Lunkers Grill** (810 E. Main St., 830/278-2060, 11am-9pm daily, $9). Satisfy your appetite with beef, green beans, and a side of carbs.

Accommodations

Amber Sky Motel (2005 E. Main St., 830/278-5602, $52-62) is your roadside mainstay, with 39 units. A restaurant is on the premises.

For slightly fancier accommodations there's the **Quality Inn** (920 E. Main St., 830/278-4511, $88). This hotel has a pool, an on-site restaurant, banquet rooms, and a cocktail lounge.

For luxury in a bed-and-breakfast atmosphere let **Live Oaks Bed & Breakfast** (6 Tanglewood, 830/591-2340, www.liveoaksbnb.com, $100-130) take care of you. Live Oaks is nestled in a secluded meadow of tall mesquite and live oak trees on a six-acre plot on the outskirts of town. When you think of a bed-and-breakfast, you may think of an old converted Victorian house, but that's not what you'll find here. Think new construction, contemporary design, clean and simple rooms, and great service.

Eastern Rim

The Eastern Rim of the Hill Country is defined by I-35, which connects San Antonio to Austin, Dallas, and everything in between. The towns along the freeway were the original settlements of the first German immigrants back in the 1800s. Today these towns are getaway hot spots for city folk who want to tube the beautiful rivers, shop for antiques, and enjoy leisurely meals on outdoor patios.

★ Tubing the Guadalupe River

One of the main attractions in this corner of the Hill Country is the Guadalupe River, which winds its way from the west and passes through New Braunfels. This ancient resource has been attracting humans for centuries. From the native populations in ancient times to the fun seekers of today, this spectacular river has been a must-see for everyone. Besides being astonishingly beautiful and even majestic, the Guadalupe River is a virtual air conditioner for locals and visitors, as it's always cool and always running. Activities include swimming, tubing, and rafting. In the summer you'll find thousands of folks from all walks of life sunning, relaxing, and drinking as they

The Hill Country's natural AC is the Guadalupe River.

bob down the river through groves of bald cypress and over mild white-water rapids.

The riverhead is at Canyon Lake, and New Braunfels and Gruene are the end of the line. The entire length is approximately 20 miles. On any given day May-October you'll find a mob of sunburned, exhausted, tipsy folks staggering out of the exit points along the river carrying inner tubes, ice chests, and empty beverage containers. It's a sight to behold. Floating the short circuit takes about an hour, and floating the long one can take about six hours. On the trip tubers encounter ancient cypress trees, miniature waterfalls, and serene settings around every bend.

Businesses offer tube and raft rentals along with shuttle service to various starting and exiting points along the river. A local favorite is tubing the Horseshoe, which is an upper portion of the Guadalupe River near Canyon Lake. The best outfit for tube rentals and shuttling is **Whitewater River Tube Rentals** (11860 FM 306, 830/964-3800, www.floattheguadalupe.com). These folks offer the best two- to four-hour float service, along with canvas tubes (more comfortable than rubber), cooler tubes, and fast shuttle service. If you want to make a day of it, plan on departing in the afternoon so you can arrive and catch a live music show at their famed amphitheater, at the end of the line. The tubing fee of $20 a day includes tube, shuttle, and parking.

Tubing also takes place on the stretch of the Guadalupe River around New Braunfels and Gruene. For tube rentals there's **Rockin' R River Rides** (1405 Gruene Rd., 830/629-9999 or 800/553-5628, www.rockinr.com) and **Gruene River Company** (1404 Gruene Rd., 830/625-2800 or 888/705-2800, www.toobing.com). Farther into New Braunfels is **Comal Rockin R** (193 S. Liberty., http://comalrockinr.com, 830/620-6262). Tube rentals for most outfits are around $15, coolers are $15, and cooler tubes are $18. Inflatable canoes run $30-55, and rafts for 3-6 people are $25.

To reach the main locations for either of these companies from I-35, exit at Loop 337 and go north toward the town of Gruene.

The Guadalupe River

THE HILL COUNTRY
EASTERN RIM

© AVALON TRAVEL

After you cross the Guadalupe River, turn right on Gruene Road. Drive up to the river and park. You can plan for a half day of tubing or you can spend a full day in the area tubing and afterwards enjoying food at a nearby restaurants.

MCKINNEY FALLS STATE PARK

A bucolic spot on the eastern side of I-35 between San Antonio and Austin is home to **McKinney Falls State Park** (5808 McKinney Falls Pkwy., 512/243-1643, 8am-10pm daily, $4). This beautiful area on Onion Creek was settled by one of Steven F. Austin's original 300 colonists, Thomas F. McKinney, back in the 1850s. Ruins of his original homestead have been preserved. Park facilities include 84 campsites with water and electricity, screened shelters with bunk beds, and picnic sites. There's also an interpretive hiking trail that's just under a mile long, as well as over three miles of paved trails. Mountain biking is available on designated trails. Camping costs $16 per site.

SAN MARCOS

Between Austin and San Antonio, on I-35, is the small river city of San Marcos (pop. 44,000). Over 12,000 years ago Native Americans lived in this area, making it the oldest continuously inhabited place on the continent. It's not hard to figure out why people have always lived here. This lush spot on the San Marcos River is where springs from an underground reservoir burst forth, creating the riverhead. The result: beauty and life.

Today San Marcos is a town that wears many hats. It's home to Texas State University and the state's largest shopping outlet center, and it's a place for ranchers and country folk to get supplies. But San Marcos's most important aspect is the ancient river. For more information contact the **San Marcos Tourist Information Center** (617 I-35 N., 512/393-5930, www.sanmarcostexas.com, 8:30am-5pm Mon.-Fri.).

Scenic Drive: Devil's Backbone

One of many scenic drives in the Hill Country is Devil's Backbone, which is out in the country near Wimberley. This is a winding country road that cuts its way along a dramatic ridge and through a valley of rolling hills. This drive is at its visual climax in the spring. To get to Devil's Backbone from San Marcos, follow RR 12 west to RR 32, where the scenic drive travels west for about 14 miles.

Sights and Activities

The fourth-most visited attraction in the state of Texas is the shopping mecca **Premium Outlets** (3939 I-35 S., exit 200, Centerpoint Rd., 512/396-2200, www.premiumoutlets.com, 10am-9pm Mon.-Sat., 10am-7pm Sun.). Every year more than six million shoppers visit the sea of concrete and buildings that make up the shopping center, in search of deals, steals, the new thing, the old thing at a discount, and an endless array of bargains. The 110-plus factory outlet stores offer everything from apparel and accessories to health and beauty items to home furnishings and housewares. The outlets have been developed with a Disneyland aesthetic, such as castle-like towers and gondola rides, that only adds to the draw. If you plan to join the hordes shopping here be sure to pick up a map of the complex as soon as you arrive, and plan on making a day of it.

Texas State University's **Aquarena Center** (921 Aquarena Springs Dr., 512/245-7570, www.aquarena.txstate.edu, 10am-5pm daily, free) is Central Texas's contribution to the science of water. At the center there's an aquarium, an endangered-species exhibit, a wetlands boardwalk, and scientific diving, all to educate visitors about the fundamental element of all life—water. The highlight of the Aquarena is taking a tour in a glass-bottom boat to explore the watery underworld without getting wet. The 30-minute boat tour costs $9.75 adults, $8 seniors (62+), $6 children 3-12, and 2 and under are free.

San Marcos's version of a theme park is **Wonder World** (1000 Prospect St., exit 202 off I-35, 512/392-3760, www.wonderworldpark.com). Along with dramatic caverns to explore, Wonder World also has an antigravity house, animals on the prowl, an observation tower, and a mini train to ride. Summer hours are 8am-8pm daily June-August; winter hours are 9am-5pm Monday-Friday, 9am-6pm Saturday-Sunday September-May. Ticket prices range $7-24 depending on what attractions you want to experience.

One of the most popular activities in San Marcos is tubing down the San Marcos River. **Lions Club Tube Rental** (in City Park across from the university, 512/396-5466, www.tubesanmarcos.com) makes the experience easy. Just show up at their site, pick out a tube, and jump in the river. The Lions Club folks will pick you up at the Rio Vista Dam (one-hour trip) or Martindale Dam (six-hour trip) and drive you back to the start point at the Lions Club. Rental rates range $7-14 depending on the type of tube. Deposits are required. Summer hours are 10am-7pm daily June-August; winter hours are 10am-7pm on weekends only September-May. Last tube rental is always at 5:30pm.

Food

The **Café on the Square** (126 N. LBJ, 512/396-9999, 6:30am-11pm Mon.-Sat., 8am-10pm Sun., $8) is where all the town's gossip goes down. Locals converge here all throughout the day and night, and sip iced tea and eat breakfast well past noon. This is the type of place where it's OK to occupy a table for hours. The food is standard American, delivered with above-standard hospitality.

Palmers (218 W. Moore, 512/353-3500, www.palmerstexas.com, 11am-10pm Sun.-Thurs., 11am-11pm Fri.-Sat., $10) offers the classiest environment in San Marcos for lunch and dinner. The menu offers a diverse selection of entrées, from pastas to steaks, all served at tables situated among plants and trees.

WIMBERLEY

The wacky little valley town of Wimberley (pop. 2,600) is in an incredible setting on the Blanco River and Cypress Creek. Many residents of Wimberley don't think the outside world knows about their quirky little town, and they want to keep it that way. I hate to disappoint, but people are on to them and their town, and visit by the thousands. Some visit and love the place so much that they move there. Wimberley has become home to artists, authors, musicians, and people seeking a simple life away from the city. This has given rise to an organic community of artists, which has made Wimberley into a bona fide art town. This identity has been grafted to an old tradition of ranching, which gives Wimberley a funky, charming, and offbeat identity crisis.

Wimberley has been struggling with its identity ever since its founding back in the 1850s. The town was first settled by a veteran of the Texas Revolution named Williams Winters, who built a mill on the location. The town was called Winters until a man named John Cade bought the mill and renamed the town Cade's Mill. A few years later a wealthy man from Llano named Pleasant Wimberley bought the mill and changed the name to Wimberley. For over a hundred years nothing changed much in the small town. Then in the 1970s and '80s hippies started showing up, giving way to the art scene. Today, you'll find a charming town; a fascinating little shopping area at **Wimberley Square,** where some artists peddle their wares; and over a hundred bed-and-breakfasts in the surrounding countryside. Although Wimberley's status as an art town draws people here, the real reason people come is to simply do nothing.

For more information stop by **Wimberley Visitor Center** (14100 RR 12, 512/847-2201, 9am-4pm Mon.-Sat., 1pm-4pm Sun.).

Sights and Activities

Wimberley's lifeline is the scenic **Blanco River,** which cuts its way through town amid extraordinarily beautiful surroundings. The best way to take in the Blanco River is to drive up River Road. It only offers about a mile of river frontage views, but it's well worth the trip.

The other feature of town is also a natural one: Cypress Creek. The spot to see this creek at its best is at **Blue Hole** (RR 3237, north of town). This majestic piece of the river has been a popular swimming hole ever since this area was settled. It's called Blue Hole for a reason—the water is a deep cobalt blue.

People from all over the area converge in Wimberley once a month for **Market Day at Lions Field** (RR 2325, in Lions Field, 6am-6pm first Saturday of the month April-Dec., free). More than 450 vendors set up booths under tree-covered paths. The scene is exotic bazaar meets country kitsch, with vendors peddling antiques, canned goods, furniture, art, and live music.

A good view of the area can be had by hiking to the top of **Mount Baldy.** The prominence got its name because the trees stopped growing and the top is as bald as Kojak. There are 212 steps to the top. To get to the trailhead from RR 12, go west on Woodcreek Drive, then take your first right. You should see the stairs and a place to park.

One of the weirdest things in Wimberley is **Pioneer Town** (333 Wayside Dr., off River Rd., $5 for parking). This is a small Wild West town created out of old buildings found in and around Wimberley. It all started when the founder of 7A Resort, old-timer Raymond Czichos, visited Knott's Berry Farm in California. He came back to Wimberley inspired, and over the course of several years built this bizarre mock town. Initially it had real businesses, run by folks in Western get-ups, but today it's more of a ghost town: 1960s-style mannequins from department stores, dressed up in Western attire, are the only remaining survivors of this dream.

One of the top attractions in town is the studio at **Wimberley Glass Works** (6469 RR 12, 800/929-6686, www.wgw.com, 10am-5pm daily). Founded by Tim de Jong in the 1990s, this incredible space has become one of the premier art glass galleries in the Southwest.

Handblown glass demonstrations take place daily, where master artists create lighting and art glass. Wimberley Glass Works is south of town on RR 12.

Shopping

All the shopping in town takes place at Wimberley Square. Here you'll find hundreds of little boutiques filled with Texana crafts, home furnishings, vintage clothes, and antiques, along with a couple of art galleries. Your shopping strategy should be to park anywhere and spend a couple hours walking around. Shops often come and go within a matter of months in this area.

Boutiques worth checking out are **Brocante** (14015 RR 12, 512/847-8577, 10:30am-5pm Mon.-Sat., 11:30am-5pm Sun.) and **Wall Street Western** (13904 RR 12, 512/847-1818, 10am-6pm daily). An interesting art gallery featuring folk art and wildlife sculptures is **Old Mill Store** (Wimberley Square RR 12, 512/847-3068, 10am-6pm Mon.-Thurs., 10am-7pm Fri.-Sun.).

Food

Blair House (100 Spoke Hill Rd., 512/847-1111 or 877/549-5450, www.blairhouseinn.com, $65) offers the best fine-dining experience in the area. A five-star fixed menu is offered at 7:30pm each Saturday evening. Any restaurant that's only open one night a week and still gets the highest of accolades deserves the title of fine dining. Entrées have included coffee-braised short ribs with baked yams and pork tenderloin with orange sauce.

Cypress Creek Café (320 Wimberley Square, 512/847-0030, 11am-9pm daily, $12) serves up American fare that keeps the locals coming back. Coconut shrimp, scampi, marlin, pork—all make this menu diverse and yummy.

On beautiful Cypress Creek is **Ino'z** (14004 RR 12 on Wimberley Square, 512/847-6060, 11am-9pm daily, $8). The setting is the best in town as restaurants go; however, the food is nothing special. The reason to come here is to sit on the outside deck and have chicken-fried steak and a beer under the bald cypress trees next to the creek.

Miss Mae's BBQ (419 FM 2325, 512/847-9808, 10:30am-7pm Mon.-Sat., $8) has the barbecue connection in Wimberley. The tradition started in 1957 in the founder's grandmother's kitchen. Using her recipe, Miss Mae's cooks up barbecue chicken, beef, ham, and turkey.

Accommodations

There are over 100 different lodgings in and around Wimberley, including bed-and-breakfasts, guest rooms, cottages, and cabins. The reservation service **Texas Hill Country Reservations—All Wimberley Lodgings** (14500 Ranch Rd. 12 #13, 512/847-3909, http://texashillcountryreservations.com) can help match you with a lodging that suits your budget and needs. If you prefer not to use a service, the following accommodations come recommended.

★ **Blair House** (100 Spoke Hill Rd., 512/847-1111 or 877/549-5450, www.blairhouseinn.com, $125-275) is easily one of the top places to get away in the Hill Country. After all, *Condé Nast Traveler* considers Blair House one of the top 25 inns in the country for a very good reason—or should I say several reasons. Here guests are seduced with all the pleasures one could wish for in a vacation getaway, with fine dining and fine linens in a fine location. In the evening, turndown service includes a beverage and a confection, and in the morning guests wake up to a gourmet breakfast.

For budget travelers, **Mountain View Lodge** (RR 12, south of Wimberley, 512/847-2992, $85-95) has excellent rooms with balconies and views of the Wimberley Valley. Continental breakfast is included in the rates.

Comfortable cottages and a serene setting are to be found at **Wimberley Inn** (200 FM 3237, 512/847-3750, www.wimberleyinn.com, $85-175). A night's stay here includes an upscale continental breakfast, along with great service. High-speed Internet access is available.

NEW BRAUNFELS

The German heritage of Central Texas all began in the town of New Braunfels (pop. 63,000), located in the Austin-San Antonio corridor off I-35. Back in the 1840s, German entrepreneurs bought a vast amount of acreage here with the intention of bringing in German colonists. The first settlers, led by Prince Carl of Solms-Braunfels in Germany, arrived to find the area far from the coast and populated by Native Americans, but they decided to settle the area anyway. These first German settlers brought their culture and traditions and integrated them into the story of the Texas Hill Country. These traditions have survived to the present day and define New Braunfels, making it the unique place that it is.

Today people come to New Braunfels for many reasons. City folks in both Austin and San Antonio come here to relax, spend hot summer days at the enormous water park, and to imbibe the vestiges of German-meets-Texas culture. People also come here to do some serious antiques shopping. There are so many junk and antiques shops here that New Braunfels has been dubbed the Antique Capital of Texas. For more information on New Braunfels contact the **New Braunfels Visitors Center** (237 I-35 N. at FM 725, 830/625-7973, 9am-5pm daily).

Sights and Activities

Most people come to New Braunfels for recreation that centers on water. Water fun comes in many forms and sizes here, such as tubing down the Guadalupe River, rafting, or fishing. For those who want water without the mud and in a totally artificial environment, there's **Schlitterbahn** (400 N. Liberty, 830/625-2351, www.schlitterbahn.com, 10am-8pm daily in peak summer months, 10am-6pm weekends at the beginning and end of season, $38 adults, $30 children 3-11). This mega-size water park with a German theme, open late April-September, draws people by the thousands all spring, summer, and fall. Featuring over 30 waterslides, pools, thrill rides, and all sorts

Cheating Death at the Guadalupe River

Driving north from San Antonio toward Austin on I-35, you will cross the Guadalupe River at the scenic town of New Braunfels. As you pass the bridge over the Guadalupe, imagine the winter of 1838. At that time, Noah Smithwick, a Texas Ranger, was making his way from San Antonio to his base in the community of Bastrop on the Colorado River. There were no bridges across the Guadalupe, and Smithwick was riding a mule. He thought he could get across, but unfortunately the river was deeper and swifter than he anticipated. He and his mule struggled but were unable to get across. After almost drowning, they both eventually emerged on the same side of the river where they had started. Unfortunately for Smithwick, he had lost his rifle, his gunpowder was wet, and he was soaked to the skin. The temperature was hovering at 30°F and a north wind was blowing at about 30 mph. The sun was going down and Smithwick was in danger of freezing to death.

He could not get a fire started since he had no dry gunpowder and no flintlock to create a spark. It was at this time he remembered a story told to him by David Crockett. Crockett had been in a similar situation and survived by gathering enough armloads of tall grass to create a hay pile. Smithwick did the same and took off his wet clothes and dove into the middle of his fresh pile of grass. Amazingly, he soon became warm as toast and survived the cold night. In the morning he mounted his mule and headed back to San Antonio, where he discovered that he had escaped death three times within 24 hours.

A large band of Comanche had struck San Antonio the previous day, and his friends in town thought that Smithwick had been caught alone on the prairie and killed by the Native Americans. This would probably have been his fate but for his mishap in the Guadalupe River. If he hadn't lost his rifle, he would have been able to make a fire and the Comanche would have spotted him. If he had successfully crossed the Guadalupe River, he would have run smack into their war party. Thus he almost died of drowning, freezing, and a Comanche attack all in the same day. Smithwick was a living example of that pioneer philosophy that what seems to be bad luck at first is sometimes the best thing that could happen to you.

---

of wet fun for the whole family, Schlitterbahn has become Texas's largest water park.

New Braunfels has a strange assortment of grassroots museums and historical sites that aren't necessarily worth driving for miles to check out. However, if you have an itch for curious historical things there are a couple places you may want to visit. The **Sophienburg Museum and Archives** (401 W. Coll St., 830/629-1572, 10am-4pm Tues.-Sat., $5) has an interesting collection of local artifacts, mostly relating to German pioneers and early folks in the history of New Braunfels. The museum is on the hilltop site where Prince Carl of Solms-Braunfels built a log fortress. There's also the **Museum of Texas Handmade Furniture** (1370 Church Hill Dr., 830/629-6504, 1pm-4pm Tues.-Sun. Feb.-Nov., $5), which features furniture items that were handmade in Texas during the 1800s. Finally, there's the **Lindheimer**

Home Museum (491 Comal, 830/629-2943, 2pm-5pm weekends, $3), where visitors can tour the home of the father of Texas botany, Ferdinand Jakob Lindheimer (1801-1879).

Just south of New Braunfels is **Animal World and Snake Farm Zoo** (I-35 exit 182 at Engle, 830/608-9270, www.awsfzoo.com, 10am-6pm daily Memorial Day-Labor Day, $12.75 adults, $11.75 seniors and military, $9.75 ages 3-12, children 2 and under free). Since 1967 this roadside shrine devoted to reptiles has been drawing in the curious from the highway. Inside the main facility there are over 300 reptile species. Some are endangered, some are poisonous, many you probably have never seen up close before, and all are intriguing and beautiful. All these curious creatures are stuck in small, dank aquariums, tanks, and cages that seem a bit precariously stacked and neglected. The smell in here is phenomenal. Snake Farm also has what I consider to be one of the weirdest gift shops in the state. As expected there's all kinds of snake-related memorabilia, as well as display cases that exhibit dusty souvenirs so old they've become relics in their own right. There's also a rattlesnake pit with live rattlesnakes.

Food

In step with New Braunfels' German heritage is the popular **Alpine Haus Restaurant** (251 S. Seguin Ave., 830/214-0205, 11:30am-2pm and 5pm-9pm Tues.-Thurs., 11:30am-9pm Fri.-Sat., 11:30am-8pm Sun., $12). If you're expecting a super-authentic basic German food experience you may be disappointed—however, if you want a fun and fancy experience with beer and wine you will love this place. Alpine offers quite a selection of imported German beers and schnitzels, which makes for an enjoyable lunch or dinner.

Want to eat beef at any time of day? **New Braunfels Smokehouse** (140 Hwy. 46 S., 830/625-2416, 8am-8pm daily, $8) has beef for breakfast, lunch, and dinner, and even for snack time. They specialize in German and American smoked meats. Here you can find any kind of meat you could ever crave—beef brisket, pork, chicken, ribs, turkey, and jerky—all hickory smoked.

Housed in the old Palace Movie Theatre in historic downtown New Braunfels is **Myron's** (136 N. Castell Ave., 830/624-1024, 5pm-9:30pm Mon.-Thurs., 5pm-10:30pm Friday.-Sat., $30). People come here for great wine, Chicago prime beef, and a classy fine-dining experience. Myron's has a full bar as well as an extensive wine list. The atmosphere is casual but elegant. Reservations are recommended.

Some of the best fish tacos in the area happen to be served up by surfers. The California-imported folks at **Wahoo's Fish Tacos** (6700 I-35, 830/627-7226, 11am-10pm Mon.-Sat., 11am-9pm Sun., $8) seem like fish out of water in Texas. The walls are lined with graphics of surfers, giant waves, and skateboarding stickers, and the vibe is straight from Santa Cruz, California. It's hard to wrap your head around the fish taco component, but the food is remarkably well put together and tasty, and the price is in the budget range.

Accommodations

The best bed in town is at **Prince Solms Inn** (295 E. San Antonio St., 830/625-9169 or 800/625-9169, www.princesolmsinn.com, $125-150). This historic inn was built in 1898 and was known as the most romantic and most luxurious hotel in this area. It still deserves this distinction, with a great central location, fluffy pillows, wines, confections, and breakfast in the morning. If you stay here ask about the ghost tale, if you dare. Speaking of creepy stuff, the inn offers a unique experience called the murder mystery weekend, when folks rent out the inn and the staff hosts a clever whodunit evening.

An excellent bed-and-breakfast just north of New Braunfels and Gruene is **Das Anwesen Bed and Breakfast** (360 Millie's Ln., 830/625-5992 or 866/526-1236, www.dasanwesen.com, $100-175). This prairie-style home is on historic Karbach Ranch, which was established when the German immigrants first settled New Braunfels in 1844. The interior of the home is filled with fine antiques, tasteful decorations, and country charm. Breakfast is served on antique china, crystal, and silver at 8:30am.

For standard roadside accommodations in New Braunfels there's **Days Inn New Braunfels** (963 I-35 N. at exit 189, 830/608-0004, $54-150). One notch above the Days Inn is **La Quinta Inn and Suites** (365 Hwy. 36 S., 830/627-3333, $80) and the **Hawthorn Inn and Suites** (1533 I-35 N., 830/643-9300, $80).

GRUENE

One of the Hill Country's best-kept secrets is historic Gruene (pop. 20). Pronounced like the color green, this small bend in the river is technically a part of New Braunfels called the Gruene Historic District. The slogan on Gruene's promotional material speaks volumes about the town's forward-looking vision: "Gently resisting change since 1872." This happens to be the year the town was born, when German immigrant Henry D. Gruene bought the land to establish a cotton farm. The town's gentle resistance becomes very apparent once you take that last turn and drive into Gruene. Suddenly you find yourself smack-dab in the middle of an old-world downtown that's straight out of a bygone era. If you enjoy a leisurely day that includes great food, walking the carbs off, and window shopping, Gruene can steal half a day from you. If you combine this with river rafting, make it a full day.

Sights and Activities

The town itself is the main attraction. It's nothing more than a few Wild West-style buildings with tin roofs, a large water tower, a historic mansion, and a few restaurants and specialty shops, all with laid-back country charm. This charm is due to the town's perfect combination of strict zoning laws that keep out big business and laissez-faire fire codes that allow nearly dilapidated buildings to continue to exist. Several of the businesses simply don't have air-conditioning. This may be a deliberate attempt at creating an old-world ambience, or maybe it's simply a way to save money. Either way it adds to the experience. A nice way to spend half a day is to simply

meander through town, going in and out of the old buildings that house new businesses. If you're so inclined, buy some horseshoe art, some locally made wine, or some antiques.

You never would guess it, but Gruene has one of the best venues for music in Texas, and one of the most distinctive venues in the whole United States. **Gruene Hall** (1281 Gruene Rd., 830/606-1281, www.gruenehall.com) is billed as the oldest standing dance hall in the state. I say "standing" with trepidation, as the building is so old and rickety it doesn't look like it's long for this world. The windows are chicken wire, the roof is tin, and the walls are those originally erected back in the 1880s. With chicken-wire windows there's no chance for air-conditioning, so the best way to cool down is with a cold beverage. Adorning the walls are hundreds of signed photos of the performers that have graced this old hall. Be sure to look for the two photos of Lyle Lovett, one when he was a young upstart without the big hairdo, and the other when he found his shtick. Many country legends and rock stars have performed here over the years, such as Willie Nelson, George Strait, Jerry Jeff Walker, Merle Haggard, George Thorogood, and the alt-country

Gruene

band the Old 97's. There's live music seven days a week in summer and 3-4 days a week the rest of the year, including Saturday and Sunday afternoons.

Shopping

In a historic town like Gruene, it's only natural that there be antiques shops to add to the yesteryear flavor. If you enter town by way of Gruene Road, coming from New Braunfels, the first antiques shop you come to will be the **Gruene Antique Company** (1607 Hunter Rd., 830/629-7781, 10am-9pm daily). Housed in the original mercantile building is 8,000 square feet of antiques, collectibles, furniture, and gifts. Ask to see the original bank vault from the Henry D. Gruene days.

Just up the road is a string of antiques shops, all in historic old houses, starting with **Dancing Bear** (1632 Hunter Rd., 830/629-2059, 10am-6pm Mon., daily). The proprietors are proud to offer unique finds, Texas trinkets, and decorative items for the country home, all at great prices. Next door is **Cactus Jacks** (1706 Hunter Rd., 830/620-9602, 10am-5:30pm Wed.-Mon.), which offers more furniture but with a European flair, along with some handmade gifts and things for the garden.

Food

There are a few great eateries in town, a couple hovering above the Guadalupe River. These riverfront restaurants have seating outside on decks and porches under the groves of trees that line the river. One of the best restaurants in all of Texas, the ★ **Gristmill River Restaurant & Bar** (1287 Gruene Rd., 830/625-0684, 11am-9pm Sun.-Thurs., 11am-10pm Fri.-Sat., $15), is right here in Gruene at the base of the water tower. With a maze of terraced decks, porches, and covered areas that weave in and out of the ruins of an historic cotton gin, this top-notch restaurant is a must for dinner. Although there is no air-conditioning in most of the restaurant, once you sit down with a cold iced tea and relax, you can forget about the heat, sort of. The fare is standard, such as sirloin, trout, shrimp, and chicken-fried chicken, but all is above standard once it hits the palate.

Gruene's Tex-Mex food establishment, **Adobe Verde** (1724 Hunter Rd., 830/629-0777, www.adobeverde.com, 11am-9pm Sun.-Thurs., 11am-10pm Fri.-Sat., $8), is a great place to bring the family or fill up before a show at Gruene Hall. I recommend relaxing on the covered patio while eating fajitas, chips and queso, or tortilla soup.

Accommodations

If you aren't hurried and can stay the night in town, Gruene has a few great options for lodgings. The most famous and certainly the place with the most mystique is **Gruene Mansion Inn** (1275 Gruene Rd., 830/629-2641, www.gruenemansioninn.com), the original house that Henry D. Gruene built. This old mansion offers 30 different rooms, units, and nooks to stay in, ranging $159-209. Rooms are brightly colored, some outfitted with claw-foot tubs, hardwood floors, canopy beds, fireplaces, and views of the Guadalupe River.

If an old mansion freaks you out, or if you prefer modern accommodations, **Gruene River Hotel & Retreat** (1235 Gruene Rd., 830/643-1234, www.grueneapple.com) has clean rooms with views of the river as well. Amenities in the rooms can include a whirlpool tub, fireplace, or a private balcony, and amenities available to all guests include a full-size swimming pool, a media room with theater, and an entertainment room including a pool table and library. Rates range $160-210 and include a hearty gourmet breakfast. Imagine cinnamon pecan-stuffed French toast, and you'll understand the use of the word *gourmet.*

Other accommodations include **Gruene Homestead Inn** (832 Gruene Rd., 800/606-0216, www.gruenehomesteadinn.com), a collection of historic farmhouses and cabins on eight acres. Prices range $175-250 depending on the room and time of the year. There's also **Gruene River Inn** (1111 Gruene Rd., 830/627-1600, www.grueneriverinn.com, $125-195), located 100 feet above the Guadalupe River. Every room takes advantage of the great view of the river. And finally, for a great bed-and-breakfast, there's **Antoinette's Cottage** (1258 Gruene Rd., 830/606-6929, www.antoinettescottage.com, $150).

Transportation

The best way to get around in the Hill Country is by car. Having the freedom to go where and when you please is the only way you can truly sink your teeth into this big pie. Car rental agencies in Austin and San Antonio include **Advantage Rent-A-Car** (800/777-5500), **Alamo Rent-A-Car** (800/462-5266), **Avis Car Rental** (800/331-1212), **Budget** (800/527-0700), **Dollar Rent-A-Car** (800/800-3665), **Enterprise** (800/261-7331), **Hertz Rent-A-Car** (800/654-3131), **National Car Rental** (800/222-9058), and **Thrifty** (800/847-4389).

On average, Hill Country towns are about 30-40 miles apart. You don't need to sweat filling up with a tank of gas at every town (that is, unless you are driving a 1960s Buick that gets 5-10 miles per gallon). That said, when you're in a small town and you're running below half a tank, it's a good idea to fill 'er up.

Finding your way around the small roads in the Hill Country can be tricky if you're not from the area. Streets in town often have a name, but as they leave town they turn into numbered roads. On maps you may see unusual abbreviations. FM means Farm-to-Market, RM means Ranch-to-Market, and RR means Rural Road. Many dude ranches, state parks, and attractions out of town simply don't have street addresses. Instead they use old-fashioned ranch signs to mark their entrances.

San Antonio

Look for ★ to find recommended sights, activities, dining, and lodging.

Highlights

★ **San Antonio Zoo and Aquarium:** This zoo carved into the side of a cliff is a blast for the whole family. See lions, gorillas, alligators, and other exotic birds and animals (page 173).

★ **Brackenridge Park:** This beautiful park is home to many of the city's main attractions, such as the San Antonio Zoo and Aquarium, the Witte Museum, the Texas Pioneer and Ranger Museum, the Japanese Tea Gardens, and a miniature train called the Brackenridge Eagle (page 173).

★ **San Antonio Museum of Art:** Prehistoric art, Egyptian mummies, Roman statuary, antiquities, and American and European paintings by the masters are all housed in the former Lone Star Brewery building (page 175).

★ **The Alamo:** The most sacred site on Texas soil is this old mission that became the site of one of the bloodiest showdowns in U.S. history (page 175).

★ **River Walk:** Walk down the old stone steps to the River Walk to find shops, boats, and restaurants with umbrella tables, all lining the twisting San Antonio River (page 178).

★ **La Villita:** The historic site of the first established village in San Antonio today houses art galleries, cafés, and funky shops (page 179).

★ **HemisFair Park:** Once the World's Fair of 1968 was over, San Antonio was left with amazing attractions like the Institute of Texan Cultures, the Tower of the Americas, the water gardens, and the Schultz House Cottage Garden (page 182).

★ **King William Historic District:** An excellent place for a lazy afternoon or evening stroll, this historic part of town was built by and

© AVALON TRAVEL

for San Antonio's upper class. The mansions are still occupied, and a couple are even open to the public (page 182).

★ **The Missions:** Stroll these sacred grounds and learn how the indigenous peoples lived before the arrival of the Spanish, and how missionaries changed them and their culture (page 183).

S an Antonio is one of the oldest continuously inhabited places in Texas. Historically, this stretch of lush and scenic land along the San Antonio River was both beautiful and rich in resources, which made it a crossroads of many peoples and cultures, including Native Americans, Spanish settlers and missionaries, Latin Americans, and even German immigrants. Throughout the centuries, all this cultural exchange and diversity provided the stage for some of the more dramatic chapters in Texas's history.

Today San Antonio has settled into its role as a laid-back, friendly, gritty, hardworking family town and is proud to still be a crossroads of cultures. It is a place where Mexico, the old Wild West, and the New World genuinely and successfully collaborate to create a unique culture and relaxed lifestyle that can't be found anywhere else. It's a place where Spanish colonial architecture and modern skyscrapers emerge out of the ancient San Antonio River's beautiful River Walk; where mariachi mass is still offered at one of the old Spanish missions; and where masterfully executed murals on city walls tell the story of Mexico and Texas.

People are always pleasantly surprised by the remarkably unique charm this city has. Most people know of San Antonio as the home of the mother of all American pilgrimage sights—The Alamo. Sure, there's The Alamo, Davy Crockett, General Santa Anna, and the fight for independence—but there's also much more. There's the beautiful River Walk, the crumbling Spanish missions, world-class museums, and even overblown theme parks. Because of all this history, natural beauty, and fun, San Antonio has grown into the seventh-largest city in the United States and is Texas's most beloved town.

PLANNING YOUR TIME

San Antonio covers a massive area, but fortunately most of what people come here for is in or around downtown, which makes planning your time fairly easy. Most people prefer to stay at one of the many hotels along the River Walk to make it just

---

Previous: two views of San Antonio's famous River Walk. **Above:** streetside shrine to the Virgen de Guadelupe.

San Antonio

To Six Flags Fiesta Texas

WURZBACH PKWY

SAN ANTONIO INTERNATIONAL AIRPORT

TEXAS TRANSPORTATION MUSEUM

STARCREST RD

WETMORE RD

JACKSON-KELLER RD

410 DINER

N NEW BRAUNFELS

AUSTIN HWY

BALCONES HEIGHTS

FREDERICKSBURG RD

HILLCREST RD

ST. CLOUD RD

SAN PEDRO

ALAMO HEIGHTS

Olmos Basin

Park

MCNAY ART MUSEUM

TERRELL HILLS

BANDERA RD

CULEBRA RD

OLMOS PHARMACY

HILDEBRAND AVE

BLANCO RD

SAN ANTONIO BOTANICAL GARDEN

BURR RD

FORT SAM HOUSTON

SAN ANTONIO ZOO AND AQUARIUM

BRACKENRIDGE PARK

SEE "BRACKENRIDGE PARK" MAP

SAN ANTONIO INTERNATIONAL HOSTEL

SPLASHTOWN

W COMMERCE ST

GEN. MCMULLEN DR

SAN ANTONIO MUSEUM OF ART

THE ALAMO

LA VILLITA

RIVER WALK

HEMISFAIR PARK

SEE "DOWNTOWN SAN ANTONIO" MAP

AT&T CENTER

E HOUSTON ST

E COMMERCE ST

KING WILLIAM HISTORIC DISTRICT

SEE "KING WILLIAM HISTORIC DISTRICT" MAP

To SeaWorld San Antonio

RIGSBY AVE

SOUTHWEST WEST WHITE RD

KELLY USA

Concepción Park

MISSION CONCEPCIÓN

THE MISSIONS

ZARZAMORA ST

NOGALITOS ST

S FLORES ST

ROOSEVELT

S PRESA ST

S NEW BRAUNFELS

MISSION
MISSION TRAIL

NEW LAREDO HWY

MILITARY DR

MISSION SAN JOSÉ

Padre Park

Espada Park

Mission Trail

MISSION SAN JUAN

MISSION ESPADA

0   2 mi

0   2 km

© AVALON TRAVEL

San Antonio Fast Facts

- Founded in 1731
- Population: 1,327,000 (2016 U.S. Census Bureau data)
- Land area: approximately 460 square miles
- Time zone: GMT/UTC-6 (Central Time)
- Second-largest city in Texas
- Seventh-largest city in the United States
- County: Bexar
- Ethnicity: 72 percent white, 63 percent Hispanic, 7 percent African American, 2.4 percent Asian, 13 percent other
- Sales tax: 8.25 percent

that much easier. If you plan on seeing the sights downtown, your trip is a cinch to plan—in fact, you can figure it out as you go. Two days should be sufficient if you're focusing on downtown. However, if you want to take in sights outside of the downtown area, such as the San Antonio Zoo, the missions, the Witte Museum, or one of the two theme parks, you will want to plan your time more carefully. Going to any of the above can easily turn into a full-day excursion, once you factor in transportation time and meal breaks.

ORIENTATION

San Antonio is only 80 miles south of Austin, just outside the Hill Country. The border of Mexico is 270 miles to the south, and the Gulf of Mexico is 140 miles to the southeast. The city itself is a massive, sprawling place that can be intimidating for the first-time visitor. For the most part, sights, activities, and points of interest are located in three main areas: downtown, Southtown, and the Brackenridge Park area. The downtown area is where you will likely spend most of your time. It's stunningly beautiful here, and most everything is within walking distance. Because of this, most visitors pitch their tent in one of the many hotels on the River Walk. This is where you'll find sights pertaining to the original Spanish settlement, such as The Alamo, the River Walk on the San Antonio River, La Villita, several museums, and Market Square. In Southtown you'll explore the mansions of the King William Historic District, modern art studios and galleries, and some of the best restaurants San Antonio has to offer. Southtown is also the starting point for the missions along the Mission Trail. The Brackenridge Park area is where you'll spend a good chunk of time if you have kids. This beautiful city park is home to the famous San Antonio Zoo as well as museums and botanical gardens geared toward families. Also in this area is the newer Pearl District, home to some of the city's best restaurants.

Outside of these three areas is an endless urban and suburban sprawl with neighborhoods, strip malls, industrial complexes, and military bases. The three attractions worth mentioning among these areas are Six Flags Fiesta Texas, SeaWorld San Antonio, and Splashtown.

Two Days in San Antonio

If you have two days to devote to your stay in the large city of San Antonio, you will want to plan your time wisely. An itinerary to maximize time but not miss anything important would include focusing on the downtown area, the Brackenridge area, and the Mission Trail. Unless big theme parks are important to you I would skip them all together and enjoy the richer things the city has to offer.

Day 1: Wake up at the Menger Hotel, get breakfast, and head over to The Alamo before the historic site gets crowded. Next up is window shopping in the old part of town, La Villita, which is close by. By now you're probably getting hungry, so a stroll through the Arneson River Theatre and down to the River Walk is recommend. After a riverside lunch at Boudro's, the rest of the day could be spent on a guided river cruise and traveling the Mission Trail by car or bike.

Day 2: Start the day with breakfast at Guenther House in the King William District. Next is an excursion up to the Brackenridge Park area. Take time to meander through the Japanese Tea Garden followed by a visit to the Witte Museum. After a light lunch (we're saving our appetite for later), a couple hours could easily be spent at the San Antonio Zoo. Before evening comes, head to the Pearl District. Here you can enjoy shopping and dining at some of the city's best restaurants, such as Southerleigh Fine Food and Brewery. Lastly, one should spend his or her final late-night hours on the beautiful River Walk, maybe stopping by the Esquire Tavern before turning in.

Sights

San Antonio is Texas's most beloved city for all things touristy. Its rich history combined with a contemporary appeal keeps folks coming here year-round. Besides being home to the two most visited attractions in Texas, The Alamo and the River Walk, San Antonio also has world-class museums, mega theme parks, and quirky attractions that are sure to amuse even the most jaded traveler.

NORTH
Six Flags Fiesta Texas

A mega theme park in the San Antonio area is **Six Flags Fiesta Texas** (17000 I-10 W., 210/697-5050, www.sixflags.com, hours vary). With over 200 acres of fun for the whole family, Six Flags is a major draw for thrill seekers from all over the state. The park features rides for all ages, as well as campy shows and theme areas à la Disneyland. The whole park has a Texas spin, flavor, and look, with cartoon-style themed areas like a Hispanic village and a German town. The real reason people come here is to get sick and scared on the roller coasters or get wet on the waterslides and chutes. Families will like how the rides are laid out, mixing the adult rides with the children's rides. This makes for a fun day for everyone, all at the same time. I pity the folks who are walking around dressed up like cartoon characters in the middle of summer. Park hours and days of operation fluctuate, so call in advance. Tickets are $55 for general admission. Purchase tickets online for a discount.

Texas Transportation Museum

The quirkiest attraction in town has got to be the **Texas Transportation Museum** (11731 Wetmore Rd., 210/490-3554, www.txtransportationmuseum.org, 9am-3pm Fri., 10am-5pm Sat.-Sun., $10 adults, $8 children 4-12, children under 4 free). Really, this is more a shrine and a personal passion dedicated to the great era of the locomotive. Here you can marvel at miniature-scale model train sets, both indoors and outdoors. The scale models and their detailed environments are a must-see for the train geek and a try-to-see for the curious. It's north of San Antonio Airport. If you can, give a donation on top of your admission to keep this independently owned operation alive.

McNay Art Museum

San Antonio's best repository for paintings by the masters is the lovely **McNay Art Museum** (6000 N. New Braunfels St., 210/824-5368, www.mcnayart.org, 10am-4pm Tues., Wed., and Fri., 10am-9pm Thurs., 10am-5pm Sat., noon-5pm Sun., $20 adults, $15 students, seniors, and military, children 12 and under free). Safely hanging on the walls of a stunning old Spanish colonial revival mansion is a spectacular collection of art. The collection focuses on 19th- and 20th-century European and American art, including notable works by Picasso, Cézanne, O'Keeffe, Gauguin, and Van Gogh, and also features sculpture. The mansion is surrounded by well-tended gardens, making this one of the most scenic and breathtaking museums in Texas. The house and much of the collection belonged to a wealthy woman by the name of Marion Koogler McNay, who donated everything to the cause of "advancement of art" upon her passing in 1950. Subsequently, the McNay Museum was the first modern art museum in the state. Free parking is available.

San Antonio Botanical Garden

The **San Antonio Botanical Garden** (555 Funston Pl., 210/536-1400, www.sabot.org, 9am-5pm daily, $10), northeast of downtown, is a whopping 33 acres of well-tended plants, all waiting to be admired, understood, and appreciated. Most of the plants are displayed outdoors in the vast landscape. A slew of well-planned theme gardens are carefully orchestrated, such as the Texas regional gardens, the Old-Fashioned Garden, the Rose Garden, the Sacred Garden filled with biblical plants, the Japanese Garden, and the brilliant Garden for the Blind.

The uniquely shaped glass building that's the focal point of the grounds is the conservatory, which houses plants that have "special needs." Within a fully controlled climate the staff are able to create mini-ecosystems for plants that otherwise would perish in the San Antonio climate. Displays in the conservatory include exotic plants, ferns, desert plants, tropical plants, and palms and cycads. Outside, the conservatory is surrounded by a sunken courtyard and tropical lagoon filled with even more plants. The overlook happens to the highest point in San Antonio, 798 feet above sea level.

★ San Antonio Zoo and Aquarium

In beautiful Brackenridge Park is the glorious **San Antonio Zoo and Aquarium** (3903 N. St. Mary's St., 210/734-7184, www.sazoo-aq.org, 9am-5pm daily, until 6pm in the summer, $14.25 adults, $11.25 children 3-11). This world-renowned zoo is home to over 3,500 animals, with 750 species represented, including some endangered species. Virtually every animal that spurs the imagination the world over can be found here, lying around in small cages and faux environments. Popular residents are the lions, zebras, tigers, and gorillas. Along with gawking at those critters in captivity, one can also learn much here, as the zoo is set up to educate and foster a love of animals. To give the kids time to explore I recommend planning about three hours for your trip to the zoo.

★ Brackenridge Park

North of downtown is San Antonio's own Shangri-la, **Brackenridge Park** (3910 N. St. Mary's St., 210/207-7275, 5am-11pm daily, free). This beautiful city park has many features and attractions that make it a special place for kids, adults, and adults that act like kids. There's the nationally renowned **San Antonio Zoo and Aquarium,** a miniature train called the **Brackenridge Eagle** (210/735-7455) that travels a two-mile circuit around the park, the **Japanese Tea Gardens** (210/735-4648), also known as the **Sunken Gardens,** and the **Sunken Garden**

Theatre. Brackenridge Park is also home to the **Brackenridge Golf Course** (210/226-5612), the oldest 18-hole public golf course in Texas. At the northeastern edge of the park are a trio of excellent museums, among them the **Witte Museum** (210/357-1900).

Besides these attractions Brackenridge Park is the location of many springs that make up the headwaters for the San Antonio River, which brings the beauty of flowing, twisting lanes of water to the park. The old stone building over the river is the pump house that operated as San Antonio's first public water supply system.

With a mini-amusement park, a mini-train to ride, boats to bob in, museums, and a zoo, who needs *Lost Horizon*? The park is approximately two miles north of downtown, and the main entrance is in the 2800 block of North Broadway. Although admission to the park is free, fees may apply to some of the attractions within the park. Plan on spending about an hour here appreciating the beautiful setting.

Witte Museum

The museum that boasts the most is the **Witte Museum** (3801 Broadway St., 210/357-1900, www.wittemuseum.org, 10am-5pm Mon.-Sat., until 8pm Tues., noon-5pm Sun., $10 adults, $8 seniors and military, $7 children 4-11), north of downtown in beautiful Brackenridge Park. The correct pronunciation is like "witty," and coincidentally the museum is pretty clever. The Witte is a spectacular institution that features all sorts of fun and interesting exhibits that are sure to pique the interests of everyone. With real *Triceratops* and *Tyrannosaurus rex* bones, mummies, dioramas, history and natural science exhibits, national touring exhibits, family events, and overnight camp-ins for children, there's almost—dare I say—too much happening here. In fact, the Witte deserves nearly a day of your time, especially if you are bringing children. The biggest draw for kids is the H.E.B Science Tree House, which consists of four floors for the mini scientist and junior anthropologist in the family to explore.

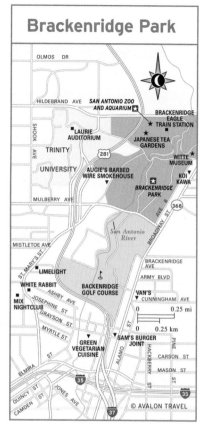

Japanese Tea Gardens

The most serene spot in town is the **Japanese Tea Gardens** (3875 N. St. Mary's St., 210/735-4648, free). Also known as the Sunken Gardens, this beautiful spot inside Brackenridge Park was the former site of a rock quarry that produced the limestone used to construct the Texas State Capitol in Austin. Someone with vision got the idea of making this beautiful and brought in a Japanese designer, Mr. Jingo, who designed and built the magnificent gardens. The gardens have been restored to their prime. Highlights of the Japanese Tea Gardens include winding walkways, a waterfall, and serene lily ponds with koi, turtles, and ducks. Walking the traditional stone Japanese bridges and exploring these tranquil, lush, overgrown gardens is a relaxing way to spend an afternoon.

★ San Antonio Museum of Art

Housed in the former Lone Star Brewery building, which dates to 1884, is the **San Antonio Museum of Art** (200 W. Jones Ave., 210/978-8100, www.sa-museum.org, 10am-5pm Wed.-Sun., 10am-9pm Tues., $10). Just North of downtown San Antonio, this truly world-class museum is one of the most comprehensive in the United States, with four floors of exhibits that contain perfectly displayed prehistoric art, Egyptian mummies, Roman statuary, antiquities, and American and European paintings by the masters. Along with all this, the museum is also home to the **Nelson A. Rockefeller Center for Latin American Art,** which is the most extensive collection of Latin American art in the nation. To give you an example of the caliber of the San Antonio Museum of Art, this museum is on the same touring-exhibit circuit as the New York Metropolitan Museum of Art and the Louvre in Paris.

★ The Alamo

The most revered historical site and most venerated landmark in Texas is **The Alamo** (300 Alamo Plaza, 210/225-1391, www.thealamo. org, 9am-5:30pm daily, and 9am-7pm daily in summer, free). Here legends and heroes of Texas history were born, died, and live on in our imaginations. Most visitors are surprised to see that The Alamo is small in size, but the history here is huge. On this hallowed ground in 1836, 188 brave Texans made their stand against 3,000 (give or take a few) of General Santa Anna's finest. For 13 days a bloody battle was carried out, culminating in the final assault on the morning of March 6. Famous Texans like Colonel William Travis, James Bowie, Juan Seguin, and, of course, the Tennessean Davy Crockett (a congressman and outdoorsman who was famous in his day for his exploits) made history by defying the dictator Santa Anna and staking their lives for freedom's sake. They lost the battle, but through their sacrifice a nation (the Republic of Texas) was born.

There is some controversy regarding what became of Davy Crockett, but whatever you do, don't let a revisionist historian tell you that Davy Crockett surrendered (the José Enrique

SAN ANTONIO
SIGHTS

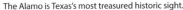

The Alamo is Texas's most treasured historic sight.

Downtown San Antonio

TRAVIS ST

Travis Park

CAMARON ST

MARY'S ST

NAVARRO

JEFFERSON ST

LOSOYA

To Hotel Havana
and Club Cohiba

● GUNTER HOTEL

SAN ANTONIO
CHILDREN'S
MUSEUM
★

E HOUSTON ST

N FLORES ST

N MAIN AVE

SOLEDAD ST

ACENAR ▼ ● ■ ■ MAJESTIC
THEATRE ★
HOTEL
VALENCIA/
CITRUS
EMPIRE
THEATRE

BUCKHORN
MUSEUM AND
TEXAS RANGER
MUSEUM ★

COLLEGE

DRURY INN
AND SUITES
▼

COUNTY LINE
SMOKEHOUSE ★

HYATT REGENCY
SAN ANTONIO ●

W COMMERCE ST

SPANISH
GOVERNOR'S
PALACE ★

SAN FERNANDO
CATHEDRAL ✝

▼
SWIG

CROCKETT ST

THE
ESQUIRE ▼

E COMMERCE ST

DOLOROSA ST

← To Mi Tierra and
Market Square

PLAZA DE ARMES

THE WESTIN
RIVER WALK ●

BOUDRO'S ●

PRESA

▼
SCHILOS
DELICATESSEN

N PRESA

MARKET ST

VILLITA ST

RIVER
WALK ✦

THE BRISCOE
WESTERN
ART MUSEUM ★

ARNESON RIVER
THEATRE ★

★ COS HOUSE

NUEVA ST

VILLITA ST

O'BRIEN
HISTORIC ●
HOTEL

FLORES ST

S MAIN AVE

ST

DWYER

LA VILLITA ✦

OLD GUILBEAU ST

INN ON THE
RIVERWALK ●

PRESA ST

FAIRMOUNT HOTEL/ ●
TRE TRATTORIA

S ALAMO ST

DURANGO

LA QUINTA INN ●
& SUITES SAN
ANTONIO
DOWNTOWN

River

SEE "KING WILLIAM HISTORIC DISTRICT"
MAP

0 ———— 200 yds
0 ———— 200 m

San Antonio

BLVD

S ST MARY'S ST

KING WILLIAM ST

PRESA ST

ARSENAL ST

© AVALON TRAVEL

What Happened to Davy Crockett?

Some of the details of the battle at The Alamo are shrouded in mystery. The legend of Davy Crockett and The Alamo is perhaps the most controversial of these mysteries. History has offered us several conflicting accounts of what happened to Crockett. Did he die or was he taken as a slave? And if he died there, where did he die? A slave of William Travis's named Joe and one of the female survivors, Susanna Dickinson, reported seeing his body at The Alamo surrounded by several dead Mexican soldiers when they departed the chapel after the battle. In 1975, a diary of a Mexican officer by the name of José Enrique de la Peña surfaced. In the diary, de la Peña reported that Crockett was one of several men taken prisoner after the battle and put to death before Santa Anna "without complaining and without humiliating themselves before their torturers." The authenticity of the diary is subject to much dispute. The diary's account of Crockett's death conflicts not only with the observations of Travis's slave and Dickinson but also with those of the Mexican *alcalde* (mayor) of San Antonio, Francisco Antonio Ruiz. Santa Anna put Ruiz in charge of collecting all the dead and burning their bodies. Santa Anna had him identify the bodies of Travis, Bowie, and Crockett, a task he would not have had to perform if Crockett had been killed in Santa Anna's presence.

de la Peña "diaries" were a forgery—Davy died swinging his rifle, Ol' Betsy, and that's my story and I'm sticking with it!). The defenders' famous stand bought precious time for the fledgling republic's first president, Sam Houston, who eventually was able to defeat Santa Anna at the Battle of San Jacinto, near Houston. Texas is the only state of the United States that was a sovereign nation before being annexed in 1845.

At the turn of the 20th century, The Alamo was almost converted into a hotel but was saved by the Daughters of the Texas Republic, who to this day impeccably maintain the historic site.

Plan on spending about 1-2 hours at The Alamo to view the old limestone buildings, artifacts, and the exhibits on the Texas Revolution and Texas history.

★ River Walk

The greatest and most pleasant surprise San Antonio has to offer is the Paseo del Río, commonly referred to as the **River Walk** (www.thesanantonioriverwalk.com). This stretch of the San Antonio River winds and twists its way through the downtown area, in the shadows of the city's historic buildings and skyscrapers. With stone bridges, stone stairways, and winding pathways at

the edges of the calm, teal-colored water, the River Walk is reminiscent of the smaller canals of Venice. Once you descend one of the many stairways and set foot on the River Walk you find yourself in a quiet, romantic, captivating subterranean world with shops, riverside cafés, bars, restaurants, hotels, and historic sites.

The River Walk almost never was. Back in the 1920s, after a disastrous flood, the city nearly filled in this part of the San Antonio River. Thanks to city officials with vision and the brilliant design of Robert H. Hugman, what began as a catastrophe ended in 1941 as the Paseo del Río (River Walk). In 1968, just before the opening of San Antonio's World Exposition (HemisFair), a second extension and upgrade was completed, which helped put San Antonio on the map as a world-class city. Then, in the '70s, the River Walk superseded The Alamo in popularity thanks to a clever campaign by the city with the slogan "Forget the Alamo. Remember the River Walk."

Today the River Walk is the historic, well-established centerpiece of downtown. The city's locals and frequenters can all too easily overlook this as something for the tourist. Sure, it has its touristy side, but it's also a unique and genuinely integral part of San

Antonio. Although the River Walk is always active, it reaches a fevered pitch during Fiesta San Antonio and the winter holiday season. So many people are down on the stone walks that it's not uncommon to see someone fall into the river. To truly appreciate the River Walk, all you have to do is take a seat at one of the riverside cafés, sip a mojito, and watch the boats and people pass by.

This River Walk area is so enjoyable I recommend strolling, enjoying dining riverside, and taking a cruise tour, all of which can add up to about four hours.

★ La Villita

While walking on San Antonio's famous River Walk you'll stumble on a historic yet touristy little spot called **La Villita** (418 Villita St., 210/207-8614, 10am-6pm daily, free). This is the original site of San Antonio's first neighborhood. It's believed it was founded as a settlement for Spanish soldiers under Santa Anna who were stationed at the Mission San Antonio (The Alamo). The buildings at La Villita are mostly historic; some have survived periodic floods and some have been transported to this location. Inside these relics there are galleries, shops, and cafés, all oozing charm. Also at La Villita is the historic outdoor **Arneson River Theatre,** which was cleverly constructed of stone with grass patches for comfortable seating, as was seen in the movie *Miss Congeniality.* Also in La Villita is the Cos House, which is believed to be the spot where General Perfecto de Cos signed the articles of capitulation for the Mexican Army after being defeated by the Texian Army. Plan on an hour or two for shopping and meandering.

San Antonio Children's Museum

The stodgy museums of adults can get pretty boring for kids. If you make a pit stop at the **Doseum** (2800 Broadway St., 210/212-4453, www.thedoseum.org, 10am-5pm Mon.-Thurs., 9am-5pm Fri., 9am-6pm Sat., noon-5pm Sun., $12) you're sure to put a smile on their faces. This three-story museum has many hands-on interactive exhibits and creative programs. Here children can pretend to be artists, a grocery store employees, veterinary doctors, or construction workers, and learn at the same time. Although the museum is designed for children ages 2-12, adults can also get into this if you let go of your inhibitions and adultness and scream, run, and play.

La Villita

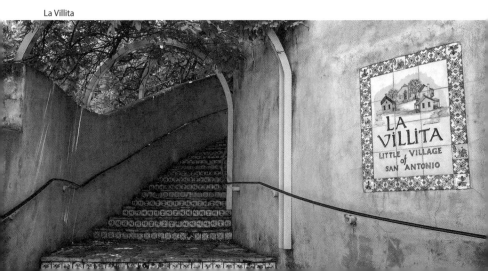

San Fernando Cathedral

The oldest cathedral sanctuary in the United States is at **San Fernando Cathedral** (115 Main Plaza, 210/227-1297, www.sfcathedral.org). Founded in 1731 by a group of families who came from Spain at the invitation of King Philip V, this picturesque, historic, gothic revival-style cathedral has seen much of San Antonio's history. Probably the most dramatic event was during the siege of The Alamo, when General Santa Anna raised the flag of "no quarter" from the rooftop. The cathedral has always been at the center of San Antonio's life, and it remains a cultural centerpiece. It is the seat of the Roman Catholic Archdiocese of San Antonio and offers mass in Spanish, English, and Latin. The popular mariachi mass is offered at 5:30pm every Saturday, and every Sunday several masses are offered. For the mass schedule visit the cathedral's website.

Spanish Governor's Palace

The **Spanish Governor's Palace** (105 Plaza de Armas, 210/224-0601, 9am-5pm Tues.-Sat., 10am-5pm Sun., $5) is considered "the most beautiful building in San Antonio" according to the National Geographic Society. The "palace" is better described as a mansion. It's a beautiful Spanish colonial home with thick adobe walls and beautiful gardens. It was built as a result of an early-17th-century rivalry between Spain and France for dominance over the territory. No Spanish governor has ever actually lived here, but, as the pseudo-home of the local authority, the palace played host to all-important Spanish officials of the Province of Texas. In short, the palace was the crash pad for big shots. The interior is simply but elegantly decorated with period furnishings and unique objects from everyday 19th-century life. For some reason ghosts inhabit the fountain in the garden. According to my research, the gurgling that comes from the fountain isn't the ghosts. The strangely low admission fee makes this the cheapest thrill in town.

Texas Pioneer Trail Driver & Ranger Museum

San Antonio wouldn't be complete without a special museum dedicated to the folks who founded and protected Texas in the beginning. The **Texas Pioneer Trail Driver & Ranger Museum** (3805 Broadway, 210/822-9011, 11am-4pm Mon.-Sat., noon-4pm Sun. Sept.-Apr., $5) is a commendable tribute that offers a rare glimpse into the early pioneer days, with exhibits that display items that kept the pioneers alive. The collection includes Texas Ranger artifacts and items from the old trail drivers.

Buckhorn Museum and Texas Ranger Museum

The **Buckhorn Museum and Texas Ranger Museum** (318 E. Houston St., 210/247-4000, www.buckhornmuseum.com, 10am-6pm daily, $19.99 adults, $14.99 for children 3 to 11) is more amusing than an actual museum. Avoiding the confines and stuffiness of the conventional museum, this weird institution has been in continuous operation since 1881. The Buckhorn was founded by Albert Friedrich on Dolorosa Street as a saloon where a man could get a shot of whiskey in exchange for deer antlers. During Prohibition the saloon became a "museum" and resurfaced after Prohibition as a watering hole. Over the years the saloon's collection of horns and antlers grew to include trophy mounts, memorabilia and "artifacts" from the Wild West, furniture made of cattle horns, art made from the rattles of rattlesnakes, antique powder horns, and firearms. In all, there are more than 1,200 dead animals, making this a temple to the art of taxidermy. If you don't know whether to take this seriously or not, err on the side of tongue-in-cheek, and you'll have a laugh. Also located here is the Texas Ranger Museum. Here you'll get up close to hundreds of Texas Ranger artifacts, including revolvers, sawed-off shotguns, badges, and all things related to law enforcement in the early days of Texas. History buffs of the great state will be impressed.

The enormous Tower of the Americas is a great way to get your bearings while in San Antonio.

The highlight of the Texas Ranger Museum is Ranger Town, a re-creation of San Antonio at the turn of the 20th century. Explore this western town complete with a replica Buckhorn Saloon, a working jail cell, blacksmith shop, newspaper, and telegraph office. Ranger Town is also home to the Bonnie and Clyde exhibit—complete with a vintage 1934 Ford V8 Deluxe, the same make and model as the couple's famous getaway car.

Tower of the Americas

The focal point in the San Antonio skyline is the **Tower of the Americas** (739 E. Cesar E. Chavez Blvd., 210/223-3101, www.towerof-heamericas.com, 10am-10pm Sun.-Thurs., 10am-11pm Fri.-Sat., $12). The 750-foot-tall tower is one of the many remnants of the HemisFair (World's Fair) that was held in **HemisFair Park** back in 1968, and it's still one of the tallest freestanding structures in the Western Hemisphere. No matter where you are in San Antonio you can see the 750-foot tower, which dwarfs the Space Needle by

87 feet and snubs the Washington Monument by 67 feet. In Texas everything is bigger—get used to it.

The observation deck is some 59 stories high and offers the very best view in town. Buying a Tower Ticket for $12 ($10 seniors and military, $9 children 4-12 years, children 3 and under free) gives you all-day access to the observation deck and a 15-minute ride called **Skies Over Texas,** which is a stadium-seating 4-D adventure that offers a short Texas history lesson through a simulated helicopter ride over the state. The tower is also home to the **Chart House Restaurant** (210/223-3101, $30), a slowly revolving eatery with mediocre pseudo-fancy food, and a low-key cocktail lounge called **Bar 601** (210/223-3101). Drinkers will be pleased to know that, unlike the restaurant, the lounge doesn't revolve. Late hours make this a must for romantics. Parking is $8 at 701 Bowie Street.

Institute of Texan Cultures

Texas, and more specifically the San Antonio area, has some of the continent's most ancient history. Many various peoples have inhabited, settled, and in some way contributed to the history and prehistory of the state. The **Institute of Texan Cultures** (801 E. Cesar E. Chavez Blvd., 210/458-2300, www.texan-cultures.com, 9am-5pm Mon.-Sat., noon-5pm Sun., $10 adults, $8 seniors, $8 children 6-17) has pulled all this history into one place and presented it in a dynamic and moving way. The populations of 26 cultural and ethnic groups are represented and explored through the items they left behind, such as tools, religious artifacts, and household items from daily life. In the 50,000-square-foot space the institute has developed fascinating permanent and rotating exhibits, educational programs, and even a multiscreen video presentation that unveils these cultures. The institute originally opened at the HemisFair back in 1968, but was so well received it has remained open since. Limited free parking is at the front of the building, and paid parking is available at 701 Bowie Street for $8.

★ HemisFair Park

One landmark event that put San Antonio on the map was the city's hosting of the World's Fair in 1968. The fair coincided with the city's 250th anniversary, and people saw this as an opportunity to boost San Antonio's profile as a world-class destination by pulling off a dramatic fair. Thus, **HemisFair Park** was created. Once the fair was over the city was left with some amazing features that were wisely preserved, such as the **Institute of Texan Cultures,** the **Tower of the Americas,** the **water gardens,** and the **Schultz House Cottage Garden.** In 1990 a children's playground was added that includes a wood-and-sand playground. HemisFair Park is downtown, adjacent to the convention center. Parking is $8 at 701 Bowie Street. Plan on spending about 2-3 hours at the park. This will give you time to experience the Tower of the Americas, the museum, and the gardens. If you want to include dinner tack on another 90 minutes.

WEST
SeaWorld San Antonio

The home of San Antonio's biggest celebrity is **SeaWorld San Antonio** (10500 SeaWorld Dr., 800/700-7786, www.seaworld.com), the biggest marine theme park in the world. And who might this celebrity be? Shamu, the gentle killer whale. Despite the controversy surrounding killer whales in captivity, the show that features Shamu is still the top-billed act at SeaWorld. With a two-story video screen, seven-million-gallon tank, and 3,800 seats, the show inundates viewers with thrills. Warning to all who like to drink water and not wear it—don't sit in the first 14 rows, where you will get seriously drenched. Shows take place throughout the day. Also at SeaWorld is a beluga show with dolphins and acrobats, the Aquatica water park with wave pool and water chutes, shark aquariums with large viewing windows, bird exhibits, and 100 resident penguins. There is also a large dolphin pool where little ones can feed dolphins.

As if this isn't enough, the park also has several roller coasters. I'm not much of a fan of overblown, mega theme parks, especially ones founded by Anheuser-Busch, but the kids *love* it! There's so much going on here that I highly suggest going online before your visit to help determine what you want to see. Also, plan on bringing swimsuits and a change of clothes because you will probably get wet. Hours fluctuate but generally are 10am-9pm in the spring and summer months. Ticket prices for day passes to SeaWorld are $55 ages 3-9 and $65 ages 10 and up; day passes to SeaWorld plus Aquatica are $80 ages 3-9 and $90 ages 10 and up. Deals can sometimes be had by buying tickets online.

EAST
Splashtown

A great place for the whole family to cool down in the hot summer months is **Splashtown** (3600 N. I-35, 210/227-1400, www.splashtownsa.com, hours vary, roughly 11am-8pm daily Apr.-Sept., $30 for general admission, $24 for children under 48 inches, $19 after 5pm). This 20-acre water theme park has hydro-related activities for every age, from Kid's Kove to the Wave Pool, from the seven-story Lone Star Luge to Starflight, a double-tube slide into total darkness. After the sun sets Splashtown offers a teen-oriented program that includes movies every Friday night and live Christian bands most Sunday afternoons. Lockers are available for a fee, and parking is free.

SOUTH
★ King William Historic District

The amazing little neighborhood just south of downtown called the **King William Historic District** is the one place in town where you can marvel at historic mansions, visit some of San Antonio's best art galleries, and get a bite to eat at one of a few fantastic restaurants. At the end of the 19th century, this little bastion of opulence initially settled by German immigrants was where the rich and notable of San Antonio lived. Today this historic district is still lined with breathtakingly beautiful historic mansions, some set on the banks of the San Antonio River. Most of the mansions are Victorian and colonial revival in style and have well-manicured gardens. If you are curious about what the interior of these mansions looks like, you're in luck. Two of the mansions, the Guenther House (205 E. Guenther St., 210/227-1061, www.guentherhouse.com, 7am-3pm daily, free) and the Edward Steves Homestead Museum (509 King William St., 210/225-5924, www.saconservation.org, 10am-3:30pm daily, $7.50 adults, $5 seniors and students, children 11 and under free), are open to the public. The King William Historic District is circumscribed by Durango Street, St. Mary's Street, Alamo Street, and the San Antonio River.

I recommend starting your day in the King William Historic District with breakfast at the Guenther House followed by a walk in the neighborhood. Plan for about 2-3 hours depending on your love of mansion gawking.

★ The Missions

Although San Antonio's history stretches back hundreds of centuries and beyond, the most visible and best-preserved relics from the past are the 18th-century Spanish missions established along the San Antonio River. There are five missions in all: Mission San Antonio de Valero (The Alamo), Mission Concepción, Mission San José, Mission San Juan, and Mission Espada. What's known as the Mission Trail historically connected the missions from the northernmost mission, The Alamo, to the southernmost mission, Espada—a distance of just over eight miles. Collectively these missions form the largest concentration of Catholic missions in North America.

Established by Franciscan friars to convert the local native population, these missions were first built of stone, wood, and adobe and didn't have walls. Because of tensions between tribes and missionary occupants, stone walls were erected as a form of

defense. Native Americans built these beautifully ornate buildings under the direction of craftsmen from Spain, using Spanish colonial architectural style.

Today, the missions are surprisingly intact, although walls are crumbling and ornamental details have eroded. Mission San Antonio de Valero (The Alamo) is maintained and operated by the Daughters of the Republic of Texas, while the other four missions are active Roman Catholic parishes run in collaboration with the Archdiocese of San Antonio and the National Park Service.

The Mission Trail has become an amazing outdoor attraction in itself. In the past the Mission Trail wasn't really an actual trail in the traditional sense of the word. The San Antonio River Authority (SARA) connected the Mission Reach Hike and Bike Trail to the Main Plaza near San Fernando Cathedral all the way down to Mission Espada in the south, making the mission trail a fun adventure by bike. Large portions of the trail are along the beautiful San Antonio River, which makes exploring the missions via bike or by foot very enjoyable. Although signage on roads helps cars and bikes navigate the trails and roads that make up the trail, it is a good idea to download a copy of the map at www.visitsanantonio.com. Be sure to bring snacks and water, as there aren't any stores to speak of along the trail.

If you don't have the time or energy for the hike-and-bike trail, you can easily explore all the missions in a long afternoon via auto. Here's what I recommend: Do The Alamo separately, and then tackle the other four missions. There's a distance of about three miles between all the missions (excluding The Alamo), so travel time is quick, unless you get lost. From downtown, drive south on South St. Mary's Street to Mission Road, where you will land at Mission Concepción. Then take Mission Road south to Mission San José. Just outside the mission is a comprehensive visitors center with video presentations, exhibits, maps (the confusing one I mentioned), and artifacts from all the missions. Then exit the mission on Napier Avenue and head south on Mission Parkway, which will connect you to Mission San Juan and the farthest of the missions, Mission Espada.

Visiting the missions is free of charge, and all are open 9am-5pm daily except Thanksgiving Day, Christmas Day, and New Year's Day. For more information contact the National Park Service's **mission headquarters** (210/534-8833, www.nps.gov/saan) or the **visitors center** (6701 San José Dr., 210/932-1001, free). Determining how much time the missions will take depends on the type of experience you want. If you walk or bike the trail and visit all the missions at a slow pace, plan on packing a lunch and snack because this can easily be a daylong adventure. If don't have a whole lot of time and want to sample the best missions via car, plan on allocating 2-3 hours.

The Legend of the Haunting Children

On the south side of San Antonio, in the vicinity of the Blue Star Arts Complex, there's a set of railroad tracks that are believed to be haunted. The story is that a bus full of children stalled on the railroad tracks and was hit by a train. All the children supposedly died. Although there is no record of this incident, people believe children haunt the tracks, especially at one crossing. Supposedly, if you go at night (especially Halloween), put baby powder on the trunk of your car, and put your car in neutral on the tracks, your car will be pushed by the ghosts of the kids. Their fingerprints are often seen in the baby powder. Local residents are tired of people stopping on the tracks and doing the baby powder test, so I won't disclose the location of this crossing. Just know that there may be the ghosts of children in the area.

Mission Concepción

Transferred to its present location in 1731, **Mission Concepción** (807 Mission Rd.) is the largest of the missions. This mission served as the headquarters for all the San Antonio missions. At one time the facade of the mission church was adorned with elaborate, colorful frescoes and detailed artistry that has faded over time. Inside the sanctuary, remnants of this colorful past are still to be found. Some of the religious paintings on the walls contain a blend of Christian, Spanish, and native influences, and they reveal how the missionaries used traditional native and religious imagery in their Christian context, in order to convey Christian teachings.

Mission San José

Founded by Franciscan missionary Father Antonio Margila de Jesús in 1720, **Mission San José** (6701 San José Dr.) became the best known of the Texas missions. The colonial baroque architecture of the limestone mission church exceeded that of the other missions, as did its capacity as a social center. These combined to help the mission earn the name Queen of the Missions. Once the founding ceremonies for the mission took place, leaders of three Native American tribes were appointed governor, judge, and sheriff of the mission community, and mission inhabitants learned to use firearms to defend themselves against the Apache and Comanche. At its height, the mission housed over 350 neophyte Native Americans; had an efficient aqueduct system for irrigation, a Spanish colonial flour mill, and a granary; there were also maintained fields and herds of livestock. In 1824 it ceased to be a mission.

Mission San Juan

Founded in 1716 in eastern Texas, **Mission San Juan** (9101 Graf Rd.) was transferred to its present location in 1731. San Juan eventually became a major regional supplier of produce. Outside the mission walls, orchards and gardens produced melons, grapes, sweet potatoes, beans, and even sugarcane. Within the mission walls Native American artisans produced

cloth, iron tools, and other items for daily life. These products supported all the San Antonio missions as well as nearby settlements, and trade was established with surrounding states and throughout Mexico.

Mission Espada

Founded in 1690 near present-day Weches, Texas, **Mission Espada** (10040 Espada Rd.) was the first mission in Texas. The mission was transferred to its present location in 1731 and is now the most remote and southernmost mission of the four. Here Native Americans were taught vocational skills such as carpentry, masonry, blacksmithing, and stonecutting. Mission Espada was the only mission to produce bricks, which were used throughout the region. Some claim these bricks can be found throughout many historical sites in the San Antonio area. The church has a unique entrance topped with a three-bell tower known as an *espadaña*. According to legend, the wooden cross to the left of the main doorway of the church was carried by parishioners in a procession around the compound as they prayed for rain during a time of drought.

SAN ANTONIO
SIGHTS

Mission Concepción

Battle of Concepción

Approximately two miles south of downtown San Antonio is the historic Mission Concepción. Founded in 1716, the mission remains one of the oldest and best preserved of all the missions along the San Antonio River. In December 1835, it was the site of an important battle between the Texas colonists and the Mexican Army. The Texas revolution had just begun, and 600 colonists, led by Stephen F. Austin, marched on San Antonio to force the removal of General Cos and his 900 Mexican troops. As the Texans approached San Antonio from the south, Austin sent Jim Bowie ahead with 60 men to scout out the enemy. Bowie camped in the bend along the San Antonio River, a few hundred yards in front of Mission Concepción. The following day, Cos marched out with over 300 infantry and cavalry to surround and crush the Texas force.

While lesser men might have considered surrendering, Bowie's inspired leadership led to a Texas victory. He had his men shelter behind the riverbank and prepare for the Mexican onslaught. The cannon fire of the Mexicans went over the Texans' heads and showered them with pecans from the trees along the bank. At each charge, the Texas long rifles fired and caused heavy casualties among the Mexican Army. After four unsuccessful assaults, the Mexicans retreated back to San Antonio, leaving their cannon behind. It was the first significant victory the Texas forces won over the Mexican Army, and it inspired the troops to subsequently attack the city of San Antonio and force the surrender of General Cos.

It is remarkable that after all of these years the battlefield (so close to downtown San Antonio) remains virtually unchanged. With just a little imagination a visitor can easily envision the positions of the Mexican Army and the defending Texians and relive the historic battle. Look for the monument marking the place where the Texans suffered their first fatality of the revolution.

Entertainment and Events

San Antonio isn't known for having a crazy nightlife scene filled with live music and all-night dancing. This came about probably because at some point the family-oriented city let Austin take the lead for nightlife and entertainment. However, if you're "in the know," you can find some pretty spectacular places to spend a memorable night on the town.

For complete listings of what's happening in San Antonio, pick up a free copy of the weekly alternative newspaper, the *San Antonio Current,* or check out the Weekender section of the local newspaper, the *San Antonio Express-News.*

San Antonio is one of the largest cities in the United States, so touring national acts often play here. Two mega entertainment venues host everything from hugely popular rock and country bands to monster-truck extravaganzas to Disney on Ice to all spectator sports. The biggest is the ginormous **Alamodome** (100 Montana St., 210/207-3663, www.alamodome.com), on the east side of I-35 near HemisFair Park. Next up is the **AT&T Center** (1 AT&T Center Pkwy., 210/444-5000, www.attcenter.com), which is home to the San Antonio Spurs and has a maximum capacity of 18,500. Finally, the big music venue downtown is **Sunset Station** (1174 E. Commerce, 210/222-9481, www.sunset-station.com). This entertainment complex is in the original San Antonio train station at HemisFair Park and can host 3,500 people. Tickets for large events can be purchased through **Ticketmaster** (210/224-9600, www.ticketmaster.com).

LIVE MUSIC

There's no real entertainment district to speak of in town. All venues for live music are scattered throughout the big city, and many venues double as restaurants and bars. For the most part bands strike up on weekend nights between 9pm and 2am, and cover charges vary.

A popular music and food district has sprouted on North St. Mary's Street near Brackenridge Park. This popular hipster area is home to the great music and DJ club **Limelight** (2718 N. St. Mary's St., 210/735-7775, http://thelimelightsa.com). Upon entry you may be a tad intimidated by the tattoos and stares at the door, but hang in there as this place is one of the hottest venues in town for indie rock. Shoe gazers, loud amps, and nerd rebellions rattle this place with sometimes mediocre, but often intriguing, talent. Cover usually starts at $5.

The other popular venue on North St. Mary's is **Mix Nightclub** (2423 N. St. Mary's St., 210/735-1313, http://themix-sa.com). This dive bar has a built-in scene that is alive most weekend nights starting on Thursday night. The beer is pretty cheap and the place is often packed.

The best place to catch a great blues, roots, or Americana act is **Sam's Burger Joint** (330 E. Grayson St., 210/223-2830, www.samsburgerjoint.com, $12). Although the name is unassuming, this highly respected venue has a great sound system and a vibrant scene after dark. Local musicians and touring acts showcase their talent while bartenders serve up the best beers on tap.

Every town has its legendary music venue. San Antonio's is **Floore's Country Store** (14492 Bandera Rd., north of San Antonio in Helotes, 210/695-8827, www.liveatfloores.com). This "country store" sells nothing but barbecue, beer, and foot-stomping country and rockabilly music. Artists such as Lyle Lovett and Willie Nelson have graced the outdoor stage time and again. Don't expect anything fancy here, just picnic tables in the dirt.

A surefire way to have a great time on the town is by catching a DJ session or live jazz big band at **Tucker's Kozy Korner** (1338 E. Houston St., 210/320-2192). Originally opened in 1948 as a burger stand, today this local food and dance spot always provides patrons a memorable night on the town. On Monday

nights catch the in-house seven-piece band headed by Jim Cullum, as the group faithfully performs early big-band jazz pieces covering greats such as Benny Goodman, Glenn Miller, and Louis Armstrong.

Leon Springs Dancehall (24135 I-10 W., 210/698-7070, www.leonspringsdancehall.com) is where you can two-step to a live country band along with hundreds of other folks. This family-friendly dance hall has a massive, 18,000-square-foot wooden floor that's packed Friday and Saturday nights. Cover charge is only $5, making this a great place to take a date for a cheap but memorable night out. Minors are welcome but must be accompanied by an adult.

Teen angst is best experienced at the famous **White Rabbit** (2410 N. St. Mary's St., 210/737-2221). Here a younger crowd sweats to indie rock, punk, and hard-core music. The venue is all ages and often there's no cover charge. Buy tickets by phone for a discount.

BARS AND CLUBS

Located in the hip Blue Star Arts Complex is the **Blue Star Brewing Company** (1414 S. Alamo, 210/212-5506). This inviting brewpub in the artsy enclave of Southtown is a welcome oasis from the hubbub of downtown. The brews cooked up here are best enjoyed on the large outdoor patio or 2nd-story balcony, where you can watch the artists and businesspeople.

Just around the corner from The Alamo is three stories of par-tay at **Bonham Exchange** (411 Bonham St., 210/271-3811). With five bars, some named after heroes of The Alamo, and three dance floors, the Bonham has oodles of space to mingle. Wednesday is college night, also known as straight night. The rest of the week it's a popular gay hangout.

Yes, the missions are old, but **The Esquire** (155 E. Commerce St., 210/222-2521) is old too. This bar is a San Antonio institution that has been around since 1933, the year Prohibition ended. Okay, so it closed for four years and was renovated, but the ancient long bar remains the main attraction. This historic saloon, which houses the second-longest wooden bar in Texas, is the oldest continuously running watering hole in the state (except for those four years I mentioned). There's a whopping 91 feet of stools, bar, and locals leaning up against it checking out the folks that walk through the door. It can be intimidating drinking a beer in this joint for the first time, because no matter who you are, "you're new in these parts," and you'll get the stare-down. The crowd in here is primarily locals and rough characters who practically live here. The ceiling is stamped copper, the walls are bordello-style, and the waiters sport black shirts and ties.

The highest barstool in town is at **Bar 601** (739 E. Cesar E. Chavez Blvd., 210/223-3101). Located at the top of the Tower of the Americas, this classy bar with a view isn't for those who pinch pennies or have vertigo.

A great spot to stop off after an evening walk in the King William Historic District is **La Tuna** (100 Probandt St., 210/212-5727). This ice house has an inviting atmosphere fit for the whole family. Drinking a beer at one of the outside tables in late spring is a popular way to be in denial about the forthcoming heat.

Next door to The Alamo is a bar rich in history called the **Menger Bar** (204 Alamo Plaza, 210/223-4361), attached to the famous (and haunted) Menger Hotel. A replica of the House of Lords Pub in London, this small, dimly lit room covered in rich cherrywood is the perfect place to sit in a dark corner and have a drink. As you sit and sip, ponder how this pub was the location where Teddy Roosevelt recruited some of his Rough Riders. Who knows—maybe you'll see his ghost if you have enough drinks.

For a modern spin on the Brat Pack approach to booze there's **Swig Martini Bar** (111 W. Crockett St. #2205, 210/476-0005). This martini bar is all about cocktails, cigars, and live music. Guys, you gotta have a collar on your shirt to not stand out here, and gals, you gotta be in pumps. With a patio overlooking the River Walk, the best selection of

The Tejano Accordion

The accordion is a 19th-century European instrument. So how did it become an integral part of Mexican music? It happened right here in Central Texas. The unusual instrument was patented in 1829 in Vienna. Only a few years later German pioneers headed out to the New World, ended up in Texas, and quickly established many of the Hill Country towns, such New Braunfels, Gruene, Boerne, and Comfort. They brought with them sauerkraut, schnitzel, and a strange new musical invention: the squeezebox. As the German and Mexican cultures mingled, a new style of music was pioneered. The final product was an accordion-based, Tex-Mex music that blended traditional Mexican forms such as the *corrido* with European waltz and polka. San Antonio was the biggest city in the region and quickly became the experimental ground for this new music style called both **Tejano** and **conjunto.** In recent years it has adopted strong influences from rock, blues, and *cumbia,* and is now not just regional ethnic music, but its own genre with wide appeal.

martinis in town, and live jazz bands to set the tone, this place is a class act.

PERFORMING ARTS AND THEATERS

San Antonio has a slew of small performing-arts groups, as well as some more-established companies that keep the local performing-arts scene eclectic, entertaining, and cutting edge. The main performing-arts company in the arena of music is the nationally recognized **San Antonio Symphony** (210/223-8624, www.sasymphony.org). Most performances are held at newly renovated Majestic Theatre (224 E. Houston St., 210/226-3333, www.majesticempire.com). Classical music filling the extraordinarily ornate halls of the Majestic can be a breathtaking experience.

When it comes to theater, San Antonio takes pride in having a handful of performing-arts companies. Most theatrical performances take place at one of several venues. The city's beloved **Majestic Theatre** (224 E. Houston St., 210/226-3333, www.majesticempire.com) is considered one of the most ornate theaters in the country, and its history alone seems to add to any drama. Built in the 1920s, this grand stage has been the center of the performing arts in San Antonio for decades. Today you can catch major Broadway productions as well as the San Antonio Symphony. The Majestic's sister theater is the **Empire Theatre** (226 N. St. Mary's St., 210/226-5700, www.majesticempire.com). This old opera house built in 1914 now puts on shows and performances of all kinds.

The Trinity University campus is home to **Laurie Auditorium** (715 Stadium Dr., 210/999-8117). It's not possible to pin down all that happens in this performing-arts auditorium. People come here to see comics like Jay Leno as well as jazz concerts, and world-renowned lecturers speak to packed audiences on all topics imaginable.

San Antonio's cutting-edge shows are put on at **Jump-Start** (108 Blue Star Complex, 210/227-5867, www.jump-start.org). This unique company focuses entirely on new creations that are dreamed up by local artists and writers. Most of what you'll see here is very avant-garde—and it all appropriately takes place on a stage in an old warehouse.

Located downtown on the River Walk at historic La Villita is **Arneson River Theatre** (418 Villita St., 210/207-8610, www.lavillita.com). This well-designed outdoor amphitheater is in a spectacular setting. The San Antonio River separates the stage from the audience, who sit on cleverly designed stone seats that are filled with patches of grass for comfort.

CINEMAS

For the magic and clarity of IMAX, there's **San Antonio IMAX Theatre** (849 E. Commerce St., 888/262-4386). Along with the usual movies Hollywood pumps out, this theater also screens those dramatic movies that make IMAX so famous. The one everyone has to see here is *Alamo, The Price of Freedom*. The theater is on the first level of Rivercenter Mall. Three hours of parking is free at the Rivercenter Mall with the purchase of an IMAX ticket.

Arneson River Theatre

COMEDY CLUBS

The one outlet for live laughs is **Rivercenter Comedy Club** (849 E. Commerce St., Ste. 893, at the Rivercenter Mall, 210/229-1420). Big-name acts come through here, such as Dennis Miller and comedians from Comedy Central and HBO. Local talent is also appreciated, especially during Comedy Potpourri on Monday. A night here can be complemented by dinner and drinks, as the club has a full kitchen and bar. Doors open at 4pm and shows begin at 8pm. Headliner shows are Wednesday-Sunday. Tickets can cost anywhere from $8 to $12 depending on the night of the week and the comedian or act.

FESTIVALS AND EVENTS

January

The yearly maintenance of the San Antonio River has turned into a filthy festival, the **River Walk Mud Festival** (210/227-4262). When the river is drained, a king and queen of mud are elected to preside over events that include music, games, and festivities related to mud.

February

Every February the SBC Center is taken over for the 16-day **San Antonio Stock Show and Rodeo** (210/255-5851, www.sarodeo. com). See live music, livestock, and daring cowboys riding raging bulls.

The week before Ash Wednesday, just before Lent, the River Walk features **Mardi Gras** (210/227-4262). Buy or browse arts and crafts made by local artists and artisans for an entire week. The end of the week is marked by the **Mardi Gras River Parade.** Watch a procession of decorated river barges transform the San Antonio River. Costumed revelers and live entertainment celebrate Mardi Gras San Antonio-style.

March

St. Patrick's Day in San Antonio is celebrated with barrels of green dye and even more barrels of beer. As floats pour environmentally friendly green dye into the San Antonio River, the river is renamed "the River Shannon." This is followed by the St. Patrick's Day Parade, which in turn is followed by mass consumption of beer. An estimated 15,000 people flood the River Walk for the event.

Contemporary Art Month (210/222-2787, www.contemporaryartmonth.com) is a monthlong contemporary arts festival—the only one in the nation. With more than 400 exhibitions taking place in more than 50 venues, such as galleries, museums, and studios, this celebration offers an amazing look at what's happening in the art world of San Antonio.

April

The most spectacular festival of all is **Fiesta San Antonio** (www.fiesta-sa.org). For 10 days in April San Antonio has a party similar to New Orleans's Mardi Gras. The citywide celebration includes carnivals, sports, fireworks, entertainment, feasts, art exhibits, and parades that float down the San Antonio River. In the past the fiesta has attracted some three million participants and spectators from around the nation. The first Fiesta San Antonio event was back in 1891, which included a parade called the Battle of Flowers, honoring the heroes of Texas history.

May

Tejano Conjunto Festival (210/271-3151, www.guadalupeculturalarts.org) is San Antonio's way of celebrating the unique form of music that developed in South Texas with both German and Mexican roots. The three-day festival features live performances from top conjunto and Tejano artists, all in Rosedale Park and on the Guadalupe Cultural Arts Center campus.

June

Texas Folklife Festival (210/458-2300, www.texasfolklifefestival.org) is an annual four-day celebration of the diverse group of folks who settled Texas. Some 45 groups bring their cultures to the Institute of Texan Cultures. Everyone celebrates unity through diversity with crafts, music, dances, and foods.

The most important celebration for African Americans of Texas is **Juneteenth** (www.juneteenthsanantonio.com). June 19, 1865, marked the day that Texas slaves received word of the Emancipation Proclamation. Observances include a picnic, jazz concerts, a parade, and other cultural festivities honoring the first step toward freedom for blacks.

September

Marking Mexico's independence from Spain is **Diez y Seis** (800/447-3372, www.sanantoniovisit.com). Every September 16, San Antonio celebrates with a street parade with floats, marching bands, celebrations at Market Square and La Villita, and other activities.

Jazz lovers from all over converge in San Antonio for **Jazz'SAlive** (210/212-8423). For two days the nation's top jazz entertainers, along with regional talent, perform in Travis Park.

October

Connect with your loved ones who have passed on by celebrating **El Día de los Muertos**. Translated as Day of the Dead, this important and ancient celebration in Mexican culture is a ritual in which the family welcomes back departed loved ones.

November

Wurstfest is a 10-day salute to sausage. You'll find a variety of entertainment options including a polka contest, games, rides, food, and drinks on the Wurstfest Grounds in Landa Park.

Shopping

San Antonio isn't necessarily a shopping town, but it does have a few interesting shops with local flavor that are worth checking out. Mexican markets, massive malls, funky galleries, and a few boutique shops are what's to be expected here. The markets are particularly interesting, especially for the first-time visitor to Texas and/or San Antonio. Although there are some shops downtown and on the River Walk, most of the interesting shops are spread out throughout town. Just south of downtown is the burgeoning San Antonio Arts District, also known as Southtown. A few boutiques and art galleries can be found on South Alamo Street. Shops are generally open 10am-6pm daily.

The majority of major chain retail shops in downtown are located in **Rivercenter Mall** (849 E. Commerce, 210/225-0000, www.shoprivercenter.com, 10am-9pm Mon.-Sat., noon-6pm Sun.). This four-level shopping complex has more than 100 retailers, including restaurants and an AMC movie theater, all under one roof. The scene inside is stunning, as there are picturesque views of the River Walk below.

The most interesting independently owned shops are in historic **La Villita** (418 Villita St., 210/207-8610, www.lavillita.com, shops open 10am-6pm daily). Here you'll find arts and crafts, souvenirs, upscale gifts and home decor, and art from all genres and media. Many of these shops are inside historic buildings from San Antonio's early days.

The largest Mexican marketplace outside of Mexico is at **Market Square** (between Dolorosa and Commerce just west of downtown, 210/207-8600, 10am-8pm daily June-Aug., 10am-6pm daily Sept.-May). This entire city block of all things Mexico was originally an open-air market founded in 1840. Today Market Square is a little city unto itself, with great restaurants like Mi Tierra and La Margarita, outdoor courtyards, and covered malls that feature unique retail shops and purveyors of imports such as tin lamps, jewelry,

Council House Fight

As you stroll around Market Square in downtown San Antonio and admire San Fernando Cathedral, keep in mind that in March of 1840 a major Native American battle known as the Council House Fight took place here. A group of 65 Comanche (including 12 chiefs) came to town to negotiate a peace treaty with the Texans. The Native Americans had promised to bring with them all of their white captives as a sign of good faith. Unfortunately for them, they only brought one white captive, a 15-year-old girl named Matilda Lockhart. The Texans were put in a bad mood when they saw that Matilda's nose had been burned off by the Comanche. Then Matilda informed the Texans that there were numerous other captives and that it was the Comanche's intention to bargain for their release separately.

The meeting took place in a one-story stone building on the east side of the square at Market Street. Colonel William Fisher was in charge of the Texan forces and marched a company of troops into the council room. He informed the Indians that their chiefs would be held hostage until they brought in all of the white prisoners. The Comanche chiefs refused to be held prisoner and fighting erupted.

A bloody fight to the death occurred inside the council house with knives, guns, and bows and arrows. At the end of the struggle, all of the Comanche chiefs and warriors were killed. Seven Texans died in the struggle and eight were wounded. Twenty-seven Comanche women and children were captured and held hostage. Seven white captives were finally returned to the Texans in exchange for the Comanche hostages.

The aftermath of the Council House Fight led to the greatest Comanche raid in the history of Texas. Late in May of 1840, over 600 Comanche (encouraged and guided by representatives of the Mexican government) raided the towns of Victoria and Linnville on the Gulf Coast. Linnville was burned to the ground and plundered, and many captives were taken by the Comanche. As the Native Americans tried to retreat to their Hill Country campgrounds, they were attacked by Texan forces at the Battle of Plum Creek, near present-day Lockhart. The Comanche suffered a stunning defeat. Subsequent attacks by the Texan forces followed the Comanche into the upper reaches of the Colorado River valley. There the Comanche suffered a string of defeats that weakened their power so much that they never again made such an attack in force against a Texas town.

---

knickknacks, Mexican papier-mâché, sombreros, handmade Mexican dolls, religious kitsch, and the popular Davy Crockett coonskin hats. Outside the market in the beautiful courtyards, local musicians perform and celebrations take place.

CLOTHES, SHOES, AND ACCESSORIES

The craft, tradition, and art form of bootmaking has been upheld by two legendary boot companies based in San Antonio. In **Little's Boots** (110 Division St., 210/923-2221, 9am-5pm Tues.-Fri., 9am-1pm Sat.), a one-of-a-kind shop operating since 1915, prepare to stomp your feet with excitement over all the beautiful and ornate boots. Western footwear made from crocodile, alligator, kangaroo, eel,

ostrich, and even lizard is sure to impress the imagination. Be sure to check out the custom and handcrafted boots here. They are great works of art in their own right.

The other bootmaker in town is **Lucchese** (255 E. Basse Rd., 210/828-9419, 10am-7pm Mon.-Fri., 10am-6pm Sat., noon-5pm Sun.). Here you'll find high quality, precision craftsmanship, and class for the cowboy or cowgirl who enjoys getting gussied up.

Paris Hatters (119 N. Broadway, 210/223-3453, 9:30am-6:30pm Mon.-Sat., 11am-5pm Sun.) is yet another historic business in San Antonio. Family owned and operated since 1917, this headgear shop has a large variety of new hats ranging from the iconic Stetson to Kangol to cowhide baseball caps. Although there is a large collection of hats in the store, this boutique specializes in custom headwear for those who have the money.

MUSIC

Swim through a vast sea of new and used CDs at the **CD Exchange** (3703 Broadway St., 210/828-5525, 10am-9pm Mon.-Sat., noon-7pm Sun.). Everything is relatively cheap and in abundance. Here you can also find those rare 1980s movies you've been searching for on DVD and VHS.

For the vinyl aficionado, music purist, and counterculture hipster, **Hogwild Records, Tapes and CDs** (1824 N. Main Ave., 210/733-5354, 10am-9pm Mon.-Sat., noon-8pm Sun.) has an astounding collection of great records and tapes. This is also an outlet in town for underground press and literature.

BOOKSTORES

If you're in the mood for strolling around a bookstore, take a short trip up Broadway to **Half Price Books** (3207 Broadway, 210/822-4597, www.halfpricebooks.com, 9:30am-9pm daily), an emporium of cheap used books and a strange array of records.

A great resource for Texana and regional books and literature is **The Twig Book Shop** (306 Pearl Pkwy., Ste. 106, 210/826-6411, 9:30am-6pm daily). Inside the Twig is a great children's bookstore called **The Red Balloon.** Books for all ages, from babies to tots to teens, are here. They also have children's book readings, which is great for parents and children.

ART GALLERIES

Perhaps the most innovative and noteworthy gallery in town is **ArtPace** (445 N. Main Ave., 210/212-4900). Hours vary depending on the ever-revolving door of artists and exhibits. This purely conceptual gallery puts a fresh twist on the idea of the art gallery, as it brings in artists from around the world, gives them a place to live above the gallery space, provides art supplies, and lets them go crazy. The stuff produced here is generally wildly bizarre but always amusing and thought provoking.

The beating heart of contemporary Southtown is the **Blue Star Arts Complex** (between the San Antonio River and S. Alamo St., www.bluestarart.org). This abandoned industrial warehouse was brilliantly converted into spaces and galleries for local artists, and has become San Antonio's repository for contemporary arts. If you're in the market for cutting-edge and unique art in all media—painting, sculpture, and performing arts—you'll find it here. Gallery spaces and showings are at random times, but chances are, if you show up sometime in the afternoon something will be open. Galleries include **San Angel Folk Art** and **Joan Grona Gallery.**

Art is to be appreciated and sometimes even worn. At the Gallery Shop of the **Southwest School of Art and Craft** (Ursuline Campus, 300 Augusta St., 210/224-1848, 10am-5pm Mon.-Sat.) you'll find an interesting collection of one-of-a-kind works of art made by students. Expect to find color, innovation, and flat-out strange stuff in here.

Recreation

For those looking for fun, the most popular activities are golf, spectator sports, and, of course, visits to the city's massive theme parks. There's not much in the way of outdoor recreation in San Antonio. For hiking, biking, rock climbing, and swimming, most people head out into the Hill Country.

HIKING AND BIKING

Perhaps the most convenient place to hike and bike is the **Mission Trail** (6701 San José Dr., 210/932-1001, www.nps.gov/saan). The trails that link some of the missions are, for the most part, scenic. However, some lengths of the trail cut through run-down urban areas that aren't too scenic. The only other place for outdoor activities in the San Antonio metropolitan area is **Brackenridge Park** (3910 N. St. Mary's St., 210/207-7275, 5am-11pm daily, free). Don't expect any dirt trails for hiking or mountain biking, though, as this park is primarily for families who want to picnic and walk a paved trail near the river.

On the outskirts of town is beautiful **McAllister Park** (13102 Jones Maltsberger Rd., 210/207-7275, 5am-11pm daily, free). This wooded area 12 miles north of downtown is the best place to get away from the city and hike or bike in semi-seclusion. Lastly there's **Friedrich Wilderness Park** (21395 Milsa Dr., 210/207-7275, 5am-11pm daily, free), which offers 5.5 miles of trails for hiking.

GOLF

What San Antonio lacks in hiking and biking opportunities is made up for by several world-class golf courses. The favorite resort-golf mecca is **La Cantera Golf Club and Resort** (16401 La Cantera Pkwy., 800/446-5387). The two top-notch courses on the resort grounds are both classic Hill Country layouts. One overlooks Six Flags Fiesta Texas.

One of Texas's best municipal golf courses is **Cedar Creek Municipal Golf Course**

(8250 Vista Colina, 210/695-5050). Considered by some to be the poor man's La Cantera, Cedar Creek can get very crowded, so patience and a tee time are absolutely necessary.

Lastly there's beautiful **Canyon Springs Golf Course** (24400 Canyon Golf Rd., 210/497-1770). No setting in golf is better than the approach to the signature 17th green and its waterfall backdrop.

SPECTATOR SPORTS

San Antonio's only major-league franchise is the ever-popular **San Antonio Spurs** (www.nba.com/spurs). This team has fought its way up the National Basketball Association food chain and has been the NBA champion five times (1999, 2003, 2005, 2007, and 2014). The season is October-May, and home games are played in the **AT&T Center.** Tickets can cost anywhere from $25 to $70, and can be purchased at the AT&T Ticket Office (1 AT&T Center Pkwy., 210/444-5819) or through Ticketmaster (210/224-9600, www.ticketmaster.com).

Another popular spectator sport is **drag racing.** The venue for this rubber-smoking speed sport is the **San Antonio Raceway** (3641 S. Santa Clara Rd., 210/698-2310, www.sanantonioraceway.com). There's also a minor-league baseball team, the **San Antonio Missions** (210/675-7275, www.samissions.com), whose season is April-September. Games are played at **Nelson Wolff Stadium** (5757 Hwy. 90 W., 210/675-7275).

San Antonio's megavenue is the **Alamodome** (100 Montana St., 800/884-3663, www.alamodome.com), which showcases anything from bull riding to football to the Texas Hunters Extravaganza.

One of the most distinctive experiences in San Antonio is spending the day at the *charreada,* or Mexican rodeo (6126 Padre Dr., 210/846-8757, Mar.-Oct., $10, children 12 and under free). *Charreada* is similar in many ways to American rodeo, but with a distinct

Latin flair and showmanship. Among many *suertes* (events) are *colas en lienzo* (bull tailing), where a rider grabs the tail of a running bull, wraps it around his leg, and pulls the bull to the ground, and *paso de muerte* (pass of death), where a rider jumps from his galloping horse onto the back of a galloping wild horse and rides it until it stops bucking.

For more than 50 years the San Antonio Charro Association has been keeping this old-world sport alive, dazzling audiences with high-stakes horsemanship, daring bull roping, and live mariachi bands. Events are held at the association's ranch, which overlooks the San Antonio River.

TOURS

Touring the downtown stretch of the San Antonio River by boat is a hoot. Tours are offered by **Rio San Antonio Cruises** (210/244-5700, www.riosanantonio.com). There are three ticket and boarding locations along the River Walk: Holiday Inn River Walk, Rivercenter Mall, and Market Street Bridge. The tour takes passengers on a 2.6-mile excursion along the river in an open, flat-bottom barge. Tours last about 40 minutes and cost $8.25. If you get an experienced tour guide who incessantly shoots out facts and anecdotes about history, famous people, and infamous events, the touristy ride can be quite entertaining. If you prefer to take a ride without the monologue, Rio offers a river taxi service that has 39 stops along the river. Taxi stops are marked by Rio Trans signs along the River Walk. One-way rate is $5, a day pass is $10, and a three-day pass is $25.

Food

San Antonio's proximity to the Mexican border and its rich Latino history make this one of the best places for Tex-Mex and Mexican food. Even restaurants that aren't billed as Mexican offer enchiladas at the very least. When it comes to Mexican food, expect guacamole prepared tableside, margaritas, breakfast tacos, live mariachi music, handmade tortillas, and some gringo-Mex variations of all the above, all at great prices.

If you are one of those few people in the world who don't like Mexican, or just want to try something different, there are lots of other eateries to choose from. Fabulous restaurants are scattered all throughout town, but many are in the downtown area. The River Walk is a popular place to eat for both locals and tourists, as the atmosphere is remarkably serene and alluring. The narrow winding paths along the river are lined with umbrella tables and charming eateries that are packed from spring to fall. There's also a slew of very popular restaurants that have popped up in burgeoning Southtown, along South Alamo Street. These special eateries, rich with character and bubbling with action, are favorite spots for hip locals and tourists in the know.

AMERICAN

A local favorite for brunch is **Madhatters** (320 Beauregard St. at S. Alamo St., 210/212-4832, 7am-9pm Mon.-Fri., 8am-9pm Sat., 9am-3pm Sun., $9). With a creative selection of sandwiches and salads, all made with breads baked in-house, as well as French toast and other breakfast items, Madhatters is the perfect place to relax in the King William Historic District. In spirit with *Alice in Wonderland,* they also offer a large selection of fabulous teas under the trees.

The best place to catch a great blues, roots, or Americana act and a burger is at **Sam's Burger Joint** (330 E. Grayson St., 210/223-2830, www.samsburgerjoint.com, $12). By day this place is a great burger joint with an upbeat atmosphere, and by night Sam's turns into a vibrant music scene. The cooks serve up top-notch food, such

The Invention of Fritos Chips

Legend has it that the tasty snack food known as Fritos Corn Chips was invented in San Antonio in the early 1900s. At the time, the city's Mexican restaurants were in the custom of frying up the day-old tortillas and selling them. One establishment that was peddling these recycled corn snacks was the Santa Rosa Macaroni Factory, which was owned by a distinguished Italian immigrant named Carmelo Ruffo. Some say it was a Mexican immigrant who created and sold the original recipe, but others say it was Ruffo, whose tantalizing day-old fried "Fritos" were made with his macaroni press. One day Ruffo was approached by an entrepreneur named Elmer Doolin, who offered Ruffo $100 for his fried chip recipe and the macaroni machine. Carmelo walked away with the $100 thinking to himself, "Who would buy those chips when everyone in town is making them already?" Well, the rest of the country bought into the idea and to this day munchers are suckered into paying for the unique taste of Fritos chips.

as the guacamole and jack burger, and bartenders serve up the best beers on tap.

One of San Antonio's best eating experiences can be had in the Pearl District at **Southerleigh Fine Food and Brewery** (136 E. Grayson St. #120, 210/455-5701, $15). The atmosphere is great here, as there is a lot to look at while you sip on one of their fine beers. The food is innovative and the décor is modern-retro. The cuisine is hailed as a modern take on Texas' cross-culture cuisine.

Although it's a chain, albeit a small Texas chain, **The County Line** (111 W. Crockett St., 210/229-1941, $14) has some of the best barbecue in the downtown area. Beef brisket is moist and smoldering with flavor, and comes with the boilerplate smokehouse sides of potato salad, beans, and coleslaw.

American, '50s-style *Leave It to Beaver* home cooking is served up at **410 Diner** (8315 Broadway St., 210/822-6246, 11am-9pm Sun.-Thurs., 11am-10pm Fri., $8). This true diner is where you'll find meat loaf and vegetables, along with a few attempts at upscale menu items, such as snapper with artichoke hearts. Its proximity to the airport makes it a great stop before an evening flight out of town.

The historic **Guenther House** (205 E. Guenther St., 210/227-1061, 7am-3pm daily, $7) offers high-society class at a great value. For under $10 one can have a fabulous meal in a mansion overlooking the San Antonio River, in the King William Historic District. The smell of breakfast with fresh baked goods wafting through the mansion's Victorian-style parlors is what keeps a steady fan base coming back. And it tastes as good as it smells. Patrons are generally older folks, but youngsters shouldn't be scared to claim this for their own. While there, be sure to take a tour of the gift shop and the historic Guenther House.

The best place for lunch and a cocktail is ★ **Liberty Bar** (1111 S. Alamo St., 210/227-1187, 11am-10:30pm Sun.-Thurs., 10:30am-midnight Fri.-Sat., $12). With interesting food, house-baked breads, and one-of-a-kind ambience, Liberty is a bona fide San Antonio legend. Although it has moved from its previous location, which was a building that was near collapsing, the style and eating experience have not changed. If you want to impress someone, or yourself for that matter, have a classy lunch or dinner in this former convent. Crab cakes, a New York strip, or a portobello sandwich go with your choice of wine. Afterwards, a stroll through the King William Historic District seems like a given.

North of town in Alamo Heights is **Olmos Pharmacy** (3902 McCollough, 210/822-1188, 4pm-midnight Mon.-Fri., 4pm-1am Sat., 10am-midnight Sun., $7), an old-style pharmacy serving up medicine in the form of milk shakes and burgers. Founded in 1938, this neighborhood fountain makes a mean root beer float at a price that hasn't changed in 30 years. Also consider the mashed sweet potatoes, which have a sweetness that melts in the mouth.

If after a trip to the zoo you are craving a smokehouse dinner, up in the Brackenridge Park area is ★ **Augie's Barbed Wire Smokehouse** (3709 N. St. Mary's St., 210/735-0088, 11am-3pm Mon.-Tues., 11am-9pm Wed.-Fri., noon-9pm Sat., noon-6pm Sun., $10). I'm not implying that the zoo may trigger in you the desire to dine on endangered animals. However, one of the three square meals in Texas is barbecue. As at all excellent barbecue pits, the brisket and pulled pork are the best items on the menu, assuming you get there before they run out, which does happen.

Nothing beats a deli sandwich for lunch, and nobody beats the classic yet upscale fixin's at **Schilo's Delicatessen** (424 E. Commerce St., 210/223-6692, 7:30am-7:30pm Mon.-Sat., $12). The interior of Schilo's (pronounced "SHEE-lows") is best described as caravan meets an Italian meat wagon. The food is remarkably tasty and summons authentic visions of German pioneers who settled in South Texas and transplanted their food heritage. Here you build your own sandwich, and between the slices of bread expect only the very best in sandwich craftsmanship. Be sure to try the homemade root beer.

MEXICAN, TEX-MEX, AND SOUTHWESTERN

Walk into ★ **Acenar** (146 E. Houston St., 210/222-2362, 11am-10pm Sun.-Thurs., 11am-11pm Fri.-Sat., 5pm-9pm Sun., $12) and let yourself be overwhelmed by the bright colors and delectable foods. The sophisticated menu is upscale and creative, and not traditional Mexican, which is refreshing. Be sure to ask for their famous guacamole made tableside. It's the best I've ever had. If it's not too hot, eat outside on the porch above the River Walk, and you're guaranteed to have one of those "life is good" moments.

Caribbean and Latin American cuisine has been skillfully brought to the King William Historic District by **Azúca** (713 S. Alamo, 210/225-5550, 11am-9:30pm Mon.-Thurs., 11am-10:30pm Fri.-Sat., 5pm-9:30pm Sun., $18). This hip bar and restaurant is known for making potent mojitos and well-crafted meat dishes. On weekend nights Azúca is the place in town for live tango, salsa, and flamenco music and dancing.

On the River Walk is upscale ★ **Boudro's** (421 E. Commerce St., 210/224-8484,

Boudro's is one of the best places to have a great lunch or dinner on the River Walk.

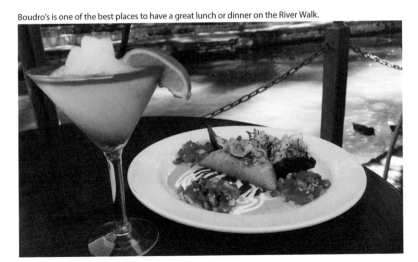

11am-11pm Sun.-Thurs., 11am-midnight Fri.-Sat., $15). This eatery on the river boasts a crafty menu, fancy drinks, fine wines, and high-caliber service. And what about that crafty menu? Try lamb T-bone with basil-lemon-mint sauce, grilled Gulf Coast yellow-fin tuna, or whiskey-soaked bread pudding and you'll know what I mean.

Locals love how **El Mirador** (722 S. St. Mary's St., 210/225-9444, 6:30am-9pm Mon.-Thurs., 6:30am-10pm Fri.-Sat., 9am-2pm Sun., $9) cooks up traditional Mexican dishes with flair. Although the whole menu is above par, the main dish people rave about here is *sopa Azteca* (Aztec soup). Tables fill up quickly, so either arrive before the mealtime rush or prepare to wait. Believe me, the wait is well worth it.

One of San Antonio's most time-tested Mexican institutions is **La Fonda on Main** (2415 N. Main Ave., 210/733-0621, 11am-3pm and 5pm-9:30pm Mon.-Thurs., 11am-10:30pm Fri.-Sat., $9). Since 1932, Mexican food has been the reason people flock here. Today the menu is a combination of regional Mexican and Tex-Mex, offering standards such as chicken enchiladas and new creations such as spinach enchiladas, shrimp with butter squash, and smoky tenderloin. The bright and cheerful environment with outdoor patio seating makes La Fonda a popular meeting place for lunch and dinner.

★ **Mi Tierra** (218 Produce Row, 210/225-1262, 24 hours daily, $9) is the local institution that serves great Mexican food 24 hours a day. All dishes are made up of beans, meats, sauces, and handmade tortillas—the staples of Mexican food. The food is okay but gets better at around 3am, when you're desperate and hungry. The old building is festively decorated with strings of lights and tinsel, and a mariachi band often strolls around the tables. Sit beneath masterfully executed murals telling the story of Mexico and Texas (notice that the breasts and noses are strangely three dimensional), and lose yourself in enchilada sauce.

The best Mexican restaurant is ★ **Rosario's** (910 S. Alamo St., 210/223-1806, 11am-10pm Mon.-Thurs., 11am-11pm Fri.-Sat., 11am-9pm Sun., $10). The proprietor has combined Mexican food with a chic, semi-retro, totally colorful dining space that makes a frequent customer out of everyone. On weekend nights chairs are removed from a portion of the dining area to make way for the dance floor, and the small stage is fired up with live salsa music. Favorite menu items are *pollo a la maria,* chile relleno, and prickly-pear margaritas.

OTHER INTERNATIONAL FOOD

If you're not quite sure what you want, but you're sure you want a drink to go with it, there's **Cappyccino's** (5003 Broadway, 210/828-6860, 11am-11pm Mon.-Thurs., 11am-midnight Fri.-Sat., $10). Both the food and drink menus are diverse and very enticing. Food items include brick-oven pizza with feta cheese and a thick golden crust, Italian-style deli sandwiches, pita wraps, and crepes. As for liquor, this place is a fan of anything fermented; it has a huge selection of scotches, brews, and martinis, from which you're sure to find just the right beverage to accompany your meal.

Texas and sushi don't sound like they go together, but **Koi Kawa** (4051 Broadway, 210/805-8111, 11am-10pm Mon.-Fri., noon-10pm Sat., noon-9pm Sun., $12) has proved all logic wrong. Two great things about this place: The chef is considered the best sushi chef in town, and the dining room affords spectacular views of Brackenridge Park and the San Antonio River. Artfully prepared black-widow rolls, devil rolls, and udon all scream healthy and tasty, and the wasabi just screams.

Housed in a converted gas station in Southtown is **La Focaccia** (800 S. Alamo St., 210/223-5353, 11am-2:30pm and 5pm-10pm Mon.-Fri., noon-11pm Sat., noon-10pm Sun., $13). The Italian food here is family-style, with blue-blood heritage. The owner was born in Rome and brought family recipes cooked for

Italian royals to San Antonio. Italian favorites such as calzones, lasagna, spaghetti, and pizzas are all worthy of a religious procession around the block.

Asian food in Alamo Heights is best eaten at **Van's** (3214 Broadway, 210/828-8449, 11am-10pm daily, $10). The combination of sushi and Chinese is tastefully set forth in a menu that can bring even the most terrified sushi disdainer to his or her senses, literally. Rounding out the experience is a great wine list. Wine and sushi at a good price make this a great low-key pick for dinner with friends.

HEALTHY AND VEGETARIAN

San Antonio is a carnivore town. However, there is one safe spot for vegans and vegetarians, and that's **Green Vegetarian Cuisine** (200 E. Grayson St., Ste. 120, 210/320-5865, 7am-9pm Mon.-Fri., 9am-9pm Sun., closed Sat., $10), not far from Brackenridge Park. Healthy-minded folks can start their day here before exploring the museums or zoo. Most everything is organic, healthy, and tasty, and all is kosher too. The menu ranges from omelets to enchiladas. The chik-n fillets are awesome in their own right.

FINE DINING

Fine dining in San Antonio doesn't get much better than ★ **Prime 1718** (321 Alamo Plaza #300, 210/377-1718, 3pm-10pm Mon.-Thurs., 11am-10pm Fri.-Sun., $30). Here you can sample from a fantastic wine list and enjoy the best filet mignon, roast quail, or blackened salmon in town. The food and service is as good as it gets. Many of the tables have a view of The Alamo, which will make your dining experience iconic and memorable.

Located inside innovative Hotel Valencia is swank **Citrus** (150 E. Houston St., 210/230-8412, 6:30am-2pm and 6pm-10pm daily, $30-50). For an amazing evening with friends, with a romantic date, or even alone, Citrus proves impeccable and divine. As soon as you are seated the knowledgeable staff makes you feel comfortable with your experience. Thanks to the brilliant selection of wines, the creative but down-to-earth entrées, and the minimalist decor, anyone can feel like a million bucks. Of course you have to have some cash to back it up, because it is expensive. Reservations are recommended.

If you are a geek about flavor but fancy yourself a refined individual I recommend fine dining at **Tre Trattoria** (401 S. Alamo, inside the Fairmount Hotel, 210/223-0401, and 4003 Broadway near Brackenridge Park, 210/805-0333, $45-65). Eating here is a serious matter. Men should look dapper and women should primp, and everyone has to be on time and follow the lead of the waitstaff. Although classy it's still a personable place. If you're irritated by pomp you won't enjoy this, but if you're out to enjoy fine wines and masterfully designed entrées in the company of the crème de la crème of society, you will have one of the best fine-dining experiences San Antonio has to offer.

Popular among locals with refined style and taste, **Silo** (1133 Austin Hwy., 210/824-8686, 11am-2:30pm and 5:30pm-10pm Sun.-Thurs., 11am-2:30pm and 5:30pm-10:30pm Fri.-Sat., $22) is the eatery that can do no wrong. This converted farmers market has a swank martini bar on the ground floor and a dining room accessed only by elevator. The short but upscale menu includes chicken-fried oysters, seared yellowfin tuna, and chocolate soufflé cake, to name a few options. Reservations are recommended.

Accommodations

San Antonio is a huge, sprawling city with accommodations everywhere. The most convenient area to stay for a visitor who plans on seeing sights is obviously downtown. All downtown hotels are within walking distance to most sights, and many are luxury hotels situated right on the banks of the famous River Walk. Rates for all hotels downtown generally start around $139. During the off-season and slow times many of these hotels offer discounts that can dip as low as $100, and deals can often be found online. Although it's almost impossible to find a room in the downtown area that is under $99, deals can be found at chain hotels and motels along the highways, just outside of downtown.

UNDER $50

The **Travelodge San Antonio Downtown** (1122 S Laredo St, 210/229-1133, $33) is by far the cheapest place to stay in town, but don't expect much in the way of accommodations other than a bed and bathroom.

$50-100

It's almost a joke having a category for $50-100 in San Antonio. Therefore I must give a disclaimer for the following cheap lodgings. Most of them aren't in the classiest and safest areas of town, and their rooms aren't particularly nice. As for amenities, expect nothing but some sheets, a small bar of soap, and maybe some lousy coffee.

For affordability with some class **Hotel Indigo** (105 N Alamo St., 210/933-2000, $89-150) offers the most basic accommodations in town near The Alamo. The River Walk is just a couple blocks away.

If you desire nothing but a bed, a TV, and an exceptionally low rate there's **Red Roof + San Antonio Downtown** (1011 E. Houston St., 210/229-9973 or 800/733-7663, $55-119). It's right off I-35, so expect some highway noise.

There are a few exceptions in this price range. A place that has yet to be discovered by the masses of budget travelers is **La Quinta Inn & Suites San Antonio Downtown** (100 W. Cesar Chavez Blvd., 210/212-5400, $89-139). Your money can go a long way here. The rooms are spacious and clean, there's a pool for splashing around in, and the complimentary breakfast is a real breakfast with eggs and waffles. The location may not be in the River Walk, but it's still centrally located.

Another affordable place to stay near all the River Walk action is the **O'Brien Historic Hotel** (116 Navarro St., 210/527-1111, $93-130). The O'Brien has the charm of being in an old building and is a step above the cheaper hotels in the price range. However, keep in mind that you get what you pay for. Nothing is superfancy here because it's more about the location and price.

$100-150

★ **Best Western Sunset Suites** (1103 E. Commerce St., 210/223-4400 or 866/560-6000, $99-169) may not be at the center of all the River Walk action, but it's a safe bet for inexpensive accommodations with clean and comfortable rooms. Amenities include nice furnishings, TVs, and mini fridges. Also included in your stay is free breakfast and free local calls.

Arbor House Bed & Breakfast (124 W. Woodlawn Ave., 210/736-4232, $140-180), situated comfortably between the King William District and the River Walk, offers the quintessential bed-and-breakfast experience. This romantic place to stay is just far enough from the hum of downtown but central to all that San Antonio has to offer. Along with all the pampering amenities of a top-class bed-and-breakfast there is a charming courtyard. Rooms are furnished with antiques, knockoff paintings, TVs, and high-speed Internet.

A great deal on the River Walk is often found at **Drury Inn and Suites** (201 N. St. Mary's St., 210/212-5200, $90-189). Amenities include free hot breakfast (the kind with eggs and sausage), free beverages, free long distance for up to 60 minutes, and high-speed Internet access. It may not be classy, but the location and value are great for budget travelers.

The **Gunter Hotel** (205 E. Houston St., 210/227-3241, www.gunterhotel.com, $99-189) is one of many hotels in the Sheraton chain. Housed in a historic landmark building in downtown, the Gunter looks like it might have back in 1909 when it was first built. Old San Antonio upscale charm makes this an enjoyable place to hang your hat for the weekend. Amenities aren't four-star, but who cares—when it comes to downtown hotels, this is the best deal.

One of three classy bed-and-breakfasts operated by Noble Inns is the **Pancoast Carriage House** (209 Washington St., 210/223-2353 or 800/242-2770, www.noble-inns.com, $130-200). Located in the King William Historic District, this carriage house has only three suites, making for personalized service and quietude. Wake up late and take breakfast at your leisure, then relax and read in the garden, followed by a swim in the full-size pool. The large suites feature queen-size beds, separate living/dining areas, and full kitchens, all with privacy. Be sure to ask about the 1960 Rolls Royce, which can be hired for transportation to and from the airport or dinner.

As you walk around downtown you will probably notice a neo-Gothic, wedge-shaped building that piques the curiosity. This is the historic **Emily Morgan Hotel** (705 E. Houston St., 210/225-5100, www.emilymorganhotel.com, $139-359), named after the Yellow Rose, a heroine of the Texas Revolution. This classy hotel is distinguished by art deco decor, spacious rooms with views, and classic jazz bebopping in the background. Amenities include Aveda skin-care products, cotton bathrobes, a full-service restaurant and bar, and whirlpool tubs. In the shadows of the hotel is the famous Alamo. Rooms on The Alamo side of the hotel offer the best views.

Affordable yet classy bed-and-breakfast accommodations can be found at **Inn on the Riverwalk Bed & Breakfast** (129 Woodward Pl., 210/225-6333, www.innontheriverwalk.com, $79-199). These three properties at the end of a cul-de-sac are tucked away on a quiet street south of downtown right on the San Antonio River, which makes it feel as though it's a hideaway right in the heart of the city.

$150-250

A swank place to stay that has a turn-of-the-20th-century aesthetic is the **Fairmount Hotel** (401 S. Alamo St., 210/224-8800, $159-229). Conveniently located on the River Walk and across the street from HemisFair Park, just down the street from The Alamo, this old San Antonio hotel is housed in a historic brick building that has been renovated for convenience and comfort. There are three floors of charming Victorian-style rooms and suites, each uniquely designed with antiques, European silk fabrics, tiling, and flat-screen TVs. Be sure to request one of the rooms with a view.

The best place to stay in town is the innovative ★ **Hotel Valencia** (150 E. Houston St., 210/227-9700, $159-300). This hotel is like none other in the state. In an age when all luxury hotels feel and look like they were cut from the same template, the Valencia appeared on the scene and completely inverted the model. The interior is dark, dramatic, luxurious, modern, vanguard, and somehow resembles a classy nightclub. The service and integrity here are the best in town, and the rooms are perfectly comfortable and unique. Faux mink throws, balconies, and bathrooms that look more like they're out of a design magazine than a hotel are all trademarks of the Valencia. It offers an upscale bar and an uptown restaurant called Citrus. Imagine all this style and class situated on a quiet bend on the River Walk and you've envisioned the

Valencia. This is why celebrities stay here, and why *Condé Nast Traveler* magazine rated the Valencia as one of the world's top 100 new hotels in 2004. Since then it has consistently made *Condé Nast Traveler*'s list of the world's best places to stay.

One of the ritziest ways to experience San Antonio is by staying in the King William Historic District at The Jackson House (107 Madison, 800/242-2770, www.nobleinns.com, $160-250). Feel wealthy for a day as you are pampered to the point of no return. Spend quiet time in the conservatory surrounded by Victorian stained glass windows; relax in the large, heated swim-spa; and return to your room to find a chocolate on your pillow. Be sure to arrange to have their 1960 Rolls Royce take you and your date to dinner.

Literally next door to The Alamo is the historic five-story ★ Menger Hotel (204 Alamo Plaza, 210/223-4361, www.mengerhotel.com, $195-215). Whether you stay here or not the Menger deserves a visit, as the backstory here is worthy of an entire History Channel special. From the famous guests who have stayed here throughout the years, such as Teddy Roosevelt, Babe Ruth, and Oscar Wilde, to the legends that were born here, such as Robert E. Lee riding his horse into the main lobby, there's lots of history to encounter. The Menger also boasts more than 40 often-seen apparitions. The hotel features a romantic courtyard, large heated pool, and a full day spa. Rooms are somewhat tiny, but charming. There's also the Menger Bar, which is where Teddy Roosevelt recruited some of his Rough Riders for the Spanish-American War. The "giant" painting in the old lobby, by F. L. Van Ness, was featured in the Western classic *Giant,* starring Rock Hudson and Elizabeth Taylor.

Early-20th-century San Antonio comes alive at the Hotel Havana (1015 Navarro, 210/222-2008, www.havanasanantonio.com, $250-400). This historic landmark building on the River Walk was tastefully renovated and designed to evoke a combination of 1920s Texas and Cuba. Rooms are decorated with vintage photographs, furnishings from around the world, plantation shutters, ceiling fans, and brick walls. On the premises is one of San Antonio's most intimate bars, Club Cohiba. This Latin bar and tapas grill is a favorite hangout for locals and travelers on the town, in the mood, and on the lam. It's best enjoyed with a stogie in hand and a flower in the lapel.

One of Texas's most historic bed-and-breakfasts is the Oge House (209 Washington St., 210/223-2353, www.oge-inn.com, $155-255). This boutique bed-and-breakfast mansion is in the King William Historic District and on the banks of the San Antonio River. The location is unparalleled. Thanks to grand verandas with views, dramatic halls lined with period antiques, and scarlet drapes, one is transported to the era of wealthy, high society, 19th-century Texas money. Most rooms have a fireplace and old-world charm with modern comfort and convenience. Prepare to be dazzled by a gourmet breakfast served on china and white linens.

Another good value on the River Walk can be found at Hilton Palacio del Rio (200 S. Alamo St., 210/222-1400, $219-300). Hilton Palacio is the longest consecutive recipient of the AAA Four Diamond Award. All rooms feature Spanish decor and have access to private balconies with spectacular views of the city. The main lobby and common areas are a bit outdated, but the fitness center has been renovated. There's also a rooftop pool and hot tub with stunning views, a full-service business center, a restaurant, and a river-level bar featuring live music and booze.

The four-star hotel on the San Antonio River is The Westin River Walk (420 Market St., 210/224-6500, $179-359). For high-end accommodations this is a good bet, as the service is impeccable and the comforts abound. From the valet parking service to the rooms with downtown views and the goose-down pillows, everything here is perfectly orchestrated. The entire hotel is decorated with art from local artists, and marble and stone are everywhere. Wireless Internet is available throughout, there's a fitness center on-site, shampoos and soaps are above average, and some showers feature spa-style double shower-heads. Among the more unusual amenities is *la merienda*, which is a Latin version of afternoon tea available to guests Tuesday-Saturday. Because of these comforts, this is one of two places where the rich and famous stay when in town.

OVER $250

For the luxury traveler, staying in the Pearl District at **Hotel Emma** (136 E. Grayson St., 210/448-8300, www.thehotelemma.com, $300-400) can't be beat. Here you can be close to all that Brackenridge Park has to offer as well as the amazing restaurant and brewery scene of the Pearl. Housed in a repurposed historic San Antonio building that was once a brewery, this modern industrial high-end hotel has a pool, terrace rooms, an in-house restaurant, and even a library.

Have you ever wanted to stay overnight at Pottery Barn or Crate and Barrel? The **Hyatt Regency San Antonio** (123 Losoya St., 210/222-1234, $249-329) rooms reflect the most current trends in decor. The bustling grand lobby is an open-air atrium with waterfall, chichi bar, and mediocre service. The location is what this Hyatt is all about. It's both on the River Walk and at the center of downtown, just a stone's throw away from The Alamo.

La Mansión del Rio (112 College St., 800/292-7300, www.lamansion.com, $239-379) is a Spanish hacienda-style hotel with everything you could want in a San Antonio stay. Of course, it comes at a hefty price. It's on one of the most beautiful stretches of the River Walk, within walking distance of all that downtown San Antonio has to offer. It has arches, antiques, verandas, wrought-iron balconies, scarlet drapes, rough-hewn beam ceilings, and amenities fit for General Santa Anna himself, and guests are encouraged to feel like world rulers. Rooms on the River Walk are very expensive and are often occupied by the rich and famous. By expensive I mean they can run upwards of $2,000.

Information and Services

TOURIST INFORMATION

The **San Antonio Visitor Information Center** (317 Alamo Plaza, 800/447-3372, 9am-5pm daily) is conveniently located right across the street from The Alamo. The helpful staff here can provide you with maps, brochures about the city's attractions, and lodging information, and are pleased to answer any questions you may have.

EMERGENCY INFORMATION

In the event of an emergency involving injury or danger dial **911.** For nonemergency police needs there's the **San Antonio Sheriff's Department** (210/335-6000). The main hospital downtown is **Baptist Medical Center** (111 Dallas St., 210/297-7000). For

information on other medical facilities call the **San Antonio Medical Foundation** (210/614-3724).

PUBLICATIONS

The best resource for all things hip, such as live music, art gallery openings, events, and festivals, is the local alternative rag, *San Antonio Current.* This free newsprint periodical can be found all over town. New editions hit the streets every Thursday. The paper with a local news focus is the *San Antonio Express-News.* Nothing special here, just politics, sport pages, funnies, and the usual *Citizen Kane* stuff. The full-color glossy magazine *Texas Monthly* is the best state magazine in the country. It can be purchased at most supermarkets and corner stores. This is a great resource for state news, politics, and celebrity gossip, and offers a great listings section in the back with restaurant reviews.

INTERNET

If you have a laptop with a wireless card you can access the Internet through hot spots in cafés. If you're staying in a hotel, chances are it has wireless or connections in rooms available to guests. For everyone else there's a **FedEx Office** (4418 Broadway, 210/821-6911) way up near Brackenridge Park. At $0.20 per minute this can get costly unless you just want to check email. For free Internet access downtown there's the **San Antonio Public Library** (600 Soledad St., 210/207-2500, 9am-9pm Mon.-Thurs., 9am-5pm Fri.-Sat., 11am-5pm Sun.).

LAUNDRY

For coin-operated laundry machines there's **E-Z Wash** (801 S. Hackberry St.,

210/359-9274). Check the phone book for more listings.

POST OFFICE

Just across from The Alamo is the most conveniently located post office (615 E. Houston St.) downtown. For other locations call 800/275-8777. You'll need a zip code to get a location using this toll-free number. If you prefer paying slightly higher prices for your postal needs, the **UPS Store** (200 E. Market St. near HemisFair Park, 210/258-8950) has mailers, envelopes, copy machines, and even maps.

MONEY

ATM kiosks are everywhere, but beware—the ATMs you find on the street all charge extraordinarily high fees. It's always best to get money from your own banking institution, but if your bank isn't to be found, at least use a national bank's ATM. You may still incur a fee but it's much less than at kiosk ATMs.

Transportation

GETTING THERE

Getting to San Antonio is a cinch. All you need is money for an airline, train, or bus ticket, or gas for a road trip. Being the seventh-largest city in the United States, San Antonio has lots of travel and commerce, by highway and by air. Since it's sort of in the middle of nowhere, with respect to the greater United States, the easiest way to get here is by air.

Air

Located about eight miles north of downtown is **San Antonio International Airport** (9800 Airport Blvd., 210/207-3433, www.san-antonio.gov/airport). This is the region's largest airport and is an international hub with both direct flights and domestic connections that can get you to anywhere in the world. Nonstop flights are offered to 41 destinations, mostly major U.S. cities and a couple of cities in Mexico. Passenger airlines that service the

airport include: Aerolitoral (800/237-6639), America West (800/235-9292), American Airlines (800/433-7300), Delta (800/221-1212), Mexicana (800/534-7921), Midwest (800/452-2022), Southwest (800/435-9792), and United (800/241-6522).

The airport provides hourly, daily, and economy parking. For hourly parking, the rates are $2 for the first 30 minutes, $3 for 30 minutes to one hour, and $5 up to two hours. Long-term parking is $11 for 24 hours.

There are several ways to get from the airport to town. The most economical way is by taking the **VIA Metropolitan Transit** bus 2. Buses run about every hour 8am-9:30pm, and it takes about an hour to get to downtown. The fastest and easiest way to get to downtown, especially if you have lots of luggage, is by buses service provided by **SA TRANS** (210/281-9900). One-way shuttle service to downtown costs $18 per passenger. For groups there's

Star Shuttle (210/341-6000). Taking a cab costs about $25-30. Most hotels offer shuttle service free of charge. Be sure to ask your hotel about this before traveling.

To drive from the airport to downtown, take Highway 281 south, which goes straight to downtown. It takes about 30 minutes to get to downtown from the airport via car, taxi, or shuttle.

Car

San Antonio has been a crossroads for centuries, and this becomes apparent when you look at a current map of the state. Major highways fan out from the metropolitan area and shoot to all parts of the United States and Mexico. The main interstate highways that connect San Antonio to the world are I-35, I-10, I-37, and I-410. It's imperative to have both a regional map and a good city map to successfully get around. Signage is good, for the most part, but exits and exchanges can happen fast the closer you get to downtown.

If you are driving from Austin to San Antonio, take I-35 south, which goes through the heart of downtown Austin to the heart of San Antonio. The drive is about 80 miles and takes about 1.5-2 hours, depending on traffic. If you are driving from Houston to San Antonio, take I-10 west. The drive is approximately 200 miles and takes about three hours.

Bus and Train

On Greyhound (800/229-9424, www.greyhound.com), you can get to San Antonio from just about anywhere in the contiguous United States, provided you don't mind a long ride. Using the service to get to San Antonio from Dallas, Houston, or Austin is very affordable. Buses to San Antonio from Dallas, Austin, and Houston are available every 2-3 hours. The ride from Dallas is about 5-6 hours and the standard fare is $39. The ride from Austin is about 1.5 hours and the standard fare is $29. The ride from Houston is about 3 hours and the standard fare is $33. The bus station (500 N. St. Mary's St., 210/270-5824) is conveniently located downtown near hotels, restaurants, and attractions.

For travel to and from many of the smaller Texas towns, including many in the Hill Country, there's Kerrville Bus Company (800/335-3733). The station for this bus line is shared with Greyhound.

As for train access to San Antonio, there's always the old American staple, Amtrak (800/872-7245, www.amtrak.com). Trains to San Antonio from Dallas are available daily and leave around noon. The travel time is about 10 hours and the standard fare is $43. Trains to San Antonio from Austin are available daily and leave at about 7pm. The travel time is about 3.5 hours and the standard fare is $27. Trains to San Antonio from Houston are available daily and leave at 7pm. The travel time is about 5 hours and the standard fare is $34. The train station (350 Hoefgen St., 210/223-3226) is located on the eastern side of downtown.

GETTING AROUND

Deciding which mode of transportation you will need while in San Antonio entirely depends on what you plan on achieving while in town. The downtown area is a self-contained tourist world chock-full of things to see and do. If you can walk, it's entirely feasible to have an enjoyable experience without ever thinking about transportation. However, the city is sprawling, and some attractions are way out there.

Car

For the first-time visitor, getting around the city via automobile can be confusing and frustrating. There are many major freeways in the metropolitan area and in the suburban sprawl. The city is best navigated and understood when compared to a wagon wheel. Two rings of highways circumnavigate the city, one in the center of downtown and the other at the outer rim of the city. Highways fan out from the center of town and shoot off into all parts of the state. The downtown area is inside the inner ring, which is defined by I-35, I-37, and I-10. Beyond this is greater San Antonio, which is circumnavigated by the outer ring, defined by I-410, also known as Loop 410.

Parking can be frustrating in the downtown area. Metered parking is available on many streets, but spots are always hard to find. If you plan on tooling around the sights downtown you might as well leave your car at a parking garage and tour by foot. Centrally located parking garages are: **LAZ Parking** (122 N. Main Ave., 210/224-2468, and 151 Soledad St., 210/224-2468) and **Market Street Parking Garage** (421 W. Market St., 210/212-4011). Most attractions outside of downtown offer parking free of charge.

All the usual rental car companies are represented at **San Antonio International Airport**, as well as around town. Car rental agencies include **Advantage Rent-A-Car** (800/777-5500), **Alamo Rent-A-Car** (800/327-9633), **Avis Car Rental** (800/831-2847), **Budget** (800/527-0700), **Dollar Rent-A-Car** (800/800-4000), **Enterprise** (800/736-8222), **Hertz Rent-A-Car** (800/654-3131), **National Car Rental** (800/227-7368), and **Thrifty** (800/847-4389). My hunch is Alamo Rent-A-Car gets the most business in this town.

Bus

San Antonio's public transportation system, **VIA Metropolitan Transit** (210/362-2020, www.viainfo.net), is the cheapest way to get around, and fairly easy to get the hang of. VIA has both buses and touristy streetcars. VIA's hub-and-spoke system offers over 85 routes, with major hubs downtown fanning out into the metropolitan area. A ride costs $1.20 a trip, and transfers are $0.15. Buses and streetcars are in operation 5am-midnight. If you plan on using VIA as your primary form of transportation, I highly recommend getting a day pass for $4, which provides unlimited rides on both the buses and streetcars for a day.

Taxi

Although taxi cabs can be hailed on the streets, you'll probably save time picking one up at the bus station downtown, by catching one at a hotel, or by simply calling in advance. **Yellow Cab** (210/222-2222) has the San Antonio cab monopoly. Cab rates start at $2.50 for the first mile, plus $2.65 for each additional mile, and there's a minimum of $3 for rides in downtown. The one-way fare from San Antonio International Airport to downtown is $25-30.

Background

The Landscape

GEOGRAPHY

The impression most people have of Texas is that it's a dry, flat, and arid land fraught with twisters, dust bowls, and cacti. That may be true for the western part of the state, but that's far from what Austin, San Antonio, and the Hill Country are like. The region at the heart of the state, known as Central Texas or the Texas Hill Country, is a lush, green land with rolling hills, crystal-clear rivers and lakes, giant outcroppings of granite rock, and plentiful wildlife. Geologists claim this remarkably beautiful landscape was formed over the course of billions of years. Geological records tell a dynamic story of activity: inundation by inland seas, volcanic eruptions, the erosion process of rivers, and earthquakes. Thanks to this extraordinary process the region is filled with great beauty both on the surface and beneath the surface. Visitors can see Central Texas geography and geology at its best by visiting any of the many parks, such as Enchanted Rock State Natural Area, or by visiting some of the many caves throughout the region.

CLIMATE

Some people say Central Texas has three seasons: fixin' to be summer, summer, and just been summer. More-informed folks say there are four seasons: flood, hurricane, drought, and tornado. Combining these two theories provides an accurate, albeit unorthodox, description of the climate in this hot and meteorologically dramatic part of North America.

When it comes to crazy weather, Austin and the Hill Country seem to be particularly prone to the drama of the Greek gods above. At any given moment the sky can go from meek and mild to a violent, spectacular show of lights, thunder, and hail. Although there are more tornadoes in Texas than any other state, they rarely rip their way through Austin. As for hurricanes, they generally downgrade to a tropical storm by the time they make it this far inland.

The climates of Austin, San Antonio, and the Hill Country are very similar, with some slight variation. The Hill Country is often a few degrees cooler, San Antonio is always more humid, and Austin is somewhere in between. Average temperatures for all of Central Texas are: summer 85°F, fall 70°F, winter 50°F, and spring 70°F. Remember this is an average—don't be fooled by these numbers. In summer months expect average highs of 90-100°F. As for the rest of the year, the temperature can range anywhere from 40 to 70°F.

Expect dramatic and crazy weather in the spring, late arrival of fall, moderate winters, and hot summers. Spring is a time when flash flooding is commonplace, hail can be the size of baseballs, and lightning starts fires. The summers are all that they're advertised to be. They're hot, and they're humid, and usually last about three months. The spring and the fall are the best times of year in terms of temperature and beauty. In the winter the weather is rarely the same for two days in a row. On occasion it will drop below freezing, and on the very rare occasion it will snow.

Previous: fossilized dinosaur skeleton at the Witte Museum in San Antonio; wagon replica in Gruene.

Ask the Weatherman

With freak hailstorms, flash floods, lightning, and thunder year-round, 90°F Novembers, 60°F Decembers, and 110°F summers, this type of climate needs a professional explanation. Local weatherman **Mark Murray,** chief meteorologist of KVUE News, has the answers.

Q: At any given moment throughout the year freak storms can envelop Austin. Flash floods, thunder and lightning, and even softball-size hail in the middle of summer. Why does Central Texas have such dramatic freak storms all year-round?
A: We do get our share of severe storms, especially in the spring, and it has to do with our location. We're close enough to the Gulf of Mexico to get plenty of moisture, but we're also not too far from that dry desert air of West Texas. When that moist air from the Gulf meets the dry air from Texas, it creates something called a "dry line." When two different air masses come together—moist and dry in this case—that's what makes the fireworks. The dramatic storms that we get here often fire up along what's called the "West Texas Dry Line" and march into Austin, San Antonio, and the Hill Country. The dry line runs north and south, from West Texas all the way up to Nebraska.

Q: I've heard people say there's no spring or fall in Central Texas—it's all summer and winter. Can you explain the seasons here?
A: Seasons can change rapidly here, it's true. Fall is beautiful, but short. It's generally mid-September through late October. It's still warm but the humidity drops quite a bit, and it becomes sunny and mild. Winter is mild. On average it freezes about 19 days a year. Every couple years we get just enough snow to cover the ground but it melts pretty quickly. Only two times has the temperature dropped below zero. Spring, which is mid-March through mid-June, is a great time because temperatures are mild and the wildflowers are in full bloom. This makes it a very pretty time of the year. Wildflower festivals are happening in the Hill Country, and people are outdoors all day. Summer, which is from mid-June to mid-September, is very hot and humid. If you're in Central Texas during the summer heat, you may want to plan your day a little differently. If you want to walk around Lady Bird Lake's hike-and-bike trail you may want to do this in the morning or the evening.

Q: When is the best time of year to visit Austin and Central Texas?
A: You can do things outdoors in Austin pretty much year-round. Festivals and outdoor events are scheduled throughout the year here. However, spring and fall are the best times of year to visit. The weather is moderate and it's beautiful.

Q: When is the least desirable time of year to visit Austin and Central Texas?
A: I think a lot of people would say the middle of summer, which is August and September. It's very hot and humid.

Q: What are the greatest meteorological threats to Central Texas?
A: There are three main threats we're faced with. Flash flooding is our biggest threat. Weak tropical depressions can dump lots of rain very quickly. Lightning is the second-biggest threat. After these two, another threat we have is tornadoes. They generally don't last long and aren't that big, but they have caused damage. Central Texas has seen only two F5-class tornadoes. Hurricanes from the Gulf of Mexico aren't a threat here as they rarely hold their strength this far inland. However, hurricanes can create a tornado outbreak and can bring heavy, flooding rains.

Q: Why do you love Austin's climate?
A: I love the weather here. When people ask me what kind of weather I like, I always say I like weather that changes. Being a meteorologist, I love to forecast the changes.

Q: What's the first thing you do every morning?
A: Look outside to see if I was right.

Plants and Animals

PLANTS

The climate in Central Texas has created a diverse plant ecosystem that includes everything from cacti to maple trees to an astounding array of wildflowers. All of the flora that exists here has the ability to survive drought conditions and extended periods of hot weather. The most common forms of plant life are oak trees, juniper (often mistakenly called cedar), and numerous varieties of wildflowers. Every spring the Hill Country explodes with wildflower color. Bluebonnets are the most prolific and popular of all Texas wildflowers. When they're in full bloom it's common to see families scrunched down in fields of bluebonnets along roads and highways taking photos. If you're tempted to pick these gorgeous flowers, be aware that this is frowned upon. (Most people think it's illegal to pick bluebonnets because they are the state flower, but this is a Texas myth.) Other common wildflowers include Texas paintbrush, the bright and delicate fuchsia-colored winecups, greenthreads (which are actually yellow), and the shockingly radiant Indian blanketflowers. The best way to experience wildflower season is by driving the Willow City Loop in the Hill Country, or by visiting the Lady Bird Johnson Wildflower Center just east of Austin.

ANIMALS

There are thousands of species of wildlife in Central Texas, but the ones that get the most press are bats, armadillos, and the longhorn steer. These have become larger-than-life icons that represent the region as virtual ambassadors. Of the three, bats are the most popular. There are more than two dozen species of bats in Texas, the most popular and well known being the Mexican free-tailed bat.

The largest colony of Mexican free-tailed bats in North America happens to be beneath the Congress Avenue Bridge in Austin. These little mammals have helped put Austin on the map, as they have been drawing tourists and the curious to the city for decades.

The prehistoric-looking armadillo is the most curious of Texas's creatures. Unfortunately, these armored mammals are known most for being roadkill. These low-key residents of the state feed on insects and vegetation. Although the ones we have today are about the size of cats, in prehistoric times they could get as big as a VW Bug. The skeletal remains of one of these monsters are at the Texas Memorial Museum in Austin.

Perhaps the most iconic of all Central Texas animals is the longhorn steer. Once the symbol of Texas pioneer ranching, the longhorn steer is now best known as the logo for University of Texas sporting teams. These majestic-looking beasts can be seen fenced in on ranches all throughout the Hill Country, grazing in fields, and resting beneath ancient oak trees. Longhorn steer are raised primarily for beef, but their unwieldy horns are also desirable. On occasion you'll see them fixed to the front of a Cadillac.

Besides bats, armadillos, and longhorn steers, Texas is also known to have more bird species than any other state in the United States. With over 600 documented bird species, including some rare birds that live only in this region, Texas has become one of the top bird-watching destinations in North America. This extraordinary number of birds is due primarily to the fact that Central Texas is a popular stopping point for migratory birds flying the Central Flyway, which runs from Canada to Mexico.

History

A history of Austin, San Antonio, and the Hill Country has to be told properly—it has to happen through the prism of Texas history. After the prehistory, the state's story unfolds in and around San Antonio and makes its way toward Austin being named the capital. Everything in between is pure drama.

PREHISTORY

Texas must have been a popular place for prehistoric creatures to congregate. Fossils and footprints of at least 16 types of dinosaurs have been discovered all around the state. According to current paleontology the following dinosaurs ruled the state: the huge and fierce *Acrocanthosaurus atokensis,* the big-toothed, meat-eating *Tyrannosaurus rex,* the plant-eating dinosaurs of the Ornithischia order, the giant crocodile-like *Deinosuchus,* and the *Tenontosaurus,* among many others. Artifacts found include bones of mammoths, horses, camels, ancient bison, giant short-faced bears, and giant armadillos.

Most of the evidence of earliest human inhabitants dates back 10,000-13,000 years. These early "Texans" are believed to be of Asian origin, having come to the North American continent by way of the land bridge at the Bering Strait in Siberia and Alaska. They are believed to have been completely modern *Homo sapiens,* as no evidence has been found in the New World that indicates evolutionary change. Archaeologists have determined four stages in development of early inhabitants: Paleo-Indian, Archaic, Woodland, and Neo-American.

Perhaps one of the earliest tribes of indigenous peoples is the Caddoes. They were highly civilized and agricultural, had a highly defined social structure, and even participated in trade.

NATIVE AMERICANS OF TEXAS

Long before Europeans arrived in the area known today as Texas, various tribes of Native Americans occupied the region. Some migrated here from other parts of North America, while others are believed to be indigenous. The history of present Texas is inextricably linked to these native populations who were in the region when Spanish explorer Álvar Núñez Cabeza de Vaca landed in 1528, and to those who later swept down from the plains on horseback. Regrettably, the story of the indigenous natives is not a pleasant one. Tribes were either wiped out by the Spanish, French, Mexican, and Anglo settlers or simply merged into and became part of the Mexican and Hispanic populations, losing their tribal identities.

Karankawans

Karankawa was the designation for several bands of coastal tribes who shared a common language and culture. They were perhaps the most successful and long-lived of the indigenous tribes encountered by Cabeza de Vaca when he shipwrecked off Galveston Island. The Karankawa people were known for their distinctive physical appearance. The men were described as tall and muscular, unlike the other natives. They practiced ritualistic cannibalism but were repulsed by the fact that some of Cabeza de Vaca's companions ate their dead to avoid starvation. After Cabeza de Vaca's encounter with the Karankawans, the tribe didn't encounter Europeans for another 150 years. In 1685, the French explorer René-Robert Cavelier, Sieur de La Salle, established a fort near what is now Matagorda Bay in the heart of Karankawa country. The Karankawans eventually killed all of those settlers except for six children who were taken captive; two survived and returned to France and told of their life with the Karankawans.

During the Spanish mission period an attempt was made to Christianize the Karankawans and to make them loyal Spanish subjects. La Bahía mission and presidio complex near present-day Goliad was established in 1749 for that purpose. However, the Spanish attempts to Christianize the Karankawans met with little success. The Karankawans were hostile toward everyone: the Spanish, the French, the Comanches, and Anglo Texans. Because of this the Karankawans were exterminated. In 1858, a Texan force attacked and annihilated the last organized bands of Karankawans near Rio Grande City. The last reported Karankawan, named Indian Tom, was raised from infancy by Anglo settlers in Matagorda County. Later he enlisted as a Confederate soldier in the Civil War. He was killed while being detained as a prisoner of war when he refused to obey his captor's commands.

The Tonkawa

The Tonkawa occupied the majority of the Central Texas Hill Country, from Llano to San Antonio. They were very mobile and hunted buffalo, deer, and smaller game. Upon the arrival of the Apache and Comanche Indians, the Tonkawa were forced into the region between Austin and San Antonio, where they existed through the Spanish period and the subsequent Texan and American periods of history. It's believed they were the friendliest of the Native American tribes in the region. They shared living space, as well as water and food sources, with the Karankawa, as well other tribes that passed through the region.

The Comanches

No tribe had a greater impact on Texas than the Comanches. The Comanches didn't exist when Cabeza de Vaca journeyed through Texas. In fact, the arrival of the Europeans was the genesis of the Comanche. Prior to that, anthropological evidence and linguistic studies indicate they were a branch of the Northern Shoshones. Originally, the Shoshones were typical pedestrian hunters and gatherers. When they obtained the horse

Origin of the Word "Texas"

One of the indigenous Native American tribes present in eastern Texas when Spanish explorer Álvar Núñez Cabeza de Vaca arrived was the Caddo tribe. Their word *techas,* which means "friend," turned into "Tejas," which eventually became "Texas." The Spanish began to use "Texas" as the name for that entire group of Native Americans—records show the word appearing as early as 1689. The transition from *Tejas* to *Texas* came easily, as the letters *x* and *j* have the same pronunciation in Spanish—the "h" sound in English. Thus, the Texas name is derived from a Caddo word, and the state's motto of "Friendship" reflects that heritage.

in the late 1600s, a revolution occurred. This obscure branch of the Northern Shoshones evolved into a mounted and aggressive warrior culture that left their mountain home for the great plains of eastern Colorado and western Kansas, where game was plentiful. They eventually migrated south, attracted most likely by the warm climate and abundant buffalo, and the presence of less-aggressive indigenous tribes they could dominate. By the 18th century, much of north, central, and west Texas was Comanche country, also known as Comanchería. This is when they became known as Comanches, a name derived from a Ute word literally meaning "anyone who wants to fight me all the time." And fight they did.

Lipan-Apaches

The Apaches are believed to be descended from Athapaskan ancestors who migrated from the forests of western Canada into the southern Great Plains. When the Apaches came to the lands of what is today known as Texas and Mexico, they were constantly forced to move due to pressure from the Comanches. In Texas they came into contact with the new Spanish settlements. By the 1600s, the Spaniards had enslaved many

The Comanche Warriors

From the early 1700s to the late 1800s, a period of approximately 200 years, the Comanches' warrior culture changed the face and destiny of what is now Texas. The Apaches, who had previously dominated the region, were forced south by the Comanches and became their mortal enemies. The Comanches completely halted Spanish and Mexican efforts to colonize Texas during the mission period. In 1758, a force of approximately 2,000 Comanches attacked a Spanish mission built for the Apaches on the San Saba River in Central Texas near present-day Menard. They sacked and burned the mission and killed most of its inhabitants, including two priests. A Spanish expedition was mounted the following year to punish the Comanches, but it also met defeat. The Spanish were never able to successfully colonize Texas because of the Comanches' continued raids on their settlements for horses and captives.

In 1821, Mexico won independence from Spain, but the armed, mounted, and aggressive Comanche warriors remained dominant. A series of unstable governments from Mexico City had no more success than their Spanish forefathers in projecting their power and presence in Texas.

The dominance of the Comanche warriors in Texas, probably more than any other factor, was the reason the weak Spanish and Mexican governments enacted laws to encourage foreign immigration to Texas. They were attempting to create a buffer between them and the Comanches and seeking someone who could match the Comanches in aggressiveness and warrior mentality. The new tribe that was invited into the Texas territory to battle the Comanches and ultimately defeat them was the Anglo-Americans. The interdependence of the fate of Comanches and Europeans in Texas is clear. Without the horses brought by Europeans, the Comanches never would have risen to dominance, and without the Comanches, Anglo-Americans never would have come to the Republic of Texas, which evolved into the State of Texas.

The Comanches still spread terror over much of Texas when Texans won their independence from Mexico in 1836. Sam Houston, the first elected president of the Republic of Texas, had lived with and was an adopted Cherokee. He wanted to institute a policy of peaceful coexistence with all the Native American tribes, including the Comanches. That policy was not favored by most Texans, including Sam Houston's successor in office, Mirabeau B. Lamar. Texans and Comanches remained enemies, committing brutal atrocities against each other until the Comanches were almost exterminated and were permanently removed from Texas to Indian Territory, now Oklahoma. Even after the Civil War, and after the Comanches entered into various peace treaties with the U.S. government, hostilities continued between them and the Texans. In reality, the Comanches and the Texans never considered themselves bound by such treaties. For them, it was a war until death or total subjugation, a war the Comanches could not win—which is why there is no Comanche presence in Texas today.

Apaches to work ranches and mines, and the Apaches often retaliated by stealing horses. The Apaches found themselves under pressure from Anglo-American settlers from the north and east, the Mexican-Spaniards to the south, and the Comanches from every direction. By the 1740s, pressure from the Comanches prompted the Apaches to migrate toward the Rio Grande. Eventually, settlements such as San Antonio encroached on the Apaches' hunting grounds. This was a period of much violence between the Apaches, the Spanish missions, and the settlers. Avoiding the encroachment of these other groups and conversion to Catholicism, Apaches eventually retreated to the Rio Grande.

SPANISH AND FRENCH EXPLORATIONS (1519-1685)

As early as 1519 the coast of Texas was mapped. Under the service of the governor of Jamaica, Captain Alonso Álvarez de Pineda sailed the Gulf of Mexico and became the first person in recorded history to explore the region. Just a few years later, in 1528, exploration in Texas was resumed by Spanish explorer Álvar Núñez Cabeza de Vaca. *Cabeza* is Spanish for head and *vaca* is Spanish for cow. How appropriate that the written history of Texas begins with the fascinating adventure of a man with the name of "Cow's Head."

Cabeza de Vaca was shipwrecked on the coast of Texas and washed up on the beach literally naked. He spent the next seven years wandering through what is now Texas. He lived with the native inhabitants until he arrived at a Mexican outpost near the Pacific coast in early 1536. Cabeza de Vaca arrived as a conquistador but during the course of his travels became a merchant, a slave, and a healer to the various small family bands of hunter-gatherers scattered throughout the region. In his role as a healer, Cabeza de Vaca removed an arrow from the chest of an Indian, for which the Texas Surgical Society honors him today as their "patron saint." He chronicled his odyssey in what is titled *La Relación* (The Account), which was first published in Spain in 1542. In it, Cabeza de Vaca describes in detail the landscape he encountered and his observations of the native peoples' cultural practices, including how they ate, raised their families, and made love and made war, all before the land and its people were irrevocably altered by the European culture, its diseases, and the introduction of the horse. Cabeza de Vaca advocated to the Spanish crown not to enslave the natives. His precise route through Texas has been the subject of considerable study but is not exactly known. Some scholars have Cabeza de Vaca's route taking him through what is now Central Texas and the area including Austin, San Marcos, and San Antonio. The Center for the Study of the Southwest, at Texas State University in San Marcos, houses a rare 1555 edition of Cabeza de Vaca's *La Relación*. Artifacts from the natives of this era are on display at the Witte Museum in San Antonio.

After Cabeza de Vaca's unintentional tour through Texas, Spain continued to have many contacts with Texas. Subsequent Spanish explorations of Texas were conducted

Discovery of La Belle

One of French explorer La Salle's ships, *La Belle,* sank in Matagorda Bay in 1686. Over 300 years later, in 1995, Texas Historical Commission archaeologists discovered its resting place and erected a cofferdam around it to salvage its contents. They eventually recovered its hull, over one million artifacts, and the skeleton of one of the crewmembers. It is one of the most important shipwrecks ever discovered in North America. Many of its artifacts are on display at the Bullock Texas State History Museum in Austin.

by Francisco Vásquez de Coronado and Luis de Moscoso Alvadaro. Forty years later, Fray Agustín Rodríguez, a Franciscan missionary, and Francisco Sánches Chamuscado led an expedition through Texas and New Mexico. In 1681 the first permanent settlement in Texas was established in the El Paso area.

REVOLVING SOVEREIGN DOOR (1685-1690)

With Spanish exploration, the region fell under the domain of Spanish rule. However, the Spaniards soon learned Texas didn't have the gold, silver, and other riches they sought, and the hostile environment of Texas wasn't providing sufficient incentive for them to wander far from the reasonable comfort of Mexico City. This left a gap for the French to try to lay claim to the New World. In 1682, French explorer René-Robert Cavelier, Sieur de La Salle, attempted to create a colony in Louisiana but mistakenly landed in Texas. La Salle's settlement was on Lavaca Bay just up the coast from present-day Corpus Christi.

Hearing that France was establishing a presence with a colony, the Spanish government became very interested in Texas. In 1689 Spanish authorities sent Captain Alonso de León to confront the French and reclaim the region. When he arrived at the French colony, he found the settlement had been decimated by Indians and La Salle had been killed by his own men. Thus Spain realized it ruled the land once again.

SPANISH TEXAS, MISSIONS, AND AMERICANS (1690-1821)

In 1690 an expedition of Spanish soldiers and four Franciscan priests crossed the Rio Grande. The Spanish were coming to establish their own settlements, bring Christianity to the Indians, and, more importantly, prevent any other European powers from claiming what they believed was rightly theirs. Thus began in earnest the Spanish mission period in Texas.

Between 1682 and 1793, 26 missions were established by Franciscan priests in Texas. The most successful were the five missions established in San Antonio: Mission San Antonio de Valero (The Alamo), Mission Concepción, Mission San José, Mission San Juan, and Mission Espada. Less successful but still with a significant presence was Mission Nuestra Señora del Rosario and its accompanying Presidio La Bahía, established on the lower San Antonio River in 1749 (the Goliad mission). The five missions on the upper San Antonio River still exist and are within a few driving miles of each other. Collectively these missions form the largest concentration of Catholic missions in North America. The goal of the missions was to convert the local native population. The buildings were first built of stone, wood, and adobe and didn't have walls. Because of tensions between tribes and missionary occupants, stone walls were erected as a form of defense.

By the late 1770s it was clear that the efforts of the Spanish to civilize and colonize Texas through the mission system had been largely unsuccessful, if not an outright failure. The population of the weaker indigenous tribes who had been the mission recruits declined through high infant mortality rates, epidemics introduced by the Europeans, pressure from more aggressive invading tribes, and

assimilation. Texas remained thinly populated and impoverished. Between 1824 and 1830, the first years of the Republic of Mexico, all the missions still in existence in Texas were officially secularized with the exception of the ones in El Paso.

One of the greatest contributions of the mission system was the establishment of ranching in Texas. Early expeditions brought livestock to the missions, and within two to three decades thousands of cattle and horses roamed the pastures and prairies from central to south Texas. The horses and cattle were the genesis of the huge cattle drives after the Civil War and were managed by the *vaqueros* (from which the term "buckaroo" is derived), who evolved into the quintessential Texas cowboy.

Around the 1800s the first Anglo-Americans appeared on the scene. Initially they were tolerated by Spanish authorities, but Spain's grip on Texas began to weaken between 1790 and 1820 as Spain focused more on Europe and Mexico. This opened the door for Anglo-Americans to continue settling in Texas, which eventually morphed into unregulated colonization by Americans.

MEXICAN TEXAS (1821-1836)

Spain's efforts to colonize and populate Texas ended in failure. When Mexico gained its independence from Spain in 1821, it inherited the results of that failure. Only three towns existed and the population was estimated at approximately 2,500. The Comanches, Apaches, and other hostile tribes ruled Texas more than the government officials in Mexico City, whether they were Spanish or Mexican.

To populate this northern frontier full of hostile natives, the Spanish and then the Mexican governments looked to Anglo-American immigration. In January 1821, the Spanish government gave Moses Austin of Missouri a contract to establish a colony with 300 families. When he died, his son Stephen F. Austin inherited the contract. The Mexican government confirmed Austin's contract after independence, and Austin and other *empresarios* (those with contracts from the Mexican government) began immigrating into Texas. By 1835, there were 21 towns, and the Anglo-American population was estimated to be approximately 20,000, with the Hispanic Texans, called Tejanos, numbering fewer than 5,000.

Antonio López de Santa Anna was elected president of Mexico as a liberal and a champion of the Constitution of 1824. However, by 1835, he replaced the existing congress with a new body dominated by centralists under his control. He then abolished the Constitution of 1824 and abolished the various state governments, including that of Coahuila y Texas. Mexico, like the United States, had then and has now a federal government and various state governments; even today, the official name for Mexico is Los Estados Unidos de Mexico (the United States of Mexico). Santa Anna had replaced the state governments with departments run by officials he appointed. When the state of Zacatecas (Texas) rebelled, Santa Anna's forces invaded the state. After defeating his opposition, Santa Anna allowed his soldiers to murder and rape the local citizens, killing thousands of them. By October 1835, Santa Anna had made himself supreme dictator of Mexico.

The people of Texas, both Anglos and Tejanos, were in conflict with the policies of the brutal dictator. They had economic interests separate and apart from Mexico City and were used to little in the way of government interference. Facing the loss of their local government and the replacement of the liberal Constitution of 1824 with the arbitrariness of a supreme dictator, the Anglo-Texans, who called themselves "Texians" at that time, decided to rebel, with the support of a significant number of Tejanos.

THE TEXAS REVOLUTION (1835-1836)
The Battle at Gonzales

The flash point that ignited the Texas Revolution occurred in October 1835 in the

Mexico's past meets San Antonio's present in HemisFair Park.

town of Gonzales, on the Guadalupe River about 70 miles east of San Antonio. The town had a small cannon given to it by the Mexican Army to defend against the native tribes. Due to the Texians' rising frustration with Mexican dictator Santa Anna, the Mexican Army sent a contingent of 100 dragoons to retrieve it. The Texians rounded up volunteers to repulse the Mexicans under their makeshift banner with an image of the cannon on it and the words "Come and Take It." On October 2, the Texians and the Mexican Army faced off. The Texians fired their cannon and charged. The Mexican Army withdrew, suffering at most two fatalities. One Texian received a bloody nose when he fell off his horse. Although not a significant battle to say the least, this skirmish marked a point of no return.

The Battle at San Antonio

Stephen F. Austin was in command of the volunteers that constituted the "Texian Army." He led his volunteers to San Antonio, where

Texas History Through the Flag

Texas has had a very interesting history filled with drama, power struggles, wars, and uprisings. From being Spanish territory to being part of Mexico to being its own republic, the state has worn many hats and flown banners of many different colors. In all, Texas has had eight changes in sovereignty and six different flags. The state flag that is in use today is the same flag that was used during the Republic of Texas period. This flag has become a popular iconic symbol, indelible in its simplicity. It's just red, white, and blue, with a large "Lone Star" on the left. A great way to see this radically shifting history is through the various incarnations of the flag that have flown over the state.

- Spanish (1519-1685)

- French (1685-1690)

- Spanish (1690-1821)

- Mexican (1821-1836)

- Republic of Texas (1836-1845)

- United States (1845-1861)

- Confederate States of America (1861-1865)

- United States (1865-present)

General Martín Perfecto de Cos, the brother-in-law of Santa Anna, had arrived and taken over The Alamo as his command center. The Texian volunteers decided to use Mission Concepción, just down the road from The Alamo, as their headquarters. The Texian Army wasn't a disciplined lot, and the lack of active fighting led to boredom among the troops, which led to lots of heavy drinking. At a point when the Texian Army was in danger of collapsing in total disarray, Stephen F. Austin was called to San Felipe, where a "Consultation" of the Texian colonists had been meeting. Edward Burleson, a veteran Native American fighter, was elected as the

Texian Army's new commander in his absence. Burleson ordered an attack on San Antonio on December 3, but the troops refused to obey. Burleson decided to pull the troops out of San Antonio and winter in Goliad. Then one man stepped up and changed history. Benjamin Rush Milam, disgusted with the decision to withdraw, went through the remaining troops with the cry: "Who will follow old Ben Milam into San Antonio?" About 300 of the remaining volunteers joined Milam in an attack that began on December 5, 1835. The battle lasted three days with the Texians fighting house-to-house, cutting holes through the adobe walls to advance and gain control of San Antonio. They inflicted 150 casualties on the Mexican forces but not without loss of their own. Ben Milam himself was killed by a shot through the head on the third day of the battle.

On December 9, General Cos retreated back to The Alamo, where he chose to surrender. The Texians were generous and allowed General Cos and the Mexican troops to leave Texas with the promise not to "oppose the reestablishment of the Federal Constitution of 1824." Interestingly, the Texians weren't fighting for total independence from Mexico. They just wanted to be free from the dictatorial government of Santa Anna.

The Battle at The Alamo

After Cos surrendered, most of the Texas Army of volunteers just went home. Approximately 100 defenders remained in The Alamo. The Consultation of 1835 had created a Texas regular army on paper and made Sam Houston commander in chief. The problem was that the regular army had no soldiers and the volunteers already in the field were not under Houston's command. The bigger problem was Santa Anna. Shortly after the new year of 1836, Santa Anna crossed the Rio Grande with an estimated 4,000 troops as well as cavalry and artillery, with the goal of punishing the Texians.

The Texas Army at this time consisted of the 100 men in The Alamo and about 400 men under the command of James Fannin in Goliad, with Sam Houston as commander in chief. When Houston received word that Santa Anna had crossed the Rio Grande, he sent a courier to The Alamo with orders to remove the cannons, destroy The Alamo, and proceed to Gonzales. Sam Houston's order to abandon The Alamo was not carried out. Nineteen cannons that had been captured from Cos bolstered the Alamo defenses. Seeing that The Alamo could be defended, Houston's orders were overruled, and William Barret Travis was sent from San Felipe to reinforce The Alamo.

In February of 1836, Travis reached The Alamo, but he only had with him an additional 29 men. David Crockett arrived from Tennessee about the same time in response to the call to arms. The Alamo's departing commander, James Neill, put Travis in charge. The men, however, were used to electing their leaders and chose Jim Bowie, who was popular among the resistance. Bowie and Travis compromised by agreeing to a joint command with Bowie commanding the "volunteers" and Travis the "regular" army. On February 24, Bowie ceded full command to Travis when he became seriously ill to the point of being bedridden. By this time Santa Anna's troops had made their appearance in San Antonio and the siege of The Alamo had begun.

Santa Anna marked his arrival by raising a red flag above San Fernando Cathedral and demanding an unconditional surrender. Santa Anna had issued a decree that anyone rebelling against his rule was a "pirate" and should be shot. Captured pirates were not entitled to the status or protection afforded prisoners of war. The red flag meant "no quarter" would be given to any prisoner. Travis responded with a shot from his 18-pound cannon, the largest in The Alamo.

The siege of The Alamo lasted 13 days and ended in the early-morning hours of March 6, when Santa Anna's troops overwhelmed the Alamo's defenders. Travis was one of the first to die, when shot through the head. Bowie was killed in his bed in the chapel, and Crockett most likely died while defending the wooden palisades erected just outside the entrance to the chapel. The Mexican *alcalde* (mayor) of San Antonio, Francisco Antonio Ruiz, put the death toll of the Alamo defenders at 182. The number of Mexican losses will never be known for sure, but modern estimates place Santa Anna's casualties in the range of 600 dead and wounded.

The importance of the battle of The Alamo as a military feat can be debated. What cannot be debated, however, is that The Alamo let all Texians know they were in a battle to the death, and it inspired them with a rallying cry and thirst for vengeance that they carried with them to victory at San Jacinto.

The Battle at San Jacinto

The Consultation of 1835 called for a convention to meet at Washington-on-the-Brazos on March 1, 1836. On March 2, the delegates to the convention declared Texas a "free, sovereign, and independent republic." The news of the Declaration of Independence did not reach The Alamo before it fell, but the defense of The Alamo certainly gave the convention delegates the time and opportunity to meet and allowed the Republic of Texas to be born.

The real military prize for Santa Anna was obtained after The Alamo, at Goliad. As Santa Anna marched on San Antonio he sent a smaller force under General José de Urrea on a southerly route through the populated areas of Texas toward Goliad.

Houston ordered Goliad to be abandoned, but the 400 men under the command of James Fannin left too late. Just six miles outside of Goliad the Texians were surrounded and caught by Urrea's troops. After a brief and ferocious battle, Fannin accepted his fate and sought surrender under favorable terms. He surrendered after receiving what he thought were assurances that his men would be treated as prisoners of war. Fannin and his men were marched back to Goliad and imprisoned in the chapel at the Presidio La Bahía. Urrea reported the capture of Fannin and his men to Santa Anna and requested clemency for them.

Santa Anna replied with a direct order to execute all the prisoners. At sunrise on Palm Sunday, March 27, 1836, the order was carried out and the men were marched out of the presidio and shot. After the initial volley of fire, 28 prisoners escaped to the woods and lived to tell the tale of the massacre. The dead counted 342, including Fannin. Fannin had requested only two things from his captors when he learned he would be executed: that he not be shot in the head and that his personal belongings be sent to his family. Fannin was not marched out of the presidio with his men. He was executed just outside the chapel by a shot to the head. His executioners stole his personal effects.

Texas was now virtually defenseless, with no army in the field. Houston went to Gonzales and rounded up several hundred men that had gathered, originally with the idea of trying to relieve The Alamo. When word reached Houston that The Alamo had fallen and Santa Anna was approaching with as many as 5,000 troops, Houston, not wanting to defend fixed positions against overwhelming odds, decided to retreat. He burned the town and sank what few cannons were available in the Guadalupe River. Within days, he learned that the Texians at Goliad had all been executed and that his men were the only hope of survival for the fledgling Texas republic.

Houston retreated to the east, passing over the Guadalupe River, the Colorado River, and the Brazos River. Many of his troops and commanders didn't like the tactic, as they wanted to fight and avenge The Alamo and Goliad. Santa Anna believed Houston and his army would not fight and were fleeing to the safety and protection afforded by United States troops at the Louisiana border. But when Houston learned that Santa Anna's force was fewer than 1,000 men, he shadowed it to Harrisburg, near present-day Houston. Santa Anna failed to capture the officials that now made up the Texas government in Harrisburg. They fled again to what was called "New Washington" on Galveston Bay.

Eventually, Santa Anna and his troops, along with Houston and his troops, arrived on the San Jacinto River, where they faced off in open prairie of several hundred yards.

On the morning of April 21, General Cos arrived with an additional 500 men. Santa Anna's forces now numbered over 1,300 while the Texas forces numbered almost 900. Santa Anna, assuming he would have to attack the Texians, let Cos's men rest after their long march while he awaited the arrival of his remaining troops. Houston, on the other hand, held his first council of war. He and his commanders decided to take the offensive. The Texians formed their line on the prairie around 3pm. The line included two small cannons (called the Twin Sisters) and a cavalry contingent under the command of Mirabeau B. Lamar. The Mexican troops were not expecting offensive operations, and many were enjoying their siesta. The Mexican sentries on duty detected the advance and opened fire with muskets and a 12-pound cannon. Most of the fire was without effect. The Texians were crouching low in the grass and were advancing through a small depression in the prairie. While riding his horse, Sam Houston was hit by a musket ball that fractured his leg just above his left ankle. The Twin Sisters fired once on the Mexican breastworks, and Houston led his men to within 20 yards of the Mexicans when the order to fire was given. After the one volley, the Texians did not reload but charged ahead. The Mexican line broke and ran. The battle lasted only 18 minutes, but the killing lasted until it was almost dark. The Texians, yelling "Remember the Alamo, Remember Goliad," ran down the fleeing Mexicans, clubbing and knifing them to death. Many were trapped in low wetlands where the Texians could reload and fire upon them from the dry shore as they struggled to get free from knee-deep mud. Houston tried to stop the slaughter, but most of his troops ignored his pleas. In all, the Texians killed 630 Mexican soldiers and captured another 730. The Texians had only two killed on the

Republic of Texas

UNITED STATES
OF AMERICA

MEXICO

REPUBLIC
OF TEXAS

THE BATTLE AT SAN ANTONIO/
THE BATTLE AT THE ALAMO

THE BATTLE AT
SAN JACINTO

THE BATTLE AT GONZALES

PACIFIC
OCEAN

Gulf of Mexico

© AVALON TRAVEL

0   400 mi

0   400 km

day of the battle; six more died later from the wounds they suffered.

Santa Anna was captured the following day dressed in the clothes of a common soldier. When he was brought into camp, his true identity became known because the soldiers began addressing him as "El Presidente." He was brought before Houston. Many of the Texians wanted to kill him immediately, and there was no shortage of volunteers for the job. Houston, however, knew that Santa Anna was more valuable alive than dead. The remaining Mexican Army, which had more troops than were present at San Jacinto, was only miles away. Houston forced Santa Anna to sign a treaty that called for the Mexican Army to return to the other side of the Rio Grande.

The freedom of Texas from Mexico won at the San Jacinto River led to annexation and the Mexican War, resulting in the acquisition by the United States of the states of Texas, New Mexico, Arizona, Nevada,

California, and Utah, and parts of Colorado, Wyoming, Kansas, and Oklahoma. Almost one-third of the present area of the American nation, nearly a million square miles, changed sovereignty.

REPUBLIC OF TEXAS (1836-1845)

With the defeat of Santa Anna at San Jacinto, the Texians had at last been freed from the tyranny of the oppressive Mexican government. The land of Texas was theirs. Immediately a government was put in place. Within months voters of the new republic chose their first elected official. Sam Houston was elected president of the Republic of Texas, and he established the capital at his namesake city in eastern Texas. Shortly thereafter the first Congress of the Republic of Texas convened. Voters also overwhelmingly approved a referendum requesting annexation by the United States, but U.S. president Martin Van Buren refused to consider the request.

Birth of the City of Austin

BACKGROUND
HISTORY

Before the birth of the City of Austin, there was nothing at the location other than a low-water crossing on the Colorado River, where the Congress Avenue Bridge is today. To the east was black-land prairie, and to the west of the Colorado were the limestone hills marking the beginning of the Hill Country. Immense herds of buffalo migrated south from the Panhandle region following the Colorado River through Central Texas.

In the early 1800s the Mexican government decided to allow Anglo-American settlers to im-migrate to this part of Mexico to help populate the region and provide a buffer against Native American attacks on the town of San Antonio. Those early American settlers loved to hunt buf-falo, and many quickly discovered the location on the Colorado where the buffalo herds would cross. These hunters set up campsites at the crossing, which grew into a small community that was known as Waterloo. One of those early buffalo hunters was Mirabeau B. Lamar. Years later Lamar was elected the second president of the Republic of Texas and chose the buffalo campsite of Waterloo as the location of the capital.

A year later the Republic of Texas was officially recognized by the United States, and later by some European countries. The new republic faced many problems. The economy needed attention, local Native American tribes were fiercer than ever, relations with the United States had to be developed, and Mexico was itching for a war. General Santa Anna was in custody and the public demanded he be ex-ecuted. Wisely, Houston kept him alive and eventually released him.

In 1838 Mirabeau B. Lamar was elected president. He was notorious for spending lavishly and exacerbating problems with Native American tribes. Since he detested Sam Houston, he refused to reside at a capital named Houston. Therefore, the need arose to find a new capital for the Republic of Texas. Many communities wanted that honor, but not one was the clear favorite. As a result, Lamar decided to create a new capital where no city existed before. The site he chose was a buffalo hunting camp. In 1839, a new capi-tal city was laid out between Waller Creek on the east, Shoal Creek on the west, and the Colorado River on the south.

The original 200 residents of Austin resided in log cabins along the street that was grandly called Congress Avenue. Unfortunately for the settlers of early Austin, this part of Texas was Comanche territory (as well as buffalo territory) and thus Austin was a very dan-gerous place to live. The diaries of the early settlers confirm that many were killed and scalped when they strayed beyond the imme-diate confines of the capital city. Many times the Comanches came into the city itself to wreak havoc and terrorize the citizens.

In 1841, Sam Houston was reelected presi-dent and quickly decided to move the capi-tal back to Houston. Houston was pro-Native American and thought it was a ridiculous idea to stir up the Comanches by creating a capital in the middle of their territory. Furthermore, the Colorado River was not navigable that far upstream. Therefore no steamboats could travel to the capital city, leaving it quite isolated.

Houston, a savvy politician, knew that the 200 residents of Austin would not be in favor of moving the capital, so he devised a plan to move it without their knowledge. He sent some Texas Rangers with a couple of wag-ons down to Austin with orders to sneak into town in the middle of the night, load up the archives of the republic, and take them back to Houston. Where the archives resided, so would reside the capital.

All went well with this plan, and the ar-chives were loaded up and moved out of town late one night. However, one woman, Angelina Eberly, remained awake. She was the proprietress of the Bullock Hotel, located on the northwest corner of 6th Street and Congress Avenue. She investigated what was going on, quickly discovered that the town had been robbed of the archives, and fired the cannon that the city had for protection against the Native Americans. The firing of the cannon woke up the community, and a large group armed themselves, mounted their horses, and rode out after the Rangers. They caught up with the wagons and at gunpoint turned them around. The archives headed back to Austin and the incident would forever be known as the "archives war." Thus, in spite of Sam Houston, the "Hero of San Jacinto," the archives remained in Austin and so did the capital.

Houston may not have been successful in moving the capital from Austin, but he was successful at obtaining annexation. Houston courted Great Britain and France and both became interested in the idea. However, the United States was very uncomfortable with the prospect of a British or French presence in the middle of the country and quickly moved to annex Texas. In 1845 annexation to the United States took place and the Republic of Texas was dissolved.

ANNEXATION (1845-PRESENT)

The entry of Texas into the United States sparked the Mexican-American War. Mexican officials were angered at Texas's annexation because they felt the region was under negotiation. By this point, the relentless General Santa Anna had gained power in Mexico and felt it was time to take his revenge. The war lasted for two years and came to a close in 1847, when U.S. troops gained control of Mexico City.

Settlers, Slaves, and Cowboys

In the 1850s the population of Texas almost doubled. This rapid growth came about primarily because of Germans and African American slaves. A significant number of German immigrants made their way to Texas,

with the largest population moving to the Hill Country. They brought with them German culture, customs, and traditions. The other factor in the dramatic rise of the population came from folks migrating to Texas from the southern states, bringing with them thousands of slaves. Slavery wasn't customary in Texas until these wealthy slave-owners introduced the practice.

During the Civil War (1861-1865), Texas seceded from the United States and joined the Confederate States of America. Texas contributed food, supplies, and some 80,000 men to the Confederate war effort. Although most of the battles took place outside of Texas, the Civil War left an indelible scar on the Lone Star State. With slavery abolished following the war's end in 1865, blacks did gain some rights, but they were limited.

It was at this time that Texas found its calling in ranching. With the advent of the railway and the state's abundance of land, Texas's identity as ranching and cowboy country quickly developed. Land barons, businesses, and money poured into the state, and small pioneer towns quickly grew into cities.

The 20th Century

In the second half of the 19th century oil was discovered in east Texas, but it was nothing to shake a stick at. It wasn't until 1901, when a drilling site east of Houston exploded with a gusher of oil, that Texas realized it was sitting on an abundant and extremely valuable natural resource. Just a few years later, Henry Ford was making his automobile available to the mass public. With millions of barrels of black gold shooting out of the ground, and amid great demand for the resource, oil made Texas rich. Although oil moguls scooped up a lot of this wealth, the tax revenues spilled into all aspects of local and state government. Schools were built, roads were paved, and homes were constructed. Then, with the fall of the stock market and the Great Depression in 1929, the state's progress and flow of money came to a screeching halt. The demand for oil hit rock bottom as the market became glutted and common people couldn't afford to fuel a car, much less own one. A section of Texas became part of what was known as the Dust Bowl, an area in the Southern Plains that was afflicted with severe drought, poverty, and agricultural decline in the wake of the Great Depression.

Texas found its way out of the Great Depression during World War II, when several military bases were established. With the manufacturing industry on the rise and the federal government spending money in Texas, the state slowly regained its wealthy and influential status. Oil value increased and production followed right in step. The following two decades saw growth in the state's economy, population, and recognition.

Texas remains a major oil producer and home to several massive military bases and facilities. Although ranching isn't as prevalent as it was in the past, the tradition still carries on.

Government and Economy

POLITICS

Being the capital of Texas, Austin is the hub of the state's politics. The legislature meets every other spring and consists of a 31-member senate and a 150-member house of representatives. Texas had traditionally been a Democratic state, but this dramatically changed when George W. Bush became governor and later when he was elected president of the United States. Following Bush's election as president, Republican Rick Perry became the governor of Texas.

Several problems plague the politics of the state capital. First, the legislative process is famous for getting bogged down and for not achieving its goals. Special legislative sessions are often called to try to tackle these important issues, but the "special sessions" often end with nothing getting accomplished except taxpayer dollars being spent while the feuding legislators get nothing done. Another problem in Texas politics is big business. It should come as no surprise that politics and business are fast friends, but in Texas this is downright cultural. Texas is home to some of the nation's largest and most powerful businesses, and their agendas are consistently integrated into legislation, right under the noses of the unvigilant and unaware public.

ECONOMY

The economy of Central Texas used to hinge on ranching and cotton, but today the region's main industries are higher education, government, and high technology. Top employers in Austin include the University of Texas, Dell Computers, the City of Austin, Motorola, Seaton Healthcare Network, and IBM. The economic force that people most associate with Austin is the high-tech industry, which took root when IBM moved here in the 1960s. Since then, Motorola, Texas Instruments, and Dell Computers have chosen Austin as their home. Today high technology is the third-largest industry in the region, and Central Texas is a major player on the global computer and technology scene.

In recent years an economic shot in the arm has been coming from the movie industry. This burgeoning interest in Austin is for good reason. Filming and production work in Austin is less expensive than in the big cities, and the industry folks here are friendly. Films made in and around Austin include *Dazed and Confused, The Alamo, The Faculty, Texas Chainsaw Massacre I* and *II, Miss Congeniality I* and *II, Second Hand Lions, Spy Kids, Slacker, Waiting for Guffman, Office Space, How to Eat Fried Worms, Sin City, Machete, Boyhood, True Grit, Transformers,* and many more. In addition, TV series such as *Friday Night Lights* have been made in Central Texas.

Lastly, one can't talk about Austin's economy without mentioning the music industry. Although there's no real "industry" to speak of, such as record companies, music executives, and tall buildings where musicians sell their souls, live music is a big source of revenue for the city. In 2012-2013, the music industry brought in an excess of $856 million per year, never mind the boost music gives the tourism industry. With high-profile festivals such as SXSW ($218 million) and Austin City Limits Festival ($102 million), live music revenue is something the city relies on.

People and Culture

Texans are bold, brash, and full of bravado. The bravado, however, is tempered with a large dose of hospitality and friendliness. The state's motto, "Friendship," has historical linguistic origins, but it is also reflected every day in its people. Who and what a Texan is can be summed up by two popular bumper stickers. One identifies the car's occupant as a "Native Texan" while the other boasts, "I wasn't born in Texas but I got here as fast as I could." To qualify as a true Texan you don't need established bloodlines like the Virginia planter class or the Brahmins in Boston. In fact, the founding fathers of Texas, almost to the man, came to Texas because they were running from the law, debts, failed careers, or failed marriages. Most will agree that being Texan is open to all classes, all races, and all religions. It is a spirit and an attitude, coupled with a pride associated with a special place that was conquered and cultivated by strong-willed and independent-minded people.

Texan pride is due in no small part to the fact that Texas was created in a revolution against a brutal dictator and stood alone for almost 10 years as an independent nation. Texas joined the United States in 1845 as a result of a treaty between two sovereign nations, not because it was a conquered territory or constituted land purchased from a European power. It is understandable that the original Texans were proud of what they created and have passed on that pride to future generations and new arrivals. That is why as you travel around Texas you will see the Texas flag displayed prominently by its people at their homes and businesses.

The strongest cultural influences that have informed Central Texas character come from Mexico and Germany. Mexico should come as no surprise, as the border is so close, and Latino heritage reaches far back into the state's history, but people are often surprised at the German heritage. Both cultures combined have shaped the cultural landscape. The Latino cultural and historical presence is especially apparent in Austin and San Antonio, where most of the food, art, and music draws heavily from Latino culture, and the German heritage is strongest in the Hill Country, where folks still dance to polka and eat schnitzels. One strong reminder of both German and Mexican heritage is in the regional Latin music, which features the accordion, introduced by early German pioneers.

POPULATION

The populations of Austin, San Antonio, and the Hill Country are largely composed of whites/Caucasians and Hispanics. Austin's significant demographic figures as collected during the last major census in 2010 are as follows: 49 percent white/Caucasian, 35 percent Hispanic, 8 percent African American, 8 percent other. San Antonio's demographics from the 2010 census are as follows: 63 percent Hispanic, 27 percent white/Caucasian, 7 percent African American, 3 percent other.

RELIGION

Religion is a major part of life in Texas. Beliefs and values are unquestionably integrated into secular culture, and a church-based way of life is the accepted norm. Texas is at the westernmost reaches of the Bible Belt, the region of the United States made up of communities that are predominantly Protestant and Evangelical. There isn't a definitive boundary for this belt, but most agree that it stretches from Dallas, Texas, down to Austin, which is at the western reaches, and continues east through the South. Although only part of Texas is in what's considered the Bible Belt, the Bible is the basis for beliefs and ideologies for the majority of Texans. According to *Churches and Church Membership in the United States,* Texas has the most Evangelical Protestants in the nation, with California a distant second. Texas rankings with other religions as compared to the rest of the United States are as follows: third-largest number of Catholics, third-largest number of Buddhist congregations, fifth-largest number of Muslims, fifth-largest number of Hindu congregations, and tenth-largest number of Jews. At least 55 percent of Texans adhere to a particular religion.

Being the most liberal piece of Texas, Austin has the most diverse representation of religions and is perhaps the most accepting and tolerant. San Antonio, on the other hand, is predominantly Catholic. This should come as no surprise due to its Mexican history and the proximity to the border.

LANGUAGE

The predominant language spoken in Central Texas is English. This may sound simple to those familiar with the language, but newcomers beware—the version of English expressed here isn't always as it seems. Besides being famous for their unique accent, Texans also have a tendency to pronounce words in a creative way. The most widely known example of this is the word "y'all." Although not exclusively Texan it has become synonymous with the state. Along with this, there's a long list of weird pronunciations that first-timers will encounter. At first this approach to English is amusing and takes a little getting used to, but its charm will win you over.

Due to Central Texas's rich Mexican history and Latino and Hispanic culture, the Spanish language comes in a close second to English. Most Texans speak a little Spanish and many are fluent. The infusion of Spanish into Central Texas culture has created a unique lexicon that is to be found nowhere else. Spanish words have merged into the Texas lexicon and have taken on their own meaning. For example, the Spanish word *grande* is pronounced like "grand" (e.g., Rio Grand), and Guadalupe is pronounced "gwada-LOOP." In Spanish "ll" is pronounced like "y," but no one would dare pronounce Amarillo with a "y" sound. The list of weird idiosyncrasies is long and amusing. Travelers, especially those with a background in Spanish, should try to go with the vernacular flow.

MUSIC AND ART

Music is a major part of the life and culture of Central Texas. Austin is the Live Music Capital of the World and San Antonio is considered the home of Tejano and conjunto music. I won't speculate as to how music and Austin became synonymous, but I will say that Austin has been greatly blessed in its calling to live music greatness. Today Austin is compulsive about music. Throughout the year Austin's hundreds of venues, bars, and clubs are full of touring national acts, local favorites, and wannabes seeking expression and recognition. Although the city is smack-dab in the middle of Texas there isn't much "tractor pop" (modern country) to be heard here. Austin is an independent artist and songwriter paradise that transcends all genres by offering music by the people, for the people. The scene is both diverse and tolerant, and most music fans here don't subscribe to any one genre.

Austin may be known for its contribution to live music, but San Antonio and the Hill

Country are known for Tejano and conjunto music. This unique form of music is the direct result of the Spanish, Mexican, Texian, and German cultures mixing over the course of two centuries in Central and South Texas. The final product is a Tex-Mex music that blends traditional Mexican forms such as the *corrido* and the Western/European waltz and polka introduced by German and Czech settlers in the late 19th century. The most distinct element of this music is the accordion, which was introduced by the German settlers. Today Tejano and conjunto music reflects influences from rock, blues, and *cumbia,* and has gone from being a local and ethnic form of music to its own genre with wide appeal in North America, Latin America, and Europe. At the core of Tejano and conjunto are songs about drinking, love, heartbreak, and dancing. Popular artists that have either pioneered or popularized the Tejano sound are Narciso Martinez, Isidiro Lopez, Joe Lopez y El Groupo Mazz, and Flaco Jimenez, who can still be seen performing around Austin and San Antonio.

Folk art is second only to music in Central Texas. Although it is something that is not easily defined, it is widely accepted as simply art by and for the folk. In Austin folk art is pop paintings of Hank Williams Sr. on old fence boards, or junk from the landfill and car graveyards that is painstakingly fitted together to form a postmodern apocalyptic "sculpture," or retro-style neon signs mounted on tin with catchy statements that echo sentiments of the obscure, or a thought-provoking social/political painting of Elvis wired to light bulbs. In San Antonio a similar modern approach is taken to folk art, but with one difference—replace Elvis with the Virgin Mary. All the above expressions of folk art can be found in galleries, shops, boutiques, and restaurants, on urban walls, and in people's front yards all over Austin, San Antonio, and in some Hill Country towns. You'll know it when you see it.

Essentials

Transportation

GETTING THERE

Austin, San Antonio, and the Hill Country, collectively known as Central Texas, is situated in the heart of the state, which is in the heart of the United States. Getting to the region is easy and affordable for domestic travelers. One can drive in by car from another region in the United States. This is the classic way of traveling, often referred to as the road trip, and it can be nostalgic and adventurous. However, most travelers fly in to either Austin or San Antonio on one of the major airline carriers.

Air

The main airports for the region are located in Austin and San Antonio: **Austin-Bergstrom International Airport** (300 Presidential Blvd., 512/530-2242, www.austintexas.gov/airport) and **San Antonio International Airport** (9800 Airport Blvd., 210/207-3433, www.sanantonio.gov/airport). Choosing which airport to arrive at depends on what you plan on doing in the region. If you plan on staying in Austin and sticking with the urban experience of live music and summer festivals, with a quick side trip to the nearby Hill Country, you should fly in to Austin-Bergstrom International Airport. If you plan on staying on the San Antonio River Walk, or going to SeaWorld, or traveling to the farther reaches of the Hill Country, you should fly into San Antonio International Airport.

Austin's airport is a converted air force base. It offers international connections that can get you anywhere in the world. Major passenger airlines include America West (800/235-9292), American Airlines (800/433-7300), Delta (800/221-1212), Frontier Airlines (800/432-1359), Southwest (800/435-9792), and United (800/241-6522).

San Antonio International Airport is the region's largest airport and is an international hub with both direct flights and domestic connections that can get you anywhere in the world. Nonstop flights are offered to 41 destinations, mostly major U.S. cities and a couple of cities in Mexico. Passenger airlines that service the airport include Aerolitoral (800/237-6639), America West (800/235-9292), American Airlines (800/433-7300), Delta (800/221-1212), Mexicana (800/534-7921), Midwest (800/452-2022), Southwest (800/435-9792), and United (800/241-6522).

Bus and Train

Although traveling by air is often more practical, travel by bus or train may offer a more adventurous and colorful experience. **Greyhound** (800/231-2222, www.greyhound.com) bus lines and **Amtrak** (800/872-7245, www.amtrak.com) train service both have stations in Austin (Greyhound: 916 E. Koenig Ln.; Amtrak: 250 N. Lamar Blvd.) and San Antonio (Greyhound: 500 N. St. Mary's St.; Amtrak: 350 Hoefgen St.). Fares are anywhere from $11 to $36 to get from one city to another.

Car

Because Texas is so darn massive, driving to Austin, San Antonio, or the Hill Country can be tedious. Depending on where you are coming from, the drive can be miles of straight and boring roadways with scorched and desert-like landscapes. Some stretches of highway are almost hypnotizing; be careful not to let yourself get sleepy. Also, filling stations and food can be scarce, especially in some East Texas regions. As you get closer to Central

---

Previous: Elvis souvenir at the general store in Fredericksburg; example of the "Don't mess with Texas" antilittering campaign.

Texas, gas stations, roadside barbecue shacks, and rest stops become more frequent. Once you arrive in either Austin or San Antonio, Interstate 35, which is the primary highway that connects the two cities, can be backed up for miles at morning and evening commute hours. For both cities, it is best to plan your arrival time so as to avoid rush hour.

GETTING AROUND

Once you have arrived in Central Texas, getting around can require some planning. If you plan on staying in either Austin or San Antonio, renting a car is highly recommended. If you prefer not to rent a car but wish to explore the area, you will quickly discover the challenges of a region that doesn't have a cohesive public transportation system. Greyhound bus line and Amtrak train system are the two primary ways to hop from one city to the other.

Getting around by car can provide the most freedom, and the best way to make the most of your time. There are only a few major freeways in the Austin metropolitan area, and only a few primary highways that connect Austin to the Hill Country and San Antonio. One minor drawback to using a car is downtown parking and freeway congestion in Austin and San Antonio. Interstate 35, which connects the two cities, can be backed up for miles at morning and evening commute hours. For both cities, it is best to plan any road trip or highway travel around these times.

All the usual rental car companies are represented at both Austin-Bergstrom International Airport and San Antonio International Airport, as well as around town. Car rental agencies include Advantage Rent-A-Car (800/777-5500), Alamo Rent-A-Car (800/462-5266), Avis Car Rental (800/331-1212), Budget (800/527-0700), Dollar Rent-A-Car (800/800-3665), Enterprise (800/261-7331), Hertz Rent-A-Car (800/654-3131), National Car Rental (800/222-9058), and Thrifty (800/847-4389).

As a region, most towns are 30 miles apart or less. Gas stations and mini-markets are easily found along routes between Austin and San Antonio, and throughout the Hill Country. You don't need to sweat filling up with a tank of gas at every town (unless you are driving a gas-guzzler). That said, when you're in a small town and you're running below half a tank, it's a good idea to fill 'er up. Also, if you plan on hitting the road, it's always a good idea to stock up on some food, snacks, and water before heading out.

ON THE ROAD

Folks in Central Texas drive very differently from folks in the rest of the country. The hospitality Texans are famous for definitely carries over to the streets. They can be some of the slowest, most patient, courteous drivers in the nation. Central Texas driving philosophy is summed up on a road sign seen throughout the state that says, "Drive Texas friendly." People who are used to roadway customs such as honking, aggressive driving, and a general lack of patience should try to slow down and take their time.

Driving Courtesy

People on the roads of Central Texas are remarkably courteous. The two most important customs regarding this are waving and letting other drivers go. Locals have the hospitable practice of waving when changing lanes, when passing on two-lane roads, and sometimes for no reason at all. The rule of thumb for waving is, the smaller the road the more important it is to give people a nod or a wave. This simple howdy-with-the-hand is especially crucial in the Hill Country. It's also not uncommon to see people getting into courtesy stalemates at stop signs, waving on freeways, and holding up busy traffic to let someone in.

Honking in Texas is a sign of an impending traffic accident, of a friend nearby, or of a child sitting behind the wheel of a parked car. People don't use the horn to say, "Get out of my way." Never start honking the second the light turns green; people will wonder what's wrong with you. If someone is sitting at a green light and not moving, be patient and just sit there until he or she starts moving. Road rage is a very rare occurrence here.

Central Texas Mileage

	Austin	Johnson City	Fredericksburg	Kerrville
Austin	—	47	77	101
Johnson City	47	—	30	54
Fredericksburg	77	30	—	24
Kerrville	101	54	24	—
Bandera	108	76	50	25
Boerne	85	52	38	34
New Braunfels	47	52	72	75
San Marcos	30	50	69	85
Wimberley	37	38	58	79
San Antonio	79	61	68	36

Traffic Police

The traffic police in Austin and the surrounding Hill Country are particularly notorious for being sticklers. Speed traps are unfairly set up all over the area, and unsuspecting folks who are good drivers are always getting tickets for going a little faster than the speed limit. Sometimes the speed cushion can be as low as four miles per hour over the speed limit. With this kind of speed enforcement, it's wise to drive at the speed limit at all times. For some reason police are particularly active on Sunday mornings when people are heading to church. This stringent enforcement creates piles of paperwork and loads of headaches. My suspicion is that some of this police zealotry is to increase city revenue, but maybe I'm just bitter because I got a speeding ticket recently.

The Austin police are also known for going to dramatic lengths to catch people committing traffic violations by setting up sting operations. My favorite is the "beggar sting," when cops dress up like homeless beggars and stand at busy intersections for the purpose of peering into cars to look for laws being violated. The moral of the story: Drive with compulsive prudence while on Central Texas roads.

Low-Water Crossings

Central Texas is prone to flash floods and mini-deluges. For some of the roads in the Hill Country this means flooding of roads and low-water crossings. In some cases these roads are designed to flood during heavy rains in order to divert water from buildings and communities. Never drive into a flooded roadway. You never have any idea how deep the water is or how fast it's moving. It doesn't take much more than a foot or two of water to sweep a car or an RV off the road and down the river. Every year people drive into these and get themselves into trouble.

Freezing Conditions

People are surprised to hear that every year during winter there's an occasional freeze. When a freeze is in the forecast the city of Austin freaks out, schools close, and everyone hunkers down as if there will be nuclear fallout. Texans are the first to admit they are completely incompetent at driving on icy roadways. Although the city applies a chemical and gravel substance in order to prevent them, crashes, fender benders, and accidents are abundant. Bridges and freeway overpasses can be especially dangerous when icy.

Bandera	Boerne	New Braunfels	San Marcos	Wimberley	San Antonio
108	85	47	30	37	79
76	52	52	50	38	61
50	38	72	69	58	68
25	34	75	85	79	63
—	25	65	80	79	46
25	—	41	57	55	30
65	41	—	18	26	30
80	57	18	—	14	47
79	55	26	14	—	56
46	30	30	47	56	—

Travel Tips

WHAT TO PACK

When visiting during the warmer months bring lots of casual clothes. It is imperative to pack plenty of shorts, comfortable shirts, and sandals or flip-flops. Why lots of these, you may ask? Everything gets sweaty in a matter of minutes. In one day you can easily go through four changes of clothes: one for the morning, one for swimming, one for after swimming, and one for dinner out. If you'll be visiting the region between June and September, don't waste any room in your luggage with jackets, sweaters, or anything with long sleeves. Believe me, you won't get chilly, except for the kind that comes in a bowl. However, during the winter months, temperatures are sometimes near freezing, so be sure to bring warm clothes.

CONDUCT AND CUSTOMS

Texas Manners

In Texas chivalry, politeness, and manners are very much a part of everyday life. Men in Texas have a respect for women that harkens back to a bygone era. Opening doors for ladies, not talking vulgarly in their company, and addressing women with a respectful "ma'am" are customs that are alive and well. Cursing in public isn't as prevalent as it is in many other parts of the country, so it's best to keep the sailor talk to a minimum. Also, when walking down the street people look each other in the eyes and say "Hi." Yankees and West Coasters may take this the wrong way at first. If someone starts talking to you in line at the store, it doesn't mean they are mentally ill or they want your money. It's just good ol' Texas kindness.

Tipping

An important part of the income of workers in the service industry comes from tips. It's considered rude to tip too little or with spare change. With the Texas minimum wage being a measly $7.25 an hour, don't be one of those cheapskates who tips low and tries to sneak out the back door. The following workers should be tipped based on the fare, bill, or fee: cab drivers 15 percent, restaurant workers 15-20 percent, bartenders 10-15 percent, bellhops $1 per bag.

Fast Facts for International Travelers

Time: Central Texas is in the central standard time zone (CST), which is GMT/UTC-6; one hour behind the East Coast and two hours ahead of the West Coast.

Measurements: The metric system doesn't apply in the United States. Distances are measured in inches, feet, yards, and miles.

Weights: Dry weights are measured in ounces (oz.) and pounds (lb.).

Temperatures: Degrees are Fahrenheit, not Celsius.

Mail: Currently domestic letters can be sent for $0.49, postcards for $0.34, and letters to most international destinations for $1.15 (except Mexico and Canada), but prices may change, so check with the post office.

Electricity: The United States uses 110V to 120V at 60 cycles. Appliances brought from Europe or Australia won't work in the United States without a 110V transformer, which can be hard to find in this country.

Liquor Laws

Liquor laws are the same throughout the United States when it comes to age and drinking and driving. However, specifics regarding what can be sold vary from county to county. Some counties in Texas prohibit the sale of distilled spirits, while others are totally dry. When it comes to these varying degrees of "dry," the counties where Austin and San Antonio are located are so wet they are drenched. You have to be 21 and older to drink in the United States, and driving while intoxicated is illegal, dangerous, and flat-out stupid. It's also illegal to have an open container in a vehicle. Also, note that you can't buy alcohol on Sundays or late at night—liquor stores close by 9pm and are closed on Sundays.

Smoking in Public

Just a few years ago most restaurants, bars, cafés, and music venues had ashtrays on tables and a plume of smoke lingering in the rafters. Thanks to a growing concern for public health, Austin's smoking laws have been changing in favor of a smoke-free environment. Smoking is now prohibited in just about all indoor public places except for bingo parlors, pool halls, and bowling alleys. It was only in 2005 that voters banned smoking in music venues and bars, and only by a very narrow margin.

Don't Mess with Texas

It's highly suggested that one not mess with Texas while visiting Austin. There are two meanings behind this directive. First off, don't litter. The popular phrase "Don't mess with Texas" was created as an antilitter campaign, which has been very successful. Because of this, the Lone Star State is beautiful and clean. The other meaning behind "Don't mess with Texas" is this: Don't slight, mock, dis, or make fun of the state in any way. Texans are very proud of their state and take great offense at people who come in from out of town and talk trash about Texas.

WOMEN TRAVELING ALONE

When traveling in Texas women should apply all commonsense safety precautions. It is no worse or better than other U.S. destinations in terms of risk. However, women who travel to Texas should be prepared for the duality of chivalry and chauvinism that can be found in Texan men. Women will find the "little darlin'" culture of Texas either charming or oppressive. The same guy who holds the door open for you might look you up and down as you walk past. In the hot summer months you won't want to wear much more than shorts and a T-shirt, yet the less you wear the more attention you will draw.

SENIOR TRAVELERS

Nearly all attractions and many hotels and airlines offer discounts for seniors. It is highly recommended to unabashedly ask for your senior discount wherever you go and whatever you do: It can save you a lot of money over the course of a week or two. What constitutes a senior? In most places a senior is someone over 60 or 65.

TRAVELERS WITH DISABILITIES

In Austin and San Antonio most attractions are easy to access. Austin is particularly easy to get around, as most of what's great about Austin is centrally located, and most museums, restaurants, and accommodations are wheelchair accessible. Although most San Antonio attractions are accessible, sights such as the Mission Trail and the attractions in Brackenridge Park are pretty spread out. The River Walk has a few accesses for wheelchairs and the city is continually improving access. As for the Hill Country, don't expect much in the way of easy access. Dirt roads, few wheelchair accesses, and just plain old rugged environs can slow you down and even be impassable. However, the bigger towns, such as Fredericksburg, Boerne, and New Braunfels, do have some ADA infrastructure.

GAY AND LESBIAN TRAVELERS

Austin is the one bastion of open-mindedness in the conservative state of Texas. The city boasts a strong, vibrant gay and lesbian community and the only kind of intolerance that's acceptable is of intolerance itself. This general open-mindedness has provided an excellent atmosphere for the gay community to flourish. With a wide array of clubs and venues, popular liberal bookstores, a viable presence in the *Austin Chronicle*, and widely respected organizations that fight for gay rights in Texas, Austin is the San Francisco of the South. However, once you leave the Austin metropolitan area you're back in Texas. When it comes to safety, gay and lesbian travelers in Austin, San Antonio, and the surrounding Hill Country shouldn't worry. Although in the Hill Country people aren't necessarily accepting, they leave "different" folks alone. Outside Austin, public displays of affection will most certainly turn heads and possibly elicit a rude remark.

TRAVELERS WITH CHILDREN

Family is first in Texas, and people traveling with children will find this a great advantage when visiting the state. All restaurants, businesses, and attractions are very proud to be family oriented, which makes traveling with children easy. Folks in Central Texas love to compliment others on their children, so don't be freaked out if someone in line somewhere strikes up a conversation through a flattering remark about your child. When it comes to the necessities for children, such as food, bathrooms, and keeping them interested in the day's activities, Austin and San Antonio are full of resources. Food is easy here, as most kids like hamburgers and tacos, which can be found on every street corner; public bathrooms are easy to find and often outfitted with changing tables; and most attractions are family oriented.

Traveling with children in the Hill Country takes a little more planning but can be well worth it. With family-oriented dude ranches, underground caves to explore, great state parks to run around in, and fun festivals held throughout the year, there's much here to create a lifetime of memories. Planning comes in handy because everything is a little spread out. Things to take into account are travel time, finding the appropriate accommodations, and making sure you land in town when the kids get hungry or need to go to the bathroom.

Health and Safety

FLOODS, LIGHTNING, AND TORNADOES

The three biggest dangers in Central Texas are flash flooding, lightning, and tornadoes—the biggest being flash flooding. People refer to the region as "Flash Flood Alley" because every year there's an immense amount of water that gets dumped here. Moisture from the Gulf of Mexico and the rocky terrain of the Hill Country (covered by just a thin layer of soil) combine into excellent conditions for water to pour and collect. Flash flood watches and flash flood warnings are very common, especially in the spring. Most of Austin's infrastructure was designed specifically to avoid flooding danger. For example, the city has special five-foot storm drains everywhere as well as many massive culverts strategically placed throughout town. Lake Travis, the second-largest lake in the area, was designed as a flood-control lake. When all the regional rivers, such as Llano River, Colorado River, and Pedernales River, boil over with water they all dump it right into Lake Travis.

The second-biggest danger is lightning, and the third is tornadoes. When a lightning storm is overhead, go indoors. Twisters are far down on the list of things to be paranoid about because they don't normally pass through the region with sustained force. The time to watch out for them is during and after a coastal hurricane.

SEASONAL ALLERGIES

According to many national surveys, Austin is one of the worst places in the United States for allergies. If you are prone to allergies, come prepared with your preferred medication or time your trip to avoid the worst periods. The peak allergy times are December-January (mountain cedar), March-April (oak), and September-October (ragweed). Adding to the irritation are numerous wildflowers and grasses. For day-by-day allergy levels and forecast information, check out www.kvue.com (click on the weather link, then the allergy forecast link).

THINGS THAT BITE

There are three main critters that bite humans in Texas: mosquitoes, chiggers, and venomous snakes. Mosquitoes are the most common and can be a nuisance during the spring and summer months. Few cases of West Nile virus have been found in Central Texas. If you plan on being outdoors for any length of time during the summer months it helps to have a mosquito repellent on hand.

The most irritating of biting critters are chiggers (mites). These common skin parasites are found throughout the central part of the United States. They are members of the genus *Trombicula*. Chiggers are usually found in the highest numbers during the spring and fall in grassy areas. They are about the size of the head of a pin and are reddish orange in color. Their 50-day life cycle begins as an egg that's laid in soil and around vegetation. Larvae hatch from the egg and crawl onto a host animal, where they attach themselves, feed on fluids in the tissue for several days, and then drop off the host. Symptoms of chiggers include severe itching and irritation of skin. They prefer to attach in cozy lower regions of the body such as underneath sock bands, behind the knees, and around ankles. As gross as it may sound, the best treatment for chiggers is to let them run their course. One method of trying to get the little suckers to dislodge is to drown them in rubbing alcohol or cooking oil.

The deadliest of all Texas creatures are venomous snakes, and the most common in Central Texas is the rattlesnake. They live under rocks, fallen trees, and in dark places in rural areas. People most often encounter snakes while hiking in parks and open spaces. Snakebites can be fatal, but if treated correctly and quickly you can survive. If you are bitten by a snake, there are a few things you should do. First of all, don't panic. Keep the area where the bite is stable and below the heart, and put a bandage over the infected area. Then quickly get to a medical facility. Antivenins are available and a full recovery is possible. If the snake that caused the bite is dead, and you have your wits enough about you to remember, bring the snake along as well. To help prevent snakebites, always be aware of your environment when in rural areas. Wearing hiking boots can help prevent contact with the venom and teeth of snakes.

Along with insect and snakebites, there's one other danger to be aware of: rabies. Animals that carry rabies are raccoons, possums, skunks, dogs, cats, and bats. It's wise to avoid contact with any wild animals, no matter how cute they may look, because rabies can be fatal.

CRIME

For its size, Austin is a very safe place. It boasts low crime rates, especially for violent crimes such as homicide, assault, and rape. The crimes most committed here are burglaries of homes and cars and bike theft. San Antonio, on the other hand, has much higher crime rates. Although crime is less than in Dallas and Houston, San Antonio has enough crime to merit a gentle word of caution when exploring outside the downtown area, beyond the safety of the tourism infrastructure. When venturing into the outlying neighborhoods expect to see the seedier side of the city, and be a little more careful than normal.

Resources

Suggested Reading

Brands, H. W. *Lone Star Nation*. New York: Doubleday, 2004. The author brings to life the epic tale of the Texans' struggle for independence. All the great figures of the Lone Star State's history are brought to life, such as General Santa Anna, Stephen Austin, Davy Crockett, Jim Bowie, and Sam Houston.

Brice, Donaly E. *The Great Comanche Raid*. Austin, TX: Eakin Press, 1987. Outlines one of the most famous Native American attacks in the Republic of Texas's brief history.

Campbell, Randolph B. *Gone to Texas*. Oxford: Oxford University Press, 2003. This well-written tome on Texas history covers everything from the first arrival of humans in the Panhandle some 10,000 years ago to the dawn of the 21st century, offering an interpretive account of the land and the successive waves of people who have "gone to Texas."

Favata, Martin A., and Jose B. Fernandez, eds. *The Account—Álvar Núñez Cabeza de Vaca's Relación*. Houston, TX: Arte Público Press, 1993. Perhaps one of the most insightful and historically important writings in early Texas history, this work documents the conquest of the region by both Spaniard and white man.

Friedman, Kinky. *The Great Psychedelic Armadillo Picnic: A "Walk" in Austin*. New York: Crown, 2004. Famous humorist, author, and Texas politician Kinky Friedman takes the reader on a white-knuckle tour of Austin—poking, prodding, and overturning every social, political, and cultural rock in town.

Greer, James Kimmins. *Colonel Jack Hays, Texas Frontier Leader and California Builder*. College Station: Texas A&M University Press, 1952. Tells the story of Texas Ranger Colonel Jack Hays, offering a peek into the pioneer Wild West version of Texas that has been immortalized in legend.

Kownslar, Allan O. *European Texans*. College Station: Texas A&M University Press, 2004. Considers the contributions of those who immigrated to Texas from Europe in the early days of the state's history. Readers learn about the life and culture of French, English, Scottish, Irish, Dutch, Belgian, Swiss, Danish, Norwegian, Swedish, German, Wend, Polish, Czech, Hungarian, Italian, Greek, and Slavic Texans.

Laird, Tracey. *Austin City Limits: A History*. Oxford: Oxford University Press, 2014. Chronicles the history of the longest-running musical showcase in the history of television, Austin City Limits, from Willie Nelson's pilot show through Season 35. Includes historical stories and anecdotes, including performances by BB King and Stevie Ray Vaughan, Bonnie Raitt, Johnny Cash, Ray Charles, Mumford & Sons, and Arcade Fire.

Long, Joshua. *Weird City: Sense of Place and Creative Resistance in Austin.* Austin: University of Texas Press, 2010. Explores the social, political, and economic origins of Austin's obsession with being weird and hip, especially as it pertains to Austin's controversial "Keep Austin Weird" slogan and its attendant movement.

Reid, Jan. *The Improbable Rise of Redneck Rock.* Austin: University of Texas Press, 2004. Chronicles the days when music hit Austin, Texas, in the early 1970s at now-legendary venues such as Threadgill's, Vulcan Gas Company, and the Armadillo World Headquarters.

Smithwich, Noah. *The Evolution of a State or Recollections of Old Texas Days.* Austin: University of Texas Press, 1984. Read about Texas's early period from someone who was there. It covers the early days of Austin's colony to the aftermath of the Civil War. Some of the content may not be perfectly accurate but it does offer a personable glimpse into Texas myth, legend, and folklore.

Wilbarger, J. W. *Indian Depredations in Texas.* Austin, TX: Eakin Press, 1985. A series of accounts of the turmoil on Texas soil when white men came along. The tales here are true accounts of the men involved in conquest and the desperate responses of the indigenous peoples being overrun and exterminated.

Internet Resources

Austin Chamber of Commerce
www.austinchamber.com
Includes general information about Austin.

Austin Chronicle
www.austinchronicle.com
Comprehensive resource for music, arts, entertainment, classifieds, restaurant reviews, festivals, events, and weather for Austin.

Austin Convention and Visitors Bureau
www.austintexas.org
Premier website for tourism in Austin.

Austin 360
www.austin360.com
Online magazine with music, arts, and entertainment listings; restaurant reviews; festivals; and a calendar of events.

Culturemap Austin
http://austin.culturemap.com
Website with Austin events calendar and stuff to do.

The Handbook of Texas—Online
www.tshaonline.org/handbook/online
Texas state history and statistical information.

San Antonio Convention and Visitors Bureau
www.visitsanantonio.com
San Antonio's primary resource for tourism information.

San Antonio River Walk
www.thesanantonioriverwalk.com
Information about San Antonio's River Walk.

Texas Parks & Wildlife
www.tpwd.texas.gov
The official Texas Parks & Wildlife site includes information on parks, camping, hiking, and park access and hours of operation.

Texas Tourism
www.traveltex.com
The official site of Texas Tourism includes maps, guidebooks, highway information, and all tourism-related information about the Lone Star State.

Index

List of Maps

Photo Credits

Also Available

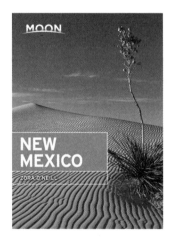

MAP SYMBOLS

≡≡≡ Expressway	○	City/Town	✈	Airport	⚲	Golf Course
─── Primary Road	◉	State Capital	✗	Airfield	Ⓟ	Parking Area
─── Secondary Road	⊛	National Capital	▲	Mountain	⬟	Archaeological Site
------ Unpaved Road	★	Point of Interest	✚	Unique Natural Feature	⛪	Church
─── Feature Trail	•	Accommodation				Gas Station
- - - Other Trail	▼	Restaurant/Bar	⌇	Waterfall	∽	Glacier
········ Ferry	■	Other Location	⚑	Park	▨	Mangrove
═══ Pedestrian Walkway			◨	Trailhead	∼	Reef
⊓⊓⊓⊓ Stairs	∧	Campground	⛷	Skiing Area	▭	Swamp

CONVERSION TABLES

°C = (°F - 32) / 1.8
°F = (°C x 1.8) + 32
1 inch = 2.54 centimeters (cm)
1 foot = 0.304 meters (m)
1 yard = 0.914 meters
1 mile = 1.6093 kilometers (km)
1 km = 0.6214 miles
1 fathom = 1.8288 m
1 chain = 20.1168 m
1 furlong = 201.168 m
1 acre = 0.4047 hectares
1 sq km = 100 hectares
1 sq mile = 2.59 square km
1 ounce = 28.35 grams
1 pound = 0.4536 kilograms
1 short ton = 0.90718 metric ton
1 short ton = 2,000 pounds
1 long ton = 1.016 metric tons
1 long ton = 2,240 pounds
1 metric ton = 1,000 kilograms
1 quart = 0.94635 liters
1 US gallon = 3.7854 liters
1 Imperial gallon = 4.5459 liters
1 nautical mile = 1.852 km

MOON AUSTIN, SAN ANTONIO & THE HILL COUNTRY

Avalon Travel
Hachette Book Group
1700 Fourth Street
Berkeley, CA 94710, USA
www.moon.com

Editor: Kimberly Ehart
Series Manager: Kathryn Ettinger
Copy Editor: Brett Keener
Graphics Coordinator: Sarah Wildfang
Production Designer: Sarah Wildfang
Cover Design: Faceout Studios, Charles Brock
Interior Design: Domini Dragoone
Moon Logo: Tim McGrath
Map Editor: Kat Bennett
Cartographers: Stephanie Poulain, Karin Dahl, Brian Shotwell
Indexer: Greg Jewett

ISBN-13: 978-1-63121-643-5

Printing History
1st Edition — 2006
5th Edition — September 2017
5 4 3 2 1

Front cover photo: © ATMTX Photography
Back cover photo: © Kan1234 | Dreamstime.com

Printed in Canada by Friesens